Complexity and Sustainability is a pillar of scholarship. Wells has shown how and why major complexity concepts are so significant to our era, done so with a critical and creative perspective, and provided crucial concepts and strategies for addressing our environmental crises. As a result, this is poised to be a widely cited, major reference. This is a very important book.

Timothy F. H. Allen is the co-author of *Hierarchy: Perspectives for Ecological Complexity* and *Towards a Unified Ecology.*

Complexity and Sustainability is a brilliant, comprehensive synthesis of complexity theories in the natural and social sciences. Wells uses complexity concepts to cast new light on pressing issues such as climate change and sustainability. Anyone who wishes to learn cutting-edge approaches to resolving global environmental problems will want to read this thoroughly engaging, lucid, and remarkable book.

Carolyn Merchant is the author of *The Death of Nature* and *Reinventing Eden.*

Complexity theories have emerged across the natural and social sciences in just the last few decades, and the relationships between them are still underexplored. In this timely and significant work, Wells draws on the reflective ideas of a diverse range of thinkers, from biologist Timothy Allen to sociologist and philosopher Edgar Morin; yet she moves beyond mere description and categorization to advance an ambitious and compelling synthesis of her own. Perhaps most importantly, she doesn't shy away from addressing the normative implications of the complexity sciences in the face of global sustainability challenges such as climate change. A valuable metacontribution to many fields!

Paul Baer is co-author of *The Greenhouse Development Rights Framework* and *Dead Heat.*

Complexity and Sustainability

Complexity has been presented as a few pieces of gold, when in fact it is a great goldmine. *Complexity and Sustainability* links complexity theories from throughout the disciplinary spectrum, distils one complex dynamic systems framework, and shows the value of complexity writ large for tackling issues of sustainability, such as climate change, extinctions, and the depletion of natural resources, as well as the twin problems of poverty and overconsumption.

Complex dynamic system studies have been studied explicitly in the natural sciences, and mostly only implicitly throughout other fields. Yet much great social theory and philosophy is in fact based in complexity, and important concepts like postmodernism, risk, and collapse all stem from complexity. Six key terms are explored: nonlinearity, feedbacks, thresholds, hierarchies, emergence, and self-organization, and dozens of related principles are discussed, with a focus on uncertainty, risk, vulnerability, learning, strategy, resilience, collapse, and sustainability. The book surveys the role of these complexity principles in the natural sciences, social theory, transdisciplinary discourse, philosophy, and ethics, and shows how this complexity framework is a valuable lens for approaching the spectre of climate change and life in the Anthropocene.

Problematizing the role of complexity in comprehending "wicked problems" and the potential for "synergistic solutions," it is argued that a comprehensive study of complexity theories is particularly helpful to addressing highly complex issues of rapid global change. Scholars and scientists throughout the many disciplines focusing on sustainability will find a refreshing new perspective on the invaluable role of complex thinking and interdisciplinary, transdisciplinary, and collaborative approaches to transforming today's social and environmental crises into opportunities.

Jennifer Wells is Assistant Professor at the California Institute of Integral Studies, San Francisco, USA

Routledge studies in ecological economics

Complexity and Sustainability

Jennifer Wells

Routledge
Taylor & Francis Group

LONDON AND NEW YORK

First published 2013
by Routledge
2 Park Square, Milton Park, Abingdon, Oxon OX14 4RN

Simultaneously published in the USA and Canada
by Routledge
711 Third Avenue, New York, NY 10017

Routledge is an imprint of the Taylor & Francis Group, an informa business

British Library Cataloguing in Publication Data
A catalogue record for this book is available from the British Library

Library of Congress Cataloging in Publication Data
Wells, Jennifer, 1969–
Complexity and sustainability/Jennifer Wells.
  p. cm.
  1. Complexity (Philosophy) 2. Environmentalism. 3. Ecosystems.
  4. Social systems. 5. System theory. I. Title.
  Q175.32.C65W45
  2012 003–dc23   2012010806

ISBN: 978-0-415-69577-0 (hbk)
ISBN: 978-0-203-09567-6 (ebk)

Typeset in Times New Roman
by Wearset Ltd, Boldon, Tyne and Wear

Printed and bound in the United States of America by Publishers Graphics,
LLC on sustainably sourced paper.

To my parents, Doris J. Wells and William S. Wells.

Contents

Acknowledgments

It is a pleasure to thank those who have contributed to my work on this book. The breadth of these ideas reflects the richness of the community that has helped to inspire them. The people who have influenced this book are too numerous to list, and I hope that I have not slighted too many.

A warm and profound thank you to my dissertation committee members who have inspired me and shared conversations with me on these ideas since the conception of the first version of the book: Daniel Andler, Amy Dahan-Dalmedico, Jean-Pierre Dupuy, Catherine Larrere, Pierre Livet, Carolyn Merchant, Richard B. Norgaard, Kate O'Neill, Samuel Scheffler, and David Winickoff.

Thank you to the many colleagues and friends who have contributed to the thinking that led to this book, commented on excerpts of it, or discussed these ideas with me: Timothy F. H. Allen, Henri Atlan, Harry Bader, Paul Baer, William R. Burch, F. Stuart Chapin III, Michael Dove, Jennifer Dunne, J. Doyne Farmer, Timothy J. Foxon, Debora Hammond, Jeffrey Goldstein, Paul Higgins, Alastair Iles, Giorgos Kallis, Kamal Kapadia, Stephen Kellert, Sean Kelly, Raphael Larrere, Mark Longo, Neo Martinez, Melanie Mitchell, Edgar Morin, Sean O'Nuallain, Peter Ralph, Kurt Richardson, Stephen H. Schneider, Peter Taylor, Sarah Trainor, Lee Worden, and Eddie Yuen. I wish to thank many mentors including: Urs Cipolat, Alan Code, Phillipe Descola, Hubert Dreyfus, Roger Hahn, Robert Hass, John Harte, Hannah Ginsborg, Daniel Kammen, Thomas Nagel, Dominique Pestre, Isha Ray, Garrison Sposito, R. Jay Wallace, and Daniel Warren.

Thanks to the following institutions for generous financial contributions and support for this research: the University of California at Berkeley, Department of Environmental Sciences, Policy and Management, the Sorbonne, Paris IV, Philosophy Department, the National Science Foundation, the Santa Fe Institute, Centre de Recherche en Épistémologie Appliquée, l'Ecole des hautes études en sciences sociales, l'Ecole normale supérieur, Ministère de l'enseignement supérieur et de la Recherche, Sciences politiques, the Yale School of Forestry and Environmental Studies, the Yale University Fox Fellowship, and the Yale Hixon Center for Urban Ecology.

I am grateful to the following institutes and organizations without which this work would not have been possible: the UC Berkeley Complexity Discussion group, le Réseau Intelligence de la Complexité, l'Association européenne du Programme Modélisation de la Complexité et de l'Association pour la Pensée Complexe, Centre Edgar Morin, the International Society for the Systems Sciences, the journal Emergence: Complexity + Organization, the Institute for the Study of Coherence and Emergence, International Society for the Systems Sciences, the New England Complex Systems Institute, and the Santa Fe Institute. Thanks to the many other systems, complexity, social and environmental thinkers who have pioneered these fields and inspired my thinking.

Thanks to all my colleagues at the California Institute of Integral Studies, and a special thank you to creative complexity thinkers Leslie Allan Combs and Alfonso Montuori. I am very grateful to my doctoral students who read excerpts of this book: Harlan Gilbert, Joe Mageary, Chip McAuley, and Cynthia Vale. Thank you sincerely to all my students for many rich discussions on these topics in the last few years.

Additionally, I wish to thank my gracious editors Robert Langham and Simon Holt of Routledge, and all the others who helped with the completion of the book, including Allie Waite and Claire Toal of Wearset.

Finally, thanks to the community, friends and family who have helped me to see this through to fruition, especially to Shastri, Scotty, Rusty, Rosy, Kent, Sara, Ken, Juan, Maurine, Claire, Peggy, Sonie, Sylvie, Orange, Cathy, Dave, Andrew, Will, Chris, Karen, Rebecca, Ron, Sam, Rochelle, Selig, and my parents, William and Doris.

1 Introduction

[T]he twenty-first century will be the century of complexity.

Stephen Hawking[1]

In the twenty-first century complexity is not a vague science buzzword any longer, but an equally pressing challenge for everything from the economy to cell biology.

Albert-Laszlo Barabási[2]

Make things as simple as possible, but no simpler.

Albert Einstein

Complexity

A compelling vision has been emerging in the last few decades, a growing understanding of the multiple patterns that make up our world. Scientists speak in terms of the interconnectivity of ecosystems, biodiversity, the carbon cycle, the atmosphere, geothermal cycles – all of which is increasingly modeled and conceptualized in terms of interactions. Social theorists think along similar lines, using terms like socioecological systems, green business, the links between social and environmental impacts, stresses and resilience, cradle-to-grave cycles of materials and waste, and adages such as reduce, recycle, and reuse. Artists and poets take up phrases like "the pattern that connects." In the end, all are speaking about a perspective on our world's complexity that, with developments in the natural sciences, environmental education, the Internet, social networking, GPS, Google Earth, and globalization, has become increasingly widespread and influential.

Crisp images of networks, nonlinear patterns, and fractals have become commonplace, mixed with a vague sense of the meanings and implications of these terms. Yet increasingly, scientists and scholars are clarifying the nature of various key aspects of complex dynamic systems – e.g., networks, uncertainty, nonlinearity, thresholds, feedback, and resilience – in the greater transdisciplinary literature on global change. All of these terms form part of a complexity framework, which will be described in Chapter 2 and discussed throughout this book.

These complexity terms and theories form a poignant new conceptual perspective. While most people using the terms, including experts, have studied them in their individual aspects, and while a growing literature on systems and complexity has traced a few patterns between them, the truly comprehensive and powerful patterns they reveal have yet to be more fully explored.

I explore the meaning and nature of complexity throughout the book. For a start, many people have defined complexity in terms of complex dynamic systems, as dynamic interactions of multiple elements engaged in self-organizing processes. My focus throughout this book is mostly on the complexity principles inherent to dynamic systems, systems such as: stars, universes, cells, brains, anthills, dazzles of zebras, families, cities, language, and the internet. The common characteristics of these systems – physical, living, social, virtual, linguistic systems, and more – are central to understanding our world and the current global challenges of social and environmental sustainability.

Complexity is bigger than this, a characteristic not just of dynamic systems, but of all systems. Two atoms of oxygen and one atom of hydrogen form a molecule and produce the emergent quality of wateriness.[3] Complexity is a profound characteristic of reality, and we need to explore it more fully. For my purposes in this book, I focus mostly on complex dynamic systems, itself a very wide-ranging topic! The implications of complexity theories just in this area are epistemological, ontological, and ethical, deep and far-reaching.

Complexity theories lead to the acknowledgment of the importance of complexification, which I explore in Chapter 6. In short, this theory holds that reality is not purely mechanistic or deterministic, but rather reality possesses qualities that we have not fully grasped, including emergence of novel properties, self-organization, and a general tendency to become increasingly complex, to complexify, after Nicolas Rescher.

This view sits much better with most of us. After all, who, while reading the Sunday *New York Times* over brunch and a cup of coffee, gets the reassuring, gratifying sense that society is on a path of truth, stability, and progress? After discussing the daily news, we are not often left with the feeling that societies are steadily unveiling and accreting certainties about an orderly world. Complexity theories, across the disciplines, have opened windows into a very different worldview for a highly dynamic world.

Complexity theories have emerged in every realm of knowledge, as we have found complex systems in all spheres of reality – physical, living, social realms, and all social sectors comprise complex dynamic systems, including economic, political, health, culture, and ideas. The term "transdisciplinary" refers to this comprehensive view, which incorporates but transcends disciplines to include physical, living, and social systems, with their many implications. While interdisciplinary research may unite data from two or more disciplines, usually employing one epistemological method such as quantitative modeling, in contrast, transdisicplinary research includes all of the necessary epistemologies and methodologies, spanning the physical, living, and social realms, usually employing both quantitative data and qualitative theory.

In my travels in the last few years I have heard the views of many eminent natural scientists and social scholars. In graduate school at Yale University, the University of California at Berkeley, the Sorbonne, École Normale Supérieur and Science Politiques in France, at the Santa Fe Institute and the New England Complex Systems Institute, in conferences and in lecture halls, I began to see links emerging across the many fields devoted to understanding the planet's current great social and ecological changes. Biologists, physicists, philosophers, social theorists, business leaders, and activists have all been increasingly using these core terms in describing global change. Uncertainty, nonlinearity, feedbacks, and thresholds – little by little, these terms began to coalesce into intriguing patterns.

Suddenly, a beautiful vision is emerging. This book is born of two powerful insights, both of which have been largely inexplicit and unnamed up until now. As complexity theories have developed in many disciplines, each in their arena, natural scientists, social theorists, philosophers, and organizational leaders are making links and sketching parts of the puzzle. Now, when we step back and look at all of their work across the disciplines, we begin to see a broad, inspiring vision. First, it's now clear these disparate studies fit together within the theoretical framework of transdsiciplinary or generalized complexity theories, or simply, complexity theories. Second, this framework is intricately linked with our aims of sustainability.

Complexity theories have become significant at the highest levels of academia, science, and policy for sustainability. Transdisciplinary, or generalized complexity theories, or simply, complexity theories, although not widely articulated yet explicitly, are already implicitly playing a central role in science, scholarship, policy, and activism for sustainability. In each of the four vignettes to follow, I explore how these leading thinkers' core arguments derive from central principles of complexity theories.

Around the world, across a wide range of fields, leaders in the natural sciences and social theory researching applied issues and working on solutions to sustainability are tapping into the broadly scattered field of complexity theories. Complexity theories, or broadly, "complex thinking," encompass and include the work done in the natural sciences, e.g., at the Santa Fe Institute, but they also encompass much more – e.g., social theory, transdisciplinary research, philosophy, and applied research – as I explore in this book.

Therefore, in reference to all of these realms, I use complexity and complexity theories as synonyms. While some natural scientists use narrower connotations of the word "theory," I use the word "theory" in the broader, transdisciplinary sense: a theory is any attempt to understand or explain phenomena in any realm – physical, living, or social systems, with any methodology. So when I speak of complexity theories throughout this book, I am speaking of both complexity and theories in the broad, general, and transdisciplinary sense of these terms.

Indeed, this is a key moment in the development of complexity theories. Recently, scientists and scholars have proven the great power and potential of these theories. Rapidly, complexity theories are being taken up by many of the world's leading thinkers and activists working towards global sustainability, with goals of increasing equity and solidarity, transitioning to green economies and technologies, and creating more sustainable societies. At the same time, everyone from military strategists, to finance profiteers, to energy moguls are trying to capture the power of complexity theories, oftentimes at cross-purposes. Never was the time so ripe for turning our best theories to our common interests, but not since the Gilded Age has there been such tragic social inequities, and never before have there been such great social and environmental issues at stake.

Uncertainty, nonlinearity, and thresholds

Walter Reid exudes an overflowing passion to share what he has learned with others. Medium build, black hair slightly fraying, sharp-eyed, he paced before a hall packed with Berkeley students, faculty and visitors, spilling over to sit on the floors throughout the lecture hall at the University of California at Berkeley, on a warm fall day in 2006. Indeed, Walter Reid had learned a tremendous amount in the preceding five years, as the director of the most comprehensive study of the environment of all time, the Millennium Ecosystem Assessment, composed of 1,360 of the world's best scientists, from 2000–2005, who studied just about every major environmental system on the planet.

Reid was reaching the high point of his lecture, the conclusions of the intensive survey of the state of the planet. "The Millennium Ecosystem Assessment made clear some issues of utmost significance for the future of the planet: uncertainty, nonlinearity, and thresholds," he said.

> There is an ongoing increase of multiple intersecting nonlinear systems and thresholds. Because of these increasing changes and interactions, because of these feedbacks and thresholds, we do not know what the next fifty years will look like. Clearly though, thresholds will play a huge role. It's surprising how much they are seen as an anecdotal issue. It's amazing how little thresholds are discussed. These are keys to understanding our future.

Clearly, he said, feedbacks are quite important to climate change and related environmental issues. A concerted effort to understand the interactions of climate feedbacks seems like a good way to frame questions of how we can intervene to reduce the rate of climatic changes. We don't have a picture of interconnections across the globe regarding effects on the global climate system. These initial generalizations are pretty crude, perhaps very crude, but advancing upon these climate ecosystem feedbacks could make a huge contribution to policy by nailing down some of these effects more accurately. This is a very clear place where targeted efforts by the scientific community should have huge policy paybacks.

Specifically, closer study of feedbacks could contribute to required policy changes in the areas of: reducing trace gas emissions, fostering reforestation, especially in the tropics, protecting and restoring vegetation cover especially in dry lands, and reducing the risk of desertification.

The benefit of the diversity of perspectives amongst the 1,360 scientists and scholars who participated in the Millennium Ecosystem Assessment was clear as soon as Reid began to speak. The talk was not a typical scientific one, but had the new ring of an effective transdisciplinary talk. The science was good, backed with the usual empirical facts, models, charts, and graphs of scientific results. However, the presentation was infused throughout with talk of acknowledging and integrating various social groups, interests and values, the role of indigenous voices, and the imperative of alleviating poverty.

These topics, previously less common in strictly scientific lectures, have become increasingly lauded and expected in recent years, for natural scientists and social thinkers alike, as each grapple with the transdisciplinary aspects of socioecological problems. While individual scientists with narrow disciplinary foci can omit the full complexity and transdisciplinarity of global environmental change, the analyses of 1,360 world-class scientists and scholars illuminated the very transdisciplinary root causes and drivers of change.

This trend can be hard to reconcile with the bitter and unresolved meta-theoretical battles of recent decades – the science wars and the culture wars. Philosophers of science and leading theorists have begun to explain how these two trends could be proceeding simultaneously. On the one hand, disciplines have continued to proliferate and to fracture, and the dominant camps – natural scientists, social theorists, and philosophers – have become seemingly even more entrenched as the theoretical battles over the nature of these domains have only shown the depths of misunderstanding between them. On the other hand, leading thinkers from all realms of academia and leading institutions of science and scholarship have increasingly lauded and prized more comprehensive and global studies. Interdisciplinary, transdisciplinary, complexity, and integral approaches and lenses have shifted to the center stage, with the leading edge of scientists, humanities, and social science scholars practicing some version of these hybridizing, integral approaches as they increasingly take on highly complex social and ecological issues. One conclusion of the Millennium Ecosystem Assessment was a unanimous call for utilizing a transdisciplinary complexity lens as the major framework for studying global change. It has also become a major focus of large-scale institutions and funding agencies, from the United Nations to the Pentagon to the National Science Foundation.

As interdisciplinary and transdisciplinary approaches gain ground as the dominant approach for issues such as global environmental issues, global social, cultural, and political change, many scientists and scholars feel this tension and rightly perceive this perspective as one that threatens the old Newtonian underpinnings of determinism, linearity, equilibrium, and reversibility. In fact, from two sides, both complexity theories in the natural sciences and cultural studies in the humanities have disproven these old underpinnings. In their place, complexity has given us, in the place of certainties, probabilities; in place of determinism, deterministic chaos in the most stable systems; in place of linearity, the tendency to move far from equilibrium and toward bifurcation, especially in more dynamic systems; in place of integer dimensions, fractals; in place of reversibility the arrow of time.[4] Moreover, in place of science as fundamentally different from humanistic thought, we have come to see that science is deeply entwined with philosophy, embedded in culture, and engaged with humanities' questions about human lives and meaning.[5]

Academics across the disciplines are increasingly confronted with the imperative of confronting highly complex issues – socioecological change such as climate change, environmental ethics and politics; global social, cultural, economic, and political change; and a great array of interactions between social, technological, and environmental change. And these issues, in their complexities and hyper-transdisciplinarity, throw light on more simplifying and stultifying dogmas, ideologies, and assumptions.

Another of the main conclusions drawn from the five-year MEA study spotlighted the elephant in the room: both widespread poverty and corporate greed drive the degradation of ecosystems and the depletion of natural resources. Both intense deprivation and overconsumption must be transformed to develop sustainable societies. Before the financial crash of 2008 made it more obvious to more people, the MEA made unequivocal what interdisciplinary ecological economists have been saying for 40 years – economics must be fully contextualized within societies and environments.

Compiling statistics of global environmental change has made this clear, but integrating these statistics and analyzing their full interactions further reveals the fallacy of understanding economics apart from peoples and places. Poverty, Reid and other leading environmental thinkers repeat, is one of the main drivers of ecological destruction. Any policy aimed at protecting the environment must take into account people and poverty. Of the myriad policies that need to be implemented, it is necessary both to reduce luxury emissions and to overcome poverty.

After spending five years deep in conversation with a great diversity of study groups and local voices, the leaders of the MEA became aware of the social intricacies inherent to the resolution of poverty, such as differences in views, attitudes, and lifestyles. After hearing many voices from many places through the MEA study, Reid said – from indigenous communities in Peru to urban areas in Stockholm – and comparing notes between hundreds of experts, it became glaringly apparent to the MEA scientists that people have very different considerations of intrinsic values and that these values are major factors in local environmental policies and practices.

Leaving the lecture hall, I reflected on Reid's talk. The Millennium Ecosystem Assessment laid out in detail how in the last 50 years humans have brought about massive transformations of every major life-support system on Earth. From 1954 to 2007 humans increased the CO_2 concentrations in the atmosphere from about 320 ppm to now over 390 ppm. Out of the 24 global ecosystem services that the MEA analyzed, we have enhanced four of these through such measures as reforesting of northern woodlands and some technological improvements such as pollution absorption; we have created mixed patterns of degradation and improvement in five of these ecosystem services; and yet, overall, we have dangerously degraded 15 of the 24 ecosystem services.

The bottom line: over the last 50 years about 60 percent of the Earth's ecosystem services studied have been degraded, many of these dangerously. Complexity theories, by highlighting systems interconnections and interactions, show that a crash in one major planetary support system may create some domino effect. It is clear that in the past few decades, this has been having serious effects on the impoverishment of many societies, extinctions of many species, some dire and perhaps irremediable changes to many of the world's ecosystems, some of which may have reached or may soon reach tipping points. Moreover, in some cases, cumulative, multiple feedbacks between various ecological and biophysical processes – such as the extinction crisis and climate change – may lead to their mutual acceleration.

This perspective helps us to consider which human interventions may affect such interrelated trends positively, social as well as ecological. Renewable energy, for instance, can help to slow both extinctions and climate change. Yet, while scientists and policymakers have known about nonlinear patterns, positive feedbacks, and abrupt changes for some time, for a variety of reasons we have been slow to integrate these concepts into scientific analyses, public discourse, or policy directives. Even the most brilliant thinkers, immersed in both hyper-specialization and a largely modernist worldview, still fail to grasp the full startling reality that we are in some ways as vulnerable as our weakest link, or in John Donne's cryptic warning, no man is an island.

All of these evolving ecosystem functions or services have nonlinear patterns, Reid had said. Most of the drivers of change we are measuring are increasing, which means that the likelihood of encountering a threshold, a point of rapid change, is increasing. And these issues intersect. If deforestation drives loss of biodiversity and extinctions, then biodiversity loss and extinctions also drives a decrease in that ecosystem's general resilience. Reid concluded,

> At the end of the assessment process, all of the scenarios showed the continued degradation of ecosystem services over the next 50 years. We don't even know if it could continue that way. We do not have enough information about thresholds, to know whether it could continue or not.

Chaos, post-normal science, and risk management

When we met up for coffee at his office, Stanford professor and prominent climate scientist Stephen Schneider was just back from speaking before the US Congress and a trip to consult for the government of New Zealand on responses to the specter of dangerous climate change. A biologist and atmospheric scientist, Schneider was among the first to see the significance of climate change in the 1970s and 1980s, and spent much of the last 40 years engaged in climate science. Intimately involved with the IPCC from its inception, Schneider was Melvin and

Joan Lane Professor for Interdisciplinary Environmental Studies and Senior Fellow at the Woods Institute for the Environment at Stanford University, before he died tragically in the summer of 2010. I visited on a fall day in 2007. Schneider was hosting a talk at a Stanford graduate seminar and I met up afterwards with Schneider, his post-doc Michael Mastrandrea, and his graduate students by a refreshments table overflowing with good wines, cheeses, and chocolate-dipped strawberries.

Stephen Schneider was in a typically ebullient mood. I always found it remarkable that having been working on the depressing topic of climate change for four decades, Schneider had such a happy disposition. Schneider had some of the classic look of the brilliant scientist. When he appeared on the Bill Maher show, Maher joked, "If you aren't really a professor, you sure look the part." But he was a bit off. Schneider often as not wore a black leather jacket and actually fell more into the category of the more hip worldly professors – speaking before Congress and vacationing with friends like Al Gore. His exuberance seemed to stem in equal parts from his fast wit, sharp mind, and acrobatic verbal skills, keeping Stanford students on their toes.

Several events contributed to Schneider's early knowledge of complexity theories and planetary complex systems dynamics. He told me the story of how he was one of the first to learn of chaos theory.

> I first learned about chaos while hiking up Long's Peak with Ed Lorenz. He had to rescue me from a very steep, deep snowy crevasse. I heard all about chaos on that trip, which at the time he was calling "intransitivity." We talked about ice age interglacial cycles. Are ice ages internal tipping points or are they forced? It was a wonderful conversation, brilliant. I loved every minute of it, except for having to be dug out of the snowfield.[6]

The bottom line, Schneider explained, is that good science, most science today, is complexity science or strives to be. The bottom line is that chaotic equations are an essential part of models today. Models, all models, are simple relative to full-blown complex systems. They are really just analogies and metaphors for the behavior of the system. It is very important to do simple models, oscillator models of climatic behavior. Then, though, you add complexity, you build up the hierarchy, and you find out how each addition of incremental change alters the emergent properties of your answer, the results of your experiments. Through that process you are building up your understanding. You are rendering your models more sophisticated, more real-life-like.

Ironically, the many ways in which scientists have advanced the introduction of complexity into their models has greatly improved the models, but it has also given the scientists glimpses of the extraordinary complexity of real life, and the concomitant ultimate impossibility of perfect models in light of that highly complex reality. Mathematics and models have grown much more sophisticated in recent decades, but in the process the idealistic goal of having the model absolutely match the reality has been overturned and transformed. The philosophy of science of the last few decades has had to come fully to grips with the disinteg-ration of notions that were essential to the classical modern project – certainty, absolute truth, and science as revelator of any kind of pure and complete grasp of reality.

But as science strives towards complexity, it is always a question of how close it gets, and what it manages and does not manage, to capture. Science in this sense is always producing, not certainties or absolute truths, but only partial indications. By rendering their models more complex, scientists are improving science, advancing it beyond what it has ever been before. But there is no such thing as perfect science, just as there is no such thing as perfect truth, in our complex, evolving reality. Policy-driven science is being forced to take on more and more complex issues, of which climate change is perhaps the ultimate example – involving just about every planetary and social system. Seen in this light, one can appreciate just how much science has advanced in our times, as scientists have had to develop their methods to capture problems of ever-increasing complexity. Talking to Schneider, I appreciated even more deeply the significance of the IPCC's work. As Schneider said,

> You are probably never going to have a mathematics that is fully representa-tive of the complexity of reality, because either, we haven't invented the mathematics, or we don't have enough empirical information to know how to come up with coefficients and values of coefficients that really matter. Empirical information is infinite in the sense that empirical conditions are in a state of constant evolution. Moreover, even minor changes can cause a wide variation of results. Change the values and you suddenly get a chaotic response. Change them again and you get a whole different response.[7]

We can understand this in light of the long, great shift in our understanding of the underpinnings of natural science in the growing knowledge of uncertainty, nonlinearity, and evolving systems. Natural scientists working on climate change have deepened our appreciation of natural science techniques of modeling, prob-ability, and the bridging and validation of natural science and philosophy – including valuation, subjective assessment of probabilities, and the transdisciplinary savvy required to make sense of model results and contextual-ize them within social, ethical, and political issues.

The advancement of mathematical models in the life sciences in recent decades has at once brought us much closer to our new goals, and farther from our original goals. At times it can appear like the infinite regress you see reflected in objects between two mirrors: the better the lens with which we grasp reality, the more complex and more elusive that reality becomes. At the same time, when it comes to the market on the truth, science has only advanced as the tool with which we make sense of our natural world; while science must be coupled with ethics, social theory, and philosophical analysis, nonetheless, there is no alternative to science. If it is no longer seen as producing absolute or eternal truths, we also now know that no such certainty exists in the evolving reality of our living planet. Rather, we have a more realistic and optimistic understanding of what science really is and can do. In fact, science generally, climate science particularly, has been on a steady path of rapid advances. While it is improving in its capacity to capture and assess the messy and rapidly changing complexities of human societies and environments at the planetary scale, it is also improving in its capacity to bridge and link the necessary scientific questions and the related philosophical questions.

Schneider often referred to the work of colleague and friend Jerome Ravetz, who coined the term "post-normal" science to describe that which must be used in highly complex situations. What this refers to however is in no way a "new" science. It is still the same science, the seventeenth century scientific method. Observation, empirical data collection, modeling, and analysis remain at the core of all scientific enterprise today. Rather, "post-normal" science is a term meant to evoke and explain the challenge of applying science to highly complex subjects today, and the perspective with which the scientist must understand his or her research.

Ravetz employed an x-y axis to make his essential point, that within the context of highly complex subjects, we see science confronting the following set of possible realms: low decision stakes, high decision stakes, low systems uncertainty, and high systems uncertainty. Low decision stakes means that the results will not have a significant impact on society. High stakes refer to cases like climate change, where the outcomes range into the catastrophic. Similarly, we can study certain systems with a considerable degree of certainty – many mechanical and physical systems behave in very predictable ways within a large range of conditions. In contrast, many planetary life-support systems behave in unpredictable ways, especially in highly interconnected, changing systems. Evidently, climate change is an issue of particularly high decision stakes and high systems uncertainties. Generally speaking, most issues of environmental sustainability are characterized by high decision stakes and high systems uncertainties. This is why complexity is so relevant to sustainability. Complexity theories, applicable to any of these realms, appear to be particularly poignant for this last category of high uncertainties and high stakes, which generally exhibit high degrees of complexity, or "hypercomplexity."

Schneider ambitiously aimed to tackle this hypercomplexity in order to link science to real policy change. In pursuit of this goal he became increasingly versed in complexity, insofar as it relates directly to the improvement of climate models, the transdisciplinary analysis that is inherent to climate change science for policy, and the dynamics between scientists, policymakers, business, media, civic groups, etc. Schneider did not consider that he had great knowledge of complexity theories; he did not write about complexity or systems theories. Nonetheless, one could say that in another sense he was developing complexity theories, by dint of his highly complex subject and his drive to derive useful applied results, he had to focus on just how to conceive of the complexity in his research. In other words, his work explicitly advanced applied complexity studies, in that his writings on uncertainty, risk management, transdisciplinarity, and ecological complexities help us to develop some of the major principles of complexity theories.

For example, aside from his considerable contributions to climate science in the last few decades, Schneider played a crucial role in addressing the related philosophical issues, which greatly contributed to the work of the IPCC. The philosophical issues are long-term and substantial. They arise from the entire paradigmatic shift of modern to contemporary thinking. Broadly speaking, this includes the general shift from the myths of certainty, truth, and progress to the realities of uncertainty, the acknowledgment of partial unknowns, unforeseen and nefarious consequences, and the evolution of social and ecological change.

Within climate science, philosophical issues have revolved around notions of uncertainty, probability, and prediction in highly complex systems. Throughout the 1990s climate scientists struggled with the comprehension and presentation of uncertainties and probabilities in climate change. These posed a formidable problem in the face of climate skeptics and deniers. In a guidance paper for IPCC scientists published in 2000, coauthors Richard Moss and Stephen Schneider suggested a way for their IPCC colleagues to advance the integration and communication of scientific uncertainty. In an elegant philosophical argument addressed to all the IPCC scientists, they discussed how scientific results and analyses must be reframed due to the paradigmatic shift from what Jerome Ravetz called the shift from normal to "post-normal" science, and in relation to this, what I focus on in this book as the shift from classical science to complexity science. Scientists heeded their advice and integrated the results into the subsequent Third and Fourth IPCC Assessment Reports.

The Moss and Schneider paper showed that despite the highly complex nature of science at the planetary scale, and the ubiquity of degrees of uncertainty in such systems, that the results in the form of Bayesian probability and uncertainty bands are just as valid and significant as other types of simpler, narrower scientific results. Bayesian probability and uncertainty bands are just what science looks like at the scale of the planet, and in the realm of highly uncertain, highly significant global change. The paper showed how degrees of uncertainty are just as inherent to the science of biophysical trends as to knowledge generally, while at the same time how tools like Bayesian probability and uncertainty bands provide helpful quantification to our understanding of major planetary change. As the authors noted,

> The term "uncertainty" can range in implication from a lack of absolute sureness to such vagueness as to preclude anything more than informed guesses or speculation. Sometimes uncertainty results from a lack of information, and on other occasions it is caused by disagreement about what is known or even knowable.... "Science" itself strives for objective empirical information to test theory and models. But at the same time "science for policy" must be recognized as a different enterprise than "science" itself, since science for policy (e.g., Ravetz, 1986) involves being responsive to

policymakers' needs for expert judgment at a particular time, given the information currently available, even if those judgments involve a considerable degree of subjectivity. The methods outlined below are designed to make such subjectivity both more consistently expressed (linked to quantitative distributions when possible) across the (Third Assessment Report) TAR, and more explicitly stated so that well-established and highly subjective judgments are less likely to get confounded in policy debates. The key point is that authors should explicitly state what sort of approach they are using in a particular case: if frequentist statistics are used the authors should explicitly note that, and likewise if the probabilities assigned are subjective, that too should be explicitly indicated. Transparency is the key in all cases.

One result of this, according to Schneider, is that uncertainty – inherent and ubiquitous in global systems that are by nature highly complex systems – must be normalized, and yet science along with the appropriate subjective analysis is still the most highly powerful tool for navigating current and future societal choices; it is in fact irreplaceable and still the most legitimate source for making such decisions. The question is not one of whether science should be trusted or when science will be certain; both of those questions are now moot. The answers are yes and never, and the latter only reinforces the former. If science only provides partial and partially uncertain knowledge, this is much better than ignorance.

What the shift from classical to complexity science necessitates is a shift towards increasing understanding and validity of science for policy. Schneider suggests a shift in language from the language of uncertainty, which may make it sound to people still thinking in a classical paradigm as if a situation is inoperable, to the concept of "risk management," which we have long relied on in coping with the uncertainties, surprises, and unanticipated consequences of living in complex systems – risks of rain, mudslides, fires, earthquakes, floods, etc.

The real obstacle is not any inadequacy in science, but the urgent need to boost public understanding of the tremendous shift that has taken place in science in recent decades. What is needed is to promote understanding of the absurdity and practical inadequacy of hubristic classical views of certainty and truth. These notions have long been debunked, and in their place, understanding has advanced over and again throughout the last century that all basic science is completely embedded in ecological and social systems and that science for policy shares some of the qualities of other areas of life for which we have long analyzed degrees of uncertainty and probabilities in risk management. Just as we make everyday choices based on probabilities of rain, so we make preventive and adaptive changes about climate change based on scientific probabilities of climate change patterns. Schneider uses simple analogies to make such points crystal clear.

If there was a ten percent chance of a fire, would you buy fire insurance for your house? Of course you would! Anybody would spend a small fee if there was a ten percent chance of a catastrophic event. You would buy it if the risk was five percent, or one percent. It's the same with climate change. We have a ten percent chance of catastrophic climate change, would we invest a small sum to prevent it? What a question. Of course we would.

Feedbacks, transdisciplinarity, and resilience

If anyone would know the answer to Schneider's question about house insurance, it is the residents of Fairbanks, Alaska, epicenter of climate change research, and one of the first regions to be hard-hit by climate change. Climate change has hit the polar regions harder than most of the rest of the globe, because the global temperature increase is not distributed evenly; in the last few decades, the Arctic has been heating four times as fast as the equatorial regions. There is even more variability throughout the year; winters in Fairbanks are 15 degrees warmer than they were 50 years ago. Moreover, the polar regions exhibit obvious climate feedbacks, including the initial poster child of climate positive feedbacks, the ice albedo effect. The albedo effect refers to the way that dark ocean waters absorb more sunlight than white ice and snow, such that a small increase in temperature that melts some ice and creates more of the darker ocean surface, thus brings about a larger amount of melting.

Among the early signals of change, the area surrounding the relatively southerly Alaskan town of Fairbanks suffered from several dramatic impacts as early as the 1990s. The permafrost shelf that undergirds the Arctic region has melted sufficiently that roads that were once flat were rumpled by the uplift of emerging soils, and trees and telephone poles slumped over as the permafrost beneath them began to liquefy. Locals refer to these respectively as "wavy roads" and "drunken trees."

Increasingly, permafrost melt is also causing houses and other buildings to collapse, while glacial melt is forcing entire villages to move inland at the economic cost of millions and incalculable social and environmental costs, as people lose their sense of place, their culture, and their subsistence security. Both peoples and whole species are being dislodged from their homes, their villages and their sources of food. Photographic evidence shows that in unprecedented events, polar bears isolated by disintegrating ice floes and separated from food sources have resorted to desperate acts of cannibalism.

It is no surprise then that many of Alaska's best scientists are involved in climate change research. A leading ecologist and now climate change scientist is the amiable Alaskan scientist, F. Stuart "Terry" Chapin, III, Professor at the University of Alaska at Fairbanks, who recently travelled to the University of California at Berkeley. He held a general lecture on climate change in the cavernous Mulford Hall auditorium, and a more specialized talk with graduate students, each of which was packed, buzzing with talk of the intricacies of climate drivers and interactions between shifting cloud cover, oceanic currents, acidification, and carbon sequestration patterns, terrestrial carbon dynamics, natural resource management, and possibilities for policy.

Immersed in this work for two decades now, Chapin was deeply influenced by complexity in ecology, and quickly saw the significance of terms such as resilience, sustainability, and vulnerability. In fact, he saw in these terms a new framework for natural resource management – "a framework based on stewardship of ecosystems for human well-being in a world dominated by uncertainty and change."[8]

Chapin developed a systems perspective, an integrated, often transdisciplinary approach framed as socioecological systems, employing terms from complexity theories, principally – resilience, vulnerability, and sustainability – to ecosystem management and governance. Like Stephen Schneider, most climate scientists have had a crash lesson in the significance of positive feedbacks, thresholds and abrupt change, and a transdisciplinary framing of how these three are linked. In Mulford Auditorium, Chapin discussed feedbacks in climate change:

> We don't have a clear picture of the net magnitude of different feedbacks yet. We don't have a picture of the interconnections across the globe regarding the effects on the global climate system. The generalizations we have managed to make about climate feedbacks are still pretty crude, but climate ecosystem feedbacks could make a huge contribution to policy by nailing down some of these effects more accurately. This is a very clear place where targeted efforts by the scientific community should have huge policy paybacks.

Studying the many patterns of climate change across ocean, tundra, forest, and clouds involves the consideration of various tools of complex systems analysis. Chapin mentioned the need to consider the biophysical interactions in terms of the appropriate scale and grain, two concepts from ecological hierarchy theory, another branch of complexity studies founded by biologist Timothy F. H. Allen of the University of Wisconsin, Madison. We need to consider how systems dynamics in one place and at one scale affect the dynamics in a related system at another place and scale. We have to learn more about the particularities of major climate feedbacks, which may help to inform potential climate policies.

For instance, scientists are now revealing patterns between terrestrial and oceanic changes in one region and how they affect other regions. Some of these patterns are simple. Land-cover changes affect rainfall patterns. Deforestation in one area will cause floods and droughts in other areas. In this way, 30 percent of precipitation has been lost over critical croplands in recent years, according to Chapin, while there has been a 10 percent increase of rainfall over heath lands, or lands covered in natural vegetation. Reversing some of these land management practices – agricultural practices, deforestation, etc. – can reverse rainfall changes as well, maintaining a better balance of rainfall patterns over areas both of vegetation or forest and cropland.

Similarly, rather than just study the impacts of fire on the climate system, we need to think about specificities of changes in different areas, said Chapin.

Changes in wildfire regimes have been variable, with mixed impacts. In southeastern Siberia, for instance, logging has brought a lessening of wildfires in neighboring areas. Of course, in some places – Southern California, Indonesia – wildfires have been increasing in number and intensity. The bottom line about wildfire trends is that across the globe land use practices are changing fire patterns, most often with a negative impact on both human settlements and ecosystems, especially in terms of deforestation in some areas, and increasing fire destruction in others.

A very important lesson emerges from these studies, says Chapin. Climate feedbacks are not something we are necessarily stuck with! Since human social change has brought about most of these shifts in rainfall and wildfire patterns, we can pinpoint which behaviors and policies are creating these biophysical shifts and we can reverse them. We have influence over climate feedbacks through policy.

Over the years, the socioecological framework has given natural scientists concerned with environmental issues an appreciation for the profound significance of human–nature interactions. It has led Chapin to speak deeply with the Inuit people of Alaska and learn from their environmental wisdom. By framing his scientific research in a way that inherently includes peoples and their activities, he has become highly sensitive to the differences between the relatively resource-sustaining Native Alaskans and the resource-plundering Westerners who have arrived in Alaska mostly in the last few decades. While some corporations deplete fishing stocks and deepen oil wells, many Native communities continue the ecological practices that have guided them through millennia. Chapin incorporates his deep appreciation of Native wisdom into his science. To truly understand the socioecological framework and the principle of resilience on the land is to understand human impact, behavior, and activities on the landscape. Striking contrasts between Native and Western natural resource management practices informs the very basis of Chapin's models. He considers such issues as how Natives think, sense, and relate to the land, and how that in turn affects the cycles of human–land interactions over time.

Chapin's core principle is one of the principles at the heart of complex dynamic systems studies: resilience. He has developed this from a piecemeal concept to an effective general resilience framework for environmental and natural resources management. His work adds to that of several leading ecologists and related social scientists, including Lance Gunderson and C. S. "Buzz" Holling, editors of an influential book on socio-ecosystems as complex, dynamic, and resilient systems, *Panarchy* (2002). Resilience in the context of environmental management, says Chapin, is the magnitude of disturbance that can be absorbed by a system without fundamentally changing it.[9] "More resilient systems are able to absorb larger shocks. When massive transformations occur, resilient systems contain the components needed for renewal and reorganization. In other words, they can cope, adapt, or reorganize without sacrificing the provision of ecosystem services."[10]

Chapin argues that managing for general ecosystem and landscape resilience rather than for specific properties, such as the abundance of a particular species, has greater potential to sustain those fundamental features of northern systems crucial to society. For example, as in the case of deforestation causing droughts and fires, one can pinpoint some drivers of change in socioecological systems and the correlated corrective policies. In these cases, policies would include the money, assistance, scientific knowledge, political power, and regulations needed to stop and reverse deforestation. "The goal of ecosystem stewardship," he says, "is to respond to and shape change in social-ecological systems in order to sustain the supply and opportunities for use of ecosystem services by society."

Ecology has long been recognized as the study of complexity in nature. The very word "eco-system" captures the central role of complex systems. Transdisciplinary scientists involved in both natural science complexity studies and in ecology appreciate the special role that complexity plays in this science, or rather, that complexity sciences and studies help to illuminate aspects of ecological and social systems; nature is comprised of complex systems. Ecologists have long appreciated this – Darwin, through the naturalists of the last few centuries, and more recently ecologists in the formal field of the discipline beginning in the 1960s.

However, in the last decade the confluence of the fields of complexity and ecology has spawned a reframing of ecology around many of the specific complexity principles, in a fruitful marriage. Use of complexity as a framework for ecology has exploded, with Chapin's work on resilience being just one example among many. Most ecologists have been engaged to some degree with work on the complex systems principles in ecology, including resilience, network studies, scale and grain, feedbacks, thresholds, collapse, and sustainability.

Sustainable commons and natural resource management

The decision to grant the Nobel Prize in Economics to Elinor Ostrom in 2009 was a radical departure from past assessments of the Nobel Prize committees in economics, a new view for which ecological economists and others have been advocating for decades. A closer look at Ostrom's propositions reveals that as in the case of Reid, Schneider, and Chapin, once again, Ostrom's core argument derives from complex dynamic systems principles, or complexity theories. In one of the papers leading to her Nobel Prize, she stated her main conclusion thus:

> Officials and citizens need to craft institutions at multiple levels built on accurate data gathered at appropriate scales given the type of resource involved. Scholars have learned that ecosystems are diverse, complex, and uncertain, and sustainable management requires substantial investment in acquiring accurate data to learn more about patterns of interaction and adapt policies over time that are better fitted to particular systems.

In other words, while science must of course rely heavily on knowledge of the particulars of our social and ecological systems, it is the interactions between different elements of these systems, long neglected throughout the disciplines, which must now be at the forefront of our understanding. Ostrom's work indicates that while complexity theories themselves need not always be part of the explanation, they are essential to theoretical framing and understanding. Insofar as complexity principles undergird many successful policy tools, they deserve to be more comprehensively unearthed and assessed.

None of the above leading environmental scholars – Reid, Schneider, Chapin, and Ostrom – utilize the terminology of complexity theories specifically as described in this book; what I refer to as generalized complexity theories, or just complexity theories, is new terrain. It is the proposition of this book that acknowledgment and advancement of the conceptual and theoretical framework of generalized complexity theories provides a major framework for sustainability efforts; it is one important piece of the puzzle. It seems to be, as Kenneth Boulding suggested 50 years ago, the "skeleton of science."[11]

Conclusion

Visions of complexity and of sustainability have been emerging and developing in consort. Complexity theories have helped to rid us of falsely assuring assumptions of control and stability, and rather, show just how our planet is uncertain, vulnerable, and resilient, in constant networked interactions, and prone to at times rapid and widespread changes. Not only this, but they help us to see more detailed processes and patterns of this newly contingent and precious world – patterns of networks, feedbacks, hierarchically ensconced processes and interactions, and the way that various systems continuously change and self-organize, change and remain the same. As such, complexity also touches the core of some of our oldest philosophical questions, and helps to show us the way forward to bridging and linking key questions between the natural sciences, the social sciences, and philosophy, all of which are necessary to understanding our current moment of momentous global change.

Internationally leading scientists and scholars working on global environmental change, climate change, and related environmental management and policy, have drawn deeply on complexity principles in understanding and addressing key issues and approaches of the twenty-first century. These leaders are framing particular aspects of sustainability in terms of complexity principles, and yet, they have had to do so without the benefit of a clear articulation of the field of complexity theories writ large, and of the implications of this for a new kind of transdisciplinary unity of the branches of knowledge. These leaders have had to present various of the core principles of complexity theories, without the benefits of a clear exposition of the general field of complexity theories, and its role in understanding and advancing sustainability. Like many other leading world thinkers, Walter Reid, F. Stuart Chapin, Stephen Schneider, and Elinor Ostrom have each taken up several different key principles from complexity theories at the heart of their own theoretical perspectives. Their analyses have been shaping the world's approach to study and policy for global change.

To date, the complexity vision has been promoted largely in a very piecemeal fashion, with each theorist mentioning a few of the core principles and focusing on one or two of the major frameworks within complexity theories. This book proposes to give an overview of the broader field of complexity theories, to capture this fascinating moment in the history of ideas, and to contribute to advancing both complexity theories and planetary sustainability.

2 Elucidating complexity theories

> I would not give a fig for simplicity on this side of complexity, but I'd give my
> life for the simplicity on the other side of complexity.
>
> Oliver Wendell Holmes, Jr.[1]

Complexity theories

Over the past 20 years there has been an acceleration of so-called "complexity theories." Useful definitions and descriptions of these theories have developed, but these have been mostly fragmented, dispersed, and lacking in systemic analysis, scope, and depth. Most people associate complexity with a few discoveries in mathematics applied to natural systems – e.g., chaos, fractals, and networks. For years we have heard that weather patterns are chaotic, the structure of snowflakes is fractal, and that ecosystems are made up of networks.

While such discoveries regarding natural systems are receiving increasingly systematic attention, so far this remains largely dissociated from substantial advances and insights into the nature and implications of complexity developed in other realms, e.g., social systems, and related areas of knowledge: quantitative social science, qualitative social theory, philosophy and the humanities. Significantly, complexity theories about each of these realms are in fact interrelated, sharing core characteristics, and in at least some significant respects, coalescing into one transdisciplinary framework.

The proposition to be explored throughout the book is that an explicit rendering of the transdisciplinary complexity principles as a framework provides a reference guide throughout many areas of science, scholarship, policy, organizations, and activism. By focusing on complexity not just as piecemeal phenomena, but also rather as a profound characteristic of our world, we radically shift epistemology, ontology, and ethics, opening the way to develop wiser thinking about the range of issues crucial to improving the human ability to survive and thrive. Complexity theories highlight an integral view of sustainability issues, which may contribute to the framing, understanding, and guidance of economics, science, technology, ethics, politics, and policy.

In this chapter, I develop one central complexity framework helpful in the case of highly complex social and environmental change and the quest for sustainability. In general, I use the term sustainability in the broadest sense of the term, meaning social and environmental well-being over the long term; I define it in more detail later. Many other approaches to complexity for sustainability are possible, and I focus on just one, the relevance of complex dynamic systems, or simply "complex systems."

Complexity theories have been presented as a few pieces of gold, while in fact they represent a goldmine. While most people still associate complexity merely with a few discoveries in math and science, in actuality there is a rich array of complexity theories about phenomena occurring throughout the sciences, but also throughout all branches of reality and knowledge. This book highlights the entire range of transdisciplinary complexity theories, and in so doing, showcases various practical applications and implications for dealing with planetary issues, and deep philosophical implications of complexity as a powerful perspective in the twenty-first century.

This view of complexity theories writ large illuminates the framework presented in this book, which can be a key reference guide for addressing many of the pressing problems confronting humanity today. Many of the global crises in recent years – mass extinctions, climate change, social injustice, poverty, natural resource depletion, toxic pollution, etc. – have existed in large part because our thinking has been more focused on single issues and disciplinary parts rather than on synthetic analysis about the interactions and processes of whole systems. For years we have been thinking about trees and losing whole forests.

The modern era has highlighted the extraction of the simple from the complex, overlooking the complex in ways that are at times useful and necessary, but often, and somewhat systematically in fact, disastrous. Increasingly, complexity theories show that seemingly innocuous oversimplification is the bane of contemporary knowledge, creating hyperdisciplinary blinders, unguided drivers of knowledge and technology production, and the lack of a clear, common sense of humanity's current path and future vision.

I admit my failure to develop a simple new definition of complexity theories. It may not be possible to define complexity. Complexity theorist, biologist, and philosopher Henri Atlan has held for decades that complexity is that which we cannot grasp. Complexity theorist, ecologist, and interdisciplinary thinker Timothy F. H. Allen calls complexity "the undefinable." He writes, "complexity theory is what we do when faced with the undefinable."[2] Nonetheless, Atlan, Allen, and many other complexity theorists have spent decades doing their best to describe the somewhat, partially indescribable. Even if we may never fully grasp the complexity of reality, we can improve our understanding of it.

I continue to develop a transdisciplinary perspective of complexity throughout the book. In articulating a starting point for this inquiry, I focus on one major arena of complexity theories, complex dynamic systems. As I mentioned in the Introduction, with this focus we might briefly describe complexity as *the dynamic interactions of multiple elements engaged in self-organizing processes.* The implications are epistemological, ontological, and ethical, deep and far-reaching. I will dig into the layers of this deeper definition and implications throughout this chapter and this book.

The rise of transdisciplinary complexity theories is at first hard to grasp because it is just so significant, and the implications so extensive. Again, when I speak of complexity theories throughout this book, I am speaking of "theory" in the original sense of the term, as any attempt to understand or explain phenomena in any realm, physical, living, or social systems. When I speak of transdisciplinarity throughout this book, I am speaking of an approach to knowledge that encompasses multiple disciplines, including differing methodologies and epistemologies, in order to grasp multidimensional, complex issues in our world. In the case of environmental issues, we often draw on the best environmental scientific data and understanding, as well as ideas and theories from our great philosophers and social theorists, from Plato or Kant to Foucault or Zizek today. When I speak of social theory then, I am speaking of it in the broadest sense of the term, as any theories or explanations of social phenomena.

The transdisciplinary focus of this complexity framework and of this book involves the nexus of three major realms of knowledge – the natural sciences, social theory, and philosophy, and on transdisciplinary approaches that integrate these fields. By the natural sciences I mean all sciences using quantitative methodologies (the scientific method, mathematical models, etc.) to understand natural systems – the physical and living worlds we inhabit, e.g., physics, geology, atmospherics, biology, ecology, etc. By social theory I mean, all academic disciplines using "theory" most broadly defined – which is to say not qualitative in the narrow methodological sense but rather qualitative in the broadest sense to mean all non-quantitative theoretical methods – to study social systems, such as: sociology, critical theory, cultural studies, postmodernism broadly defined, etc. While I do not focus as much on the quantitative social sciences, I include most academic fields related to understanding society today, including those that utilize quantitative data as well as qualitative theory, e.g., sociology, psychology, economics, politics, demography, etc., under the general monikers of social systems and social theory. Philosophy, of course, includes ontology, epistemology, ethics, and the philosophy of science. In each of these three general realms – the sciences, social theory, and philosophy – my focus is the fields most relevant to sustainability. A central aim of the book is to show the value of this transdisciplinary perspective to global issues.

While the book is transdisciplinary, there are, of course, many disciplines that I omit. I mostly omit computer sciences, and details of most natural sciences, as these are covered elsewhere by specialists in those fields. I mostly omit the quantitative social sciences and the humanities, e.g., agent-based models applied to social systems and the study of complexity in history, anthropology, and literature, as these fields are often relevant but less central to my focus on sustainability. While there is now literature on complexity throughout various areas of the arts, media, and diverse fields, again, I leave these areas to specialists in those fields. However, I discuss some aspects of ecology, climate science, and other scientific fields relevant to environmental crises.

Complexity and sustainability

Our era is witnessing massive global change of innumerable types, many of them novel, and evolving in ways that are networked, interacting, and interdependent. Our societies and environments are not only not stable and not predictable – not Aristotelian, not Laplacian. They are also inherently complex, linked together via hierarchically structured networks of feedbacks, and capable of at times rapid changes.

Ironically, this profound lesson comes just as we have entered what geographers now call the Anthropocene. We have realized that human impacts on the environment are quite powerful, and in fact that we are undermining the natural fabric upon which our lives depend. Due to these vast networks of intricately interdependent, coevolving systems, due to the power of positive feedbacks and nonlinear, rapid change, we suddenly realize that humanity is not only powerful, but also vulnerable.

 And yet complexity theories also inform us that as agents in the environment we are capable not only of impacting and degrading environments, but also that we are capable of learning, adaptation, strategy, change, and caring for environments.

Because complexity theories are transdisciplinary by nature – in the sense that all realms of reality physical, living, and social are complex and in many ways interacting – they necessitate and explicate the need and the way to validate and integrate some transdisciplinarity into our thinking. Seeing complexity as transdisciplinary helps to comprehend global change, and to pinpoint drivers, feedbacks, network causality, and potentially even networked, integral solutions. In contemplating what drives societies today at the global level, it is apparent that there is no one global mastermind. There is no Wizard of Oz, behind the curtain, pulling all the levers that drive global change. Quite the contrary, amongst the lot of us, there is not even a very deep understanding of life's complexity.

Complexity theories are developing rapidly throughout every realm of knowledge – a kaleidoscopic new view of life's intricacies and dynamics – revitalizing our sense of awe, wonder, and enlivenment. The more we see the world in terms of dynamic systems, the more we also illuminate how overly simplistic our thinking has been, and the more we see the deep problems brought on by overly simplistic thinking. Social theorist Bruno Latour has argued that we are living in a "non"-modern era; "we have never been modern" in that the simple and simplifying precepts underlying modernity are illusory. Our postmodern era is commonly lamented as somehow negative or nihilist. Rather if there was a nihilist vision, it was the dulling, mechanistic lenses of modernity. In contrast, with a vision of complexity renewing our sense of life's extraordinary qualities, perhaps "postmodernity" can become quite a promising era.

Complexity frameworks

In this chapter I build a series of conceptual frameworks, leading up to one complexity framework, and one framework linking complexity and the quest for sustainability. This is not a comprehensive, singular or final project, but rather one initial exploration.

In developing complexity theories, a major pitfall is to overly simplify, systematize, or reify them, or to try to create a singular unified theory – all of which would be just as antithetical to complexity as the most reified classical scientific assumptions and ideologies. Attempting to avoid these pitfalls, it would behoove us to move beyond our current largely piecemeal understanding of complexity theories, towards a more comprehensive, integrated view. With sufficiently deep, ongoing, critical thinking, developing such general complexity frameworks explicitly and comprehensively will advance social and environmental thinking, science, politics, policy, and ethics in the decades ahead.

The field of transdisciplinary complexity theories is now well underway. Even in its dispersed, fragmented state, complexity has already become widely used and lauded. Study of complex systems has been advancing in every branch of knowledge, regarding the physical, the living world, and social and philosophical realms, as well as brain sciences, consciousness studies, psychology, art, and literature. Understanding contemporary issues in terms of complex systems gives us a powerful perspective for addressing them not just with reductionist precision but also in terms of life's vibrant interrelated processes.

A brief history of complexity theories

A few major challenges plague a clear account of the history of complexity theories. First, in a certain sense, the exposition of complexity theories to date contains landmines of discord between and amongst different disciplines and epistemologies, and this has yet to be more fully revealed. Complexity studies have been taken up in highly disparate disciplines with only partial accord between them over several decades. Second, terms like chaos, equilibrium, organization and even "theory" are used with very different connotations from the perspective of the different disciplines. A physicist and a social theorist use the same term "theory" with different meanings. Furthermore, natural scientists and humanities scholars often are scantly aware of the different theoretical frameworks and underlying assumptions that undergird these different connotations of key terms.

Moreover, the field of complexity has developed in many different languages across the globe, and the terms have evolved somewhat differently in these different societies and languages. For instance, the precursor to complexity theories, systems theories, varied in some significant ways in Anglophone and French schools of thought. Some major works have not been translated from one language to another, and other works are translated without a full consideration of disciplinary epistemology or discourse, or of transdisciplinary meaning.

I focus here on a sketch of main events, discoveries, and thinkers in the complexity field. To clarify the parameters, I see transdisciplinary systems theories largely as the precursor and core of what has more recently blossomed under the larger umbrella of transdisciplinary complexity theories. I will refer to these simply as systems theories and complexity theories throughout. Systems theories were first developed from the 1920s through the 1970s; complexity theories have extended beyond and subsumed systems theories from the 1980s through today. Though this distinction is certainly crude and open to debate, I think it is a useful organization of the history.

As such, I divide the history of these studies into three major phases: pre-systems theories (ancient history to 1921), systems theories (1922 to 1976), and the contemporary phase of complexity theories (1977 to today). There is much overlap and also some divergence. See, for instance, Kurt Richardson's series, "Systems Theory and Complexity."[3] Whether or not one accepts this general, somewhat crude description of the relationship between the two sets of theories, both have deep roots. Seeds of complexity were planted from antiquity through modernity, and again throughout the systems phase, while systems theories are to a degree and in various respects perhaps, still a distinct domain. Complexity theories have mushroomed into a broad literature within and across the disciplines. While systems thinkers made the shift from objects to subjects and parts to interactions, complexity scholars in the last three decades have added crucial new dimensions that significantly advance upon systems theories, that is, the processes of emergence and self-organization. These concepts in turn have revolutionized all the other major principles of complex dynamic systems studies – nonlinearity, feedback, network, hierarchy, uncertainty, and many more, which will be described in this chapter.

The pre-systems theories phase is significant. Many or perhaps all indigenous societies in times past and present have been and remain attuned to systems and complexity concepts. Western thinkers, such as Heraclitus, Pascal, and many others, expressed core elements of complex thinking. Heraclitus noted phenomena that today may well be called complexity, emergence, and self-organization. One could argue that thinkers like Pascal were already complexity scholars, allowing the glimmerings of complexity thinking to reverberate in the background of the modern age. Karl Ludwig von Bertalanffy traced systems concepts to the philosophy of Gottfried von Leibniz and Nicholas of Cusa's *Coincidentia Oppositorum*. Eastern thinkers evoked complexity as well. Charles West Churchman identified the *I Ching* as a systems approach sharing a frame of reference similar to Heraclitus' pre-Socratic philosophy.[4] Joanna Macy draws rich parallels between Buddhist philosophy and systems thinking.[5]

Significant precursors to contemporary complexity theories in the natural sciences first emerged not in the natural sciences, but rather in philosophy. Specifically, complexity principles in the works of Pascal, Kant, and Nietzsche began overturning classical scientific assumptions, e.g., Newtonian mechanics, as Morin argues. Whereas, in the natural sciences, complexity emerged with the second law of thermodynamics, Gödel's theorem, and Heisenberg's uncertainty principle.[6] One important strand of transdisciplinary thinking first articulated in modern times by the French Enlightenment thinkers was the desire to unify knowledge, to somehow weave back together some threads of the growing ensembles of disciplines. The *Encyclopedia* of Denis Diderot and his colleagues spurred thinking on whether and how the branches of knowledge may ultimately be reunited.

Nineteenth century thinkers noted various central aspects of complex systems dynamics. The French biologist Claude Bernard developed the first extended analysis of feedback in physiological and other biological processes, and the French mathematician Henri Poincare was the first to note deterministic chaos, later developed by Edward Lorenz.

A source of early general systems theory was the reaction against a later attempt to unify knowledge, the logical positivists of the early to mid-twentieth century. Moritz Schlick organized the Vienna Circle, a group of philosophers and scientists who met regularly beginning in 1922. The group aimed to develop a rigorous, empirical perspective on the potential unity of knowledge, the subject of their main project, *The Encyclopedia of Unified Science*. Regular members included Rudolph Carnap, Otto Neurath, and Hans Hahn. Ludwig Wittgenstein and Karl Popper influenced the group, meeting with them occasionally. Kurt Godel, W. V. Quine, and A. J. Ayer also visited the group.

Like the social theorists of Diderot's *Encyclopedia*, these philosophers were also attempting to model their ideas and methods for social systems on the same basis as the natural sciences, to base social theory on the methods and concepts of classical science, such as Newtonian mechanics. This attempt to transfer the underlying assumptions of the natural sciences to social systems failed both the social theorists and the philosophers. Ironically, the radical idea at the heart of complexity theories – self-organization – shows how and why attempts to apply the natural sciences to social systems have always failed, and continue to fail throughout a great deal of science and scholarship today, even that which otherwise incorporates or espouses complexity principles. Thus, complexity has come full circle to shed new light on how a partially unified, though still partially disunified, pluralistic view of knowledge might take hold.

In the first half of the twentieth century many precursors to today's complexity theories were developed. The modern version of the notion of complexity emerged perhaps as early as the theoretician of population dynamics in ecosystems, Alfred J. Lotka's 1925 classic, *Elements of Physical Biology*. Other early developments included in 1925 mathematical theoretical biology and in 1944 the study of biospherics.[7]

During and after World War II a group of engineers, mathematicians and others developed cybernetics, a branch of early systems studies. Norbert Wiener coined the term cybernetics in the seminal article published in 1948, *Cybernetics: Or the Control and Communication in the Animal and the Machine*, or the study of communication and control theory in animals or machines, concerned especially with the comparative study of automatic control systems, such as the nervous system, brain, and mechanical-electrical communication systems.[8] This view brought in one side of complexity thinking, but omitted another side. First-wave cybernetics focused on mechanistic feedbacks, and omitted other feedbacks involved in self-organization. The reverberations of this philosophical error are still playing out in various areas such as biology and cognitive science today.[9]

However, a fuller view of self-organization has been developing all through-out. John von Neumann early set out the principles of self-organization with respect to self-organizing automata. Various thinkers – Ross Ashby, Heinz von Foerster, Gottard Gunther, and several others – developed a meta-cybernetic theory of self-organizing systems at three meetings on self-organizing systems in 1959, 1960, and 1961.[10]

While cybernetics was developing, General Systems Theory (GST), founded by biologist and philosopher Karl Ludwig von Bertalanffy. Bertalanffy had been working throughout the 1940s on a unified view of knowledge, a response to and repudiation of the Vienna Circle's positivist approach. While Bertalanffy, who was from Vienna and a doctoral student of Moritz Schlick, shared the Vienna Circle's goal of rigorous analysis of important transdisciplinary dynamics, he also disagreed with what he saw as the positivist approach of the Vienna Circle. Bertalanffy saw systems concepts as a broad, interdisciplinary bridge that could ultimately unite all the sciences in a more inclusive fashion, with implications extending throughout the natural and social sciences. GST was an attempt to the-orize the connections between disparate types of systems, which provided a major basis of subsequent systems theories. Bertalanffy's work on GST was published as a book in German in 1948, an article in English in 1951, and a book in English, *General System Theory: Foundations, Development, Applications*, in 1968.

In the post-war period, from 1946 to 1953, Bertalanffy Gregory Bateson, Margaret Mead, and other major systems thinkers gathered regularly in New York City for a series of groundbreaking meetings called the Macy's Confer-ences. They discussed general system theory, cybernetics, and system dynamics and their possible implications in diverse fields, mainly mathematical modeling, engineering, biology, and psychology – laying the groundwork for the birth of complexity theories. Meanwhile, from 1956 to 1960 a group formed consisting of Bertalanffy, Anatol Rapoport, Ralph Gerard, Kenneth Boulding, and Ross Ashby. They were officially called the Society for General Systems Research (SGSR), and informally called the "Stanford Group." The span of the group's work was short but the results were prodigious, including four major volumes on GST. They began a journal by the same name, a central resource in systems studies through the 1960s and 1970s.

The SGSR influenced a group of philosophers who took up some of the ques-tions lingering in the wake of both the Vienna Circle and the advent of systems theories. This group, sometimes called the "Stanford School" of the philosophy of science, included Nancy Cartwright, John Dupré, Ian Hacking, Patrick Suppes, and Peter Galison. These five philosophers have had a considerable influence from the 1970s to today in shaping ideas in the philosophy of science, including the nature and consequences of systems and complexity theories.

The 1960s was a fertile time for the systems sciences. Several major related fields had their start, including artificial intelligence (Herbert Simon and others, 1956), ecology (Rachel Carson, 1962), chaos theory (Edward Lorenz, 1963), and catastrophe theory (Rene Thom, 1967). Though some might say that ecology began as early as 1866, with Ernest Haeckel's *General Morphology of Organisms, General Outlines of the Science of Organic Forms based on Mechanical principles through the Theory of Descent as reformed by Charles Darwin*, most see the field as starting with *Silent Spring* in 1962. While Rachel Carson was neither a founder of ecological science nor of complexity thinking per se, nonetheless many see her book as launching both the environmental movement of the 1960s and 1970s, and scholarly interest in the field of ecology, which quickly came to be seen as a complexity science par excellence, overturning modernist assumptions through revelations of complex dynamics, and hence called the "subversive science."

Major dates for early complexity theories from 1970 to 1980 included the following: Gregory Bateson published *Steps to an Ecology of Mind*, and Humberto Maturana and Francisco Varela introduced autopoesis in 1972; Benoit Mandelbrot coined the term "fractal" in 1975; and in 1977, Edgar Morin published the first volume on what was to be later called generalized complexity theories or simply complexity theories, *The Method, Volume I*, to be followed by five more volumes, between 1981 and 2006; also in 1977, Conrad Hal Waddington pubished the founding book on operations research, *Tools for Thought*; and in 1980 a major French Cerisy conference was held on complexity theories.

Complexity was coined and the synthesis of all of these major endeavors and fields began. Jean-Pierre Dupuy published *Orders and Disorders: Quest for a New Paradigm* (*Ordres et désordres: Enquête sur un nouveau paradigm*) in 1982.[11] The Santa Fe Institute formed in 1984. A popular book appeared on chaos in 1987 by James Gleick, and two on complexity in 1992 by Mitchell Waldrop and Roger Lewin. Dupuy critiqued the cybernetics movement and its legacy today in *The Mechanization of the Mind* (1994).

By the 1990s, thinkers were applying systems and complexity theories in intriguing new directions. Joanna Macy explored links between systems theories and Buddhism in 1991, and N. Kathryn Hayles applied systems theories to the arts, literature, and posthumanism (e.g., 1990, 1999). Three major complexity institutions began in the years 1998 to 2000: the New England Complex Systems Institute (NECSI), the Institute for the Study of Coherence and Emergence, (ICSE), and the French organization founded by Jean-Louis Le Moigne and Edgar Morin, Modeling of Complex Systems and the Association for Complex Thinking (MCX-APC). ISCE publishes the major journal, *Emergence: Complexity + Organization* (E:CO), covering the full spectrum of complexity studies, from organizations, to social and environmental issues, to philosophy.

Transdisciplinary complexity theories or "generalized complexity theories," have blossomed with the work of ISCE, E:CO and many other organizations. French transdisciplinary scholar – sociologist, philosopher, filmmaker, social critic, and more – Edgar Morin, a pioneer of contemporary transdisciplinary or "generalized" complexity theories, argues that complex thinking will help us to overcome destructive past paradigms and assumptions more fully, and to open our minds to a more effective worldview. His work is only slowly appearing in English, including his six-volume series on complexity theories (1977–2006) with many other books that can be seen as extensions of this project, including

La Voie, published in 2011. Morin has written approximately 2,000 pages in primary texts on complexity theories, and about another 1,000 pages on their implications. He is a leading intellectual in Europe, Latin America, and French-speaking Africa.

With many research institutes, journals, publishing houses, academic departments, and degree programs around the world, the field of complexity studies is flourishing.

Complexity framing and terms

Any highly complex theories will prove unsatisfying and even sacrilege to those who wish to condense reality into one simple unified theory, one discipline, one ideology, one doctrine, or one triumphant Nobel Prize.

Contrary to popular opinion, simplicity and significance are not always correlated. Not every useful theory can be as elegant as $E = MC^2$. Increasingly, social theorists have realized that in social and environmental systems, many types of descriptions must be "rich," "thick," or "complex." In fact, I argue that complexity is especially powerful in the treatment of so-called "wicked" problems – those that by nature are challenging due to their complexity and do not always yield easily to simple solutions.

Over the last century, scientists and scholars increasingly have broken with simpler notions, and begun to accept a more intricate view of reality. Those most interested in tight, logical, precise arguments may be perplexed by transdisciplinary complexity theories. Because complexity theories aim to articulate a more intricate and comprehensive view, complexity terms seem to suffer from vagueness, incoherence, and inadequacy. One of the operating principles of this book is to discard the notion that for something to be worthwhile it must be simplified or simplifiable, concise or cryptic. Indeed, complexity is that which we cannot model fully; we inevitably lose complexity in the modeling, even if complex processes may preexist and persist in terms of the patterns and processes under study. Yet, we can render our thinking, models, and theories "more complex," more adequate to grasping fuller complexity.

Complexity is paradigmatic. It has been described as a shift beyond the paradigm of classical science and the modern era, alternatively viewed either as a new paradigm or as beyond paradigms. I stick with the former out of intellectual humility and uncertainty, but I admire the latter for its potential to underscore the nature and significance of the shift.[12]

In either case it is significant to define complexity in contrast to the classical science paradigm from which it emerged. The term "classical science" or "modern science" refers to the dominant mainstream Western scientific worldview based on the 1600s frameworks of Bacon, Descartes, and Newton, their founding ideas and underlying assumptions about the nature of science, including a belief in pure reductionism. Even when today's scientists and scholars assiduously incorporate complexity concepts in their models and analyses, most still sneak in some degree of flawed underlying modernist assumptions in their framing and interpretations, as leading social theorists have shown in recent decades.[13]

Historically, complexity is breaking out from the confines of classical scientific thinking. Hence, complexity theories have emerged across the widest span of disciplines, when in fact complexity also evokes the very transdisciplinary fabric capable of articulating these disparate disciplines. They reveal how disciplines are both necessary and often inadequate. Disciplines are one side of the Möbius strip of reality, which can only become more fully representative when integrated with the other side of the strip – transdisciplinarity.

It must be noted how much has yet to be articulated to make sense of this paradigmatic novelty. It's useful to distinguish between the dominant, classical paradigm and the complexity perspective. However, this is no easy task; the boundary between so-called "classical" or "modern" vs. "complexity" views are difficult to articulate. At this historical moment, science and scholarship are prolific, diversified, and undergoing multiple transitions. While some science and scholarship and most interpretation and understanding of it still eschews complexity too much, at the same time, in other ways, much contemporary science and scholarship already incorporates much complexity. The question now is improving our methodologies and analysis, knowing when and how we fail to incorporate it effectively, and how to encourage effective incorporation and advancement.

One step is in clarifying common confusions about the emerging complexity perspective. In just one example, take the ongoing confusion of chaos and complexity theories. Complexity is an extremely broad term – a general epistemology and ontology, a paradigm. So complexity is a broad term like sustainability, nature, human nature, or social change. Whereas, chaos is much more delimited, albeit common; chaos refers to mathematically bounded infinities in physical and chemical systems. Chaos is intriguing, significant, and has far-reaching implications.[14] However it is a quite delimited concept in contrast with complexity. True, this chaotic pattern can be extended metaphorically to describe the restructuring phases in social systems, one specific aspect of the configuration of social change. Yet chaos describes one set of patterns, while complexity describes a once-in-500-year paradigmatic shift.

Yet, perhaps because chaos sounds catchier than complexity; perhaps because people are complexity averse, but can instantly relate to "chaos"; perhaps because James Gleick's book on chaos appeared several years before Mitchell Waldrop and Roger Lewin's books on complexity, the term chaos went viral, while the greater significance of complexity lurked in the shadows. Chaos is of course a major discovery! In the last 15 years, with the rise of journals, institutes, and degree programs devoted to it, complexity's significance has become clearer.

Key terms: complex, complexity, complexity science, complexity sciences, complexity theories, and complex thinking

Key complexity terms used in different disciplines reveal some of the differing viewpoints to be reconciled and articulated in this process of advancing comprehension of complexity. Major complexity terms that are used mostly orthogonally within different disciplinary contexts are: complex, complexity, complexity theory, complexity science, complexity sciences, complex thinking, and complexity theories.

The terms complex and complexity have several connotations. I focus on the broad, transdisciplinary sense of these terms as synonyms for the terms complex dynamic systems. All of these terms refer to dynamic interactions of multiple elements engaged in emergent, self-organizing processes in all kinds of systems – e.g., physical, biological, and social systems. Complexity theories focus on the intricacy and interactions of processes that occur within and between parts and wholes. Paradoxically, we see that this highlights both interdependence and disjunction. Complex systems are infused with both constraints and emergence; both interdependence and independence; both congruities and incongruities. Ultimately, again, complexity speaks to more than just dynamic systems, but the latter is the focus in this book.

I use the term complexity sciences to highlight the pluralistic epistemologies embedded even within the domain of the natural sciences. Physics, biology, and ecology require various diverse epistemologies and methodologies, simultaneously in various ways congruous and incongruous. The term "complexity sciences" accurately captures the fact that the sciences are not in fact either ontologically or epistemologically unified in the sense that the logical positivists have pursued. While mathematics underlies the sciences, this does not mean that physics, biology, and ecology collapse fully into one discipline.

For these reasons I try to avoid the terms "complexity science" or "complexity theory," unless I'm talking about one specific science or theory. "Complexity science" is widely used by complexity scientists, so I share their use of the term. Yet, generally speaking these two terms can be seen as holdouts from the very dreams of a unified science or unified theory that transdisciplinary complexity itself paradigmatically refutes. This in absolutely no way demotes the scientific method, which is of course an essential aspect of complexity theories. There is no demotion of "complexity science," only its expansion into a greater ensemble of theories and dimensions. This remains anathema to some engrained disciplinary thinking, which holds that one disciplinary methodology and approach provide the greatest perspective, the most "generalized" knowledge. Complexity shows otherwise.

The Möbius strip is a useful metaphor. Quantitative reductionist methods are necessary to one side of the strip, while qualitative, synthetic, pluralistic, and transdisciplinary theoretical methods are necessary to the other side. Classical complexity sciences are necessary to one aspect of complexity, but the reductionist aspect of mathematics must be complimented to provide for articulation of the greater transdisciplinary dimensions. It's true, complexity scientists do important quantitative work in the social sciences, such as work on cities and economics. This perspective provides the necessary basis with which to articulate the other side of the Möbius strip – the transdisciplinary. Quantitative and qualitative complexity studies are interrelated.

Nonetheless, modernist attempts at basing social theory on the same principles as the natural sciences, Newtonian mechanics, or the nomothetic approach to social sciences has been fully debunked by decades of scholarship.[15] While some physicists still hold firm to the belief that mathematics is the *only* valid language of reality, this view has been firmly rejected throughout all of the disciplines of social theory and philosophy. For this reason, the terms complexity science and complexity theory can be misleading, modernist holdovers, distorting and impeding a deeper comprehension of complexity. This is why they do not apply well as general monikers for the greater transdisciplinary field. For the same reason complexity sciences and complexity theories are more useful general terms.

Because complexity for sustainability necessitates transdisciplinarity, I use the term "theories" in the general, historical, and transdisciplinary sense of the term, to mean, as in this definition from the mid-1600s (in the original English), "contemplation, speculation, deepe study, insight or beholding."[16] This is in contrast to more specific uses of the term within, for instance, physics. This is not an incidental, but rather a deliberate move on my part, to promote the use of the term as it does and can apply in social systems, in philosophy, and in any inquiry with a transdisciplinary dimension. This is the case for all of our major social and environmental issues, such as climate change ethics and policy. In fact, this more general sense of the term "theory" is useful in transdisciplinary analyses even in the case of primarily natural science issues.

So I say complexity theories to refer to the study, sciences, and theories of complex systems dynamics throughout all intersecting realms of reality, to portray complexity in its truer depth and scope. Since my perspective is largely based in Morin's meta-theoretical inclusion of both science and philosophy, quantitative and qualitative, constraints and emergences, congruities and incongruities, I use the term complexity to refer broadly to "complexity theories," "generalized complexity," and "transdisciplinary complexity." This broader sense of the term becomes imperative when we want to understand the interrelated social, environmental, ethical, economic, and political issues inherent to sustainability.

The term "complex thinking" captures the way in which transdisciplinary complexity theories move beyond awkward attempts to integrate plural epistemologies and methods, to a general perspective on reality. Since the articulation of transdisciplinary complexity theories involves philosophical theory, as much as social theory and scientific theory, complexity is a question not just of method or methods, but rather of a whole approach to knowledge and policy. I take the term "complex thinking" to mean: the use of a set of ideas, principles, models, and conceptual tools to explore the nature and the dynamics of any systems –

physical living, social, linguistic, meaning, etc. – in terms that incorporate the interactions of their elements in emergent, self-organizing processes. Simply put, if the world desperately needs one thing, it is an antonym and antidote for the disastrously "simple thinking" that has contributed to our current world crises, the simplistic assumptions at the root of classical science, and the many other simplifying assumptions and ideologies that have dominated the modern era.

Fundamental and relative complexity

A principle epistemological shift in complex thinking is the shift from the belief in abstract and totalizing objectivity, the removal of the observer from the systems, to the central role of subjectivity that arises when we put the observer back into context.

Flowing from this, it is useful to think about two categories of complexity, fundamental versus relative complexity. Fundamental complexity is the quality of the dynamics expressed by all the major complexity principles I will describe in this chapter. It has meaning only in distinction from relative complexity. Relative complexity is the degree of complexity observed relative to an observer or a particular issue or instance.

Subatomic particles, the smallest elements we have found in physics, behave in complex ways. The dynamics of physical entities like rocks can be seen as simple relative to those of living systems. For instance, a rock is composed of atoms exhibiting complex behavior, yet with respect to humans, the rock's behavior is simple! It goes through almost no discernible internal dynamics or exchanges with the environment for very long periods of time. So in relation to the human observer, the relative complexity of a rock compared to any living entity is very small. Moreover, even if there may be complex processes at the subatomic level, the behavior of the rock as a rock, as a part of the ecosystem, is not complex, but simple. Until an avalanche!

 Complexity is not an inherent material property or substance of some kind; rather complexity is relevant relative to systems, interactions, observers, and particular inquiries. One cannot extricate the observer from the system, and this has major consequences. What we see as simple one moment can be complex the next, depending upon the relationship of the observer to the system and the nature of the inquiry.

If we are asking how many lobes the brain has, it's simple: the brain has four lobes. If we ask about the evolution of the brain, this is also simple: it evolved from one lobe, to two, to three, a simple progression. Yet, of course, the human brain is characterized by complex processes – neuronal networks in webs of chemical and physiological interactions, producing emergent processes involved in phenomena like emotions, consciousness, experience, ideas, and meaning. So if we are asking about emergent processes, then the brain is a highly complex entity. Based on the degree of variables and interactions, the most complex entity is the human brain. Could we predict how much else there is to know about the brain?

Some thinkers have described relative complexity as a heuristic. One approach to complexity is to map systems as simply as possible, and then build up models and interpretations to include increasing degrees of relative complexity. Kenneth Boulding developed a typology that defines and describes degrees of relative complexity in a seminal article in 1956, "General Systems Theory: The Skeleton of Science."[17] More recently, Jean-Claude Lugan and Steven Jay Kline have developed further versions.[18]

Boulding's typology for instance, describes nine levels, ranging from simplest to most complex. The first level consists in an abstract static description of the elements and interactions within a system – "the patterns of electrons around a nucleus, the pattern of atoms, in a molecular formula, the arrangement of atoms in a crystal, the anatomy of the gene, the cell, the plant…" etc.[19] Disciplines are based upon first extracting this kind of static map, and then factoring in the dynamics. The second level he called simply a dynamic process involving somewhat predetermined, necessary motions, like the mechanical motions of a clock. The third level included the receipt of information and the process of feedbacks, control mechanisms, or cybernetic loops. It might be nicknamed the thermostat level, since thermostats function due to both predetermined processes and programmed information, as well as via reception of new information and subsequent adaptation, feedbacks.

Subsequent levels progress through biological and social systems dynamics to include entirely new kinds of phenomena. Already, Boulding included the next obvious levels of symbols and language. We might also include sensation, experience, consciousness, and spirituality. Boulding contemplated the inclusion of a final level, "a transcendental level." There may be a similarity to the nature of complexity across the levels with respect to any given example. Clearly though, the degree of complexity increases as one moves up the typology from the first to the ninth level.

This axis of degrees of relative complexity has also been described in terms of the disciplinary spectrum with physical systems at the one end and consciousness or perhaps "the transcendental" at the other. The spectrum is intriguing, but one should not assume implicit reason or order. Perhaps subatomic particles are as complex as processes producing human consciousness. What seems clear is that the more variables, interactions and feedbacks are involved, the greater the degree of relative complexity.

Restrained and generalized complexity

In order to articulate the two sides of the Möbius strip that comprise both quantitative and qualitative, both scientific and philosophical, Edgar Morin distinguishes between the work of more purely quantitative complexity sciences researchers such as the Santa Fe Institute, and the methodologically transdisciplinary, quantitative and qualitative approaches such as his own, which he calls, respectively, "restrained complexity" and "generalized complexity."[20]

It's important to note that because most scientists do not have the professional need or inclination to become fully versed in transdisciplinary perspectives, much of Morin's views may remain foreign or anathema. This is unfortunate, because Morin's view is not to eschew the work done by most complexity scientists, but rather to show even more fully its value to a more transdisciplinary enterprise. Morin develops the complexity sciences himself in the first two volumes of *The Method*.

For many issues, you cannot fully extricate the transdisciplinarity of complexity from the issue at hand, and retain a robust comprehension. For the aim of fuller understanding of the meaning and implications of science, according to Morin, such as science for sustainability, the results of quantitative research must be integrated with the broader qualitative context.

Morin begins by naming the three principles of the rejection of complexity by classical science: universal determinism, the idea of perfect knowledge and prediction of the past and the future; reductionism, the idea of knowing any composite from only the knowledge of its constituting elements; and disjunction, the principle of isolating and separating cognitive difficulties from one another, leading to the separation between disciplines, which have become hermetic from each other.[21] Essentially, he says, it is these three principles that now divide restrained from generalized complexity, as the former maintains some degree of each of the three classical principles, while the latter begins with the attempt to surpass the pure forms of these three classical principles.

Natural scientists may reject the term restrained, because they see their aim as entirely generalized, which is true. Morin is making, I believe, a subtle philosophical distinction, though this may seem foreign, especially to less transdisciplinary thinkers. Morin also bases his work on good quantitative science. In fact, a fuller marriage of the sciences and other branches of knowledge only further clarifies that value of the sciences.

Restrained complexity, says Morin, makes possible important advances in quantitative methods, which contribute to our fuller understanding. But one still remains partially within the epistemology of classical science. "When one searches for the 'laws of complexity', one still attaches complexity as a kind of wagon behind the truth locomotive, which produces laws."[22] The scientists at SFI, says Morin, succeed in their aims, producing important basic science. On the other hand, according to Morin, the "restrained" approach:

> …avoids the fundamental [philosophical] problem of complexity, which is epistemological, cognitive, paradigmatic. To some extent, one recognizes complexity, but by decomplexifying it. In this way, the breach is opened, then one tries to clog it: the paradigm of classical science remains, only fissured.[23]

Generalized complexity is an epistemological rethinking, bearing on the organization of knowledge and the nature of reality itself. It is paradigmatic. A paradigm of simplification controls classical science, by imposing principles of determinism, reduction, and disjunction to knowledge. To more fully engage with complexity, it is necessary to adopt a paradigm of complexity "that would impose a principle of distinction *and* a principle of conjunction." In opposition to reduction, complexity requires that one tries to comprehend the relations between the whole and the parts. The knowledge of the parts as parts is not enough, the knowledge of the whole as a whole is not enough, if one ignores its parts. Thus, the principle of reduction is substituted by a principle that conceives the fuller implications of reduction and synthesis, wholes and parts, together. It appears that we require a degree of restrained complexity in order to produce and develop generalized complexity. Ultimately, we need both disciplinarity and transdisciplinarity.

Complexity frameworks – towards an evolving comprehension of complexity

My aim is to clarify and inform ways in which complexity theories advance knowledge, and specifically, knowledge for sustainability. Complexity principles illuminate work within a multitude of individual disciplines. At the same time, seen together, these principles link and interrelate all the disciplines and the major realms of knowledge in a way that does not subsume or reduce one to another, but rather allows us to analyze issues in more of their plurality and multiplicity, with a transdisciplinary vision. Finally, it permits us to apply these lenses and insights to many kinds of interrelated social and environmental issues.

Complexity is briefly defined as the dynamic interactions of multiple elements engaged in self-organizing processes. A more adequate definition of complexity theories seems to be inherently long, complicated, and qualitatively multidimensional. When a definition becomes too long, it may seem to dilute its force. Actually, the very fact that the definition of complexity theories continues to grow in scope and detail and prove useful throughout many disciplines, indicates that there are processes in the world which are highly complex, and that we may need to pay attention to this, with regards to some issues, in some ways, and at some times. Current planetary environmental crises – extinctions, climate change, resource depletions, oceanic threats, poverty, and injustice – are one example.

Clearly, complexity theories are at times unnecessary or inappropriate, and they are never a panacea. Quite the contrary, they show the impossibility of "silver bullets." Many study subjects require a largely reductionist or restrained analysis, and not the more synthetic or generalized approach that this book examines. Complexity theories have sometimes been off base, wrongly applied, or misconstrued. In this book, I focus on the field's considerable successes.

From modernity to postmodernity, from mechanism to complexity

First and foremost, we can define complexity with respect to simplicity, as we understand postmodernism against the relief of modernism arising from the presumptions of classical science at the dawn of the Scientific Revolution.

Complexity is that which was eschewed by the simplistic assumptions of the early modern era, and has been increasingly coming to light.

In the last few decades of the twentieth century, many have noted the shift away from the narrower, simpler view of the simplistic mechanistic metaphors and assumptions of classical science – such as order, mechanism, atomism, positivism, monism, determinism, universalism, control, progress, etc. – towards the dawning complexity perspective. Carolyn Merchant's classic *The Death of Nature* argued that assumptions of a mechanical clockwork universe, one that is ordered and controllable, were overturned by a new view of nature based on chaos and complexity.[24] Richard B. Norgaard's book *Development Betrayed* focused on overturning major myths of classical science and modernity – mechanism, objectivism, positivism, monism, universalism – as well as both cultural and environmental deterministic thinking, and the problem with focusing on single causal mechanisms.[25]

Edgar Morin's voluminous *The Method* argued that each of these previous assumptions – mechanism, objectivism, positivism, etc. – were part of a binary. In classical science, just one side of the binary reigned – order, stability, invariance, exclusion, etc. Rather, complexity includes both parts of the binary, focusing on the dynamic interrelationship between the two. Rather than just order, our world exhibits a deep and continuous interrelationship, dialectic or dialogic, between order and disorder, known as self-organization; neither order nor disorder exists in isolation or abstraction, but rather always in interrelation with the other. This central notion of self-organization is one of a litany of changes replacing the classical scientific assumptions with a new complexity perspective that subsumes and transforms the older principles.

Complexity frameworks – approaches, promises, and pitfalls

With the aim of developing an initial framework of complexity for sustainability, several questions are useful: What do we see when we look at complexity? What epistemological tools do we use to look at complexity? What are the theoretical constructs we use in order to study complexity? And finally, in what ways are complexity theories most relevant to sustainability? I will offer an initial exploration of these four questions, focusing on the last. My aim is not to provide a comprehensive or final account of these new fields of study, but to explore some significant patterns.

One of the striking aspects of these complexity principles is that they refer to processes occurring throughout all kinds of systems – physical, living, and social – showing the transdisciplinary nature of this field. Ultimately, such explanations must be developed by thinkers from a variety of fields, from physics through biology, ecology, economics, sociology, and philosophy, alongside transdisciplinary thinkers.

Philosophical interpretation is crucial in developing a deeper understanding of complexity. One pitfall is strong naïve realism or foundationalism, which see complexity as a property of matter. According to this view, things are complex in an overly modernist, objectifying framing, whereby some things, in themselves, are simple or complicated and others are complex. Rather it seems that ultimately perhaps all reality is complex, but that given phenomena are relatively simple or complex with respect to given observations and questions. The brain is both simple and complex with respect to what we look at – four lobes are simple; consciousness is complex.

Another pitfall is strong naïve holism, whereby the complexity principles are over-generalized. We commonly hear, "everything is interconnected," which is true in a simple sense, but false once it's over-generalized. Yes, things are "interconnected" in some ways, but not in other ways. Complexity breaks down the simplicity of such terms. Not everything is interacting, or interacting in any significant or meaningful ways. Some things are deeply incongruous and orthogonal. The realms of social lives, ideas, and meaning are rife with incongruities.[26] Most electoral politics provide examples of incongruities, for instance, between ideas, ideologies, beliefs, and worldviews.

The more we look, the more we see complex dynamic systems. This is not to fall into either naïve strong realism or naïve strong holism. Nor is it to imply that we should always talk in terms of complexity! We use the concept of system, with its rich heritage from Leibniz to Bertalanffy, as a label to delineate one complex entity or process from another. The complex dynamics that we see are imbued with constraints and emergences, obfuscating absolute or permanent "identities" or "interconnection." Nonetheless, physical, living, and social systems are profoundly interdependent. More accurately, the natural world is not so much dependent upon us, as we are upon it.[27]

In the physical world, we see that all the systems we previously thought of as objects are in fact subjects in the sense that they are complex, dynamic, emergent, and self-organizing – from subatomic particles to solar systems. Likewise, all living systems appear to manifest in nested hierarchies of self-organizing systems – from the level of cells throughout the body, to organs, to the fantastically complex brain, to animal colonies and plant communities of all kinds. At the material–human interface, human cities are self-organizing ecologically, materially, economically, culturally, and socially.

Repeatedly, the significance of the observer's position and relationship within complex systems asserts itself, continually rebutting tenacious modern notions that we can isolate and objectify effectively. Physicists, to their astonishment, have found that the results of some experiments are altered by the presence of the observer. In biological and living systems, the position and influence of the observer in the system can always be significant. This fact, so surprising in the face of classical views of physics, becomes obvious in the case of human impact involved in global environmental crises like climate change and the sixth great extinction event.

All systems involve feedbacks and nonlinearity. All physical processes involve nonlinear energetic buildup and release. All living systems are based on intricately enmeshed feedbacks of information, material, and energy, and all social systems additionally possess feedbacks, also called reflexivity, in the realms of ideas, emotions, the virtual and the spiritual. Networks appear like the ubiquitous extension of feedbacks. While absent from physical systems, networks become a central feature in living and social systems. Similarly, the way that systems are organized can be understood with the concepts of hierarchies, which provide a host of organizing principles in terms of scale, grain, nestedness, and control.[28]

Within hierarchies, all living and social systems are enmeshed in continuous constraints and emergences. A major constraint in physical systems is gravity. Indeed, Newtonian gravity is law-like within broad parameters. In living and social systems, constraints are ubiquitous; all living systems are dependent upon other living systems, and ecological reproductive processes and functions – reproduction and maintenance of fresh water, clean air, food, and other interdependent temperature, moisture, and atmospheric conditions. Social systems are anchored in ecological constraints, and create additional social constraints – norms, regulations, and laws. Social constraints are not as deterministic as physical constraints, but rather are flexible and prone to being transformed – ideas, agency, habits, strategies, and choices.

Emergence has been defined as the process by which relatively simple rules lead to complex pattern formation.[29] Emergence describes the processes that allow for the properties at the scale of the system, that cannot be discerned by examining only the parts individually, but must be understood through dynamics throughout the system. For instance, dynamics throughout a cell allow for the qualities and properties of the cell. The same is true for organs and whole organisms.

Emergence appears as the Janus face of constraint; where there is constraint there is emergence. While emergence is difficult to comprehend, it appears to be common to physical, biological, and social realms. In a sense, emergence appears to be central to the story of life. Yet like "complexity" it can seem so abstruse that some leading scientists will not yet even use the term. Emergence in physical systems involves the development of novel realities – from physics emerged chemistry, from chemistry emerged life, from life emerged subjects, brains, consciousness, and ideas. Constraint and emergence are articulated or outlined by nested hierarchies, and these become a useful heuristic in living and social systems. Hierarchies are particularly useful in framing and grasping various key variables in socioecological issues, and thus understanding their various axes – level proximities, scales, grain, codes etc. – helpful in framing social issues. Codes are the rules or functions of emergence, and thus interrelated with functions of constraints.

Self-organization is likewise ubiquitous but largely not yet truly understood. Universes and stars self-organize. The Big Bang created a vast expansion of emerging stars, solar systems, and other physical phenomena. On the planet Earth, it was from the self-organizing properties of physical systems that the first chemicals emerged. The self-organization of chemicals produced the first living systems. The self-organization of living systems produced autonomous individual creatures, from the amoeba and algae to the great proliferation of species through the history of Earth.

When we are looking at complex systems dynamics, we use a wide variety of tools. Complexity has been called the undefinable. A phenomenon is always and only relative and partially "known" to observers. Yet, complexity is apparent throughout all disciplines, and all have developed their own means and methods of grasping and describing it.

In each discipline, we have found ways to explore and express aspects of complex, dynamic processes. In science this is done through the quantitative methods – the scientific method, modeling, probability analysis, and more. In social theory and philosophy it is done through qualitative conceptual theories, models, and frameworks. Specifically these fields use a wide array of methods including narratives, historical analysis, "thick" description, and the prolific fields of social theory, such as postmodern theories, critical theory, science studies, and cultural studies.

We only begin to see the extraordinary nature of complexity when we put aside the primacy of disciplines, and learn to draw from disciplines as one means to greater ends. Complexity is not another ghettoized discipline, isolated in a disciplinary silo like the rest, but rather it's a paradigmatic response to that diaspora of knowledge, a unifying theoretical framework. Seeing it in this light, various insights emerge.

As we begin to see complexity as paradigmatic, we see how it is central to – if often eschewed or distorted within – all the disciplines. In this sense there are no special tools or methods specifically for complexity. Just like there is no special complex substance or property out there in the world. However, some of our old tools become increasingly helpful in looking at complexity – for looking not at the static, but at the dynamic; looking not at analysis of the parts, but comprehension of the wholes; generally speaking, looking with the aim not of some kind of totalizing analytical "understanding," or "truth," but rather merely for an improved comprehension.

So it is primarily with our old and trusted tools and methods, but with new vision, that we can finally no longer eschew complexity. We have found complexity everywhere – with all the tools of science and scholarship, with telescopes and microscopes, with all varieties of multivariate analysis, with quantitative models and qualitative models. Simply put, we use old and new tools to shift the focus to dynamics, from the parts to the wholes, from snapshots to interactions. We improve and combine tools to see life more fully, more realistically.

So for instance, shifting the gaze from parts to wholes, we concern ourselves with sets, groups, and clusters, and increasingly, with dynamics, novelty, and transformation. Analytic tools that allow us to look more at sets and dynamics include cluster analysis. By looking at dynamics, we notice the significance of rate change. For rate change in physical systems we use quantitative models. In biological systems, we use quantitative models, simulation models, power law analysis, and feedback models. In social systems and socioecological systems, we increasingly use interdisciplinary, multidisciplinary, and transdisciplinary conceptual models, theories, and frameworks, such as integrated socioecological systems (SES) frameworks.

Table 2.1 What do you see when you look at complex dynamics?

	Physical systems	Biological systems	Social systems
Complex dynamic systems	Ubiquitous, e.g., stars, suns, whirlpools, atoms, subatomic particles	Ubiquitous, e.g., tree stands, ant colonies, brains, cells	Ubiquitous, e.g., families, cities, societies, ideas
Observer in system, involving rate dependence vs. rate independence	Mostly rate dependent, some rate independence, e.g., crystals, particles	Many systems include both rate dependence and rate independence, e.g., persons in ecosystems and societies	Mostly rate independent rules, e.g., peoples' ideas and habits with respect to communities and environments
Feedbacks, nonlinearity	Common, e.g., chaos, fractals	Common, e.g., chaos, fractals, exponential rate of change, as in the case of disease outbreaks, climate change	Common, many types of examples, e.g., spread of ideas, panic in crowds, economic fluctuations, and rapid changes in ideas, policies, and behaviors
Networks	Various, e.g., percolation theory of fluids traveling in matter, dynamical ice melting	Many, e.g., food webs, neuronal networks, energy flows, material flows, information flows	Many, e.g., language, ideas, knowledge, friendships, the Internet, airline networks, road networks
Hierarchy, level structure	Clear, self evident, easily distinguished, e.g., solar systems relative to geophysical formations, atoms	Ubiquitous, requires observer and assertion, flexible, e.g., ecosystems can be large like rainforests or small like puddles	Ubiquitous, requires observer and assertion; sometimes obvious as in socioeconomic classes, but other times more subtle as in some social dynamics
Hierarchy, level proximity	Distant, e.g., solar systems	Close, closely packed or enmeshed, e.g., ecosystem dynamics	Close, very closely packed or enmeshed, e.g., social dynamics, academic knowledge
Hierarchy, coded constraints	Perhaps, e.g., crystals	Many, often not overt, e.g., DNA, hormones, species attributes like plumage, stripes, etc.	Many, often overt: regulations, laws, cultural norms, spoken language

Hierarchy, non-coded constraints	Yes, e.g., gravity	Ubiquitous, e.g., ecosystem functions like water purification needed for biological survival	Ubiquitous, e.g., cultural norms, emotional needs, artistic drive
Scalar hierarchies	Scales clear	Scales unclear, often could be better clarified	Scales unclear, not clear how clarified it can be
Nested hierarchies	Yes, but taken for granted; required for closed systems in thermodynamics	Many and obvious, e.g., taxons: cells, tissues, organisms	Many, e.g., in social groups and institutions like: schools, companies, communities, governance, militaries
Non-nested hierarchies	Less useful, incidental	Many, pecking orders, food chains	Many, common and taken for granted, e.g., most social relations
Control hierarchies	None	Many, often not overt, e.g., temperature, moisture, or atmospheric constraints	Some, often overt, like state and military oppression and violence
Emergence	Not stabilized with codes; dependent on scale differences	Negative feedback, constraints are coded and stabilized	Codes important but more labile, e.g., the existence and meaning of words and regulations change
Self-organization	Ubiquitous, e.g., the Big Bang, the birth of stars, atoms	Ubiquitous, e.g., the reproduction and maintenance of all life	Ubiquitous, e.g., the reproduction and maintenance of all aspects of societies and ideas

In social systems, the narrative theoretical approach captures dynamics like networks, constraints, and emergence and the tensions and experience of these. Moreover, narrative permits us to reconcile partially incongruous phenomena.[30] Social theory, philosophy, literature, theater, and poetry all employ types of narrative theorizing. Similarly, historical analysis captures rich tapestries of the networks, constraints, and emergences of complex social dynamics. In anthropology, Clifford Geertz coined the term "thick description" to contrast with regular "thin description," as that which captures more layers of life's complexity – epistemologically, ontologically, and experientially. Similarly, a rich array of specific social theoretical fields such as critical theory and cultural theory and the broad umbrella of postmodern theory, capture considerable complexity in social and socioecological systems.

In some ways of course, long before today's social theory, literature, poetry and theater captured rich layers and tensions of complexity in the social sphere. Precursors to the complexity leaders in modern literature include for instance Greek and Elizabethan dramas and worldwide mythologies. Nineteenth to twentieth century social theory and literature saw a shift in method from more formulaic or simpler grand narratives, to subtler, richer, more multifaceted narratives. Masters of complexity in literature include Proust, Joyce, and Faulkner.

As complexity has emerged, scientists and scholars have developed an array of theoretical constructs. While it may be impossible to cryptically define complexity, we can advance comprehension of it. Initial theoretical constructs include the first definitions of complexity, which are based on principles such as self-organization found in every realm.

Comparisons are made between the complicated and the complex, to highlight the nature of the latter. This in turn highlights the centrality of the observer to the system, as one entity can be both complicated and complex with respect to different issues. A mass of jam is complicated; shake it and it falls apart with no coherent structure. A mass of atoms or cells is complex; it maintains a coherent organization. The complexity principles are used to distinguish complexity from the background of complication, relative to the observer.

Similarly, the axes of objective to subjective and quantitative to qualitative can be articulated with respect to complexity in different systems. Physical systems are studied primarily objectively with quantitative tools, while the social realm is understood primarily subjectively with qualitative tools.

Chaos, nonlinearity and feedbacks highlight the nature and role of scale, grain, and rates of change. As networks and network causality become more apparent, so do coevolution and coproduction. In living and social systems, networks of social systems, e.g., psychological, ideas, institutions, material, economic, technological, ethical, scientific, and political systems coevolve and coproduce our world.

As uncertainty, contradiction, risk, and change become more apparent, so do vulnerability, nonrenewability, and irreversibility. In turn, in living systems this highlights adaptation, strategy, and resilience. In turn, in the realm of consciousness – in conscience animals and humans – this highlights reasoning, planning,

Table 2.2 What tools do we use to look at complex dynamics?

	Physical systems	Biological systems	Social systems
Sets	Experiments	Organizational criteria, quantitative and qualitative cluster analysis	Mostly qualitative cluster analysis
Rate change	Quantitative models	Quantitative models, simulation models, power law analysis, feedback models	Qualitative conceptual models and theories e.g., generally narratives, historical analysis, thick description, and specific theories such as critical theory and cultural studies
Power laws	Power law analysis common	Power law analysis common e.g., re ecological, geophysical (earthquakes), atmospheric patterns (ice melting, temperature shifts), technological and energy systems	Theory, power law analysis may be of significance in socio-material issues like urban studies or economics; or of little or no significance to purely social realm, e.g., emotions, ideas, behavior
Levels	Microscopes, telescopes	Multivariate analysis, taxonomy (type), resolution (scale), microscope, binoculars; radiotracers (in cells and ecosystems)	Theory, e.g., factor analysis (multivariate analysis)
Dynamics, behavior	Experiments	Differential equations	Theory – sociology, psychology, ethics, economics, etc.

Table 2.3 What are the theoretical constructs we use in order to study complex dynamic systems?

Theoretical constructs	Physical systems	Biological systems	Social systems
Preferred definitions of complexity	Emergent and self-organizing processes	Emergent and self-organizing processes and behaviors, and the many dynamics within and between natural and living systems	Emergent and self-organizing behaviors, and the great many dynamics within and between brains, minds, language, culture, economies, politics, values, ethics, etc.
Observer and systems	At least at times significant, e.g., in certain physics experiments' the observer's presence can alter the results	Always significant, e.g., generally, human environmental impact; specifically, an ecologist in a field will impact the field experiment in numerous ways	Always significant, e.g., a person has an influence on their community, as in Jimmy Stuart's influence in the movie "It's a Wonderful Life."
Complicated vs. complex	Emergence and self-organization distinguish complexity in physical systems	All the primary six complexity principles distinguish complexity in living systems	All the 50 (See Table 2.4) plus complexity principles distinguish complexity in socioecological systems; modern vs. "postmodern" theories, network causality, social reflexivity, etc.
Objective vs. subjective	All objective study; seen through subjective filters	Mostly objective study, seen through subjective filters	Mostly subjective study seen through subjective filters; though some objective aspects through subjective filters
Quantitative vs. qualitative	All quantitative, seen through qualitative filters	Mostly quantitative, seen through qualitative filters	Mostly qualitative theory, incorporating relevant quantitative data

Rate-dependent vs. rate independent	Mostly irrelevant in relation to human concerns	Common, e.g., scale, rate and grain are important in environmental issues	Common, e.g., scale, rate and grain important in social and socioecological affairs, risk analysis, precaution, proaction, etc.
Coevolution, coproduction	Not applicable	Most all complexity principles, e.g., regarding socioecological feedbacks and network causality	All complexity principles, e.g., regarding precaution, proaction, strengthening community solidarity, protecting the commons, ethics, democracy, wisdom
Vulnerability, nonrenewability, irreversibility	Not applicable	Resilience, equilibrium in ecosystems	Resilience, adaptation, strategy, precaution, proaction, biomimicry, environmental conservation, commons resource management, e.g., permaculture, agroforestry, aquiculture, ethics, democracy, wisdom
Dealing with uncertainty, contradiction, risk and change	Experiments and theory	Probabilities	Theory, e.g., probabilities, risk analysis, ethics, democracy, wisdom

and agency. The extraordinary success of classical science led to the strange ideology whereby the relative stability and laws of the physical realm were falsely imputed to living and social systems, obfuscating central qualities of the social – such as the power of subjectivity, ideas, and the ability for radical changes in ideas, attitudes, worldviews, behaviors, and social systems.

While all the realms have shifted towards analyzing ways to interpret and approach uncertainty, contradiction, risk, and change, there is particular power for this in social systems. Many of the ideals and values developed throughout the modern and contemporary era are based in this dual great potential of and great need for social change. Ethical, political, spiritual, environmental, and social philosophies are based upon the individual and social capacities to change the world.

General complex dynamic systems framework

For this book, I distill from the greater complexity literature just one framework of a few dozen principles of complex dynamic systems. Separately, they have all already proven their value as conceptual tools. It is worth examining their power together.

The first set is the set of six complex dynamic systems principles I will detail most closely throughout – nonlinearity, feedback, networks, hierarchy, emergence, and self-organization. These six principles are found throughout all realms and all disciplines. The second set consists in another some 50 common principles that flow from these major six. This second set of principles is useful for all kinds of issues, among others, they are useful for thinking about sustainability. Finally, from these sets, I derive a third set of another 50 or so principles that relate more explicitly to thinking about sustainability.

I have focused on those principles that seem most significant to social and environmental issues. Together, this group of over 100 principles appears to be central to our understanding of the complexity of our world and insights about sustainability.

Complexity Principles I – six major principles of complex dynamic systems

Many scholars have defined complex, dynamic, adaptive systems in terms of nonlinearity, networks, hierarchy, feedback, emergence, and self-organization.

These six major features of complex dynamic systems are found throughout the complexity literature.[31] Scientists and scholars frame this in a variety of ways. I adopt this initial, exploratory framing as one way to examine useful, central principles.

The ubiquity of these six characteristics of complex processes in all kinds of systems – physical, biological, ecological, social, economic, political, consciousness, and ideas – provides one basis for articulating complexity. These transdisciplinary principles are inherently interrelated, both within and between the three

Table 2.4 Complexity and sustainability framework: complex dynamic systems, general complexity and sustainability principles

Complexity Principles I: Complex dynamic systems	Complexity Principles II: General for many issues including sustainability	Complexity Principles III: Particularly for social and environmental sustainability
Nonlinearity	Rate, unpredictability, rapid change, surprise, thresholds, tipping points	Irreversibility, nonrenewability, cradle to grave accounting, long-term thinking
Feedbacks	Dynamic processes, uncertainty, unknowability, degrees of risk, probability	Social and environmental thresholds, tipping points, rapid change, and abrupt change
Networks	Network causality, networked consequences, coevolution, coproduction, unintended consequences, counterproductivity, interactions, interdependence	Environmental and social interdependence, myriad coevolving social and environmental crises, full systems accounting, synergistic approaches
Hierarchy	Observers, contexts, disciplinarity, interdisciplinarity and transdisciplinarity, systems boundaries, degrees of openness/closure, scale, grain	Physical, environmental and social contexts, levels, and transdisciplinarity
Emergence	Complexification, coherence, novelty, codes, constraints, evolution, species differentiation, human individuation, identity, autonomy, culture, meaning	Human learning, adaptation, strategy, and change, e.g., changes in human impact on societies and environments
Self-organization	Life, reproduction, dynamic disequilibrium, vulnerability, subjects, subjectivities, identity, autonomy, creativity, vision, epistemological and methodological pluralism of both quantitative and qualitative, reductionism, constructivism and narratives, precaution, proaction, crisis, opportunity, and wisdom	Collapse, resilience, and sustainability in social and environmental systems, limits to growth, degrowth, and regrowth, limits to natural resource depletion, and learning and self-organization for changes in ideas, policies, lifestyles, worldview, and current and future societal visions

sets. Within the primary set of complex dynamic systems principles, nonlinearity, feedbacks, networks, and hierarchy, are in turn central principles for understanding the processes of self-organization and emergence. Self-organization and emergence are central concepts in complex physical, living, and social systems.

Exploring how all these other complexity principles shed light on self-organization is a rich area for research, and has become a significant question for complexity scientists and scholars in many disciplines. Emergence and self-organization have been called the hardest problems in every branch of knowledge, from material systems, to social systems to the realm of consciousness and meaning. See, for instance, Jacques Monod (1970) in the philosophy of biology, Daniel Andler *et al.* (2002) and David Chalmers (2006) in philosophy, and Morin (1994) on emergence in multiple disciplines.[32] Complicated systems may be organized – mechanisms and machines; only complex systems are self-organized – stars, vortices, cells, ant colonies, and humans.

In some ways, complexity also validates the long-standing divide between physical and biological systems, even as it helps to show the interrelations between them. In terms of complexity, differences between biological and social systems become trivial since in both the biological and the social we have not been able to fully model that which has a model for itself – the inner "codes" or "programs" which allow both living and social systems to self-organize; that is, to manifest, reproduce, and evolve. It is unclear to me how much physical systems have an inner "code" or "program." Perhaps they do. One might argue that crystals have a code.[33]

Sustainability and other highly complex contemporary issues require that we examine how complexity provides nontrival transdisciplinary principles, tools, models, and narratives, even and especially across the major gaps in our knowledge systems. Nonlinearity, networks, feedbacks, and hierarchies, emergence and self-organization, are all substantively similar across different kinds of systems. In fact, a major contribution of complexity theories is to assist in breaking down the false notions that have caused us to keep physical, biological, ecological, and social systems in such isolated academic silos. While not the only cause, this disjunction in our thinking is a major flaw at the root of multiple environmental crises.

Physical systems maintain themselves in certain states of dynamic disequilibrium, phase states, and attractors. In a non-trivially parallel fashion, ecosystems and societies are found in states along an axis from unsustainable or collapsing to sustainable or flourishing. Ecosystems undergo processes whereby they are more or less maintained in certain states of connectivity, biodiversity, and ecosystems functioning, which can be more or less relevant to sustainability. Generally, one axis provides a useful reference point; at one end is an entirely depleted or degraded ecosystem, collapse, and at the other end, a healthy or vibrant ecosystem, sustainability.

The sustainability principles include phenomena in both living and social systems, most relevant to sustainability. The table points to the ways in which these six ubiquitous aspects of complexity dynamics manifest in different realms

– physical, living, social, ideas, etc. – all of which are significant to issues of global sustainability. For instance, how societies and ecosystems maintain themselves between states of collapse and flourishing depends in part on these sets of complexity principles. These principles are reference points that inform the various ways in which ecosystems and societies can foster or avoid collapse, learn, comprehend and practice how to increase resilience, and maintain themselves sustainably.

Again, because systems are composed of dynamic elements in interaction, they also are interacting not in isolated or linear patterns, but rather in patterns of network causality, or processes of multiple elements in interrelated, causal interactions. Network causality explains why interactions of complex systems generate multiple, unintended consequences. Network causality, nested hierarchies, and transdisciplinarity all help to explain why methodological pluralism, including both quantitative and qualitative methods, is necessary to highly complex systems.

Ultimately, with pluralist epistemologies and methodologies we can explore these processes at all scales, in the context of their greater systemic interactions. Regarding societies and sustainability, these processes help to illuminate various aspects of global change, such as irreversibility, nonrenewability, the limits of natural resources, the limits to economic growth and material consumption, and the vulnerability and resilience of both societies and environments, incorporating issues of human ideas, values, and strategies and the integrity of nature's ecosystem functions or anthropomorphically speaking, "ecosystem services," such as: purification of water and air, reproduction of topsoil, proper nutrient cycling, and stable climatic patterns.

Reflections on the complexity and sustainability framework

Complexity has taken time to emerge; it is still misunderstood and considered strange, untrustworthy, or worse by some scientists and scholars, and still largely unknown to the public. The reasons for this are numerous, but a primary reason is that you can successfully study and manipulate many systems without knowing about complexity theories. Thermostats are used as examples of feedbacks in machines, the Internet as an example of a scale-free, communications network, and a poodle is an example of a self-organizing biological system. Yet, without ever cracking a book on complexity theories, thermostats regulate heating, the Internet connects millions, and poodles are poodle-like. Though much of our daily lives can be better understood in complexity terms, most of our daily lives function without complex thinking, and in fact with rather simple thinking, and of course, classical science and scholarship, largely devoid of complexity, have been astoundingly successful in many ways.

However, again, classical science and thinking have proven insufficient for coping with major global changes, such as protecting drinking water, maintaining food security, natural resource conservation, biodiversity protection, and climate change policy. When it comes to thinking about societies and environments, it seems increasingly necessary to include some reference to and transdisciplinary consideration of complex, dynamic systems. This is the aim of the complexity framework laid out in Table 2.4 that I will explore.

Conclusion

Complexity has long been eschewed in pursuit of certainty, order, and control. Today, complexity is emerging onto the scene in all directions. Scientific and scholarly discoveries and analyses have been cracking open and exposing the dangerous simplicities of classical thinking. Finally, the dam of modernity has broken. Meanwhile, the rising specter of great global turmoil and various threads of apocalyptic discourse are rendering more adequate conceptual tools increasingly urgent. Complexity theories are inexorably seeping through the crevices into every realm of knowledge.

Adequate definitions and descriptions of this major new, broad view of complexity theories are necessarily extensive and elaborate. Some suggest that complexity is "the undefinable" and therefore "what we do when faced with the undefinable."[34] Nevertheless, we have created a starting point, describing complexity as *the dynamic interactions of multiple elements engaged in self-organizing processes.* Yet, the many recent developments described in this book shed new light on complexity as an increasingly powerful and well-developed set of principles, perspective, and way of thinking.

The proposition to be explored throughout the book is that this broad description and analysis of complexity theories sheds light on the related sustainability framework, and as such contributes to the framing, understanding, and guidance of economics, science, technology, ethics, politics, and policy.

In line with this perspective, I propose that an explicit rendering of the transdisciplinary complexity principles as a framework provides a valuable reference guide throughout many areas of science, scholarship, policy, business and activism. By focusing on complexity not just as a piecemeal phenomenon, but rather as a common characteristic of our world, thus radically shifting our epistemology, we open the way to develop wiser, better thinking in a range of areas crucial to improving the human relationship with nature and our ability to survive and to thrive.

Through a series of tables, I have attempted to show some of the intricacies, transdisicplinarity, scope, and power of complexity theories. Throughout the book, I refer back to "Table 2.4. Complexity Framework: General Principles of Complex Dynamic Systems," inquiring into how these three sets of complexity principles may and may not illuminate our quest for a humane and environmentally sustainable future.

The complexity frameworks outlined here suggests that the central principle of self-organization may provide both a powerful lens and it may provide us with a way to look at more deliberately conceiving of and proactively planning for sustainability. At this moment in late industrial capitalism and growing global crises, it serves to illuminate some of the social, economic, and political challenges that have to be addressed, and battles to be won. As much as complexity may shed light on the difficulties of these current and coming social and environmental battles, in providing a more adequate and realistic framing of social and environmental change, it only brings us closer to a realistic path towards greater success.

The work of scientists and scholars like Walter Reid, Stephen Schneider, Stuart Terry Chapin III, and Elinor Ostrom discussed in Chapter 1 suggests that complexity principles shed light on some of the major factors involved in developing more sustainable societies. Though mostly implicitly, many leading ideas on social and environmental change lie in this greater goldmine of complexity theories. Complexity theories provide a range of analyses, models, concepts, and conceptual frameworks that could help global societies to shift from our current blind and blundering path, toward greater social solidarity and environmental sustainability. It is the aim of this book to explore this vision. This project may be ambitious, but it is justified by both the urgency of environmental crises, and the beauty of complexity theories.

Due to vast networks of intricately interacting, evolving systems, due to the power of positive feedbacks and nonlinear, rapid change, we suddenly realize that humanity is not only powerful, but also vulnerable. And yet, complexity theories also inform us that we as agents in the environment are capable not only of impacting and degrading environmental systems, but also that we are capable of learning, agency, adaptation, strategy, great solidarity, and rapid social change.

3 Complexity in the natural sciences

If I find a being capable of seeing things in their unity and their multiplicity, there is a man who I would follow as a God.

Plato

All reality is a complex unity.

Alfred North Whitehead

In the life sciences, brain science, and social sciences, the more carefully scientists look, the more complex the phenomena are.

Melanie Mitchell[1]

The Santa Fe Institute

Alfred Hubler paced theatrically before an eager crowd at the Santa Fe Institute, in July 2005. A stout man with volatile arms and a broad mischievous grin, in his heavy Bavarian accent he announced that this first lecture would be on the topic of the meaning of the word "complexity."

Hubler obviously meant business. Strutting about the room, he and his assistants began to pull shut the huge heavy window curtains until the bright lecture hall was almost black. A light shone at the podium. Next he carried a large jug of gasoline up to the podium. My teammates and I looked nervously at each other and scanned for the exits, but curiosity prevailed. It later turned out that the gasoline jug was filled with water. Now he was standing at the podium looking rather intense, as experimental physicists are wont to do, wearing gloves and holding wires.

"Complexity," cried Hubler, "is an explosion." With this he connected two electrical wires and set off a set of a series of sizzling lightning bolts! They were lecture hall-sized lightning bolts, about ten inches long, between wires, but we were duly impressed. With this, Hubler explained his first basic definition of complexity in physics:

> Complexity is when a large degree of throughput in the system leads to an explosion. A large degree of throughput builds in a system, which

eventually leads to an explosion, a release, and later a slow buildup of tension as throughput again is greater than a system's capacity. Complexity means explosions![2]

To drive home the point, he set off more lightning bolts.

As the month-long complexity program progressed, we explored other definitions and aspects of the fascinating complexity sciences – watching chaotic patterns of beads, metal filings, and separating liquids in petri dishes, playing with pendulums in sand boxes, and exploring an impressive display of life's lovely fractals.

Yet Hubler's first definition is certainly true and central, taking us back to our cosmic roots, and of course the greatest explosion we cannot imagine, the Big Bang. Explosions are central for a physicist looking at energy flows. And Hubler loves energy flows. In a Promethean moment in the laboratory later that week, he announced he would teach us a few easy ways to create lightning bolts. With his joyful grin he intoned, "Do this at home." He showed us how to slit a grape, stick it in a microwave oven, and zap it with the oven to produce a cute little ½-inch lightning bolt. Chatting with one of Hubler's six daughters, a charming teenager who assisted Hubler in the wet laboratory where we observed chaotic patterns throughout the week, I quietly asked her if Hubler ever did things like this at home. Her eyes lit up. "Oh yes!" she said, "We have at least six fried microwave ovens in the basement."

Obviously complexity is more than a lightning bolt. Hubler's definition is one of many useful definitions, interrelated and contributing to a fuller view of complexity. For the twentieth anniversary of the SFI the year before, 2004, the institute posed the challenge for all the scientists there to give their best current definition of complexity, and the results were almost as varied as the scientists. And yet, the various definitions patched together gradually are contributing to a richer sense of the complexity sciences.

The Santa Fe Institute was founded in 1984. By summer 2005 the SFI had reached a mythic status – having passed the twentieth anniversary the institute had been around just long enough to show that complexity must have some significance, but not quite long enough for most people to grasp what this was. Yet as the Santa Fe scientists argue, it takes a while to gain clarity about new ideas. Isaac Newton did not have a good definition of, and was not fond of, the term "force"; geneticists still can't agree on what the term "gene" refers to at the molecular level; and although they say that 95 percent of the universe is made up of them, astronomers have yet to truly define either "dark matter," or "dark energy."[3] So it's no surprise that people are still discussing the possible definitions of terms like complexity, emergence, and self-organization.

Nonetheless, scientists at the Santa Fe Institute and their colleagues have stacked up an impressive list of accomplishments in the last 25 years, giving us a new perspective on everything from cells, ant colonies, heartbeats, fractals, strange attractors, ecological networks to social networks, and much more – what many call a new paradigm of knowledge.

The Santa Fe Institute is perched in a set of gorgeous, sleek, glass-walled buildings overlooking the ethereal Sangre de Cristo Mountains. Every afternoon, researchers emerge from their offices to gather for "tea," a social hour in a spacious open area with one huge wall-length white board and another glass wall looking out over the sage shrubs and pinion trees. Imbibing fine teas, hors d'oeuvres, and chocolate, complexity scientists discuss the latest advances, squiggling long equations on the white board. Visitors mingle with a colorful array of Santa Fe founders, a sprinkling of Nobel Laureates such as Murray Gell-Mann, SFI resident faculty such as theoretical physicist and former SFI president, Geoffrey West, a colorful array of resident visitors like Cormac McCarthy and Sam Sheppard, and the occasional passing celebrity like Steve Martin.

I had been invited there for a month, along with 50 others, mostly in computer science, physics, and artificial intelligence, mostly doctoral, post-doctoral students, and professors. My team of three was the one team based in the social sciences, like economics, and qualitative social theory, such as the sociological fields of critical theory and science studies. Like my teammates Debora Hammond and Timothy Foxon, professors working on systems theories, social, and environmental issues, I had come to the Santa Fe Institute to get a fuller sense of complexity's applications for sustainability.

An old, familiar, often unspoken line zigzags through the complexity sciences – the same one that has always run between the realm of the quantitative natural sciences and that of the qualitative "humans sciences," or social theory, philosophy, and the humanities, which C.P. Snow called the culture gap, largely based on the use of quantitative and qualitative methods. The science wars of the 1990s proved many mainstream scientists and scholars alike fatefully unable or unwilling to bridge this gap.

But where many mainstream thinkers failed, complexity scientists and scholars seem primed to succeed. Within the complexity sciences, this faltering line is becoming fuzzier and weaker, from both "sides" – quantitative and qualitative – it appears to be dissolving.

The synthesis will benefit everyone. I will return to explore this at the end of the chapter, when I introduce a few different perspectives on the growing complexity sciences. Inspiringly, my overview of the complexity sciences shows that the focus within complexity research on interconnections and interactions gives complexity scientists a particular advantage over mainstream scientists working in other areas. By looking at interconnections within and between areas within their work, they also illuminate interconnections between disciplines and realms of knowledge. Moreover, complexity sheds new philosophical light, which in turn helps to reconcile the culture gap and other significant issues in the philosophy of science, as I explore in Chapter 6.

A wide range of thinkers – scientists, sociologists, philosophers, and more – have informed my perspective on the complexity framework. Both quantitative and qualitative methods are important to this perspective. While the basis of this work is based on basic science – quantitative empirical studies and analysis – it is also partially based on qualitative theory, social and philosophical.

While there are many other possible foci and framings, the complexity framework I outline in Chapter 2, Table 2.4, provides one example of the way in which different epistemological views – even across the culture gap – are converging into a coherent worldview.

The complexity framework in the natural sciences: six principles of complex dynamic systems

In this chapter, I focus on the six principles that I have distilled from studies on complex dynamic systems, which are relevant to aims of sustainability.

Work at the complexity science institutes – such as the Santa Fe Institute (SFI), Center for the Study of Complex Systems at Michigan State University (CSCS), New England Complex Systems Institute (NECSI), London School of Economics (LSE) complexity group, Ecole Normale Superieur (ENS) complexity lab in Paris, and major complexity science labs in Tokyo and Seoul – is much broader than the very narrow swath that I present here.[4] Santa Fe scientists, for instance, have focused on topics such as: cognitive neuroscience, computation in physical and biological systems, economic and social interactions, evolutionary dynamics, network dynamics, and robustness. In January 2005, during a week-long intensive course at NECSI in Boston, I listened as President Yaneer Bar-Yam made forays into the application of complexity theories to music and art. We learned, for instance, that you can use complex algorithms to create innumerable Mozart and Beethoven symphonies. What would classical music aficionados Barbara Zuck or Peter Davis say! The range of explorations at the complexity science institutes has been far-reaching. I focus on areas that have proven to be substantial.

Specifically, I focus on the core principles from the complexity framework presented in Chapter 2: nonlinearity, feedback, networks, hierarchy, emergence, and self-organization. This list of key terms has been distilled from work based in both quantitative and qualitative methods.

I argue that these six principles are important for various reasons. First, in the now almost 30 years since the founding of SFI, these principles appear to be central to the basic science and scholarship of complex dynamics systems. Second, specifically, they also seem to hold up in many if not most instances in transdisciplinary analyses encompassing all realms of reality – physical, biological, social and the many manifestations of the social, such as ideas, emotions, and meaning. Third, they appear both in theory and in practice to be significant for various applications regarding understanding and actualization of sustainability. In this chapter, I focus on these six principles from the complexity sciences, and a few of the principles that flow from them.

It should be noted though, that there is still more to the story. Not just dynamic, self-organizing systems, but all systems are complex in various ways. For instance, the elements that make up water produce the emergent properties of water – its cohesive behavior, its capacity to moderate temperature, etc. So the category of adaptive, dynamic, self-organizing systems – brains, ants, and cities – does not include all instances of that which is complex; complexity appears to be more ubiquitous still. Therefore, this chapter, like this book, is not a fully comprehensive treatment of complexity writ large – quite a task. But it is one important introduction to some central concepts of particular importance to science for sustainability.

As mentioned in the brief history of systems and complexity theories in Chapter 2, all the different groups of complexity scientists and scholars were all influenced by the first wave of work in the fields of general systems theory, developmental biology, cybernetics, systems theories and more in past decades, especially the 1940s and 1950s. A series of discoveries from the 1970s, such as Rene Thom's Catastrophe Theory and Edward Lorenz's discovery of chaos in atmospheric data, both of which took place in 1974, fueling the fires that led to the founding of the Santa Fe Institute in 1984.

Measuring complexity

Santa Fe scientists, beyond these three primary definitions, have defined and described complexity by measuring particular aspects. Accurate though it is, Hubler's notion of the explosion is evidently one focus among many. As noted in Table 3.1, scientists have defined complexity with reference to many different ways to try to measure aspects of complex systems, e.g., features of physical systems such as degrees of entropy, information, and fractal detail. In 1995 the science writer John Horgan catalogued 32 such definitions based upon measuring different aspects of complexity.[5] More recently, SFI professor and computer scientist Melanie Mitchell distilled eight examples of definitions of complexity based on approaches to measurement, listed in Table 3.1.[6]

As Mitchell points out, definitions based on measurements of complexity do not support any singular, general definition of complexity even when looking at various narrow specific aspects of natural systems. Genomic size, for instance, may be a significant measure for addressing certain questions within genomic science, however for understanding broader dynamics – biological identity, evolution, etc. – it seems to be inconsequential. As Mitchell says, you can measure the size via various factors – genes, genomic base pairs, etc. We have all heard the facts about genes – e.g., humans share 60 percent of the same genes as fruit flies – which make obvious the need to question the role and meaning of "genes." The same goes for genomic base pairs. An amoeba has 225, as many base pairs as a human, while clearly a human is vastly more complex in many significant ways than one of its earliest evolutionary predecessors.

Entropy is clearly a central facet to understanding the complexity sciences. Shannon entropy is defined as the average information content or amount of surprise that a message source has for a receiver. Mitchell points out that the only way to measure entropy is to frame an "object or process" in the form of "messages" of some kind. "This isn't always easy or straightforward," says Mitchell, "how, for example, would we measure the entropy of the human brain?" Similarly, complexity as logical depth, says Mitchell,

Table 3.1 Definitions of natural complexity based on measurement

Domain	Measurement, sometimes used as a definition
Genomic size[1]	Comparison of number of genomic base pairs
Entropy[2]	The amount of entropy or disorder of a system (Shannon entropy) as measured in thermodynamics (physics, biology)
Algorithmic information	"The size of the shortest computer program that could generate a complete description of the object."[3] (mathematics, physics)
Logical depth	"A measure of how difficult that object is to construct."
Thermodynamic depth	"The most plausible scientifically determined sequence of events that lead to the thing itself," that measures, "the total amount of thermodynamic and informational resources required by the physical construction process."[4]
Statistical	The minimum amount of information about the past behavior of a system that is needed to optimally predict the statistical behavior of the system in the future.[5]
Fractal dimension	Quantification, e.g., of the "cascade of detail" in an object, or how much detail you see at all scales as you diver deeper and deeper into the infinite cascade of self-similarity[6]
Degree of hierarchy[7]	Measure of the degree of hierarchy and/or nestedness of a system[8]

Notes
1 M. Mitchell, *Complexity: A Guided Tour*, Oxford: Oxford University Press, 2009, p. 96.
2 Ibid., pp. 96–98.
3 Ibid., p. 98.
4 Ibid., p. 101.
5 Ibid., p. 102.
6 Ibid., p. 107.
7 J. Horgan, op. cit.
8 M. Mitchell, op. cit. p. 109.

has very nice theoretical properties that match our intuitions, but it does not give a practical way of measuring the complexity of any natural object of interest, since there is typically no practical way of finding the smallest Turing machine that could have generated a given object, not to mention determining how long that machine would take to generate it.[7]

Similarly, in the case of thermodynamic depth or computational capacity, measurements may have utility. However, as Mitchell summarizes:

> ...the ability to perform universal computation doesn't mean that a system by itself is complex; rather, we should measure the complexity of the behavior of the system coupled with its inputs. For example, a universal Turing machine alone isn't complex, but together with a machine code and input that produces a sophisticated computation, it creates complex behavior.[8]

The other measurements lead to the same general results: each measure appears to be useful within a certain type of reductionist experimental method. It is reductionist in the sense of both the methodology and the result, even if looking at examples across realms discerned with a more synthetic or non-reductionist conceptual criteria. These measurements have contributed to the development of a wide array of basic science discoveries and applications. They capture what other methods and analyses alone cannot, even if alone, ultimately, they cannot fully capture that complexity.

Most complexity scientists have reached an intriguing dual consensus, fueled by these tensions in the development of complexity sciences. On the one hand, they agree that finding definitions for complexity are problematic and perhaps should not even be a primary goal. As Mitchell describes above, while there is much to be discovered with quantitative methods, there appear to be limits, so far, to how much quantitative methods alone can say about the complexity of living and social dimensions of reality. You can measure and describe many aspects of complex systems. Yet, quantitative measurements only say so much about complexity. Complexity scientist Deborah Gordon laments that terms such as complexity, emergence and self-organization appear only "to provide names for what we cannot explain."[9] Some have suggested a reason for this sentiment, to which I return at the end of the chapter.

On the other hand, even as complexity scientists run up against the limits of attempts to analyze complexity, they enthusiastically agree that complexity is one of the most exciting fields in science today, and one of the most promising.

The field of complex dynamic systems

Early on in the work of SFI, many researchers focused on one general definition of complexity as that which exists, in the term coined perhaps by Norman Packard, "at the edge of chaos."[10] Norman Packard, Doyne Farmer, Jim Crutchfield, and Rob Shaw were members of the University of California at Santa Cruz "Chaos Group," a group of doctoral students who developed chaos theory in the wake of Edward Lorenz's famous discovery of chaos in atmospheric data.[11]

The "edge of chaos" was one important early complexity concept at SFI and other science institutes in the 1980s and 1990s. Today, many complexity scientists, such as Jim Crutchfield, are said to refute the term.[12] Nobel Laureate Murray Gell-Mann has called it meaningless. According to one account, Gell-Mann was scheduled to speak at an ecology meeting once, just after a talk called "The Edge of Chaos," and started his own talk by stating loudly, "First I have to clear the air. There is no such thing as the edge of chaos!"[13]

Nonetheless, perhaps the early description captured something that remains central to the field throughout complexity camps and disciplines, regarding the interplay of oppositional forces, as in the interactions of order and disorder that comprise the central property of complex dynamic systems: self-organization.

Today, the term "complex system" has various definitions, slightly broader than either Hubler's energetic explosion or the edge of chaos. The precise definitions remain somewhat contentious. In Mitchell's most recent definition a complex system is, "a system in which large networks of components with no central control and simple rules of operation give rise to complex collective behavior, sophisticated information processing, and adaptation via learning or evolution."[14] Though some details are still debated, such as the precise meaning and ubiquity of adaptation.

Some aspects of older definitions still play a role in this framing. John Holland gave a slightly longer definition, referring to complex adaptive systems (CAS) back in 1994:

> A dynamic network of many agents (which may represent cells, species, individuals, firms, nations) acting in parallel, constantly acting and reacting to what the other agents are doing. The control of a CAS tends to be highly dispersed and decentralized. If there is to be any coherent behavior in the system, it has to arise from competition and cooperation among the agents themselves. The overall behavior of the system is the result of a huge number of decisions made every moment by many individual agents.[15]

Complexity scientists have used the term adaptive to differentiate between adaptive systems, such as cells and institutions, and nonadaptive systems, which are interactive but not necessarily adaptive, such as a hurricane or a turbulent rushing river. In one long-standing view, a complex system is a complex adaptive system (CAS): a system of many parts, which are coupled in a nonlinear fashion, which may be discrete or continuous, e.g., difference equations or differential equations. A CAS involves top-level properties and features like self-similarity, complexity, emergence, and self-organization. Complex adaptive systems are also dynamic and self-organizing, such as: cells, nervous systems, brains, ant colonies, forests, human cities, and human economies.

The basic units of the CAS are often called agents. Agents react to their environment by developing rules for interpretation and action, subject to evolution. The control of a CAS tends to be highly dispersed and decentralized. Coherent overall behavior of the system is the result of a huge number of decisions made every moment by many individual agents.[16]

Complexity scientists call one group of complex adaptive systems self-similar, which might be seen as one instance of what Morin calls more generally the holographic principle, by which the whole is in the parts, which are in the whole.[17] In mathematics, a self-similar object is exactly or approximately similar to a part of itself, i.e. the whole has the same shape as one or more of the parts. The term self-similar is used for physical, chemical, and other natural systems, whereas the term holographic is used in a broader sense, encompassing more kinds of systems – biological, social, ideas, etc.

Coastlines are statistically self-similar; parts of them show the same statistical properties at many scales. This is obvious from the perspective of a pelican and now from satellite photos. We see this more clearly in nature's great Fibonacci sequence display, the self-similar growth pattern that produces the spirals we see in leaves, pinecones, broccoli, pineapples, and sunflowers. Another way to understand this, in biological systems, is that the system grows, while retaining a certain form, thus producing a physical shape that reveals both the maintenance of form and the new growth. Thus, a complex adaptive system is a complex collective of interacting adaptive agents. The widespread presence of fractal, self-similar patterns is a fascinating and significant insight into the complex fabric of nature.

Flowing from the focus on dynamics and adaptation, other important properties of CAS are: communication, cooperation, specialization, spatial and temporal organization, and reproduction. These processes occur at all scales: both cells, the whole animals they compose, and groups of those animals, specialize, adapt, and reproduce themselves. This is what is meant by self-similar behavior at different scales. Communication and cooperation also take place on all levels, from the individual agent to the overall system.

Complexity scientists are in consensus that fields in which complex adaptive systems are studied that can provide useful advances include computer science, artificial intelligence, game theory, and neural networks. Some scientists also think that the concept of CAS may also be usefully applied to: the stock market, termite colonies, dynamics of cities, and many other domains.

Nonlinearity

Nonlinearity is disproportionality between causes and effects. It is thus the principle behind chaos theory, which is the study of small causes leading to large effects, or sensitive dependence on initial conditions, leading to infinite yet bounded patterns of effects. Chaos occurs in the borderlands between more highly ordered and highly disordered states in various physical and chemical systems. The swing of a pendulum will follow certain general patterns, but each swing will be slightly novel. The patterns created by these chaotic processes are called fractals. In fractals we clearly visualize how the self-similar or holographic principle plays out in patterns that are at once bounded and infinite.

A particularly common nonlinear pattern in nature is the power law. A power law is a mathematical ratio between the size and the frequency of an event. For instance, an earthquake that is twice as large as another earthquake will be four times as rare. This pattern holds for earthquakes of all sizes, thus the distribution is said to scale. Power laws effectively describe various natural phenomena such as Kleiber's Law, the metabolic rate of a species and its body mass.

Through basic complexity science, we see and understand our world's beauty more fully. Where before we saw only differences between coastlines, broccoli, and sunflowers, now we can see that they all manifest fractal patterns.

Santa Fe scientists have largely focused on chaos and fractals in computer simulations and physical and chemical models. The most studied examples of chaos theory include patterns to be found in the behavior of: water wheels, sand piles, heartbeats, and spinning disks of particles or glass beads. Ecologists also have benefitted from the use of power laws in ecosystem studies. For instance, Santa Fe touts the theory by Geoffrey West, James Brown, and Brian Enquist to explain power laws that describe the ratio of metabolism to mass of animal species.[18]

Climatologists and their colleagues focus on another set of power laws. Perhaps the most familiar expression of nonlinear phenomena in the case of climate change is the common chart in science journals and popular media, sometimes referred to as the "hockey stick" chart: an X–Y grid showing a long gradual increase followed by a very large, rapid increase. In Al Gore's 2006 movie, *An Inconvenient Truth*, a room-sized hockey stick chart was used to show how rapidly anthropogenic climate change is accelerating. The upswing in this chart was so sharp that Gore needed to climb a tall ladder to show the trajectory in a few years' time. We have been swinging, crawling, and walking through a nonlinear world from the beginning. Yet only now, faced with striking nonlinear change in societies and environments, is it becoming such an obvious aspect of our lives.

Nonlinearity is certainly not new; it has long been noted that nonlinearity is more frequent than linearity in the natural world. Mathematician Stanislaw Ulam famously drove this point home: "To call the study of chaos 'nonlinear science' was like calling zoology the study of non-elephant animals."[19]

The polyglot mathematician Henri Poincaré discovered chaos theory at the dawn of the twentieth century. Poincare was analyzing the three-body problem, the question of whether the solar system as modeled by Newton's equations was dynamically stable. The three-body problem consisted of nine simultaneous differential equations. In 1903 Poincaré wrote:

> If we knew exactly the laws of nature and the situation of the universe at the initial moment, we could predict exactly the situation of that same universe at a succeeding moment. But even if it were the case that the natural laws had no longer any secret for us, we could still only know the initial situation *approximately*. If that enabled us to predict the succeeding situation with *the same approximation*, that is all we require, and we should say that the phenomenon had been predicted, that it is governed by laws. But it is not always so; it may happen that *small differences in the initial conditions produce very great ones in the final phenomena*. A small error in the former will produce an enormous error in the latter. Prediction becomes impossible, and we have the fortuitous phenomenon.[20] (My italics)

Further evidence and understanding of nonlinearity evolved over time. In the early twentieth century, nonlinearity appeared in mathematics, in physics, quantum mechanics, chemistry, meteorology, and finally in chaos theory. In 1974 Edward Lorenz published his discovery of chaotic weather patterns, spawning the metaphor "the butterfly effect." Lorenz's recognition was that certain systems exhibit steady-state flow patterns, others oscillate in a regular periodic fashion, and still others, chaotic systems, vary in an "irregular, seemingly haphazard manner, and even when observed for long periods of time, do not appear to repeat their previous history."[21]

Chaos, or deterministic chaos, is characterized by both order and disorder – it is partially deterministic, but manifest infinitely unpredictable patterns, or "bounded infinities." Examples of such systems include the atmosphere, the solar system, plate tectonics, and turbulent fluids. It is also said that economic and demographic systems exhibit the non-random dynamics of deterministic chaos.

Thus the formal scientific meaning of chaos is at odds with common parlance, the poetic and everyday connotations of chaos, which often implies total disorder, or even disintegration. Chaotic patterns in nature are part of the very structure of the world, which we have for so long, seen as stable. Yet, arguably some metaphorical parallels can be made between physical, biological, and social chaos.

Like most facets of complexity, the notion of nonlinear effects – small initial changes leading to large outcomes – captured the public mind in part because it was a contemporary scientific expression of an age-old truism. Before the phenomenon was found in scientific experiments, common sense long had held that small changes lead to larger ones. For instance, sociologists have noted that a small group of activists could bring about major social reform, as evoked in a famous quotation from Margaret Mead, "Never doubt that a small group of thoughtful, committed citizens can change the world. Indeed, it is the only thing that ever has," or in adages like "the straw that broke the camel's back."

Mathematicians and physicists, ecologists, biologists, atmospheric scientists, and climatologists all find nonlinearity within their separate studies. As we look at the interactions between their domains, we see more nonlinear dynamics. As we focus increasingly on rapid global change, the greater implications of nonlinearity in societies and environments have become increasingly apparent to us all. Large-scale issues of population, scientific, technological, and environmental change turn on nonlinearity. For the greater public, images of nonlinear patterns in environmental change, such as the hockey stick graphs of global warming in Al Gore's *Inconvenient Truth*, brings the connection between nature and society – between nonlinear phenomena and human security in the biosphere – into sharper focus.

Networks

Networks are another aspect of world that was always apparent, but largely ignored under the modernist focus on parts, mechanism, and control. Cybernetics, computer science, ecology and other fields each in turn showed the significance of networks. Recently, in our complex and globalized contemporary societies, in the era of the Internet and Facebook, network studies have taken off dramatically.

Simply put, networks are dynamical systems composed of nodes with links of interactions between them. Networks seem to appear in every realm – abstract (e.g., mathematics, concepts, ideas), material (ecosystems), ecological (food webs), biological (living matter), digital (computers), virtual (the Internet), and social (friendships). So nodes might be numbers in mathematical systems, species in ecosystems, or friends at the local pub.

Much of scientific network studies occur in mathematical fields such as network theory or graph theory, in computational ecology, and in simulation-based social and virtual network studies. Analysis includes descriptions of structure, such as the key concepts of small-world networks or scale-free networks, and tools for observing and managing networks – such as critical path analysis and PERT (program evaluation and review technique).

Natural scientists employ network analysis in the study of natural patterns, such as much recent work done by physicists studying ecological systems. Here, networks and nonlinearity conjoin, as we see nonlinear patterns manifesting themselves throughout networked processes. For instance, network ecologists study how biological networks are comprised of self-similar patters, e.g., the fractals we see in broccoli, seashells, and mountain ridges.[22]

Networks are comprised of nodes and links; nodes are the entities interacting and links are the interactions. A hub is a highly connected node. Social network hubs are popular or famous persons; Internet hubs are Google or Apple; and ecological hubs are keystone species that can eat or be eaten by many different species. Sea otters or coyotes, though a tiny part of the ecosystem materially, play a disproportionately large role in ecosystem dynamics because they eat many other species.

Increasingly, observations of networks across different kinds of systems have revealed various commonalities, which show that networks are not fundamentally random, but display coherent behaviors in some respects. For instance, network scientists discovered numbers at which synchronous (or "clustering") behavior begins to occur, including: clapping in a theater, calling of insects, and flashing of fireflies. The discovery that clustering is common throughout different kinds of networks elevated it from an observation about certain social behaviors to a generic property of networks in complex systems.[23]

The concept of "scale-free networks" took many researchers by storm because so many real-world networks appear to possess this quality, and multiple implications might ensue. In scale-free networks, some nodes act as highly connected hubs, while most nodes are much less highly connected. In contrast, in random networks nodes are more evenly connected. To get a sense of the distinction, an aerial map of airports and airline flights is a scale-free network. Airports are all nodes, but airports in New York and LA are large hubs with many links, whereas airports in Scottsbluff and Chattanooga have few links.

In contrast, picture a roadmap. While there are nodes, road nodes have a maximum of one or two links to other roads; they can never grow to be large hubs like airports. The Parisian planner Le Corbusier managed to avoid the stultifying grid of two and four links, by conjoining as many as five or six roads, creating lovely stars, like ferris wheels, throughout Parisian streets. And Jane Jacobs wisely advocated for small, curvy, natural roads and the avoidance of major arteries in residential neighborhoods, like the West Village in New York City. But there are only so many options within the constraints of random networks. The laws of random networks necessarily reduce the number of links.

Airport-type networks are called scale-free because this pattern of more and less densely connected exists at both larger and smaller scales revealing a self-similar or holographic property. If you squint and envision airport networks from above the Earth, you will see the patterns of highly connected nodes; whereas, no such pattern exists across scales in a random network, such as road networks. When you squint and examine an Atlas of the United States, all roads interconnect with all other roads through widely dispersed small hubs, the ubiquitous four-way intersection.

The fact that many real-world networks are scale-free has some major implications, e.g., how to find a mate. As Mark Granovetter pointed out, those hubs that link disparate clusters of social contacts are highly useful, because one is then connected to new groups of resources. This is why only a few people make it into the Who's Who. This is why people often find mates or jobs not through their immediate social circles, but through secondary social circles, adjacent hubs linking more social circles.[24] According to Google Scholar, Granovetter's seminal article on this subject, "The Strength of Weak Ties," has been cited over 17,500 times.[25]

Network rules and patterns like the strength of weak ties are also important in ecological studies of food webs, the "who eats whom" of the natural world.[26] In 1880, Lorenzo Camarano, an obscure Italian scientist, published perhaps the first food web diagrams.[27] Over the last decade, a number of general models for the structure of food webs[28] and population dynamics[29] have been developed and tested, with additional work undertaken to integrate structure and dynamics.[30]

Important discoveries in recent food web studies include regularities in how interactions are organized across habitats and through deep time,[31] and the importance of observed predator–prey body size ratios for enhancing the persistence of species in complex model networks.[32] The focus on ecological networks may also help us to better understand processes of extinctions. Food web ecology scientists have also studied how complex ecological networks mediate extinction dynamics, for instance by conducting "in silico" experiments to remove species from webs, in order to understand the patterns of species co-extinctions and extinction cascades.[33] Further, they have used complex dynamical network models, for instance to make simple predictions of the effect that losing one species will have on other species.[34]

The rich literature in this branch of network studies, food web ecology, provides one example of the ways that complexity sciences may contribute very directly to our understanding of sustainability. As food web ecology research progresses it may prove important for fields such as resource management, conservation biology, and restoration ecology. The more we look, the more we find dynamical networks. Ecology was called the subversive discipline because of the way it clearly reveals interacting systems and complex dynamics. We have discovered that not just ecology, but all disciplines, are subversive.

Feedback

Feedback is the process by which the output of a system is passed back (or fed back) to the input. It is the looping causality by which systems adapt and adjust themselves.

Thinking in terms of feedbacks is every bit as significant for our future as thinking about networks. Feedbacks are increasingly understood as the critical factor in both natural and social dimensions of climate change and other major socioecological problems.

Feedback was first extensively documented in the fields of physiology, cybernetics and control theory, and electronics, and to varying degrees in biology, engineering, architecture, economics, cognitive science, and brain science. Nonetheless, like all the other major complexity principles, the concept of feedbacks has been with us through the ages.

In modern times, feedback was popularized by the father of physiology, Claude Bernard (1813–1878). For Bernard, feedback – the looping causality by which systems adapt and maintain themselves – was a central issue in physiology and, by extension, throughout medicine and the life sciences. Bernard was a strong champion of the scientific method in the field of physiology – observation, hypothesis, experiment, confirmation, and new information – noting the basic feedback pattern in both the method and content of his research, making contributions to physiology and neuroscience. Perhaps the largest contribution was to understand homeostasis, the fundamental principle of organic life, or controlled stability of the internal environment of cells and tissues through feedback interactions with the external environment.

Feedback was also an early, core concept in cybernetics, where it was defined as a process whereby some proportion or, in general, function of the output signal of a system is passed (fed back) to the input. Norbert Wiener, one of the founders of cybernetics, called feedback a central feature of cybernetics, which he defined as "the science of control and communication."[35] While Warren McCulloch defined negative feedback as,

> the art of the helmsman, to hold a course by swinging the rudder so as to offset any deviation from that course. For this the helmsman must be so informed of the consequences of his previous acts that he corrects them.[36]

In 1943, in the philosophy of science, Arturo Rosenbleuth, Norbert Wiener, and Julian Bigelow defined feedback a bit more strictly. Previous scientists had defined positive feedback as a force that adds to the input signals of a system, but does not correct them. Rosenbleuth and his colleagues defined negative feedback more subtly as a process by which the behavior of a system is controlled within a margin of error relative to a fairly specific goal of the system.[37] Positive feedbacks lead to escalating of forcing or change in a system, whereas negative feedbacks dampen or equilibrate forcing or change in a system.

This was the great contribution – to understand feedback as the process that allows a system to adapt to its environment as if there were a helmsman, when in fact there is none. There is no control central, but rather feedbacks throughout the system produce effects at the scale of the whole system. The metaphor of the helmsman was called into question as the cybernetics scientists looking at a variety of systems found that there was no singular "actor" doing the steering.

Later, founder of organization management Stafford Beer defined cybernetics as, "the science of effective organization."

In ecology, a well-known example of feedback is the population dynamics cycles of snowshoe hares and lynxes. There is no external or central control. Rather, both groups interact dynamically, coevolving in tandem with each other and with other species and systems in their environment. In the life sciences, a much noted example of positive feedback driving climate change is the ice albedo effect, in which melting white ice increases the dark sea surface, the darker color absorbs more heat, and this feeds back into a vicious cycle of accelerated melting.

Hierarchy

Hierarchy describes the way that complexity dynamics occur in terms of interrelated nested systems. Like sets of Russian dolls, physical, living systems and social systems exist in interrelated sets of different spatial scales. Micromolecules exist inside a molecule, within human cells, within organs, within the human body. Hierarchy theory is rooted in the work of philosopher Arthur Koestler, economist Herbert Simon, chemist Ilya Prigogine, and ecologist Timothy F. H. Allen.

In 1962 Herbert Simon published, "The Architecture of Complexity," a classic paper in which he argues for the ubiquity and importance of hierarchies in complex systems.[38] Simon showed the links between hierarchy and evolution: for evolution, it is more efficient for complex systems to be composed of hierarchically organized subsystems. Thus, hierarchy is not a coincidental or accidental feature of complex systems, but an essential one.[39]

Just as the concepts of feedback and homeostasis have already proved to be essential features of diverse systems, so was hierarchical structure an inherent feature of our world. Simon expanded the meaning of the term, which had existed previously, referring to a system in which each of the subsystems is subordinated to the system to which it belongs.

Hierarchies help us to see various aspects of complex dynamics. For instance, in Morin's terms, complex systems are always reacting to both "emergences and constraints" – emergence coming from the smaller scale systems within, and constraints from the larger-scale systems within which a given system is embedded. In Timothy Allen's terms, both "codes and constraints" continuously and inherently influence a systems dynamics, which is to say, codes drive emergences influencing the system from within, while constraints influence the system from the larger scales.

In Simon's terms, in a hierarchically nested formal human organization, each system consists of a dominant system and a set of subordinate subsystems; each of the subsystems has a dominant system and subordinate systems. This terminology raises alarm bells for social theorists, as the term hierarchy has dark connotations associated with totalitarianism and oppressive regimes. "Subordination" may be natural in natural systems, and harmful in social systems. Nonetheless, various nontrivial parallels in hierarchical structures help to reveal patterns of complex dynamics even in different types of systems, e.g., natural and social.

Herbert Simon noted some of the key features of hierarchies, later developed by Timothy Allen and others. For instance, he noted that physics pursued "receding elementary particles"; the atom used to be an elementary particle, but by the 1950s they had become complex systems. Whereas, for some purposes of astronomy, whole stars or even galaxies can be regarded as elementary subsystems. And how, with respect to one biological study an elementary subsystem would be a cell, in another a subsystem would be a protein molecule, and in another, an amino acid residue. Hierarchy theory – looking at complexity across grain, scale, rate, codes, and constraints – helps both to identify and explain such patterns.

At the same time, Simon moved beyond some of the all-encompassing grander hopes of early general systems theory study, and pointed to the significance of hierarchical structure as just one feature among many with far-reaching promise. He pointed out that systems of greatly diverse kinds cannot share all properties in common, and thus that metaphor and analogy across the disciplines can be misleading in some instances, even though helpful in other instances. All depends, he says, on whether the similarities the metaphor captures are superficial or significant. Indeed, this insight can be usefully applied to many areas of transdisciplinary understanding of complex systems dynamics.

Hierarchy theory is clearly significant to theoretical ecology, where Timothy Allen and Thomas Hoekstra presented a model that maps and explains the interrelated concepts of hierarchy and scale in ecology, but also in socioecological systems.[40] Among other implications, they took one important aspect of science and scholarship, which had been obscured and distorted by classical science – the role of the observer in the observation, and the observer in the system. They showed the importance of the observer to the system in ecology, or how the observer defines the system. A given entity may belong to any number of levels, depending on the criteria used to link levels above and below. For instance, a human being may be a member of the level, (i) organism, (ii) primate, (iii) human, or (iv) host of a parasite. Different levels may be significant relative to different inquiries.

The role of the observer in the system is manifold. Not only does it show the ways in which the observer and the observation is significant to any analysis – any science or scholarship. It also requires considerations of the way in which, in studying complex systems, we gain only partial understanding through singular posts of observation. The epistemological issues of perspectives and contexts thus lurk in the background of all complexity studies. While this may be less significant in physics, it is significant in biological, ecological, and social systems.

Ecological hierarchy theory also highlights various related terms central to understanding environmental systems, of which two critical terms are: scale and grain. Scale pertains to size in both time and space; size is a matter of measurement, so scale does not exist independent of the scientists' measuring scheme.

Something is large-scale if perceiving it requires observations over relatively long periods of time, across large expanses of space or both. With all else equal, the more heterogeneous something is, the larger its scale.[41] Scale is thus intrinsic to grasping hierarchy. Levels of organization vary according to the object of study. Thus we can talk about: hierarchical levels, organizational levels, observational levels, levels of criterion of observation, and ordering of levels. Grain refers to the degree of detail we wish to examine at a given scale, in the sense of the grain of a photograph. Study systems are more fine-grained – requiring details at a smaller scale; or more coarse-grained – requiring details at a larger scale.

Finally, hierarchies fall into nested and non-nested hierarchies. The distinction between them divides two large groups of hierarchical systems. The most general kinds of hierarchies are *non-nested*, or a set of interacting parts. An army is a nested hierarchy, a collection of soldiers. However, a military commander is a non-nested hierarchy; a general does not consist of a collection of his soldiers. Other common non-nested hierarchies include pecking orders and food webs. In ecological systems, nested hierarchies are rarer. Like a set of Russian dolls, for most purposes, they are completely ensconced in distinct levels of the hierarchy. Examples are the layers in highly structured systems, such as crystals or frozen amber. Such structure is found only in physical systems – it is impossible in social systems, and probably in biological ones.

Generally speaking, hierarchy theory helps us frame and understand functions and processes in systems. Fundamental concepts are codes or constraints and emergences or possibilities. Codes or constraints can influence the system from the bottom up or the top down in hierarchical living or social systems; while possibilities and emergences are produced from lower to higher hierarchical levels. We are only starting to explore the ways in which such patterns help to better understand the world we wish to sustain.

Emergence

Even while some scientists feel they cannot define the term emergence well enough to merit using it, many argue that prodigious work on emergence in natural systems already has been paradigm changing, and important to many disciplines. Implications include important components of change and novelty in every realm, and the system-wide properties of phenomena, from the emergence of stars, chemicals, and life, to animals and humans capable of learning, adaptation, strategy monitoring and change. In physics it helps to explain the evolution of the universe, and in biology it may help advance Darwin's theory of natural selection to explain how rare and specialized features like eyes are made possible.

Emergence has been defined as the process by which relatively simple rules lead to complex pattern formation.[42] John Holland, a complexity theorist specializing in genetic algorithms, laid out some founding assumptions of emergence in mathematics and the natural sciences. Holland is clear about the extent of his research. He puts aside the social sphere, also rife with emergence, since his aim is to begin with an analysis of what he sees as the most readily examined systems. Holland restricts his study to "systems for which we have useful descriptions in terms of rules or laws. Games, systems made up of well-understood components (molecules composed of atoms), and systems defined by scientific theories (Newton's theory of gravity), are prime examples."[43]

Among the important instances of emergence he also considers significant but omits he mentions for instance, "ethical systems, the evolution of nations and the spread of ideas." Like many Santa Fe scientists, he appears to think that ultimately, methodologies from the natural sciences can be applied to social systems. The lack of rules in social systems, he says, is a prohibitive factor. Though he thinks that if better laws governing their development could be developed, then his ideas on emergence could be applied to them.[44] Regardless of the exact ways in which emergence studies can be advanced throughout the disciplines, the complexity scientists discussed in this chapter already have made major contributions to our understanding of change, novelty and strategy in the natural world, likely to shed some light on the study of emergence in social systems.

Holland explains the basis of his particular approach, which covers topics from physics to the underpinnings of biological evolution. While other valid scientific uses for the term emergence may exist, the domain of rule-governed systems provides a good starting point.

> Recognizable features and patterns are pivotal in this study of emergence. I'll not call a phenomenon "emergent" unless it is recognizable and recurring; when this is the case, I'll say the phenomenon is "regular".... Understanding the origin of these regularities and relating them to one another, offers our best hope of comprehending emergent phenomena in complex systems. The crucial step is to extract the regularities from incidental and irrelevant details.... This process is called *modeling*.[45]

Holland synthesizes his findings about emergence in such rule and law-bound systems in eight key lessons, of which I recap just a couple here. First, emergence occurs in systems that are generated. Examples include cellular automata, chess games, eddies in streams, sets of neurons, and organisms over time. The systems are composed of copies of a relatively small number of components that obey simple laws. Typically these copies are interconnected to form an "array" – e.g., a network, a checkerboard, or points in physical space – that operates within certain codes and constraints and within these parameters, may change over time.[46]

In these generated systems, the whole is more than the sum of the parts. The interactions between the parts are nonlinear, so the overall behavior cannot be obtained by summing the behaviors of the isolated components. Thus, there are regularities in system behavior that are not revealed by direct inspection of the laws satisfied by the components. These regularities both explain parts of the system's behavior and make possible activities and controls that are highly unlikely otherwise. An example is the way in which a strategy, based on uncertain pawn structures, may enable a player to win consistently at chess. Evaluating emergence requires extended or repeated examination and experiment, as the results are not evident from the starting point. In this sense "more comes out than was put in."[47]

Typically, emergent phenomena in generated systems are persistent patterns with changing components. A simple and elegant example is an eddy – water in a fast-moving stream forms a standing wave pattern in front of a rock, where the water particles are constantly changing though the pattern persists. Other examples include the pattern of a moving, changing, pawn formation in a chess game, or the reverberations in a set of neurons. Another familiar example is an organism, also a persistent pattern; organisms turn over all their constituent atoms in something less than a two-year span, and a large fraction of their constituents turn over in a matter of weeks. Only persistent patterns will have a directly traceable influence on future configurations in generated systems, and thus lend themselves to a consistent observable "ontogeny."[48]

Interactions between persistent patterns add checks and constraints that provide increasing competence as the number of such patterns increases. A simple example is the way in which in the duplication process DNA code facilitates correction of local errors. A more sophisticated example takes place in ant colonies and neural networks. As the number of individual ants or neurons increase so does the emergent competence of the network. Both nonlinear interactions, and a rich context of such behavioral patterns, increase both the number of possible interactions and the system's competence. As the number of interacting agents increases, the possible sophistication of the response rises very rapidly (factorially).

A typical consequence of the laws that generate emergent phenomena is called differential persistence, or the persistence of emerging novel attributes and strategies over a period of time long enough to allow for the development and verification of the most successful attributes and strategies. The emergent traits that prove to be the most useful and successful tend to persist and be adopted over time. So emergence is a means by which a system learns. A key aspect of emergence is learning.

Holland gives a relatively simple example, based on thinking in terms of the simplest sets of rules you might imagine in an organism. According to Holland, a default hierarchy of previous decision rules informs the behavior of organisms. For instance, an ant may be guided by a number of interrelated rules, more general and more specific. Rule #1 may be the general rule: If an object is moving (e.g., a falling rock), flee. This rule persists because it has served well in many contexts, often saving the ant's life. However, this same rule alone would cause the ant to avoid other moving ants, with deleterious effects. What if that moving object was the Queen herself, ready to reproduce? A second specific, Rule #2, corrects the general rule: If the object is moving, ant-sized, and exudes a friendly pheromone, then approach it.[49]

If a specialist rule such as this holds whenever these more particular conditions occur, then a symbiotic relation results; in other words, the ant cooperates with the other object – be it ant, plant, etc. The generalist rule provides general guidelines, while the specialist rule corrects for potential errors ensuing from the generalist rule.

Over time, more complex sets of interactions form more complex sets of rules, or enhanced persistence of certain codes, constraints, rules and behaviors lead to the generation of new rules overlaid on the original set. Cross supporting interactions, e.g., symbiosis between ants and plants, often provide enhanced persistence for the component patterns. When these patterns with enhanced persistence satisfy simple macrolaws, then a new generating procedure is overlaid on the original generating procedure, says Holland.

A gorgeous example appealing to poets as well as biologists is the eye. Emergence complements natural selection to help explain the evolutionary development of seemingly unlikely attributes. Before Darwin, many argued that only a designer could allow anything so exquisite as the eye. Indeed, if one looks at their likelihood only as a random selection from the vast number of objects that could form from atoms, it seems unfathomable, not only that nature would create one eye, but that it would create such an extraordinary feature again and again.

However, as Holland explains, emergence in molecular biology now helps to explain the gap. The generation of both micro and macro-level rules and developments radically increases the chance for nature to design via strategy. It is now understood that light alters the bonds of certain relatively simple biomolecules, setting off a chain reaction that can, for instance, cause neurons to fire. Light-sensitive compounds, lens-like crystalline compounds, neurons, and so on, serve as building blocks (generators) from lower to higher hierarchical levels, for the higher-level generating procedure that eventually produces eyes. Darwin's step-by-step lower-level generative procedure for the origin of eyes can be recast in terms of this higher-level generative procedure. Once we take into account the formation of a higher-level, overlaid generative procedure, what had been extremely unlikely when taking into account only the lower-level generative procedures – interactions of atoms to form molecules, etc. – becomes likely, indeed, perhaps inevitable. Here we see how hierarchies, with their inbuilt rules of codes and constraints, are fundamental to advancing upon some cherished scientific theories, such as Darwinian evolution.

Looking across systems at different evolved groups, we see that the eye-generation process has been repeated at least twice across evolutionary branches, in mammals and in cephalopods, using different building blocks (compounds, cell morphologies, and so forth) to achieve the complex design of an eye with the familiar parts (lens, adjustable focus, retina). In some ways, Holland conjectures, the eyes of cephalopods (e.g., squid, octopus), are better designed than those of mammals. And of course eyes of some mammals are vastly superior to human eyes at these specialties, such as long-distance predators, e.g., hawks, and night-time predators, e.g., cougars. Comparing across living systems, it seems that once such hierarchical levels and higher-order generative levels are taken into account, eyes become rather more understandable.

Emergence of new rules thus occurs on multiple levels, with self-reinforcing capacity between these levels. Once successful new patterns emerge, then there is a strong tendency for them to persist, making them candidates for combination with other persistent patterns (other copies or variants). Thus, larger patterns with enhanced competence and persistence is an aspect of biological evolution. Once some initial building blocks are discovered – simple membranes, Krebs cycle, differential adhesion of components, etc. – the number of combinations yielding viable organizations increases dramatically. The common argument that evolution is slow, requiring long sequences of improbable discoveries, misses the point. The unlikely becomes likely, if one allows for a layered series of generating procedures.

By studying the varieties of emergence in the natural world, other biologists have expanded on Holland's view of emergence. Emergent behavior in natural systems includes the dynamics of social species such as insects and birds. Canonical examples include the processes by which social insects develop and work in colonies, and those by which bird flocks form and maintain the V pattern in flight. Another compelling example is the existence of stars and matter. Classical physics taught us that no energy or matter is ever created or destroyed. But this is only partially true. It turns out that matter as we know it did not always exist, *it emerged.*

After the big bang, the universe was a great gaseous, starless, cloud – a vast sea of hydrogen atoms, helium atoms, neutrinos, and photons, of various densities and sizes, spreading out and developing. Within this space, filled with the simplest molecules, were molecular clouds, held together by gravity, surrounded by zones of lower density. As gas clouds became hotter and denser, they emerged into protostars.[50] Various processes led from the gaseous clouds of protostars to the emergence of stars. Nucleosynthesis or nuclear fusion reactions occur, with two results: they release more energy, and they produce new kinds of atomic nuclei. Star formation thus presents a clear case of emergence; the birth of a star creates an array of new elemental nuclei, changing the composition of the universe.

We begin to see the Periodic Table as sets of various steps in a chronological movie taking us back through a long series of emergences, back into deep time, when most all of what we recognize as life did not yet exist. From the Big Bang forward, simple constituents gradually contributed to the emergence of more complex constituents. Newton had it only partially correct. Matter in its present form is not eternal; it emerged.[51] As a result of stellar emergence, the universe ultimately developed into a great variety of stars, galaxies, occasional novas, pulsars, quasars, black holes, and an array of unknown entities generated by the laws of gravity, mechanics, thermodynamics, and nuclear synthesis. The more the cosmos complexified, the more complex the Periodic Table of elements, the greater the potential for new types of emergence.[52]

In the biological world, a major emergent event was the advent of multicellularity. Prior to multicellularity, prokaryotes emerged via macromolecular chemistry; chemical networks emerged with metabolism and three main areas of early biological emergence were: autotrophy (largely photo-autotrophy), ingestion of soluble molecules excreted into the environment by other organisms, and eating of other organisms.

Meiotic replication already resulted in the single-celled stage of an organism. Multicellularity arose as adult organisms consisting of many cells with different functions began resulting in more complex forms.[53] Morphogenesis arose, a subsequent series of cell divisions, starting with the unicellular diploid form, and transforming, with differentiation taking place to produce the multi-celled form of the organism. At each stage of emergence to more complex forms of organisms, the hereditary material had to contain the program for the entire life cycle of an organism. In one elaborate example, the butterfly genome must contain the specification for the butterfly, but also for the caterpillar.[54] Like the emergence of eyes, multicellularity emerged in the evolution of the taxonomic tree not just once, but on independent occasions.[55] We continue to find numerous and widespread examples of emergence.

In fact, emergence appears to be rather ubiquitous. Indeed, to many it appears that everything emerges, from physics to philosophy, from the primordial stars and elements, through biological evolution, social evolution, and agriculture, to technology, urbanization, philosophy and the spiritual.[56]

I stick to examples from natural systems here, but the study of emergence in social systems is also flourishing, exploring emergence as a common characteristic of a very wide range of systems. See Jeffrey Goldstein's excellent introduction, which gives a history ranging from Aristotle and Zeno through John Stuart Mill, James Crutchfield, on to diverse fields today.[57]

Goldstein, Harold Morowitz, and others have examined the chronological development of major instances of emergence throughout both natural and human history, drawing on examples from a wide range of disciplines, and illuminating examples such as the emergence of the wheel, agriculture, the printing press, steam engine, and urbanization.

Self-organization and self-organized criticality

Self-organization is a process found throughout every realm and every kind of complex dynamic system. Self-organized criticality (SOC), coined by physicist J. S. Katz in 1986, is a specific class of self-organization in physical and chemical systems, for an attractor at a "critical point." An attractor is a state between physical phase transitions that a dynamic system tends to slip into. Self-organized criticality is considered to be one aspect of the way in which complexity arises in physical and chemical and thus living systems.[58] While the concept derived from physics, it has been applied in fields such as: geophysics, physical cosmology, evolutionary biology and ecology, quantum gravity, solar physics, and plasma physics.

Self-organized criticality is typically observed in slowly driven non-equilibrium systems with extended degrees of freedom and a high level of non-linearity. Since a seminal 1988 paper by Per Bak, Tang Chao, and Kurt

Wiesenfeld, many individual examples have been identified, but to date there appears to be no known set of general characteristics that guarantee a system will display SOC.

The physicist Per Bak employed SOC to describe sand piles. Sand dripped continually onto a surface eventually produces a sand pile that will wax and wane, fluctuating around a critical value, a crucial amount of sand. The same principle holds – from sandpiles to Rocky Mountain avalanches. In each case, the critical value determines when piles of varying sizes are followed by phases of reorganization. Similar examples include the self-organizing processes of rice, metal filings, beads, and liquid drops. Next time you watch the steam rising off of your latte, watch the self-organizing patterns emerge, evolve, and dissipate.

As we move from physics to biology a new perspective has been needed to distinguish the processes of emergence in biological systems, adding a new dimension that has long been missing from our understanding of biological evolution. Since Darwin's work was first published, various scientists have attempted to show that self-organization is a part of evolution.

Recently complexity physicist and biologist Stuart Kauffman has argued that the self-organizing properties of organisms are a significant aspect of evolution. As he argues in *At Home in the Universe* we are not merely the results of accidental natural selection, devoid of meaning or purpose in the universe. Rather, self-organization is always at the heart of physical and living systems, a central process of life. The fate of all complex adaptive systems in the biosphere – from single cells to large economies – involves evolving to a "natural state between order and chaos," a grand compromise between structure and surprise. Kauffman rephrases Shakespeare to say,

> We will find a place in the sun, poised on the edge of chaos, sustained for a time in the sun's radiance, but then disappear – untold actors may come and go; each strutting and fretting its hour upon the stage.[59]

Perhaps most striking in this perspective is the way self-organization appears to have been a central property of life from its very inception through to today. Just as Morin and Morowitz have detailed the ways in which every phase from the Big Bang to today entailed new types of emergence, so Morin argues that all emergences were from the inception, self-organizing. As Morin wrote in 1977, "We know today that all that ancient physics conceived as of simple element is in fact organization. The atom is organization; the molecule is organization; the aster is organization; life is organization; society is organization…"

Kaufmann has theorized about the way in which biological life itself initially emerged from chemistry as a self-organizing ensemble. Sufficiently complex mixes of chemicals spontaneously crystallize into systems with the ability collectively to catalyze the network of chemical reactions by which the molecules themselves are formed. Such collectively autocatalytic sets sustain themselves and reproduce. This is what we call a living metabolism, the tangle of chemical reactions that power cells. Life is a self-organizing phenomenon! It arose as molecular diversity reached a certain threshold of complexity beyond which self-organizing pre-biotic chemical systems spurred life.

This view posits that life is inherently emergent and self-organizing. Life does not exist in the form of some elemental parts; it only exists as processes, interacting ensembles. Life is not located in the property of any single molecule; we cannot discover the meaning of life in the details alone. Rather, life is a collective property of systems of interacting molecules. Life emerged whole and has always remained whole.

Democritus and all of his followers have been wrong, or at least mostly wrong; there is no elemental particle, and the world is not composed like a set of Lego blocks building slowly in intricacy. Complexity, emergence, and self-organization were there from the birth of the universe, and from the very first physical and chemical reactions. True, reality also complexifies, it becomes even more complex through continuous emergence over time. But to begin with, it was already complex and self-organizing.

Nonetheless, no vital force or extra substance is present in the emergent, self-reproducing whole. Life itself is the force and substance in this emergent, self-reproducing system. Insofar as this discovery in contemporary biology is correct, it would go a long way in explaining both the incredible intellectual excitement, and the ultimate failure of the earlier biological notion of vitalism, e.g., in the philosophy of Henri Bergson. Bergson catapulted to fame with the great popularity of his notion of "élan vital" or a vital life force that transcends the explanations of reductionist science. The brief firestorm of interest lasted from 1907 to 1914 and was later sharply refuted. Perhaps the utter rejection of vitalism helped spur even stronger reductionism to guide the first phase of microbiology and genetics research in the latter twentieth century.

Now, studies of self-organization may reconcile these views. Both atomism and vitalism are dead. There is indeed something "vital," but it is not an extra or mysterious force; it is found in the self-organizing emergent properties at the level of the whole organism. The collective system possesses a stunning property – it can reproduce itself and evolve. When the number of different kinds of molecules in a chemical soup passes a certain threshold, a self-sustaining network of reactions – an autocatalytic metabolism – will suddenly appear.[60]

Life is the natural accomplishment of catalysts in sufficiently complex non-equilibrium chemical systems. Relatively simple behaviors of nonequilibrium chemical systems are well studied and may have varied biological implications. Systems can form a standing pattern of stripes of high chemical concentrations spaced between stripes of low chemical concentrations. Examples include the stripes of the zebra and the banding patterns on shells. Such chemical patterns are intriguing, but not yet living systems. By what laws, what deep principles, might autocatalytic systems have emerged on Earth?

In Kaufmann's view, aside from reconciling atomism and vitalism, we are also reconciling science and myth; the study of self-organization may be seen as the search for a new creation myth. The diversity of molecules in our biospheric system increased. The ratio of reactions to chemicals (or edges or nodes) increased. Molecules are themselves able to catalyze reactions by which the molecules themselves are formed. As the ratio of reactions to chemicals increases, the number of reactions that are catalyzed by the molecules in the system increases. Through ongoing catalyzing reactions, a giant catalyzed reaction web forms, so that a collectively auto-catalytic system snaps into existence. Thus, in a splendid phase transition, a living metabolism crystallizes and life emerges![61]

Many great biologists have noted aspects of the self-organizing nature of life. In nature, qualities are born of associations and combinations. The association of an atom of carbon in a chain of molecules promotes stability, a quality indispensable to life. As Francois Jacob noted, nature makes more than additions; it makes integrations. Similarly, the living cell has emergent properties – to nourish itself, to metabolize, and to reproduce.[62] While this notion goes all the way back to Aristotle, the specific concept of self-organization, as expounded by Monod in 1970 and scholars like Morin and Kaufmann today, takes on a new significance in biology.

In general, self-organization arises not from interactions of parts in their isolation, but from the whole-systems scale of systemic processes. Emergent processes retroact on parts and imbibe the whole. The qualities of an organism arise from the cellular level, while the genetic pool of a species arises from its genome. Even while integrating evolving emergence and complexity, self-organization somehow marches onwards.

Pluralist epistemological perspectives on complexity in natural systems

Scientists from SFI and now an array of institutes have produced a great flourishing new field of complexity sciences.[63] In what follows, I open up the methodological lens, from primarily quantitative, to qualitative methods from the realms of the social and philosophical. I explore a few groups who have incorporated insights from the qualitative side, namely social theory and philosophical domains of study. The scientific method, as Kurt Richardson has said, the best metaphor in history, has brought us extraordinary new insights into our world, a whole new paradigm. Yet, it appears that this new paradigm is most fully understood via a richer, more pluralist epistemological perspective.

A new paradigm often acts as a kind of Trojan horse. Just as complex processes themselves are not always visible, there is more to complex dynamic processes than meets the eye. Like the Trojan horse in *Monty Python and the Holy Grail* (or rather, the Trojan rabbit), what is hidden inside may contain various game-changing surprises (or may not). I assert that the complexity sciences contain some special surprises, ones that may even help to reshape science and knowledge more generally.

In this final section, I discuss the added perspectives of a few groups of natural scientists and scholars who bring more pluralist epistemologies to their interpretation of complexity in the natural world.

My basic contention here is that a pluralist epistemology is necessary to grasp the fuller implications of complexity theories. In this section, I show that interdisciplinary and transdisciplinary views – ones that are inter- and transdisciplinary not just in their subjects of study, but rather also in their methodological approaches to these subjects – are necessary to more fully grasp the nature and implications stemming from the sciences of complexity.

One of the most striking things about complexity is that it is transdisciplinary. This is why it is so helpful in the case of highly complex, transdisciplinary issues of global change – such as poverty, extinctions and climate change. This same transdisciplinary quality of complexity leads us to look at knowledge itself in a new light.

As I discuss further in Chapter 6, one of the lessons of complexity theories is that the very nature of life's complexity and the way in which knowledge about this complexity is expanding helps us to see two things, a seeming paradox. On the one hand, this growing transdisciplinary knowledge of complexity improves our comprehension of reality. On the other hand, it also shows how and why our comprehension of reality can only ever be partial and limited. Complexity involves seemingly contradictory forces in intricate interrelation, e.g., order and disorder, and it appears that these cannot be fully extricated, and cannot be fully known from one point in space and time. Complexity is a moving, dynamical, target. This is why a degree of transdisciplinary study is necessary in grasping a fuller sense of our world's complexity.

However, this epistemological and methodological transdisciplinarity also sheds light on another seeming paradox. On the one hand, quantitative methods necessarily build up the most rigorous view of reality, while qualitative methods are necessary to grasping the fuller meaning of that reality. On the other hand, we can never fully conjoin the quantitative and qualitative, for the same reason that we can never fully comprehend complexity. Efforts at articulating the various views – quantitative and qualitative – of the complexity sciences in their ensemble, therefore, reveal the challenge and, ultimately, impossibility of any fully, purely "transdisciplinary complexity theories," just as there is an impossibility of any "comprehensive disciplinary complexity theories." Fully transdisciplinary complexity theories are impossible; yet they are just as possible as any other attempts at knowledge once we accept an inherent degree of uncertainty and incompleteness. Complexity is only partially knowable. And yet, as we attempt to understand issues of global change and sustainability, we come closer by articulating the results of pluralist methods and epistemologies.

Epistemologically and methodologically interdisciplinary and transdisciplinary views of the complexity sciences

A multitude of interdisciplinary and transdisciplinary complexity researchers have emerged in recent years. I explore them a bit more in Chapter 5 on transdisciplinarity.

Here, I focus on one group of transdisciplinary philosopher scientists who have developed and contemplated complexity theories for over 40 years. This group got their start in a 1970s intellectual Parisian circle called the Group of

Ten. Several scholars in this group began to explore the wide-ranging nature and implications of the dawning complexity sciences. I will discuss two leading transdisciplinary scholars here: Edgar Morin and Henri Atlan. Again, all complexity scientists are transdisciplinary in the sense of their interests and subjects; scholars like Morin and Atlan are also transdisciplinary in their methods. They have conducted quantitative science, or integrated the results of quantitative data and analysis from other quantitative scientists into their interpretation, while they have also employed plural, interdisciplinary, and transdisciplinary epistemological lenses and methodologies in their thinking.

Of course, these categories, such as the SFI and the Group of Ten, are not cut and dry. Many brilliant scientists are also philosophers, humanities scholars, novelists, artists, etc. Moreover, many scientists have successfully applied quantitative approaches to social systems, at least to a degree for certain kinds of issues. The Santa Fe Institute has successfully applied quantitative methods to social systems in some instances, such as quantitative research by SFI professors Geoffrey West and Luis Bettencourt on cities, and by former SFI visiting scientist Peter Turchin on history. Much of this work is relevant to understanding sustainability. While the bulk of the work at SFI is primarily quantitative there are exceptions; the philosopher and novelist Rebecca Goldstein had a stint at SFI. Moreover, there are very few scholars doing rigorous complexity research from a pluralist epistemological basis, even though there are some brilliant leaders – Timothy Allen, Henri Atlan, Paul Cilliers, Jeffrey Goldstein, Simon Levin, Sandra Mitchell, Edgar Morin, Ilya Prigogine, Kurt Richardson, and Isabelle Stengers come to mind.

However, those scholars with the most fully transdisciplinary approach – in both focus and methods – appear to be in consensus that the applied aims of sustainability call for us to understand the multiple perspectives described here in their ensemble as much as possible. In other words, all of these approaches are necessary, but then they must, to a degree, be integrated to get a fuller picture of social and environmental systems dynamics. We may not have many philosopher-scientist renaissance thinkers today, but they may have an especially important vision.

The need for a transdisciplinary perspective, for science to be conjoined with ethics, for instance, is a long-held view. How many great thinkers, from the Frankfurt School of social theorists, to Enrico Fermi, Rachel Carson, James Hansen, and Edgar Morin, have called for science to be guided by ethics.

By advancing complexity studies in both disciplinary and to some degree methodologically transdisciplinary complexity, we may move complexity from the margins of academia to the center of our knowledge institutions – colleges and universities, but also K-12 school systems, research institutes, funding agencies, governments, and international organizations. Sustainability may require nothing less.

Complexus

Interweaving the domains of quantitative and qualitative complexity, according to Morin, is necessary to reach better understanding of the nature of our reality as "complexus," or interwoven. Everything is complex, from the Big Bang, to the evolution of life, to our most highly complex societies today. One might add, humorously, that focusing on complexity as explosions does point back to the Big Bang, which certainly situates Hubler's conception of complexity as foundational.

The physical realm is based in energy flows, implosions and explosions. The Big Bang led to an incomprehensively great cloud of matter dispersing. Billions upon billions of suns emerged, all destined at one moment or another to implode or to explode. Our cosmic story is explosive. Demonic paroxysms of that strange force of gravitation drive suns to emerge and to explode, says Morin. "The Sisyphus of gravitation has the obstinate mania of assembling and condensing the dispersed, but sooner or later, the condensed, burning too brightly, explodes, and all begins again, but with greater dispersion."[64]

The relationship between physics and self-organization is fundamental, as many have argued. As Morin puts it:

> Organization is the marvel of the physical world.... How is it that an incandescent conflagration, a boiling ball of photons, electrons, protons, neutrons could self-organize at least 10^{73} atoms, that millions and millions of suns are grinding and convulsing in 500 million discovered galaxies, (and beyond two to three billion light years away, we don't find much at all...)? In what way, out of this great ball of fire, could have emerged billions of these machines of fire? And of course: How life?
>
> We know today that all that ancient physics conceived as simple element is in fact organization. The atom is organization; the molecule is organization; the aster is organization; life is organization; society is organization. But we ignore the true meaning of this term: organization.

Paraphrasing from Morin, it is because of organization that we speak of "physis" – Latin for nature and a historical root of today's science of physics – and yet it is the key concept absent from much of today's physics! Order was the notion that, in crushing all the others, crushed organization. After the resurgence of disorder, we saw that interactions became central to modern physics. Interaction is effectively a crucial notion; it is the point on which turn the ideas of disorder, order, transformation and organization. Rather, physics must focus on, not merely interactions, but also organization.

The generative source of organization is the complexity of cosmic disintegration, the complexity of the idea of chaos, the complexity of the relation of disorder, interaction, encounters, and organization. "Yet, science alone cannot comprehend organization," says Morin, "to do so would be to reduce a complex question to a simple one, which would be to disorganize organization."[65] To surpass this problem is to surpass the focus on objects and objectivity, and shift the gaze to subjects and systems. To understand organization more fully, says Morin, we must shift our gaze to see objects as systems.

Comprehending complexity involves understanding and integrating into our thinking the ways in which we are now overturning all the previous ideologies and assumptions of classical science, and what we are replacing them with. Primary among these is the replacement of pure determinism, pure order, and pure certainty, with degrees of disorder, chaos, change, and uncertainty.

Atlan was perhaps the first to more closely examine the notion of self-organization in both physical and living systems, both scientifically and philosophically, in his 1979 publication *Between Crystal and Smoke: Essay on Organization of the Living.*[66] In Atlan's account, both nonliving and living systems exist in this state involving inherent interactions comprised of order and disorder in fundamental interrelation. On the one hand there are highly ordered systems like crystal, on the other hand, highly disordered systems like smoke. Every complex system, every dynamic system, capable of change and adaptation, exists in a state within these extremes – its existence is predicated on processes of interacting order and disorder in the form of self-organization.

The death of the ideal observer and the rise of subjects

A striking moment in the history of physics and philosophy, which has bearing on our interpretations, framings, and understanding of complexity in the natural world, is the death of pure determinism. Laplace pinned determinism on an abstract, absolute point, ironically, a conceptual *construction*. Early in the history of the Scientific Revolution, Morin recounts, the cosmologists (physicists) were the first to come up against complexity, in the form of the limits of human observation and the limits to the possibility of pure determinism. In other words, the early modern physicists hit upon the irritating issue of uncertainty.

The problem was resolved, which is to say suppressed and ignored, says Morin, by the postulate of the ideal observer, Laplace's demon, situated at the optimal post from which to perceive all reality. Laplace made major contributions to celestial mechanics, physics, mathematics, and the theory of probabilities, and envisaged such major later discoveries as the black hole. For most of modern science, an absolute version of his speculations of determinism underlay an assumption of universal certainties.

This perfect observer, postulated Laplace, "would embrace in the same formula both the movements of the largest bodies in the universe and those of the lightest atom; to it nothing would be uncertain, and the future as the past would be present to its eyes."[67]

As Morin explains, proponents of total cosmic order, in attempting to uphold that obfuscation of disorder, would have no other recourse but to invent an abstract observer. And only a true acknowledgement of disorder could then reveal the real, concrete observer.

Even after the pure version of Laplace's determinism was refuted, the corollary beliefs, the role, nature, and implications of the results of purely reductionist methodologies, have persisted. Of course there is determinism, a major feature of reality, as in deterministic chaos. But there is no "pure" determinism, only determinism that is coextensive with autonomy, novelty and change, as in the infinity of new patterns in deterministically chaotic systems.

For centuries, classical science's abstract myths of order effectively eliminated uncertainty from much of the thinking of our science and scholarship. This obstacle in our thinking created the strangely flawed perspective in which all subjective certainty took itself for objective reality. In the experience of the observer, disorder is that which brings out and reveals uncertainty. This uncertainty, reflected to the observer, brings about self-questioning, self-reflection. The observer becomes aware of internal and external, subjective reflexivity.[68] Real observers quickly obliterate notions of pure order, pure objectivity, or pure determinism.

The loss of Laplace's single abstract point of view forever destroys the classical scientific myths of pure objectivity, pure order, and pure determinism. In their place, the rebirth of multiple points of view on a reality that is everywhere dynamic, indelibly infuses uncertainty and subjectivity into our worldview, and demonstrates their supreme significance.

With the "discovery" of the observer, we are forced to integrate our selves and our subjectivity more effectively into our thinking, including the entire practice of science. This has been explored extensively in science studies and related fields in the last two decades. We are, after all, the main perpetrators of most of the social and environmental crises we are now studying. Like Pogo, we do not need to look farther, just more accurately.

As such, we must study the observer as much as the observed, which is to say, we must include the subjective. We are cultural, social, and biological beings, inventors of a way of knowing called science. The subservience of science to forces of private interests, corporate power, and the general fragmentation of power and agency in contemporary societies, has called for a reevaluation of the role of scientists interested in sustainability. This brings to light, with a new degree of urgency the role of observers, subjectivity, agency, and responsibility.

The death of pure or total determinism calls us to integrate, not the much degraded connotation of "subjectivity" referring merely to contingency and affectivity, but rather the considerable role of the much greater sense of the term – the role of our individuality, perceptions, experiences, and agency; our great potential to strategize and to change individual and social human behaviors.

Thus the earliest moments of modern physics saw the emergence of the subject from the physical, and with it, profound uncertainty. The subject emerges, says Morin, with all its insufficiency, limitation, egocentrism, ethnocentrism, but also will, conscience, interrogation, and inquiry. The subject emerges, with disorder, uncertainty, and contradiction; with awe and alarm before the great cosmos; with the loss of any privileged point of observation; but also and simultaneously, with the realization of our cultural and social roots in the here and now.

This calls for a fuller appreciation of transdisciplinarity necessary to reframing our view of global crises today. After all, humanity is not just a by-product of our cosmic roots; today more than ever, the cosmos and our biosphere within it are also a by-product of our emergence as anthropo-social beings.[69] We are in coproduction with our natural environment.

Shifting the gaze from objects towards subjects, subjectivities, and contexts produces myriad results. Most generally, it highlights the entire complexity framework that I present here – bringing to light the centrality of complexity, dynamics, and systems, and how various kinds of systems are inherently dynamic and complex, and in the process shedding light on issues of feedbacks, networks, and the other major principles.

More specifically, in the case of environmental sustainability, the death of pure determinism, pure objectivity, and pure certainty, highlights issues of human impact within socioecological feedbacks, networks, and hierarchies. For instance, we are increasingly discovering how heavily humans impacted the Earth's environment in the past. Early humans brought about numerous mega-fauna extinctions, and late medieval European deforestation likely caused the Little Ice Age.[70] We are not just further manifestations of a physical and ecological planet; we are now the greatest force influencing and altering those biophysical and ecological systems. Incorporating the death of pure determinism and pure objectivity fully shifts the entire picture, and calls for greater integration of insights from many disciplines in the quest for understanding the complexity of the natural world – from physics, ecology, biology, and neuroscience, to sociology, politics, economics, and ethics.

Immanuel Kant and "names for what we cannot explain"

Perhaps, complexity even may be the paradigmatic turn that can break down the centuries-old culture gap. Many of the complexity scientists across the quantitative-qualitative divide may not even know of each other's work. And yet, the reconciliation – that many of them may not even know they needed – may in fact already be occurring. In contrast to the science wars within mainstream science and scholarship, amongst the complexity scientists, perhaps never having declared differences, there appears to be a convergence of visions.

Both quantitative scientists at SFI, and qualitative thinkers in the Group of Ten, have highlighted the philosophical tensions underlying the entire project of complexity theories – tensions that arose and remain unresolved by the science wars and the many only partially debunked classical ideologies. These tensions, left unresolved, can dilute or distort the meaning and implications of complexity theories. But throughout these approaches to complexity science, these researchers appear to be on the way towards resolving them.

Mitchell suggests that complexity terms are plagued by only partial and incomplete meanings and understanding. General principles, she says, may be too vague to be very useful, for example, "complex systems exhibit emergent properties." Mitchell quotes the complexity scientist Deborah Gordon as lamenting the seeming weakness of the field, which at times appears only, "to provide names for what we cannot explain."[71]

That we may only partially discern complexity is a theme I explore further in Chapter 6. Complexity reveals and explains the processes by which life and knowledge becomes more complex, or complexifies, and the resultant partial unknowability. One of the great roles of complexity quantitative sciences and qualitative theories has been, in fact, to show just why and how there are limits to science and knowledge, even while both science and knowledge most generally continue to expand. Mitchell indicates this when she writes:

> Imagine that string theory turns out to be correct – physics' long sought-after (Grand Unified Theory) GUT. That would be an enormously important achievement, but ... it would be far from the end of complex systems science. The behaviors of complex systems that interest us are not understandable at the level of elementary particles or ten-dimensional strings. Even if these elements make up all of reality, they are the wrong vocabulary for explaining complexity. It would be like answering the question, "why is the logistic map chaotic?" with the answer, "Because $x_t + 1 = R x_1 (1 - x_t)$."

Perhaps complexity itself is at the heart of the reason that we cannot fully know the living and social realms "in themselves." Even if physics seems more knowable, as Mitchell points out, perhaps the complexity of physics may also evade our direct grasp. It appears that the complexity principles – such as complex systems, nonlinearity, feedback, networks, hierarchy, emergence, and self-organization – are at the heart of the reason that mathematics is central to explaining complex phenomena, and yet alone cannot fully explain things. And it appears that we can only get a step closer by conjoining pluralist methodologies – mathematics, social theory, and philosophy. Perhaps our dawning vision of life as complex and dynamic inherently implies that knowledge is only and always necessarily partial, precisely because of life's complexity.

If so, then we must always speak partly in terms of labels for that which we cannot explain. Mathematics applied to natural systems works extremely well – as Richardson says, the best metaphor humans have invented. But it appears that in the case of biological and social systems we will always be dealing largely with partial uncertainties, contingencies, unknowability, and unknown unknowns. This appears to be a puzzle, only if our aim remains partially mired in the modernist goal of possessing and attaining certainties and any reified sense of "truth." However, when we shift more fully into complex thinking, we see the many benefits, as for instance, the explanation and legitimization of the irrelevancy of the inability to precisely define terms like complexity or sustainability. After Derrida, who showed the impossibility of defining any words precisely, the richness of terms like complexity and sustainability rather indicates their great significance and relevance.

The seeming conundrum of inescapable degrees of unknowability was perhaps first most fully articulated by one of the most influential philosophers in the history of Western philosophy, Immanuel Kant (1724–1804), who argued, "We cannot know things in themselves." Kant's contributions to metaphysics, epistemology, ethics, and aesthetics have had a profound impact on almost every philosophical movement that followed. He is perhaps most famous for his metaphysics and epistemology in *The Critique of Pure Reason*.

A large part of Kant's work addresses the question "What can we know?" The answer, if it can be stated simply, is that our knowledge is constrained to mathematics and the science of the natural, empirical world. It is impossible, Kant argues, to extend knowledge to the supersensible realm of speculative metaphysics. The reason that knowledge has these constraints, Kant argues, is that the mind plays an active role in constituting the features of experience and limiting the mind's access only to the empirical realm of space and time.[72]

Moreover, for Kant, organization was the irreducible characteristic of life. Kant contrasted organization of living systems with the machine, of which the model was the pendulum, then the watch, then the steam engine – all of which was absent of organization. In machines, one found, in contrast to living beings, no internal functions of control driving finalities. Life possessed the profound property of *organization, irreducible by scientific methods.*[73]

Kant was not even the first to speculate about the nature of these complex properties of the living. History is full of queries into complexity, e.g., concepts of emergence, a property that perhaps epitomizes that which reductionism cannot fully capture. Pierre Louis Moreau de Maupertuis, President of the Berlin Academy of Sciences and a natural philosopher, described what we would now call emergence in the mid-1700s. Maupertuis was interested in the modes of transmission of "genetic" information. He described living minima that he terms "molecules" endowed with desire, memory, and intelligence. According to Charles Wolfe at the University of Sydney, Maupertuis was a Leibnizian of sorts. His molecules possessed higher-level, "mental" properties, recalling La Mettrie's statement in *L'Homme-Machine*, that Leibnizians have "rather spiritualized matter than materialized the soul."[74] In debating this issue with Diderot, Maupertuis attributed higher-level properties to his living minima, while Diderot argued that these can only be "organizational," i.e. properties of the whole.[75] In a sense, these views might now be seen as not mutually exclusive, but rather compatible, correlative perspectives on what we now call emergence and self-organization.

Both Atlan and the leading science and technology scholars who would follow two decades later were inspired in part by forewarnings from the early systems scientists and cyberneticians themselves. In 1979, Atlan echoed the concerns of these early complexity pioneers about the use of scientific metaphors such as "information" and "program." In systems theories, cybernetics and other precursors of complexity theories, scientists use the central metaphor of "program," or as stated at times, "a program of internal origin," Cybernetic metaphors like program have an undeniable operational value in biological practice, said Atlan. The problem arises when scientists tried to apply the metaphor beyond that obvious operational value, in attempts to comprehend their meaning or to explain things more fully. Such misuse, rather than leading to the desired goal of comprehension, actually causes more confusion, and argued Atlan, inevitably leads to raising new questions.

In 2000, science scholar Lily Kay would publish the groundbreaking *Who Wrote the Book of Life*, on much the same thesis. As her publisher wrote:

> Kay draws out the historical specificity in the process by which the central biological problem of DNA-based protein synthesis came to be metaphorically represented as an information code and a writing technology – and consequently as a "book of life." This molecular writing and reading is part of the cultural production of the Nuclear Age, its power amplified by the centuries-old theistic resonance of the "book of life" metaphor. Yet, as the author points out, these are just metaphors: analogies, not ontologies. Necessary and productive as they have been, they have their epistemological limitations. Deploying analyses of language, cryptology, and information theory, the author persuasively argues that, technically speaking, the genetic code is not a code, DNA is not a language, and the genome is not an information system (objections voiced by experts as early as the 1950s).[76]

All of this leads to an important set of insights about the nature of the complexity sciences. It leads to the question, what are we doing when we do complexity science? What do the results explain or help us to comprehend? It speaks to why it is that complexity scientists are left with the sense of inadequacy when labeling phenomena like emergence, which in fact we cannot fully explain; we cannot give simple definitions for words like complexity, emergence, and self-organization.

By 1979, of course, the classical problematic of reductionism of biology to physics and chemistry was outmoded. Since that time many thinkers pursued a natural philosophy that would take this into account.[77] It is common in natural science circles, lamented Atlan, to retain the old "negative," as in passive stance, and say "Of course we see well that we are only speaking in terms of metaphors, and that modern biology is not really *explaining*, in these physico-chemical and mechanistic terms, the phenomena of the living…" In such an attitude though, the passive becomes counterproductive and loses legitimacy. New questions must be posed in new language, not just a reduction of the living purely to the physico-chemical, but rather "the broadening of the living to a bio-physics of organized systems, applicable to both artificial machines and natural systems."[78]

Scientists must acknowledge the problem of this flawed extrapolation from the operational to the implication of comprehension. This acknowledgement could help us to prevent the misuse of technological "truths" to found and foster ideologies – as was done in the Lyssenko Affair, the holocaust, and various other incidents throughout the twentieth century – "of which the deadly power could reach catastrophic dimensions."[79] As societies continue to become more complex in the last few decades, this admonition has only become more important. Enmeshed in webs of social, technological, economic, political, and ideological forces, science in various ways contributes to the aims and understanding underlying any projects for "sustainability." Especially as the term sustainability has been wholly co-opted, swallowed, regurgitated, repackaged, and resold by a long list of governments, militaries, and transnational corporations.

When Kant said, "we can't know things in themselves" he put a wedge under the entire edifice of pure objectivity in classical science. Like the death of Laplace's ultimate point of objectivity, Kant's injunction also dismantles the foundations of these pure classical assumptions. To accept that there is no pure objectivity, we cannot know things from an imaginary point of objectivity, and that there is no "full direct knowledge," we cannot know things directly in any totalizing or full sense, is to begin to gain a deeper perspective on complexity.

Complexity sciences may be informing us about interconnectivity, interactions and the fascinating new studies of emergence and self-organization. However, in the context of sustainability, we must ask for more. We must inquire into how the complexity sciences inform knowledge, understanding, and perspectives on other subjects, such as ethics, politics, and economics.

Complexity – including the studies of feedbacks, networks, and hierarchies – has much to inform us about the nature of simplifications and ideologies in a world of crisis. Not just science, but all knowledge, as it progresses, must be increasingly understood in a transdisciplinary context. Many scientists have given stark warnings about this through the twentieth century. Francois Jacob warned: "We no longer study life in laboratories; it's the algorithms of the living world that we are interested in." Which is to say, very dangerously, we have lost the focus on fuller knowledge about our lives, and we have become focused on knowledge for careers, utility, political aim, and profit.

Losing sight of the bigger picture can permit logic which construes organisms as programmed machines, cybernetic systems about which the goal is to discover the programs and the logic of organization, for other aims.[80] In other words, a lot of very powerful and successful science in the last few decades – including systems and now complexity sciences – has been at least partially embedded in ideologies based on seeing what works for human aims, rather than what scientific results truly mean, and thus how they might actually play out in the world. Science becomes prey to marketability, production, technocracy, and consumption. Science becomes a tool of collapse, rather than a means towards sustainability.

Science is embedded in human societies rife with ideologies. Mathematics may be objective, but the way that humans employ it can never be so. Leading thinkers from across every disciplinary area have come to realize this. Science and reason alone do not guide societies; and science and reason in the absence of philosophical interpretation and ethics can lead societies dangerously awry. As Henri Atlan warned to his fellow scientists,

> Whether we think like Galileo that the universe is a book of which the language is mathematics, or like Poincare that mathematics is the language of humankind when we study nature, god has changed status. He began by becoming a mathematician, then he disappeared in progressive stages, replaced by physicists – mathematicians themselves – as soon as he could

do without the former. In any case, the guarantee (goal), of a unified moral law or a unified natural law was no longer God as creature-legislator, but rather, human reason. Of that period of grand ideologies of the 19th century, when reason would discover the rules of conduct and the organization of society, in harmony with the laws of nature.

Today, all that is over. Those ideologies failed, and the free deployment of critical reason has reached the failure of using reason itself to found an individual or social ethic. Moreover, we have reached a very particular point, specific to Western civilization and this particular aspect of its history. In this case, while the laws of nature are better and better described and understood by this particular exercise of reason that is the scientific method, we nevertheless resign ourselves at the same time, that this method has practically no help whatsoever for *the individual or social experience, or the elaboration or development of ethics*.[81]

From Einstein to Enrico Fermi and Rachel Carson to Stephen Schneider and James Hansen, scientists in the twentieth century have been profoundly concerned with the problem of relying too heavily on a scientific method that contributes to bombs but not ethics, a science that is capable of deciphering facts about the world, but not what they mean, and not how that meaning is significant to human well-being. Today, to ignore such considerations is a death wish for scientific institutions, who, like it or not, must respond to a world that is going through a profound crisis of sustainability.

Conclusion

In just a few decades, complexity science has flourished into not just a major new field, but also the basis of a new paradigm. Discoveries of complex dynamic systems, relevant across the widest range of areas of reality – physical, living, and social systems – may play a central role in rearticulating our goals of sustainability.

Suffice to say, a highly cryptic complexity framework such as the one I've proposed in this book, must be seen in light of the more fully detailed, articulated explanation of complexity; found in the now prodigious literature on complexity, including all the branches of the complexity sciences discussed here – from the most disciplinary to the most transdisciplinary. However, the transdisciplinarity of the complexity framework I propose permits it to incorporate the necessary insights from broad epistemological perspectives. In this way, it permits exploration of just how much and in what ways – in a transdisciplinary world – we can and cannot simplify, as we attempt to follow Einstein's suggestion to simplify as much as possible, but not more. It extends upon this dictum, by shedding light on the ways in which we must in fact contextualize the results of quantitative, partially reductionist analysis, within a fuller study of global change.

As complexity science reveals nontrivial similarities in all types of systems, outlined in the complexity framework, it becomes a perspective from which to assimilate insights about the role of disciplinary, interdisciplinary and transdisciplinary perspectives on scientific research. Ultimately, complex dynamic systems science highlights the significance of transdisciplinary perspectives in gaining a fuller understanding of socioecoogical systems dynamics central to our global social and environmental crises – from vicious cycles of poverty and oppression, to climate change and the sixth major extinction.

Complexity, focusing as it does on dynamics, interactions, interdependency, and change, has a unique role to play in advancing our understanding of science and scholarship generally. Complexity scientists have helped to put the final nails in the coffin of pure objectivity, pure determinism, pure certainty, or pure truth. They are therefore well placed to examine some of the deeper philosophical implications of complexity.

This seems to be happening on many fronts. Melanie Mitchell writes:

> Such discoveries will *require* science to change so as to grapple with the questions being asked in complex systems research. Indeed, as we have seen ... in recent years, the themes and results of complexity science have touched almost every scientific field, and some areas of study, such as biology and social sciences, are being profoundly transformed by these ideas.[82]

The challenge is to proceed while also freeing complexity science from the constraints and blinders of the ideologies within sciences, like scientism, in John Dupre's sense of the term, and the tendency to extrapolate from operational metaphors to overall meaning. Complexity science highlights the way in which, as Kant pointed out so long ago, we can only understand our reality partially via mathematics, and beyond that, "we cannot grasp (complex) things in themselves."

We are at a rich moment, when complexity science helps to once again legitimate science as the most successful metaphor we have produced, crucial for our knowledge and our vision. The challenge is for scientists now to support the greater implications of their work, in order for the complexity sciences to become not just one more silo of knowledge, but rather a reflection on the reorganization of knowledge itself.

"Finally, complex systems research has emphasized above all interdisciplinary collaboration, which is seen as essential for progress on the most important scientific problems of our day," writes Mitchell.[83] Scientists must ask how our dawning understanding of complexity leads us to contextualize science more fully within the realities of a multidimensional, transdisciplinary set of global crises. Much complexity science, as other science, aims in one way or another at goals of sustainability. And yet, an epistemologically transdisciplinary perspective is necessary for clarifying the ways in which complexity can and must contribute to sustainability, more generally. We cannot achieve sustainability through solely piecemeal, isolated scientific results, but also through the transdisciplinary complex thinking capable of negating the stultifying ideologies that are driving our current crises. The philosophical comprehension fostered by integrating work from the various branches of complexity science and scholarship is necessary to sufficiently integrate and articulate the deeper implications of complexity science for sustainability.

Mitchell cites a recent survey in which many leading complexity scientists agreed with the statement: "I see some form of complexity science taking over the whole of scientific thinking."[84] If this takes place within the confines of the current dominant system in which knowledge grows primarily in its own isolated branches, blind to the contextual social and philosophical dimensions of our global crises, then let's hope not. If, however, the truly powerful transdisciplinary nature of complexity as paradigmatic comes more fully to light; if we are able to draw on the insights coming also from social theory and philosophy, giving a fuller and richer interpretation of the myriad discoveries in complexity science; if this enriches our view not just of complexity science but also of complex thinking; then complexity may truly contribute to aims of sustainability. Such collaborations of disciplinary, with interdisciplinary and transdisciplinary research and thinking, could shift the complexity sciences from the peripheries of science to the center of our knowledge and our worldview.

4 Complexity in social theory

It is provided in the essence of things that from any fruition of success, no matter what, shall come forth something to make a greater struggle necessary.

Walt Whitman

Hunter-gatherer societies contain no more than a few dozen distinct social personalities, while modern European censuses record 10,000 to 20,000 unique occupational roles, and industrial societies may contain overall more than 1,000,000 different kinds of social personalities.

Randall H. McGuire[1]

Order and disorder

Order, stability, and control still have a special place in our thinking and our imagination. For instance, when we picture the United States it often evokes pleasing images of eternal natural scenes. We envision, for instance, landscapes of the Hudson River school of American art of the 1850s to 1870s. We can still imagine the mystical countryside of Cole, Church, and Bierstadt, brimming over with the myths of Western Progress, American Exceptionalism, and Manifest Destiny, and portraying the United States as befitting a new home: orderly, stable, abundant in nature, void of Native Americans, and infinite in its grace – purple mountains, rolling wheat fields, winding rivers, and wide-open skies.

Gazing across the United States today little remains of these visions. We have lost 99 percent of tall-grass prairies, 96 percent of American redwood forests, and over 90 percent of Californian wetlands. Radical change has made it increasingly hard to overlay visions of bucolic order onto today's continent. Superimposed over Cole's landscapes is a kaleidoscopic collage of bulldozed wetlands and forests, sprawling roads and strip malls, monoculture lawns and fields, swelling populations, technological proliferation, bulging waste dumps, and economic inequity and strife.

Two centuries of economic expansion have siphoned much of America's natural resources into cities and bank accounts.[3] One hundred years after reaching the limits of the frontier, we are reaching some limits to ecological integrity and economic growth.

Physical explosions like Albert Hubler's lightning bolts are not the only kinds of explosions or rapid change. Much of our lives are infused with this facet of complexity – the nonlinear buildup and sudden release of biophysical and environmental phenomena, storms, hurricanes, and fires, but also social ideas, projects, and movements.

A rainstorm is a common example. Moisture gradually builds in the atmosphere, until reaching a critical point of buildup transforms warm, thick, cumulus clouds into a storm. As Mike Davis recounts:

> The two-week-long Kona storm of January 1995 differed little from the classic pattern, except perhaps in the unusual intensity of rainfall in the (Los Angeles) South Bay area – forcing the evacuation of low-lying neighborhoods … and in Santa Barbara County where ten inches of rain fell in 24 hours. Otherwise, the scenes were those of ordinary, familiar disaster: Power was cut off to tens of thousands of homes. Sinkholes mysteriously appeared in front yards. Waterspouts danced across Santa Monica Bay. Several children and pet animals were sucked into the deadly vortices of the flood channels. Reckless motorists were drowned at flooded intersections. Lifeguards had to rescue shoppers in downtown Laguna Beach. Million-dollar homes tobogganed off their hill-slope perches or were buried under giant landslides.[4]

To see the world we want, we have to see the world we have, including not just the order and stability, but the natural and necessary disorder and change, such as the novelty of increasing extreme weather unleashed by climate change. We have to see storms, not just in the moment, but also as part of the very fabric of life, a part that we can influence.

Consider for instance, John McPhee's depiction of the moment when another big storm collided with Per Bak's critically self-organized sandpiles. As McPhee writes, in the blue light they saw "a massive blackness, moving." In the words of Jackie Genofile, the mother of the family of four who witnessed the spectacle, "It was just one big black thing coming at us, rolling, rolling … one big black hill coming towards us."[5] The big black thing was a "debris flow."

> They consist of water mixed with a good deal of solid material, most of which is above sand size. Some of it is Chevrolet size. Boulders bigger than cars ride long distances in debris flows. Boulders grouped like fish eggs pour downhill in debris flows. The dark material coming toward the Genofiles was not only full of boulders; it was so full of automobiles it was like bread dough mixed with raisins. On its way down Pine Cone Road, it plucked up cars from driveways and the street. When it crashed in to the Genofiles' house, the shattering of safety glass made terrific explosive sounds. A door burst open. Mud and boulders poured into the hall. We're going to go, Jackie thought…. The debris flow, entering through windows as well as doors, continued to rise. The house had filled up in six minutes, and the mud stopped rising near the children's chins.[6]

The drama of the natural world – with its long lulls and its sudden storms, debris flows, and social riots – is a truer backdrop on which to comprehend the networked consequences of our myriad technological interventions: chainsaws and bulldozers, coal plants, military bases, fishing trawlers, plastic bag factories, cars, and much more. Complex dynamic systems with their nonlinear changes and varieties of periodic explosions, is a truer backdrop to the way all of these forces are coevolving and coproducing within our dynamic, hierarchically enmeshed, interconnected world.

Social change throughout human history has occurred when long periods of societal ideas building over time erupt in great change – as in the agricultural revolution, the steam engine, and the printing press. Likewise, social movements erupt when long periods of oppression lead to sudden releases of rage. On December 17, 2010, Mohamed Bouazizi, enraged at police harassment and humiliation, stood in the streets of Tunisia, doused himself in gasoline, and set himself ablaze. By January 14, 2011, the Tunisian people had successfully ousted President Zine El Abidine Ben Ali. On January 18, 2011, 26-year-old Asmaa Mahfouz posted a fiery YouTube video calling for mass street protests. One week later, January 25, 2011, hundreds of thousands of Egyptians took to the streets, and within three weeks ousted Egyptian President Hosni Mubarek. The world watched as Middle Eastern countries burst into revolutionary protests, deposing or disposing of long-term dictators. Major social movements erupted in Chile, Spain, England, China, and throughout the world.

On September 17, 2011, revolutionary fervor finally sparked in "the heart of empire," as Arundhati Roy has called it, as a group of two hundred people in Manhattan's Zucotti Park began to self-organize and call themselves Occupy Wall Street. By October 15, 2011, Occupies spread across every corner of the United States, and the number of total Occupies had reached 951 cities in 82 countries. Like rain storms, these social storms were the result of long phases of building energies, in this case, the build-up of myriad frustrations.

There is a non-trivial parallel between Hubler's explosions in physics, and the patterns of slow buildup and rapid release we see throughout all realms – ecology, science, technology, individual emotions and ideas, societal policies and patterns, and social movements.

Inspiringly, while there is more determinism built into the chaos and explosions inherent to physical systems, there is considerable freedom in social systems. The fact that physical systems and social systems can be relatively unstable and dynamic in similar ways is nontrivial. The qualitative difference by which social ideas and systems can be much more unstable and dynamic is also nontrivial. There are many examples throughout history and the present world of economic, political, social, and environmental management systems that are not more resilient to such instability. In fact, humans can create quite chaotic, unstable systems, like the deregulated, free market, capital, and financial policies that brought about the 2007 to 2008 economic collapse. Yet, we also can create a variety of much more stable social systems, like Ostrom's examples of strongly communally enforced, regulated, agricultural and economic systems that have stayed within the bounds of regional ecological limits. Much of the world, throughout much of history, developed in social, economic and technological systems that were relatively environmentally stable, even when they were simultaneously socially dynamic.

History is replete with examples of long buildup and sudden release; but also with examples of longer-term relative sustainability with no need of violent release or social explosions. It is possible to choose systems that are less prone to social unrest, but rather tend towards long-term peace and sustainability.

Complexity in social theory: uncertainty, disorder, and rapid change

Generally speaking, the last one hundred years has seen an exponential increase in the complexity of societies, technologies, and economies. Compared to any past era, today's societies appear to be incredibly complex. Moreover, this rapid growth in complexity has largely coevolved with a modern worldview based largely in reductionist and simplifying thinking. This complexification, this simplistic thinking, and the clash between them, are all significant to comprehending our current global crises, creating more sustainable societies, and envisioning better futures.

Current rapid, major global social and environmental change requires major change in our thinking. In qualifying the nature of change today, an outstanding feature is the hypercomplexity of many contemporary societies. Hypercomplexity has been defined simply as what it sounds like, a very high degree of complexity, or a very high number of elements and interactions between those elements. Complexification, after Nicolas Rescher, refers to increasing complexity, simply put: increases in the number of elements and interactions, which is to say, increases in the number of feedbacks, the density of networks, and the number of hierarchically enmeshed systems – including societal, technological, economic, institutional, and other social systems.[7] Our era is characterized by an exponential increase in societal complexity, including many realms of societies, e.g., social, technological, economic, and knowledge.

Even as many increasingly embrace complexity in various ways, much of our thinking is still largely anchored in more simplistic myths, false assumptions of atomism, posivitism, and determinism; a way of thinking that promotes delusions of boundaries, dichotomies, ideologies; and characterized throughout by one of the most powerful and dangerous perceptions, the illusion of the separation of the social and natural spheres. As Robert Pursig pointed out in *Zen and the Art of Motorcycle Maintenance*, we live in a world of entangled, interconnected real systems, but we approach that world largely via unrealistic, overly reductionist analysis. We think in terms of greatly oversimplified, which is to say distortional, ideas of dichotomies, boundaries, and separations. As Robert Frost pondered, "Something there is that doesn't love a wall/That sends the frozen-ground-swell under it/And spills the upper boulders in the sun/And makes gaps even two can pass abreast."[8]

This simple thinking, in its many forms, is one major driver of the current environmental crisis. Simple thinking has roots in language and lives in everyday thinking as well as ideologies. Professor of literature and the environment Timothy Morton has said that one of the most dangerous words – as if it somehow exists apart from us – is "nature."[9] Likewise: "society" cannot survive apart from "nature."

A notable feature of our era is the mix of imagined and real calamities in the headlines. People are afraid of imagined issues like Y2K, distant Ebola outbreaks and statistically rare serial killers, and become immune to much more serious calamities like distant poverty and wars along with extinctions, and climate change. Meanwhile, the steady depletion of drinking water and topsoil doesn't even make the news.

There are a few striking things about this. First, is the way that we focus on negativity, but often "the wrong negativity." For various reasons, we are riveted by reports of Britney Spears going on probation, the latest serial killer, or far-off Ebola outbreak. But we fail to be adequately motivated to act on very real and pressing threats to our well being, like the depletion of aquifers and topsoil, oceanic collapse, or climate change.

One reason is the power of the amygdala, which evolved to protect us from predators and other immediate threats, but which serves now to skew our focus from the bigger, more systemic threats, to the cheap thrill or passing calamity. Another reason is that we are less developed in thinking in terms of systems and complexities. Generally, we are attuned to singular events, single causes, and silver bullets, and less prone to thinking about the big picture and the long term.

Yet, as complexification proceeds we pass social and environmental thresholds. Increasingly, the more gradual, systemic issues that for many years were primarily just future risks have become catastrophes for growing numbers. The first ravages of climate change storms, droughts, and floods are creating an increasing number of victims – killed in extreme weather events like hurricanes and cyclones, evicted by mass flooding, and driven into famine and starvation by prolonged droughts.

We are partially geared toward self-destructive behaviors of simplistic thinking, denial, greed, hubris, and violence. It is all the more vital then not to lose sight of the great lesson that the complexity framework offers about social systems, namely: the innate potential for agency, intentionality, learning, adaptation, responsibility, and action, both precautionary and proactive. Great change in social ideas and behaviors is possible, it is historically evident, and it is increasingly necessary.

This must be contextualized within today's rich social theory – whether under the labels of social theory, social sciences, human sciences, humanities, or philosophy. Great social thinkers and philosophers, as well as the great scientists, have articulated considerable complexity. In this sense, complex thinking is not new; it is a trait of all great social thinking and philosophy. In another more specific sense, complex thinking is new. It implies the articulation and application of various complexity principles, such as the complexity framework I present, as it plays out in the social sphere. Nonlinearity, feedback, networks, nested hierarchies, emergence, and self-organization appear to be just as significant in both social and natural systems.

It is in this latter sense that I approach the work in this chapter. I look at several recent examples of prominent social theories that are based very specifically on the major complexity principles, usually implicitly and not explicitly. There are innumerable examples, of which I choose just three literatures significant to sustainability: postmodernity, risk, and collapse.

It should be noted though, that the groups of thinkers I mention working on these particular issues, represent just a very few specific examples. A fuller picture requires many other great philosophers and social theorists of the last century, such as, for instance, those dealing with power, identity, class, domination, autonomy, and freedom. Ultimately, this greater cadre of diverse social thinkers is the necessary context and backdrop within which to better understand the sparse examples given in this chapter. Only within this greater context does an adequate picture form to show how complex thinking sheds light on rapid social change, the specter of social collapses of various kinds and the aims of social sustainability, or thriving. The discussion that follows must be contextualized within the greater postmodern canon of the last half-century, including fields such as critical theory, cultural studies, and science studies, all of which are also essential to the framing and conceptualization of our responses to social and environmental crises.

Given the current ecological changes, undermining our planetary life-support systems,[10] it is striking to see how much daily news, science, and scholarship blindly proceeds with atomistic, isolated analyses, knowledge which is insignificant with respect to greater social and natural crises or which our environmental crises may soon render moot. What does it mean to study individual fish species if we may face oceanic collapses?[11] What does it mean to study social dynamics in Rangamati, Bangladesh, if the whole nation may be underwater by 2100? Certainly, particular studies illuminate larger trends. However, in order to have the world to study in a few decades, we also have to open our scopes to a broader, more realistic framing. Major global change requires major changes in our thinking.

The complexity framework and social theory: scholarship for sustainability

There are beacons of light in the maze of current affairs, a few scholarly fields that have been making advances in capturing and expressing major social trends involved in today's multiple global crises. Theorists in the social and philosophical realms have been articulating a rich, synthetic, complex perspective on the significant issues of our era.

For years and decades, a wide array of social thinkers already have been articulating a lot of complex thinking, implicitly if not explicitly. I divide this wide area of literature that has already been advanced on complexity in social affairs into two categories – social theory and transdisciplinary approaches. Though the line between them is often blurred, it's a useful distinction for exploring a range of scholarly literature. I look at social theory (e.g., sociology, political theory, critical theory) in this chapter, and transdisciplinary approaches (e.g., socioecological studies, science and technology studies, etc.) in the next chapter.

Infusing these threads of social theory with explicit concepts from complexity theories can advance some of these ideas to a new level. My argument is that social theory has been very successful by implicitly evoking isolated instances of the complexity principles, and that it will advance farther still by rendering these principles more systematic and explicit, and by utilizing not just individual principles, but rather greater complexity frameworks, exploring their more systemic applications and implications. Many leading theories across the whole range of social theory in the last few decades have succeeded precisely because of their incorporation of one or more of the complexity principles. Rather than continuing to focus on isolated principles, social theorists should engage with and take up the whole complexity framework and its ensuing implications.

The complexity framework I present in this book is increasingly powerful when taken up as a whole framework, which incorporates the understanding from the natural sciences, but integrates this with sociological, philosophical and transdisciplinary theories. This approach balances sufficient variables with appropriate simplifications in order to interpret and engage with the overwhelming news of our times.

Take just one example: nonlinearity. How many headlines in the last decade talked about changes happening "faster than predicted." While change at first happens slowly, in many cases there is a threshold after which change occurs more rapidly, nonlinearly. Again, a common example is the power law that occurs throughout every kind of system from plate tectonics, to the size and metabolic rates of animals, to the rate that teen videos go viral on YouTube. Change has accelerated rapidly, faster than predicted, in innumerable instances – the eutrophication of lakes, acidification of oceans, collapse of markets and economies, and the meltdown of the Polar Regions. The buzzwords of so many social and environmental issues today are "nonlinear," "rapid," "accelerating," "thresholds" and "tipping points."

The complexity framework explains and puts these terms into context, reveals why various phenomena change at first slowly and later rapidly, and why interacting physical, biological, and social systems can produce even greater nonlinear change.

Postmodernism, risk, and collapse

In addressing this theory I look at three areas of theories loosely grouped around three of the complexity principles – postmodernism, risk, and collapse. I use the term "postmodern" here not to refer to the subset of social theories of Lyotard, Baudrillard, Derrida, prominent in the 1970s and 1980s, but rather to the entire range of social theory having to do with the shift beyond the modernist paradigm of the Scientific Revolution. This includes the subset of Lyotard and others, but is much broader, encompassing much of the social theory of the last half-century, some would say since 1914.

In each case, these terms are explicated by recourse to other interrelated complexity principles. The "postmodern" perspective is imbued with complexity, explained by complex systems dynamics, chaos, unpredictability, uncontrollability, etc. – in brief, by overturning the entire cadre of modern myths of pure reductionism, stability, predictability, and control.

Risk is closely interrelated with openness, feedbacks, uncertainty, uncontrollability, vulnerability, thresholds, resilience, mitigation, and adaptation. Once we take into account the whole complexity framework, we see that one central axis is comprised of, at one end, collapse, and at the other end, sustainability. And this entire axis is best explained by understanding the overall complexity theories framework – interdependent self-organizing systems, prone to external impacts, nefarious unintended consequences of human interventions, feedbacks, and thresholds of rapid change. Naturally, this set of presuppositions is being explored by the social theorists and transdisciplinary scholars, who incorporate the fruits of natural science into their work, and expand on it with their synthetic, complex thinking.

In the examples that follow, I analyze three important areas of social theory of the last two decades – postmodernity, risk, and collapse – and in each case show how the complexity principles invoked are central to the theory; how these influential insights are predicated implicitly, though not explicitly, on complexity principles. Generally speaking, I posit that postmodernity in this broad sense of the term is intimately based on complexity; risk is usefully framed in terms of probability, agency, responsibility, and strategy; and collapse can be best understood in terms of all of these complexity principles, along with the addition of resilience and transformation theories. Social theory, philosophy, and ethics are central to such analyses. Yes, we must utilize the best scientific data, interpretation, statistics, political theory, and economics. Yet, only a perspective that incorporates transdisciplinary data and transdisciplinary theory can do justice to such complex issues.

I focus this chapter on the way that these three areas of social theory in the last two decades have taken up the complexity principles in a broader, more comprehensive, more interrelated fashion, which is reflective of intricacy of real world issues, and applicable to improving them.

Postmodernity

In recent years, a wide spectrum of social theorists and philosophers has been utilizing complexity principles, albeit largely implicitly, to advance understanding and specific knowledge to explain, inspire, and guide rapid social change. Social theory, mostly implicitly, has shown sensitivity to, integrated, and utilized increasingly multifaceted aspects of the complexity framework.

Throughout the history of the social sciences, and particularly in the last half-century, we might say that complexity, transdisciplinarity, and postmodern social theory have all coevolved together, and all help to explain each other. A full examination of this within the realm of social theory is far too extensive for this book. I will examine but one thread of this greater trend. Throughout the twentieth century, influential theories were strewn with complexity principles, with many implications. This is not to over-generalize or to claim that all social theory is about complexity, far from it. Nonetheless, there is a significant pattern throughout many schools of thought and branches of social theory, particularly in the last half-century. It is illuminating to unearth and articulate this pattern.

The term postmodern writ large is problematic, if for no other reason that it complicates the naming of the subsequent phase in history! "Post-postmodern" won't do. Moreover, postmodern is more descriptive of what is not, rather than what is. Of course modern used to mean contemporary.

Yet, the ambiguity of the term postmodern is a reflection of the paradigmatic nature of the current shift in worldview. I use "postmodern" for lack of a better term, a placeholder, and because I am aiming my discussion precisely at the way that postmodernity points to complexity, representing the paradigmatic shift away from the modern worldview. Thus, I use the term "postmodernity" both to make a broad-brush distinction from more purely reductionist aims and methods of nineteenth century social sciences, and to inquire into the significance of complexity theories to contemporary societies.

Throughout the twentieth century, social theory has taken on the specter of complexity. There are multiple strands and potentials for further unearthing these trends. While an adequate description would be longer and more detailed, drawing more from original works, just to give a sense of this perspective I will focus on one wide-ranging example – critical theory and the influential Frankfurt School. Complexity is central to critical theory, witnessed by the fact that major complexity terms – complexity, chaos, strange attractors, reflexivity, identity, risk, uncertainty, etc. – are included in the glossaries of critical theory.[12]

Replicating the model of networks and hierarchies, there is an appreciation of the whole field of social theory as an interactive, historically contingent ensemble. While modern theories attempted to create systematic, holistic, "grand narratives," postmodern theories favor the "little narrative": "the opposite of grand narrative, little narratives comprise groups of like-minded individuals who attempt to subvert the power of grand narratives ... and refuse to allow themselves to be turned into authoritarian ideologies of the kind they are rejecting."[13]

Critical theorists trace their roots to Marxism, one of the most influential of the modern era's grand narratives, or all encompassing explanations of complex social phenomena. While there has been a proliferation of social theories that fall loosely into the category of critical theory, the social theorist today can pick or mix from the catalogue of theories – cultural materialism, structuralism, post-structuralism, deconstruction, postcolonialism, etc. – to put together synthetic models for any particular study. Critical theory is inherently cross-cutting and transdisciplinary.

Central to critical theory are the concepts of culture, identity, subjectivity, reflexivity (feedback), networks, rhizomes, power structures throughout societies (hierarchies), change and transformation (emergence and self-organization), specifically in the form of social movements and social change.

Roland Barthes declared the death of the author, to demystify the significance of the singular individual actor and thinker, highlight the relative significance of the entire social network of readers, and to describe the process by which individual texts never remain that of an author, but rather take on a life of their own, reverberating through networks of readers. Ultimately, meaning is not determined by authors, but by branching and evolving networks of readers.

In social theory and philosophy, the terms reflexivity and dialogic refer to the interactivity and feedbacks within systems of societies as well as their systems of meaning. Mikhail Bakhtin conceived of meaning as "a constant process of negotiation between individuals in a given society ... dialogic. Rather than being fixed, meaning is plural and always open to reinterpretation – and the same can be said of any narrative."[14] Reflexivity, or self-consciousness, has become central to the practice of social theory; the application of the theory is a defining factor in social theory and the humanities today. Scholars must define their "theoretical framework," and develop their theories in dialogical relation with the major theoretical framework from which they are operating.

As Paul Cillers points out, Derrida showed how ideas, theories and meaning play out not statically, but rather in idea histories and networks.

> [T]here is not a one-to-one correspondence between a word and its meaning. Meaning is the result of ... interplay between all the words (or rather, all the signs) in the system. It is an effect of the dynamics within the system.... [T]he success of the system depends largely on the effectiveness of the interaction between the system and its environment. What it does deny is that these relationships can be unpacked in determinate terms when we deal with a complex system like a brain or a language. Complexity cannot be simplified into direct relationships without losing exactly those capabilities of the system we are interested in – the capabilities that emerge as a result of the non-linear, distributed relationships between the constituents of the system."[15]

Furthermore, some social theorists argue that social structures should possess horizontal rather than vertical structures of power, communication, and cooperation. Gilles Deleuze and Felix Guattari developed the notion of rhizomatic network structure as "how systems ideally should develop. Rhizomatic structures (such as tubers or moss) can make connections between any two points on their surface; a process which these thinkers considered to be inherently creative and anti-authoritarian."[16] Such ideas have been taken up effectively in recent social movements, such as the antiglobalization and Occupy movements.

Various terms have been developed to describe the major aspects of social actors in social networks, dealing with the principle social dynamics. For instance, "critical realism," is George Lukacs's term for literary narratives that demonstrate how the economic system feeds back to influence human character. For instance, capitalism is assumed to encourage the development of competitiveness and self-interest.[17]

Evidently, this is but a very brief overview. I aim simply to give a sense of the reach and depth with which complexity has developed throughout the social theory disciplines in recent decades, and how much further it could develop. A broader overview of the influence of complexity throughout other areas of critical theory, cultural studies, media studies, literary theory, political ecology, and related fields would be a boon. Critical theory is one example of the ways that complexity theories have imbued and informed social theories in the last half-century.

The shift from modern to postmodern has been described in various ways across social theory disciplines. In her seminal book, *The Death of Nature* published in 1980, Carolyn Merchant sketches one central aspect of this shift, describing the prior shift from a worldview that posited nature as organic, to the worldview that arose from the fifteenth through the seventeenth centuries, by the founding fathers of modern science, Bacon, Descartes, Hobbes, and Newton, who saw nature in terms of a mechanistic, clockwork universe. She shows how a more accurate worldview including disorder, change, and uncertainty was defeated by the tenets of this mechanistic worldview, and how it was challenged in the 1960s and 1970s by such forces as the "subversive science" of ecology, the environmental movement, and the women's movement.

In her 1990 preface she refers to several other areas of science that contribute to the overthrow of the modernist worldview – quantum mechanics in physics, which shows that motion is not continuous but occurs in leaps and not constant but is context-dependent; Prigogine's far-from-equilibrium thermodynamics, which allows for the possibility that higher levels of organization can emerge out of tensions between forces of order and disorder; and chaos theory in mathematics, which shows how nonlinear chaotic relationships govern many types of environmental and biological systems, such as weather, population, heart fibrillations and ecological patterns. She concludes, "What all these developments point to is the possibility of a new worldview that could guide twenty-first century citizens in an ecologically sustainable way of life."[18]

From the view of nature as mechanistic, linear, predictable, and controllable, flowed many simplistic myths of the modern era. An example is the myth of inevitable and constant progress, shored up by beliefs in scientific determinism, and the slow and inevitable revelation of absolute truth and certainty. The progress myth was used to rationalize the ongoing imperialism, colonialism and globalization. The absurdity of this great oversimplification is more palpable with each year of global change, and it is easy to forget how much it infused Western thinking and rationality throughout much of the last century.

Richard B. Norgaard showed how five major tenets of the Scientific Revolution and subsequent modernist worldview were being replaced by more accurate, complex principles developed in twentieth-century social theory.[19] Specifically,

Table 4.1 Dominant and alternate premises (Norgaard 1994)

Dominant premises	Alternate premises
Atomism: Systems consist of unchanging parts and are simply the sum of their parts	Holism: Parts cannot be understood apart from their wholes and wholes are different from the sum of their parts.
Mechanism: Relationships between parts are fixed, systems move smoothly from one equilibrium to another, and changes are reversible.	Chaos and evolution: Systems might be mechanical, but they might also be deterministic yet not predictable or smooth because they are chaotic or simply very discontinuous. Systems can also be evolutionary.
Universalism: diverse, complex phenomena are the result of underlying universal principles which are few in number and unchanging over time and space.	Contextualism: Phenomena are contingent upon a large number of factors particular ot the time and place. Similar phenomena might well occur in different times and places due to widely different factors.
Objectivism: We can stand apart from what we are trying to understand.	Subjectivism: Systems cannot be understood apart from us and our activities, our values, and how we have known and hence acted upon systems in the past.
Monism: Our separate individual ways of understanding complex systems are merging into a coherent whole.	Pluralism: Complex systems can only be known through alternate patterns of thinking which are necessarily simplifications of reality. Different patterns are inherently incongruent.

the modern premises of: atomism, mechanism, universalism, objectivism, and monism, were overturned by alternate premises of: holism, evolution, contextualism, subjectivism, and pluralism. These new views overturned the inevitability of progress, revealing how issues of unintended consequences and degradation can undermine progress.

Already in 1994, Norgaard wrote:

> These premises are implied in the arguments of academics, capitalists, environmentalists, and politicians with diverse and frequently opposing interests.... [These] suppositions are so widely embedded in Western institutions that they cannot be questioned. To question publicly these premises is to disempower oneself from effectively working in large organizations, serving as a scientific or technical expert, or publicly engaging in political discourse.

Atomism, mechanism, universalism, objectivism and monism are not poor philosophical suppositions from which to reason. They have proven to be extremely productive for both Western science and other institutions. The problem is that these beliefs are embedded in our public discourse to the exclusion of other metaphysical and epistemological premises which are more appropriate for understanding the complexities of environmental systems and which are more supportive of cultural pluralism.

Against this backdrop many thinkers began to overturn modernism altogether. In *We Have Never Been Modern* (1996), Bruno Latour suggests that society has entered a "non-modern phase," in which we have become aware of the failures of modernity. In fact, the myth of modernity is breaking down, and we are realizing that our past notion of modernity was illusory, and in fact, "we have never been modern." Latour focuses on rectifying two false premises of modernity: that reality collapses into one kind of realm, the physical, and thus that nature and culture are distinct and can only be approached as separate entities.

Specifically, for Latour, the term modern designates two sets of different practices that must remain distinct if they are to remain effective, but in fact have become confused. The first set of practices is the biophysical practice of altering natural forms, the creation of new hybrids through the processes of science and technology production. The second set of practices creates distinct ontological zones and thus "purifies" the real world. I would interpret this latter to be a description for simplistic thinking, such as making the distinctions of dualities, without also then imbuing our understanding of these entities with principles such as interactions, feedbacks, and self-organization.

Two important zones thus purified by practices of mind and management are nature and culture. And one would add, of course that this practice of mind is deeply interrelated with all the other splitting, reductionist, dichotomizing ideas, such as Descartes' influential dualistic philosophy of body and mind. Though, we do not want to throw out the baby of analysis with the bathwater of reifying dichotomies. To account for this, one must articulate Latour's argument more fully.

Latour does not use all of the complexity terms, but his theory grafts onto these elements of complex dynamic systems theory. According to Latour, the first set of practices involves creating hybrids and networks, the actual intricacies of the natural world that explain how change is really occurring, at local or global scales, which is to say, throughout enmeshed hierarchies. The second set of practices involves the way we think about this world, which continues to create false ontological distinctions, in an abstract, purifying process.

This second process – the false purification of the real networks of the world – in fact spurs the first process. The way we think of course deeply influences and constructs our biophysical context. The more we purify and imagine an order that is not there, the more impurity and disorder we set loose. In other terms, the more we ignore networks and imagine them into neat categories, the more we create hybrids, and complexify networks. Not only does the world function according to complex processes regardless of the simplifying processes of our thinking, but also, when we act onto the world as if it were simple, we end up creating impacts in the form of proliferating complexities. Until of course, human impact overwhelms a system thoroughly, at which point a natural system may in fact collapse and become "simplified" to a degree, as when a patch of rainforest becomes savannah, or savannah becomes desert.

Latour's two sets of practices can be defined in terms of the modernist science worldview versus the complexity worldview. The first process represents the way that complexity theories explain reality, with the principles of uncertainty, incongruence, and incommensurability. The second process represents the way modernity construed reality – presupposing atomism, linearity, and universalism, and layering on false assumptions about certainty, congruency, and commensurability.

Breaking down Latour's main concepts, I show that we find complexity principles at the heart of each one: hybrids, networks, "local and global scales" or nested hierarchies, immutable mobiles, incommensurabilities, the Gordian knot, and the very concept of "non-modernity." Next, I examine Latour's definitions and my reframing for each of these terms in turn.

Latour defines hybrids as new types of being that are part nature and part culture. I reframe this with the concepts of coevolution, emergence, and self-organization, to examine the relationship between classical thinking and dualistic thinking, and to examine in more detail how and why modern simplifications have destructively omitted or misconstrued the interrelationships of nature and culture.

The problem is more negative than positive, in the philosophical sense. Which is to say, it is not so much that early modern scientists set out to falsely portray nature or culture, legitimize faulty dualistic thinking, or misrepresent socioecological systems and processes. In a certain sense, we should not give the founders credit for this positive project. Rather, classical, modernist thinking, with its over-emphasis on atomism, reductionism, and universalism, just tended to focus on reductionism and isolation to the exclusion of all else; it tended to omit, overlook, and thus also negate the significance of continuous and critical processes of transdisciplinarity, interrelationships, and coevolution.

In the creation of an immutable mobile, a model or experiment is reified in one context, replicated only in that context, and then transferred for use across highly heterogeneous social and ecological lines – across cultures, norms, and environments, according to Latour. Plumbing the history of classical science, Latour shows how Tycho Brahe's astronomy experiments reversed the notions of what counts as center and what counts as periphery. Of course, we must clarify; this reversal was appropriate and beneficial to Brahe's aim – to assemble a correct model of planetary positions and relations.[20] What is lamentable is that scientists extrapolated from such instances and reified the idea that knowledge makers can proceed from one center of operation, and create "immutable mobiles" in various realms of reality such as societies and ecologies, where such immutability and imposition of knowledge from one place to another, in fact, does not hold up. It does not hold up because processes of continuous change, emergence and self-organization prevent absolutist or universalist truths from operating in sociology or ecology as they may do effectively in astronomy and other realms.

Seeing Latour's term immutable mobile within the greater complexity framework, shows how it refers to the conjunction of two classical science terms, reductionism and universalism, and highlights the way in which these two modernist principles can be mitigated with more synthetic, complex thinking. In this way, classical science falsely projected results obtained from the parameters of a model or experiment within one context to another one. Laboratory science proceeded as a self-legitimizing phenomenon, reified as law and treated as a tool with which to manipulate and dominate across time and space, and across socioeconomic and cultural borders. Frequently, this flawed interpretation was transferred from wealthy nations to poor ones, largely at the expense of the latter.

Latour also speaks to "incommensurabilities," which means what it sounds like: things that cannot be compared or commensurated, or incongruent things, what Zizek would say produced "a parallax gap."[21] Latour sees incommensurabilities as one of the products of casting a modernizing (over-simplifying) gaze on the natural world (imbued with complex processes). One scholar amusingly boiled down Latour's oeuvre to the study of the "hyper-incommensurability of postmoderns."[22] Latour describes incommensurability in this excerpt:

> The same article mixes together chemical reactions and political reactions. A single thread links the most esoteric sciences and the most sordid politics, the most distant sky and some factory in the Lyon suburbs, dangers on a global scale and the impending local elections or the next board meeting. The horizons, the stakes, the time frames, the actors – none of these is commensurable, yet there they are, caught up in the same story.[23]

This raises the question of how to effectively cope with the complexity that is unearthed from overcoming modernist simplifications and taking on the many processes and interactions involved in socioecological systems. To this, Latour just points out the over-simplifications of our thinking and their dangers.

The complexity framework doesn't provide a magical formula for describing all issues, but it provides two things. First, it reminds us how and why all humans should come with large yellow labels plastered on their foreheads that read: "Warning: Do not oversimplify." And second, it provides a conceptual reference from which to proceed when one problem involves various incommensurable dimensions – a reference guide that highlights such incongruities in its very focus on the seeming paradoxes of intermingling constraints and emergences involved in self-organizational processes.

Latour debunks the proposed opposition between realism, the view that the facts of science exist independently of us, and constructivism, the view that scientific entities are always partially socially influenced or created. Rather, Latour says, both parties in this war share the fallacy that the real and the constructed are opposites or are mutually exclusive in some way. In fact, the real and the constructed are naturally interrelated facets of the real world.

Again, within complexity theories, we see that reality and construction are two sides of what complexologists call the process of emergence and organization –

variably referred to in terms of tetralogical loop,[24] feedback,[25] or panarchic loops[26] – by which the real is reconstructed and the reconstructed becomes real. The process by which, in complex systems terms, entities evolve through continuous self-organization, interrelation, and emergence, to maintain certain system-wide qualities over time, while at the same time continuously going through cycles that produce novel qualities.

Latour himself appears at times to contest the complexity sciences or the links between networks and the overall complexity framework. Perhaps this is because he is disavowing certain overly methodologically reductionist analyses and portrayals of complexity, or overly "holistic" descriptions. He does explicitly utilize the term "network," but not the other complexity principles.

He does, however, I believe, acknowledge the very significance of transdisciplinary complexity in the sense that I use it here. In one passage, for instance, Latour argues that part of network analysis can be the acknowledgement of the validity of disparate lenses that different social scholars use in analyzing their study systems. For example, he alludes to three realms of knowledge, the material, social and meaning, via analogous concepts, the "naturalized, sociologized, and deconstructed."[27] Many scholars focus on one or another of these at the exclusion of the others. So for instance, respectively, E. O. Wilson, Pierre Bourdieu, and Jacques Derrida, are "emblematic figures" of these three approaches to environmental knowledge, "naturalized, sociologized, and deconstructed."[28] When E. O. Wilson speaks of naturalized phenomena, then societies, subjects and all forms of discourse vanish. When Bourdieu speaks of fields of power, then science, technology, texts and the contents of activities disappear. And when Derrida speaks of truth effects, then it may appear that to believe in the real existence of brain neurons or power plays would betray naiveté. Each of these forms of criticism is powerful in itself; yet it is discussed in isolation. Ultimately, we need to be able to conceive of these facets of reality in their interrelation.

Latour feigns horror at a hypothetical study that would treat one socioecological issue, e.g., the ozone hole, as at once naturalized, sociologized, and deconstructed. Wryly, he says, such a study might be firmly empirically established, with predictable power struggles, "but nothing would be at stake but meaning effects that project the pitiful illusions of a [separate] nature and … speaker…. Such a patchwork would be grotesque."[29] Rather, the realms of natural, social, and discourse comprise three interrelated aspects of reality, and all three must be synthesized to foster our understanding of this reality. He is arguing for a shift from disciplinary or interdisciplinary approaches to transdisciplinary comprehension, as I explore in the next chapter.

What we must realize and work from, says Latour, is the fact that networks are simultaneously real like nature, collective like society, and narrated like discourse. I add that we must see the complex systems that make up the study systems of the social sphere in a more realistic fashion than classical, modernist social theory permitted; we must acknowledge that all social systems are pluralistic, polysemous, and multifaceted.

Many aspects of complexity theories provide tools for this approach. Latour's actor network theory in social theory, for instance, helps gain a more realistic picture of climate change policy by highlighting the necessity of moving beyond archaic epistemological and metaphysical underpinnings of modernist scientific thought, and acknowledging the very different nature of different realms of knowledge and the radical epistemological shift that this implies. Complexity theories go a step further, in articulating not just the difference between different systems – nature, social, and discourse – but also the coherent complex systems dynamics running throughout all three, the principles in this book.

Latour's argument, stated in complexity terms, is that hierarchies, networks and feedbacks traversing all realms of our world are significant to how we think, and this is the basis of human impact on the world. Specifically, he argues with many other great social commentators and critics that dichotomies like social-nature and rich-poor are distinct in our thinking but not so distinct in the messy world of network causalities and interdependence.

The complexity framework takes this thesis a step forward. Complexity illuminates both the incongruities and the interdependence, by illuminating order and disorder in terms of their interrelations, self-organization. By being explicit regarding the fact that they are all referring to one reality, that they are qualitatively different realms of knowledge (requiring different methodologies, quantitative but also qualitative and theoretical in the social and philosophical sense, etc.), but also that complexity theories do actually reveal substantive, non-trivial patterns throughout, we may develop better means of engaging with global change.

Risk

It was not so long ago that thinkers like Merchant and Norgaard challenged the notions of stability and progress, revealing a world imbued with risk. Three decades after *The Death of Nature* we are taking a crash course on risk. Rapid social and environmental change has brought to light complexity principles of networked causality, nonlinear change, and unintended consequences. As societies become increasingly complex, they become prone to greater degree of risk.

Risk must always be problematized, which is to say critically and contextually interrogated, against the background of irrational fears. The popular X-files defined the anxiety-prone 1990s. Other big "risks" that millions worried about but we are not statistically very often affected by include: killer asteroids, Ebola fever, maddog teenagers, recovered memories, Chinese atomic spies, and the like. Millions lived in terror of Y2K.[30] Yet, with nonlinear ecological and social changes, real risks are on the rise.

Leading social theorists and environmentalists long have spoken of the significance of the complexity principles of nonlinear change, uncertainties, and risks, even long before we could asses them within a fuller framework. The founder of future studies and science fiction, H. G. Wells, showed the significance of risk in his 1901 essay *Anticipations: Of the reaction of mechanical and scientific progress upon human life and thought.* Rather than a mere isolated list of possible gadgets or trends, Wells weighed human scientific, technological and social progress with risks. To a significant extent he foresaw: the rise of the individual car, "Boswash" (the Boston to Washington city-suburban corridor), the World Wide Web, Wikipedia, and much about what he calls with disdain the "irresponsible wealthy class."[31] Though while he correctly anticipated many of the risks of social issues such as corruption and greed, he fails to anticipate much of the environmental risks. While he anticipates class struggles, his own somewhat eugenicist, sexist views prevented him from foreseeing the risks of racial oppression and the power of the social movements ahead.

As early as 1864 George Marsh decried the possible risks of human impacts on nature, including the collapse of human civilization. Throughout the twentieth century philosophers such as Hannah Arendt, Gunther Anders, and Hans Jonas advanced the theme of risk, and the ensuing themes of agency and responsibility. These themes were taken up successively by a series of environmental leaders from Aldo Leopold and Rachel Carson to Bill McKibben and Vandana Shiva today. Certainly, the social movements and especially environmental movements elevated the issue of risk.

It was not until 1992 that risk was taken up more fully, becoming a full academic field. Ulrich Beck's 1992 *Risk Society: Towards a new modernity* put the spotlight on the issues of vulnerability, risk and rapid change. Beck, who had studied sociology, philosophy and other social sciences, had also been interested in how we can describe the shift away from false modern assumptions of stability, security, and inevitable progress and safety. Linking postmodernity and risk, he subtitled his work, "towards a new modernity."

In *Risk Society*, Beck argued that the gain in power from techno-economic progress was being increasingly overshadowed by the production of risk and harm. From the modern era to today increasingly complex societies brought about increases in feedbacks and reflexivity. While in the classical industrial society wealth production was more dominant than risk production, in today's society, this relationship is reversed. Hence, we can refer to our current era in Western societies as the "risk society."[32]

Beck's description of the shift from net benefits to net risks associated with industrial society is one part of the overall shift from the classical science worldview to the complexity worldview, and thus is best explained within that framework. By framing risk with respect to uncertainty, nonlinearity, thresholds, agency, responsibility, human potential, social change, sustainability, and collapse, we develop a fuller, more adequate picture of risk. Not surprisingly, many of Beck's main terms fit within the complexity framework – e.g., reflexivity, tipping point, local effects, and extra-local effects. A tipping point is a threshold; reflexivity is a term for feedback in social systems; and local and extra-local effects are explained by the complexity terms of hierarchy, scale, and grain.

Moreover, Beck uses these terms across scales and realms of reality. Beck uses reflexivity as a general term with meaning throughout social, institutional realms, material, and organic spheres. Beck invokes transdisciplinary analysis by contextualizing these terms with respect to the overall coevolving trends that have occurred in the last 60 years: as human population increased three and now six-fold, science and technology also accelerated, intensifying planet-altering technologies manifold.

In the context of classical science and its metaphysics, all realms of reality were construed to some extent as pure, certain, and linear. And classical science focused on isolating parts in what was perceived as an overall mechanical system. In contrast, in complexity studies it is generally acknowledged that what benefits one aspect of a system may harm another, and that finding overall progress for any one part of a system is far from simple. Reflexivity or feedback in interrelated systems results in both beneficial and harmful output, some integrated into a system, some becoming externalities to that system.

When the human population was smaller and our technologies less developed and fewer in number, nature still dominated on the planet. As our population and our technological impacts concomitantly expanded in recent decades, we have come to dominate the planet. Humans now compose about 50 percent of the planet's organic biomass, consume 40 percent of planetary biomass, have altered 80 percent of the earth's land surfaces, and have polluted 100 percent of air, land and water by climate change, as Bill McKibben pointed out in 1989.

In 1992 Beck echoed McKibben's observations about human impact on climate, applying this thought to the entirety of human actions and impacts. He noted that as human impacts were globalized, risks came out of the closet and achieved a central importance in social and political debates.[33] While preceded by a considerable body of literature in the form of science fiction and horror stories, such as *Frankenstein*, Beck's work contributed to academic and popular literature in the 1990s – risk and fear studies.

Now almost 20 years later, risk is clearly central to social and political debates. In 2006, a wave of popular education on climate change marginalized the skeptics throughout most countries and even, briefly, in the United States. Debates turned to focus on the details of climate change, carbon emissions reductions, and the energy transition. Al Gore's 2006 film on climate change put the spotlight on the consensus of climate scientists, riveting public attention to climate change. Yet, within weeks, pundits jumped straight from climate denial to climate despair, claiming it was too late to do anything about climate change. One might say that the mainstream discourse in the United States surpassed the phase of the risk society, jumping directly from the discourse of denial to that of crisis, reminiscent of Oscar Wilde's quip, "America is the only country that went from barbarism to decadence without civilization in between."

Similarly, Beck argues that part and parcel of the shift from wealth production to risk production was the shift from local effects to extra-local effects. The complexity principles of hierarchy, networks and scale are all significant in clarifying human impact. In fact it is with the industrial age that many pollutants emerged that are not local but global. Notably air pollutants such as greenhouse gases have rapid global reach. But perhaps the biggest issue is the way that atomist, reductionist, individualist, dichotomizing, modernist thinking encouraged us to focus on local and isolated impacts, masking the significance of the way the externalities of human industrial activities have large-scale and at times irreversible impacts across global systems.

Only with the rise of the early systems and then complexity perspective did we begin to see more clearly the way that acid rain produced in Detroit fell in Quebec, manufacturing of luxury items for Americans polluted rivers and soils in Mexico, Africa and then East Asia. Only recently is it obvious that industrialization in wealthier places contributed the most to climatic changes wreaking havoc on poor peoples, from American fires, floods and tornados, to droughts and floods, to sub-Saharan Africa, Pakistan and such environmentally besieged nations as Bangladesh. As Beck said, invoking networks, interactions, and feedbacks, "In view of the universality and supra-nationality of the circulation of pollutants, the life of a blade of grass in the Bavarian forest ultimately comes to depend on the making and keeping of international agreements."

Risk society became world risk society. In complexity terms, Beck argued that the side effects and unintended consequences of science and technology occur throughout a global ensemble of interconnected complex dynamic processes impacting the entire planet. Beck's focus on reflexivity, referring to critical thinking and reflection on our postmodern condition, exemplifies the complexity principles of adaptive systems – in the face of risks we have agency for learning, strategizing, and adapting.

Thus, the policy answer to the reality of increasing global risks is to recognize the importance of feedback in our institutions and policies, but also to recognize the other dynamics of complexity that become tools for constructive policy and change: understanding network dynamics, nonlinear dynamics, and the resultant, ever-present lessons of uncertainty, unpredictability, agency, and responsibility. New lessons emerge, that, for example, precaution and proaction are not mutually exclusive, but imperatively conjoined. By grasping the full dynamics of reflexivity, adaptation, learning, and strategy, we are better placed to cope with the multiple facets of global change.

Collapse

The specter of societal collapse has been with us throughout recorded history, the reference point most indelibly seared into the Western imagination being the fall of Ancient Rome. While Ancient Roman society also spurred ecological devastation, such as deforestation and soil erosion, it was not until the rapid rise in environmental collapses in the last 50 years that we have become more fully cognizant of both societal and ecological collapse.

Collapse is an abrupt simplification of a system amounting to a loss of systemic properties. In other words, a reduction in the nodes and links of networks induces a reduction in the greater emergent properties and qualities of the systems involved.

If we are to take the lessons of postmodernism and risk seriously, such as entwined environmental and social hierarchies, networks, and interdependence, then we must begin with the premise that in the case of large-scale anthropogenic collapses, we can only avoid either social or environmental collapse by conceiving of them jointly in terms of socioecological collapse. Moreover, we need a transdisciplinary approach to see the many social dimensions of collapse – complex social, economic, political, cultural, and ethical issues. And we need to understand these issues in terms of feedbacks, network causality, vulnerability, resilience, adaptation, learning, and strategy.

Social and socioecological resilience have been continual features of human societies, critical aspects of our ongoing human evolution. Yet, consensus holds that we are already passing thresholds of collapse in various areas, and in other areas, also hurtling towards novel types and degrees of potential collapse. As stated in the Introduction, the Millennium Ecosystem Assessment showed that out of the 24 global ecosystem services analyzed, humans have enhanced four of these through such measures as reforesting of northern woodlands and some technological improvements such as pollution absorption; we have created mixed patterns of degradation and improvement in five major ecosystem services; but overall, we have dangerously degraded 15 out of the 24 ecosystem services.

The complexity framework, Table 2.4, may reveal and explain ways in which degrees and types of societal, technological, industrial, and energetic complexity are related to issues of collapse and sustainability. Scholarship has been progressing towards more thorough analyses of the relationship of societal complexity to sustainability.

One area of sustainability studies is the relationship between societal complexity and collapse. On the one hand, a certain degree of complexity is necessary in order to maintain various aspects of desirable levels of quality of life. On the other hand, overshooting a certain degree of societal complexity appears to contribute to socioecological collapses. It seems that the optimal complexity for societies within the potentials and constraints of the Earth's environmental systems may lie somewhere in between. Due to the significance and complexity of these issues, and to recent advances in both complexity theories, and critical social and economic theory, collapse theories need to be advanced.

To discard the tenets of modernism is to discard dichotomous notions that oversimplify into under- and over-developed – e.g., the myth of either total degrowth or infinite growth, pure Luddism versus infinite progress – and develop more realistic complex concepts. Evidently, the issue is not only one of luddites versus luxuries, if the entire system collapses undermining any desired gains. The biophysical world has absolute limits – to resource depletion, economic growth, greenhouse gas emissions – and thus imminent limits to our way of life.

More specifically, relationships between several of the major complexity principles serve to elicit and explain patterns that show both why societies tend towards collapse and also some ways and perhaps principles regarding how human agency and strategy can counteract collapse and support sustainability. In this section, I look at the first part of this formula, the way that literature on collapse in the last few decades has been based, mostly implicitly utilizing complexity principles only in piecemeal analyses, and how evoking these systematically may advance our understanding of this arguably most important issue in human affairs – the causes of collapse in complex societies. In Chapters 10 and 11, I look at the latter part of this formula: in the face of wicked issues and Gordian knots, what are the lessons regarding agency, learning, and strategy.

The overarching idea that I want to contribute to this debate is the fact that the broad-ranging complexity framework I have suggested is both comprehensive and simple enough for a very important task: to articulate key principles about the whole spectrum of collapse to sustainability, which can serve to guide efforts for the latter. Placing collapse as one of the key references points in the complexity framework permits the advancement of studies of, conjointly, both collapse and sustainability. Understanding this collapse to sustainability axis involves factors such as network causality, strategy, resilience, self-organization, hierarchy, scale, and grain. Missing from the major discussions around collapse in the last few years is the contextualization of collapse within a framework that incorporates the rich ensemble of complexity principles that together begin to articulate and clarify the seemingly intractable puzzles or wicked problems of sustainability.

In the United States, George Marsh raised the specter of human environmental impact leading to society's collapse, in his 1864 classic *Man and Nature*. Thoreau famously raised the alarm about how Americans were radically reducing the biota of the continent, driving passenger pigeons and other species to extinction, "tearing a page from the book of nature." Almost a century passed with only a few luminaries and Cassandras. The lack of ecological and socioecological knowledge impeded greater insights into human impact. They did not know, for instance, that human reforestation after Europe's great plagues had likely caused the Little Ice Age of the late Middle Ages, or that the vast deforestation of the seventeenth and eighteenth centuries had then spurred a phase of minor global warming. There were of course some notable insights into human impact. The Swedish scientist Svante Arrhenius developed a greenhouse effect theory in 1896 that turned out to be remarkably accurate. But such exceptional isolated science was a side note to the concurrent pressures of rapid capitalist expansion, Westernization, imperialism, development, and globalization.

In 1988, Joseph Tainter published *The Collapse of Complex Societies*, in which he introduced a key insight of the Dutch economist Ester Boserup. During the rise of industrial agriculture, events like the Dust Bowl raised consciousness about both the significance of topsoil and our intensifying depletion of it. In 1965, Boserup published an important principle about the nature of agriculture in a complexifying society, the theory of marginal returns of agricultural development. In brief, Boserup's thesis was that over time a disproportionately larger investment of labor is necessary in order to bring about a smaller increase on returns. In other words, though intensified agriculture productivity per unit of land increases, nonetheless over time productivity per unit of labor decreases. Over time, more and more labor inputs are needed, but yield less and less proportional agricultural returns. This produces a bell curve, whereby intensified agricultural practices can produce more for a short time, but then gradually produce smaller and smaller yields.

The principle of increased labor and marginal returns coevolves with the specific type of agriculture and the rate and nature of the way it depletes natural resources over time. Even if there are short-term gains in crop yield and economic profit, over time industrial agricultural systems deplete the natural resources upon which they depend at an irreversible rate. The Ogallala Aquifer that undergirds North American agriculture, for instance, has been shrinking since the 1950s. Meanwhile, the increase in fertilizers needed to maintain more intensive agriculture, also spur ecological degradation of rivers and oceans witnessed by current increases in eutrophication, acidification, CO_2 levels, and now lifeless or "dead zones" in our oceans.

To illustrate this point, Boserup derived an idealized, arbitrary, typology of agricultural systems. Boserup's typology shows that over time more productive systems become both more labor-intensive and less sustainable. An increase in industrial complexity undermines the sustainability of the system. Eventually, overshooting societal, technological, and economic complexity, leads a system towards collapse. This may indicate that to maintain sustainability we must keep systems within a certain medium range of complexity.

Boserup included five representative systems, the first being the least intensive, the most ecologically reproductive, and each one increasing in intensification of impact, and decreasing in ecological reproductivity. Forest fallow – including swidden, milpa, and fallow-style slash and burn – involves using plots of land for a number of years and then letting them sit fallow for up to 25 years for ecological rejuvenation. Bush fallow cultivation involves a short enough fallow period, six to ten years, that forests cannot fully regenerate. Though perhaps topsoil and groundwater may be renewed at a sustainable rate. Short-fallow cultivation involves a fallow period of one to two years and annual cropping involves fallow for a few months between one harvest and the next planting.

The most intensive system of all is the one that most industrialized societies depend upon – multi-cropping, only possible in a few favorable seasons, and necessarily depleting the necessary natural resources since crops are constantly rotated with no fallow period. Various inputs must be increased throughout this sequence, including land preparation, fertilization, irrigation, energy and human labor per unit of agricultural output. Intensive industrial agriculture is promoted both by the corporations and global institutions that most benefit, and pressure other societies to comply, via laws, tariffs, and subsidies. Agricultural policies based on higher economic profits in the short term for the few, has been leading us towards agricultural collapse for all.

Boserup's sequence, as Tainter showed, is generalizable to various other food systems such as animal husbandry, fisheries, and dairy production. In one example, various technological improvements increased the labor requirements of the American dairying industry, though yields increased at a much lower rate. Between 1850 and 1910, the American dairy output per unit of labor declined by 17.5 percent.[34] Indeed, marginal returns on increasing complexity is also generalizable to diverse realms of advanced societies, including resource production, information processing, sociopolitical control, scientific and scholarly specialization,[35] and overall economic productivity.[36]

By correlating Boserup and Tainter's principle of the marginal returns of increasing complexity, with two principles discussed in the next two chapters – transdisciplinary complexity theorists' synthetic view of highly complex social and ecological systems and Rescher's principle of complexification – we advance insights and questions regarding the nature of collapse and sustainability.

Tainter examined how to define and characterize complex societies and how or why they develop.[37]

> Complexity is generally understood to refer to such things as the size of a society, the number and distinctiveness of its parts, the variety of specialized social rules that it incorporates, the number of distinct social personalities present, and the variety of mechanisms for organizing these into a coherent, functioning whole. Augmenting any of these dimensions increases the complexity of a society.[38]

Hunter-gatherer societies contain no more than a few dozen distinct "social personalities," roles or jobs in society – such as hunters, gatherers, elders, shamans, etc. – while modern European censuses by the early 1980s recorded some 10,000 to 20,0000 unique occupational roles and today's industrial societies may contain overall more than 1,000,000 kinds of social roles.[39] Technological revolutions in our digital and information societies have driven up these numbers, while recent economic turmoil have driven them down in some late industrial societies, and up in recently growing economies like China and Brazil.

We can derive some general principles from this. As Tainter pointed out, more complex societies are more costly to maintain than simpler ones, requiring greater levels of energy per capita. As societies increase in complexity, individuals form into more networks, "more hierarchical controls are created to regulate these networks, more information is processed, there is more centralization of informational flow, (and) there is increased need to support specialists not directly involved in resource production…"[40]

Moreover, all of this complexity has tended to use energy at a scale exponentially greater than those characterizing small groups of self-sufficient hunter-gatherers or agriculturalists. Historically, increased complexity in societies has brought about the desire for increased amounts of energy. Timothy Allen and Thomas Hoekstra captured this in a comparison of the Ancient Anasazi society and a tiny subset of society in the contemporary United States.[41] The energy flows of the entire ancient Anasazi villages in Southern Utah were orders of magnitude inferior to the present energy flows of a tiny set of tourist buildings that now surround them, which use computers, the internet, cell phones, a fleet of fossil-fueled cars, sundry materials transported to Utah from around the globe, and the maintenance of an interrelated network of physical buildings and social institutions.

Furthermore, Tainter argues that as societies increase in complexification there is a tendency towards the increase in three variables in society – heterogeneity, inequalities, and the degradation or dissolution of democratic structures and processes. This refers to heterogeneity not in the sense of social "diversity," but rather is the sense of the number of distinctive parts of components to a society, and to the ways in which a population is divided among the occupations and roles of a society, to be more homogeneously or heterogeneously distributed. Tainter claims that the more a society becomes complex and heterogeneous, the more it may fall prey to socio-economic inequalities.

These concepts from Boserup and Tainter provide several fundamental parameters regarding the relationship between different degrees of societal complexity and trends that lead towards resilience or collapse. It appears that there are some correlations between the degree of complexity and trends of vulnerability and resilience, collapse and sustainability.

The man who put collapse on the map of the public imagination was Jared Diamond. In 2005 Diamond's *Collapse: How Societies Choose to Fail or Succeed* was a best seller, for many months in both the academic and popular limelight. Diamond's thesis was that societies like the Napa Rui or Easter Islanders, the Greenland Norse, the Anasazi of the American southwest, and others collapsed because in the process of exhausting the natural resource base they depended upon they either failed to anticipate the consequent collapse, or they saw it coming but failed to adapt and thus to prevent catastrophe. Meanwhile, other societies in similar situations, such as the Tikopians and Tongans of the South Pacific and the Highland tribes of New Guinea survived because they were able to see the problems and thus discard their previously tightly held core values, which in fact had brought about long-term environmental degradation. Thus they were able to change behaviors and replant forests, conserve soil, change diets, and adopt the necessary reforms to maintain a sustainable environmental base for future generations.

Diamond draws parallels between these historical examples and societies today, and concludes that contemporary societies are on a precipice, engaged in activities that are putting our very existence at risk. Modern modes of consumption and destruction have already driven several societies towards collapse, including Somalia, Haiti, Rwanda, and Congo. Indeed, advanced industrialized societies appear to be pushing the entire planet towards collapse. For the first time in history, Diamond says,

> We face the risk of global decline. But we also are the first to enjoy the opportunity of learning quickly from developments in societies anywhere in the world today, and from what has unfolded in societies at any time in the past. [42]

Diamond states this as his motivation in writing the book, to realize that we have the advantage over past societies, like the Maya and Easter Islanders, to reflect on and learn from these failures and successes, and to follow positive examples to make the choices for our own survival.

Diamond lists four principle reasons for the collapse of societies: (1) *failure to anticipate problems*, (2) *failure to perceive problems*, (3) *failure to engage in problem-solving* and (4) *failure to solve problems despite engaging with them*.[43] Generally speaking, I posit, one major reason for the failure to anticipate, perceive, and manage problems has to do with the failure to see the nature of systems as complex. Predominant ideas of the last 500 years have held that the universe is static and inevitable; we see stability where there is complexity and dynamics; and that human ideas, agency, or strategy will have little impact on nature. The subject of collapse turns this view squarely on its head, by showing that in every sense it is human agency that has brought about past collapses, and that only human agency may prevent future ones.

Diamond focuses mostly just implicitly on a few parts of the overall complexity framework. The failure to perceive accurately that Diamond discusses derives from the complexity principle of unknowability. Many social and environmental issues are literally imperceptible to us much of the time. Descartes lamented that the naked eye cannot estimate either the true size or distance of a planet or star. The modern era he helped to usher in, not only focused on what we can measure and control, but also included a set of highly hubristic ideas about what we ultimately could control. Long-held myths about stability, control, knowability, and progress have reduced our awareness about just how much we do not accurately perceive or understand. Complex dynamics highlight evolution, interdependent positive feedbacks, networked causalities and consequences, and unintended consequences, revealing that in significant ways we must acknowledge degrees and types of unknowability.

Diamond invokes in his analysis mostly implicitly a few of the epistemological complexity principles. Failure to anticipate problems and failure to perceive them can be highlighted through the issues of the position of the observer in the system, hierarchy, scale and grain. The problem of our literal capacity to perceive is just one of many problems illuminated by the role of the position of the observer in the system. Hierarchy, scale, and grain permit us to account for the place of the observer within multiple nested interacting systems. We may perceive some major aspects of a system, but not perceive the complex interplay of causality across levels of a hierarchically enmeshed set of systems. Factors or agents in a system may be linked in more or less obvious or visible networks, more or less directly, which may or may not include other hierarchies one might be considering.

This backdrop of the position of the observer and nested hierarchies relates to several issues Diamond touches upon – uncertainty, unpredictability and unknowability. Uncertainty is related to the four ways our thinking contributes to ecological collapse. The systematic uncertainty, unpredictability and unknowability of complex systems both explains and is explained by three of Diamond's four errors in thinking. Once a problem is perceived, uncertainty is closely related to the second two errors. In terms of the failure to engage with a problem, high uncertainty in the systems that we are trying to more successfully manage can lead people to: a rational impasse, an overwhelming analytical puzzle, or even a sense of paralysis and hopelessness. Uncertainty is also closely related to the third problem, the failure to successfully address a problem rationally. This relationship has haunted the quest for knowledge throughout human history and remains a deep concern in philosophy and science today. It is also at the heart of this book, and the question of how to rationally address sustainability issues like global climate change.

When there is high uncertainty, it may be difficult or impossible to make a decision on strictly rational terms, given issues such as unknown unknowns, ignorance and the need for action. The philosopher Alasdair MacIntyre has argued that in the absence of the means to make a strictly rational decision, sometimes the rational choice is to make the best possible irrational choice.[44] The previous myths of inevitability, certainty, linearity, and controllability, led to a greatly simplified and distorted view of rationality. Once again the significance and role of the subject and the observer become prominent. Rationality always takes place within the minds of irrational – emotional, biased, motivated – human minds. As Latour has pointed out, our desire to control and manipulate a certain world, only feeds further interventions and ripples of causality in our uncertain one. An antidote is more complex thinking, including proactive and precautionary strategies in the face of degrees of risk. Finally, Diamond raises the question of how we fail in our attempts to resolve problems, instead clinging to irrational ideas and behaviors. Fear of uncertainty, more than uncertainty itself, may be the greater force causing us to continue unwise behaviors. In a world of dynamics, risk, and uncertainty, we tend towards ideas and ideologies that seem to provide reassurance.

Throughout human history these examples are common – both ecocidal behaviors, and our willful habits of failing to perceive, strategize, or act on them. As scholarship on collapse advances, the perspectives are expanding.[45] Few books have received such a quantity of both praise and critique as Diamond's *Collapse*. The overriding critique is that Diamond falls prey to environmental determinism, focusing exclusively on ecological factors at the expense of other intertwined issues. Diamond at times focuses on singular issues where it appears that there are a whole array of transdisciplinary, intertwined, causes, networked causality and networked consequences. Diamond omits crucial factors from the fuller panoply of contexts and causes of collapse, but particularly social issues such as colonialism, political and economic domination, ideology, war, and genocide. While critics have also pointed to other environmental factors that Diamond at times omits or underestimates, such as the role of invasive species. All throughout the modern era colonized areas were ravaged by the ecological impacts of invasives like beetles, goats, and rats.

As social, economic, and political domination appear to be central features of the collapse of complex societies, ultimately, the relationship of the increasing complexity of social, economic, technological, and institutional systems to collapse appears to be significant. First, complexity principles help to discern why complex societies collapse, after Tainter. And second, complexity principles help to articulate resilience stemming from our role as subjects with agency, after Morin. Despite tenacious modernist beliefs otherwise – Hobbesian, Laplacian, and other debilitating dogmas – examples from the recent literature show over and again that humans have the agency to choose more successful strategies. Indeed, the literature on collapse is replete with examples of resilience, wisdom, moderation, and social, cultural, and environmental success and sustainability.

Norman Yoffee provides an alternative interpretation of the infamous collapse of Easter Island, which is known to its inhabitants as the island of Rapa Nui, in which the demise was not solely human-induced ecocide, but involved a multifaceted set of concurrent drivers and impacts including: indigenous peoples' pressures on the ecosystem, but also colonizers' political domination and genocide, as well as two guests that came with European colonizers' boats – a human disease and an invasive rat. Diamond often asks, when a human was cutting down the last tree on Easter Island, what was he thinking? To which Yoffee coyly replies, when a rat ate the last tree seeds, what was he thinking?!

Yoffee provides as evidence only one quote from a French ethnographer, Alfred Metraux, writing in 1957 that what happened on Rapa Nui after Dutch colonization was "one of the most hideous atrocities committed by white men in the South Seas" and it was "the catastrophe that wiped out Easter Island's civilization." While the evidence is scant, the general point is well taken that invasive species are known to devastate many an island habitat, and that we have numerous recorded instances in which colonial forces not only destabilized, or rendered vulnerable, but rather ruthlessly slaughtered indigenous societies. Insofar as Metraux's account of Napa Rui is accurate, then overlaying a theory that places all the blame on environmental mismanagement of the indigenous may be misleading indeed.

The Ancient Maya, Patricia McAnany and Tomas Gallareta Negron suggest, did not perish due to human-induced "ecocide" alone, but rather due to a mix that also included conquest, colonialism, racism, and genocide. As these scholars looked through late-terminal Classic Maya society and try to understand the rapid changes it underwent, they found that political and economic factors were inextricably intertwined. Monetary interests, racism, and colonialism may have contributed to political and economic turmoil that drove such negative impacts on both the Mayan society and environment. In a similar vein, Frederick Errington and Deborah Gewertz have suggested that Diamond's interpretation of the collapse of Papua New Guinea underplayed a crucial factor: economic exploitation of the poor.[46]

Each of these cases may possibly further support Tainter's insights about correlative tendencies between increased complexification, increased heterogeneity of socioeconomic systems and increased socioeconomic inequities. According to this view, complexity speaks to the interactions and dynamics inherent to economic globalization. For instance, for many years, first world countries such as the United States subsidized their own sugar industries operating in places like Papua New Guinea, while at the same time discouraging or effectively preventing poorer countries like Papua New Guinea from subsidizing their own sugar industry, and thus also protecting the first world's sugar industry. Organizations like the World Bank and World Trade Organization heavily pressure local agencies and governments to eliminate all tariffs on imported sugar. These free-trade policies are strongly supported by international corporations like Coca-Cola, which imports cheap sugar for use in soft drinks and then sells it at a great profit to Papua New Guineans.[47]

Radical theorists take the argument one step further. Richard Smith, for instance, suggests that capitalism is not only at the heart of the critique about "goods" in Papua New Guinea, but also is a main driver at the heart of eco-collapse generally. In the current dominant global capitalist political economic system, says Smith, "...the choices we need to make are not up to 'society,' while the ruling classes are incapable of making sustainable choices."[48] They are incapable, that is, in that the special interests of corporations and the wealthy overrides and constrains the choices that would foster the common interests of local peoples. Smith seems to support Tainter's argument that after a certain point, highly increased social complexification is correlated to increased social domination of the majority by a small minority of elites. Many small groups of independent agriculturalists, pastoralists, or indigenous groups still make decisions by common consent, and elites are not able to wield power over group decisions. In contrast, decisions in most contemporary industrial societies are enmeshed in complex networks that promote considerable power and special interests, where corporate lobbyists, advertisers, politicians, and other special interests promote private gain at the public expense through increasingly complex and expensive campaigns.

Such issues lead Smith to dismiss Diamond's solutions, what he calls the "standard tried-and-failed" strategies of: lobbying, consumer boycotts, eco labeling, green marketing, asking corporations to adopt best practices, and so on – the stock-in-trade strategy of the environmental lobbying industry that has proven so impotent to date against what he calls the "global capitalist juggernaut of eco-destruction."[49] While reforms and campaigns have made significant impacts on environmental issues, and even some significant victories, the overall trend is towards global ecological degradation.

The underlying problem, for Smith, is that the big issues – climate change, resource exhaustion, deforestation, overfishing, pollution, species extinction, and environmentally caused human health problems – are getting worse. He argues that they are getting worse generally, despite successes here and there, "because environmental reforms are always and everywhere subordinated to profit and growth,"[50] and because it is not simply "societies" as Diamond loosely describes, but quite specifically a handful of individuals who are making the most influential decisions driving today's crises. To reverse this requires addressing the many oversimplifications of economic indicators and theories, such as the GDP.

Ultimately, collapse by definition involves emergent properties of those systems in which it occurs, and thus requires the whole systems perspective of complexity theories. We must view these issues within the greater understanding of increasing societal complexity discussed by thinkers such as Boserup and

Tainter. We should explore the ways in which societal complexification may relate to collapse and sustainability: the theory of the generalization of marginal returns on increasing investments; and the potential implications of societal complexification, like issues of heterogeneity, inequities, and other forces that alternately degrade or support democracy and sustainability.

Problematizing postmodernity, risk, and collapse

The last ten years have seen a great proliferation of confusion and despair in the literature on global change. Mixed amidst this are very productive problematizations, explanations, and prescriptions for advancing sustainability. Complexity has proven powerful both in showing qualitative differences between the nature of physical and social "explosions," social change and sustainability, and also in showing the qualitative similarities that help us to comprehend what it would mean to develop new visions of sustainable and desirable ways of living.

As we have seen in the development of ideas about the non- or postmodern era, risk, and collapse, we need rich thinking to capture the complexity of our contemporary lives. In the poem "Harlem," Langston Hughes offered a few metaphors for the nature of social change and at times social "explosions."

Harlem

> What happens to a dream deferred?
> Does it dry up
> like a raisin in the sun?
> Or fester like a sore –
> And then run?
> Does it stink like rotten meat?
> Or crust and sugar over –
> like a syrupy sweet?
>
> Maybe it just sags
> like a heavy load.
>
> Or does it explode?
>   (Langston Hughes, 1925)

The personal and political suicide of Mohamed Bouazizi illustrates dramatically that sometimes, a dream deferred does literally explode, and with it, the hopes of the world.

Yet, one of the most compelling lessons of social and environmental complexity is that it is not necessary to live with very high social instability, with its often tragic social turmoil. Emergence exhibits the striking feature of learning, and with that adaptation and transformation. The learning and adaptation central to John Holland's neural networks also are significant in social change.

Ironically, by more fully acknowledging and adapting to life's innate instabilities, we might learn, adapt and increase societal stability. Complexity, providing insights into coevolution, network causality, and self-organization, highlights the danger of failing to conceptualize the dynamic and transdisicplinary nature of the social sphere – ecological, social, political, cultural, ethical, technological, economic – in efforts of social reorganization. Just as clearly, complexity emphasizes our ability to do just that, to adapt and alter the ways that we self-organize. What complexity shows about social explosions is that we can influence them; we create them and therefore we can avoid or minimize them. Insofar as we were never modern, then we have not fully exercised this power. Social explosions can be seen as signs of anachronistic thinking, still based in overly rational, overly technocratic solutions, control, stability, and certainty.

Rainstorms, hurricanes, mudslides, and debris flows all operate according to self-organized criticality; the deluge, the storm, the mudslide, or debris flow all starting at tipping points. Social movements and social riots also operate in part via the same underlying principles of self-organization. In the case of social change though, explanations consist not just in the physical or biophysical aspects, but rather in a great tangle of economic, ethical, political, cultural, and social dimensions. We facilitate these explanations by developing not just a few isolated complexity principles, but by contextualizing social issues at the crossroads of many of these principles, outlined in Table 2.4.

As witnessed in the revolutions and protest movements throughout the world in 2011, social frustrations do sometimes explode, and lead to periods of change. Yet the complexity principles of the social realms – subjects, identities, agency, responsibility, and strategy – highlight the capacity and the need to be preventive, proactive, and visionary in ways that will lead to more stable, which is to say sustainable, societies. Beyond modernist myths of permanent or total stability, we can nonetheless strive towards greater social as well as environmental sustainability.

As F. Stuart Terry Chapin pointed out in the Introduction, pinpointing specific drivers and feedbacks driving social and environmental change, we often have the opportunity to change them. The rich necessarily transdisciplinary literatures on postmodernity, risk, and collapse have to be complemented with ongoing problematizing and reconceptualizing. Postmodernism is not just a set of theories, but also an era and its worldview. We must continue to develop its sense, meaning, and direction. We should not systematize and idealize utopia like the moderns, as a future world; we must actualize a livable world today. Living with complexity teaches us not only to plan for imagined futures, but to strategize for the dynamic present.

Postmodernism highlights that we have never been modern and yet, despite the lack of absolute certainty, truth, and control, nonetheless we must actualize a more livable world. Risk society elucidates the outlines of precisely what we must avoid – increasing risk in high stakes, high uncertainty situations, increasing vulnerability, or the risks of collapses. Understanding uncertainty, vulnerability and collapse helps us to plan for sustainability. In these examples and many more, the complexity framework may inform our path. Conceptualizing, envisioning, and carrying out changes in policies and practices for sustainability also may be one of the best means to revitalizing our democracies.

Conclusion

Looking at the social theory literature on postmodernity, risk, and collapse reveals important patterns. I have invoked only a few examples here to show that social theory literature of the last few decades provides insights into complexity and vice versa. Increasingly, social theorists have invoked complexity theories in their analyses. Albeit not explicitly, many prominent social theorists of the last two decades have based leading social theories on the complexity principles. We may advance this more explicitly.

Such ideas are just the tip of the iceberg, to use a now unsettling metaphor. I have shown that many complexity principles have been crucial to developing and explaining postmodernism, risk, and collapse. The development of complexity theories within social theory has been significant in outlining various major parameters of our era: the presence of social networks, the lack of effective large-scale social self-organization, the perils of modernity, the rise of real risks, and the proliferation of both more and less sustainable practices and trends. Complexity has helped to illuminate trends in societies – towards collapse and towards sustainability. A more explicit and generalized study of societal complexity may help to show the way towards socioecological sustainability.

5   Towards transdisciplinarity

Complexity is not analyzed; it is conceptualized.[1]

Jean-Louise Le Moigne

Ecocide and the wisdom we have lost in knowledge

Homo sapiens, Latin for wise or knowing people, arguably was a premature name. In recent decades we have driven our planet into a phase of growing social and ecological crisis. Some of these problems are new in type, some are new in magnitude, as our complexifying societies see a rise in numerous feedbacks and consequences. These changes are interacting, and it appears that some are mutually exacerbating.

Take extinctions, for example. From the moment homo sapiens began to spread out from the African plains perhaps 50,000 to 100,000 years ago, humans have brought about extinctions of mega-fauna around the world.[2] Today, humanity has pushed an alarming number of all plants and animals to endangerment, and has increased the rate of overall extinction by between 100 to 1,000 percent.[3] We are losing about 20,000 to 30,000 species per year.[4] Scientific consensus holds that "if current extinction rates remain constant, humans will drive another twenty percent of all species extinct by 2040 and fifty percent by 2100."[5] We have unwisely, nonrenewably depleted essential resources for generations, using topsoil and groundwater faster than we let it replenish. We have unleashed climatic changes increasing the existing pressures on ecosystems and their life-supporting services, endangering agriculture, oceans, and forests, and increasing damage through intensifying fires, floods, droughts, and storms.

"All else being equal," if we continue on a "business as usual" pathway, the situation may worsen. However, complex systems dynamics highlight that phrases such as "all else being equal," and "business as usual" rely perhaps too heavily on modernist notions of linearity, stability, and control. How often reading the news today does one feel that much is proceeding in a linear, stable, or controllable way!

One of the things that transdisciplinary perspectives highlight is that events taking place in networked, hierarchical, social, technological, and environmental systems, are not linear, not stable, and not under control. Transdisciplinary thinking highlights the contrast between our limited natural resources, and an economic model based on unlimited growth. Solely within either discipline – economics or ecology – we do not clearly see the clash; only by looking at both does it become evident. The very basis of our economic and business model is not stability or linearity, but continuous growth. Expressions like business as usual of course still have a role, for some issues, within some contexts. But the more we look at overall patterns, the more we must shift to a more complex view in which the exception is stability, and the norm is dynamics and change.

In brief, transdisciplinarity can be defined as an approach to knowledge that draws on multiple disciplines and transcends disciplines in pursuit of real world, complex, multidimensional inquiries. I will further explore the distinctions between interdisciplinary, multidisciplinary, and transdisciplinary approaches below.

Of course this must be problematized, critically and contextually interrogated. We might ask what exactly the term transdisciplinarity can mean, if it is, to a degree, the nature of all thinking, while at the same time there can be no such thing as absolute or fully transdisciplinary understanding, an oxymoron by defi-nition. Transdisciplinarity may be inherently hard to pin down, yet in the same way the delineation of disciplinary research is partially arbitrary and shifting. Complexity theories, as we have seen in the first few chapters, help to articulate how physical, living and social systems have evolved together, or coevolved, how the living and social emerged from the physical, and how they remain deeply interrelated. It appears that epistemology is necessarily multifaceted in the face of emergent, self-organizing realities.

Finally, transdisciplinarity is not new. Throughout the history of disciplines, of course, most great thinkers developed richly transdisciplinary ideas. Indeed, transdisciplinarity may have always been one marker of great thinking in the social and environmental realms, even if subsequent generations often begin to construe the work of our greatest thinkers within narrower academic perspec-tives. Most of the work in Chapter 4 is transdisciplinary, and this chapter expands on the arguments presented there. In recent decades, the great thinkers in social theory and continental philosophy have based their theories in increas-ingly complex social issues.

Sociologist Immanuel Wallerstein, for such reasons, prefers to talk in terms of what he calls the "unidisciplinary," based in the idea that all reality might be conceived as one multifaceted realm. Most social issues are so thoroughly multi-dimensional and interrelated, says Wallerstein, that it makes more sense to root out our strange modernist fixation on disciplines, and focus more on grappling with reality as a unified disunity of complex reality.[6] Whatever we call it, com-plexity for sustainability calls for an articulation of disciplinary, interdisciplinary and transdisciplinary approaches. In socioecolgoical systems, finding the most important drivers and feedbacks across and between systems requires that we conjoin the best of disciplinary riches and transdisciplinary vision.

Transdisciplinarity is vulnerable to the same weaknesses as disciplinary and interdisciplinary approaches. It is challenging, requiring skills, knowledge, and sensibility about multiple disciplines. These challenges though should not be overblown. For one thing, they exist within disciplines also to a significant degree. Secondly, it is not necessary for everyone to do this research, though it is surely desirable for everyone to develop some of this more multidimensional comprehension and vision. Perhaps what is needed in the quest of sustainability is to have some percentage of fully transdisciplinary theorists for every group of disciplinary specialists, perhaps one transdisciplinarian to ten disciplinarians. These numbers may already exist, in which case, what's really needed is respect, funding, and reorganization of universities and institutions to more fully support and promote this dimension of research.

Complex dynamic systems bring to light interdependencies which are necessarily transdisciplinary. Thus, complexity theories, interdependent as they are to transdisciplinarity, help us to root out and correct false classical assumptions. Much discourse on global social and environmental change is still tinged with overly modernist phrases exuding linearity, certainty, and normality, such as "if current extinction rates remain constant," "business as usual," and "all else being equal." Reframing the discourse around social and environmental change with insights of the transdisciplinarity inherent to complex thinking, we gain a more realistic perspective on changes, trends, and scenarios.

Part of developing complex thinking is a continual disavowal of simplifying strands of classical scientific thinking. When complexity – e.g., nonlinearity, networks, and thresholds – is framed within purely disciplinary and modern concepts: pure linearity, atomism, and control – the results can be even worse than that of classical or complex thinking alone, even more distorting. Such portrayals can highlight complex dynamics and rapid change, without also highlighting our ability to cope, strategize, and adapt. In fully shedding the modernist perspective we get a sharper sense of the capacities for learning, adaptation and change, which may revitalize our vision, courage, and optimism.

By framing social, ecological, economic, political, and climatic dynamics in terms of their interactions, we are better placed to see the patterns driving change more realistically. Given the recent turbulence in ecosystems, economies and politics and weather patterns around the globe, clearly rates are not often "constant," business "usual" or all else "equal." Given the great complexity of global systems involved, and the significance of feedbacks, thresholds, and nonlinearity, some of the common predictions – perhaps 20 percent more extinctions by 2040 and 50 percent more by 2100 – raise questions. We must explore how scenarios for extinctions may differ if we include other variables like climate change, population increase, and stresses to the oceans.

What we are coming up against is not just complexity, but also transdisciplinarity. The two are inextricably intertwined, and both may be needed to advance towards sustainability. Sustainability requires a radical shift that construes humans not as passive objects, but as constructive subjects – agents of change. It compels us to face our humanity, our subjectivity, agency, and responsibility.

Transdisciplinarity and sustainability

Most simply, we might define sustainability as "improving the quality of human life while living within the carrying capacity of supporting ecosystems."[7] Only by incorporating transdisciplinarity, as well as disciplinarity and interdisciplinarity, can we recognize and piece together all the elements of this cryptic definition as discussed throughout the rest of this book – poverty, justice, subsistence versus luxury emissions, wicked problems, synergistic policies, and more.

We can speak of three broad reasons that transdisciplinarity is necessary to sustainability. For each of the three reasons, complexity is at the heart of why and how transdisciplinarity is beneficial. A first reason is that isolated scientific disciplines alone are insufficient for resolving planetary change such as extinctions or climate change, which have diverse, interrelated drivers – social, economic, political, ethical, and ecological. Predictions about extinctions, for instance, often are made using particular disciplinary or interdisciplinary lenses, omitting transdisciplinary lenses. They have tended to come from one or another group of scientists speaking primarily or exclusively of their own turf. But often these areas are interacting in significant ways.

So biologist E. O. Wilson speaks to general biological trends, with a particular interest in insects. His affection for insects is evident when he points out that if humans went extinct all life would gravitate back to a richly biodiverse paradise, whereas if all insects went extinct, the planet would be plunged into a spiral of further extinctions. Scientific consensus holds, and conservation biologists like Wilson, Richard Leakey, and Michael Soule often point out that the greatest degree of biodiversity is found in the equatorial regions, in ecosystems such as coral reefs and rainforests. Yet, even leading scientists like Wilson, Leakey, and Soule tend to stay within their area of specialization to an extent, and do not fully incorporate all of the necessary drivers of extinctions and the general extinction crisis.

Of course, natural scientists have become increasingly aware of this issue, and they have been doing their best to note or even incorporate data on interrelated issues. Most have taken steps in this direction, acknowledging where sufficient interdisciplinary work has not been done yet that it is necessary, for instance, to take into account interactions between global issues like invasive species, pollution, extinctions and climate change. Already, the increase in interdisciplinary research has been providing a somewhat fuller picture about the significance of these interacting, and in some instances accelerating, issues.

For instance, in spring 2011 an interdisciplinary team of leading experts on the oceans assessed the cumulative reality of their various areas of expertise. One of their research objectives was to "Determine the synergistic effects of multiple stresses on the ocean and what this may mean for the future."[8] While they had been concerned individually, when they analyzed the issue collectively the picture began to look even worse. In June 2011 they reported that oceanic life is going through various interrelated, major ecological stresses and small-scale collapses, such as dead zones, and could be heading towards an overall collapse, or loss of life.[9] Multiple drivers of oceanic stress include climate change, over-harvesting, invasive species, agricultural synthetic fertilizer, and pesticide run-off. We have already lost over 20 percent of coral reefs, the most biodiverse oceanic system, due to climate change, and it is likely that we will eliminate the rest within a few decades. With a transdisciplinary lens, one might more wisely inquire into how oceanic malaise and potential collapse might factor into the predictions of the extinction of another 20 percent of all species by 2040 and 50 percent by 2100.

Climate scientists are exploring the significance of climate change to the extinction crisis, and cataloging cases in which climate is a key factor in extinctions. Ecologists have shown the considerable and often singular role of invasive species in extinctions, as in the classic cases of invasive rats, pigs, or foxes on islands. Also, it's estimated that at present rates of land clearing for agriculture and grazing in the tropics, humanity may lose 80 percent of the tropics by 2030. Two-thirds of life's biodiversity is found in the tropics. While I'm not a math whiz, I can calculate that 80 percent of two-thirds of life's biodiversity is more than 20 percent of the total, which could mean losing more than 20 percent of all remaining species by 2040. This is without adding in the potential of oceanic collapse.

Our problem is not science or lack of science, but the effective transdisciplinary integration of science and knowledge more generally. Scientists have not been deceptive; the power of science is precisely to free us of the deceptions of irrational thinking. It's just that we have all been largely myopic, deeply trained in the fragmented thinking of disciplinary training. Obviously, all of the disciplines are necessary to understanding our changing world. Disciplinary and interdisciplinary approaches provide essential bases of knowledge. But solely relying on disciplinary sciences has proven to be tragically insufficient.

A second reason that transdisciplinarity is necessary to sustainability, is in assessing not just the scientific aspects of global change, but also the social aspects – politics, ethics, economics, and social theories. Addressing a news conference at the UN Conference of Parties conference in Cancun on December 9, 2010, Bolivian President Evo Morales, himself an indigenous former coca farmer, announced, "We came to Cancún to save nature, forests, planet Earth; not to convert nature into a commodity or revitalize capitalism with carbon markets." Without strong, mandatory emissions reductions, he said, the world's governments would be "responsible for ecocide."

Yet, Bolivia is enmeshed in a set of difficult decisions. As one of the poorest countries in South America, Bolivians have harder choices than most, and must ponder to what extent their nation should exploit environmentally degrading but economically profitable resources. Bolivia has one of the world's largest supplies of lithium, as well as substantial gas and petroleum. Yet, with a large population much more vulnerable to extreme poverty, their economic losses have more serious impacts than those of the wealthy. Only a thoroughly transdisciplinary perspective can navigate such issues, which are at once technological, cultural, ethical, political, economic, and ecological. Moreover, ultimately,

Bolivia's policies are interdependent with those of the richest nation of the Western hemisphere, the United States. If our interests were purely economic, then we could imagine making decisions purely in isolation and in competition. However, if our joint interests are in fact planetary survival, then the very poorest and wealthiest countries must realize that ultimately they are mutually interdependent.

A third reason that transdisciplinary work is increasingly important is that the scale, degree, and novelty, as well as dynamic interactions, of global social and environmental change and crises today require us to move beyond isolated analyses to a richer perspective. Complexity theories are arising across and contributing to all disciplines. A single human cell in enmeshed in physical, chemical, biological and social systems; a single human involves all of these as well as the entirety of psychological, emotional, economic, political, and cultural systems.

Since the sixteenth century Western thought has been largely dissociated in analytical, reductionist methods and isolated disciplines and discourses. Today's crises require us not just to analyze, but also to attempt to conceive and to conceptualize more synthetically. This predicament was evoked in the first stanza of T. S. Eliot's *Choruses from the Rock*: "Where is the wisdom we have lost in knowledge? Where is the knowledge we have lost in information?"

> The Eagle soars in the summit of Heaven,
> The Hunter with his dogs pursues his circuit.
> O perpetual revolution of configured stars,
> O perpetual recurrence of determined season,
> O world of spring and autumn, birth and dying
> The endless cycle of idea and action,
> Endless invention, endless experiment,
> Brings knowledge of motion, but not of stillness;
> Knowledge of speech, but not of silence;
> Knowledge of words, and ignorance of the Word.
> All our knowledge brings us nearer to our ignorance,
> All our ignorance brings us nearer to death,
> But nearness to death no nearer to GOD.
> Where is the Life we have lost in living?
> Where is the wisdom we have lost in knowledge?
> Where is the knowledge we have lost in information?
> The cycles of Heaven in twenty centuries
> Bring us farther from GOD and nearer to the Dust.
> (T. S. Eliot, *Choruses from the Rock*, 1934)

A year before publishing this poem, Eliot also wrote a series of lectures delivered at the University of Virginia in 1933, published under the title *After Strange Gods: A Primer of Modern Heresy* (1934), in which Eliot supported what he called "cultural homogeneity." He wrote, "What is still more important [than cultural homogeneity] is unity of religious background, and reasons of race and religion combine to make any large number of free-thinking Jews undesirable."[10] Eliot never re-published the book or the lecture.

How complex the human being who could write some of the deepest poetry of the twentieth century at the same time as such socially, ethically, and politically troubling statements? Of course, broad goals like sustainability involve some of the depths and inner complexities of our humanity. Many great thinkers, past and present, have been prone to racial, ethnic, sexual, or religious prejudice. Oliver Wendell Holmes cited in Chapter 2 argued for the forced sterilization of women he deemed unsuitable parents.

Complexity theories introduce the principle of coproduction, whereby ideas we are influenced by, we can also influence. The modern notion is that Eliot was "a product of his times." Today, we have the responsibility to be more. We should consider that we are not just a product of our times, but also, that we coproduce our times through our ideas and actions. We have a far-reaching potential for plasticity, reflection, adaptation, and change both individually and collectively, enabling us to influence our times, just as we are influenced by the contingencies of our times. Collectively we coproduce and co-create the ethics, values and the society within which we live. Even the failure to act on the issues of our times requires a set of other actions, the choices of avoidance and apathy. History shows the possibility and the necessity of proaction.

Clearly, as we address today's crises, more than ever we should strengthen our understanding of central complexity principles of action – the nature of the subject, identity, solidarity, ethics, equity, and justice, as well as learning, adaptation, strategy, responsibility, and agency. Transdisciplinarity allows us to articulate the many facets of individual and societal actions and ecological imperatives. A persistent and thorough exploration of our profound interdependence on each other and on nature may help to foster the choices to survive or thrive in the twenty-first century. We may or may not all be interrelated, but most significantly in many ways we are all interdependent.

We are all dependent on topsoil, fresh water, food systems, other species, and on society. Transdisciplinarity and complexity shed new light on old truisms. Divided we fall, united we stand.

Disciplinarity, interdisciplinarity, multidisciplinarity, and transdisciplinarity

Complexity highlights the importance of hierarchically nested networks, consistently raising issues of scale and grain. Epistemological principles flow from this, such as the significance of context, heterogeneity and the position of the observer relative to the system. Factor in the principles of multiple, intersecting, multidimensional or trans-sector feedbacks impacting all kinds of systems processes, along with consequences that are unintended and unpredictable.

The result is that complexity theories illuminate the need for disciplinary, interdisciplinary, multidisciplinary and transdisciplinary approaches. While the term multidisciplinarity is still used as well, for our purposes, it may be largely subsumed into interdisciplinarity or transdisciplinarity. We might say that disciplinarity and interdisciplinarity are needed to develop varying degrees of reductionist analysis, but they must be contextuzlized within transdisciplinarity. Moreover, some research that was previously labeled either interdisciplinary or multidisciplinary may now be reframed as part of the transdisciplinary canon, such as Steven Jay Kline's work on multidisciplinarity, which I include in the transdisciplinary approaches below.

Complexity theories highlight the significance of transdisciplinarity in relation to the other categories – disciplinary and interdisciplinary. In the end, disciplinary, interdisciplinary, and transdisciplinary approaches all are necessary and must ultimately be synthesized to some degree in order to comprehend issues of global sustainability. The academy has often resisted interdisciplinary and transdisciplinary research. In each case, they were created through persistence in the face of forces promoting solely disciplinary and reductionist approaches. As these approaches are born out of struggle, it is not surprising that considerable confusion remains around these approaches and the distinctions between them. In recent years, academic scholars are advancing towards consensus about the definitions of these terms, and the necessity of these approaches.

However, in much common discourse the terms remain conflated and confused. The three terms are still given as synonyms in most dictionaries. The *Oxford English Dictionary* defines interdisciplinary as, "of or pertaining to two or more disciplines or branches of learning; contributing to or benefiting from two or more disciplines." Multidisciplinary has precisely the same definition. When I first checked in 2009, transdisciplinary was not listed.[11] Perhaps, I thought, having two false synonyms struck the editors as enough already. But then I checked in July 2011 and transdisciplinary was also listed as, "Of or pertaining to more than one discipline or branch of learning; interdisciplinary"![12]

Generally speaking, it seems commonly agreed upon that multidisciplinarity combines different analysis in one reflection, but in a way that is primarily aggregative, whereas interdisciplinary research is in some way more integrative. In multidisciplinary work, researchers each maintain their own assumptions, values and methods. While in interdisciplinary work, there is more integration of the disciplinary assumptions, values and methods.[13] Interdisciplinary research is seen to allow for deeper questioning of disciplinary assumptions, and thus greater generation of new perspectives.

However, in practice, this often breaks down. Much work that is truly multidisciplinary is called interdisciplinary, and in some cases, vice versa. In many instances, perhaps the majority, "interdisciplinary" work still is based largely on only one of the disciplines' methods, values and assumptions. For these reasons, I will just use the term interdisciplinary, to indicate researchers working in teams, sharing data, however primarily using just one discipline's sets of assumptions, values, and methods.

Within the natural sciences, the term interdisciplinary is taken to mean utilizing one methodology, usually modeling and other quantitative approaches, and applying this to the study of data from at least two or three disciplines that bring to bear for a specific aim, usually applied. So for instance, different ocean experts – hydrologists, atmospheric scientists, conservation biologists, etc. – worked together to combine and integrate related quantitative data about the resiliency of a particular ocean ecosystem, e.g., the Gulf of Mexico, or the entirety of the oceans. Much of the data by environmental scientists is based on this kind of fertile interdisciplinary scientific research.

Within the social sphere, Julie T. Klein has helped to articulate the nature and role of interdisciplinary approaches. Klein notes four ways that research by social theorists has been interdisciplinary: borrowing across disciplines, solving problems across disciplines, the increased consistency of subjects or methods, and the emergence of an "interdiscipline," or hybrid discipline, such as social ecology or ecological economics.[14]

Yet, interdisciplinary scholars often do not achieve this level of fuller integration, and transdisciplinary scholars often call this the cornerstone of their work.

Transdisciplinarity has been defined as "an approach to research that involves the integration of multiple disciplines..." based on the idea that many pressing issues "can only be understood and solved if viewed holistically and not artificially broken down into narrow research purposes that suit different disciplinary lenses."[15] In recent years, transdisciplinarity has become more clearly differentiated from disciplinary and interdisciplinary work. While all of these approaches are necessary, transdisciplinarity plays an especially significant role as it provides a fuller counterweight in contrast with philosophical and methodological reductionism.

Lima de Freitas, Edgar Morin, and Basarab Nicolescu formalized the current definition and view of transdisciplinarity in the *Charter of Transdisciplinarity*, adopted at the First World Congress of Transdiscipinarity, in Portugal in 1994, which begins:

> Whereas, the present proliferation of academic and nonacademic disciplines is leading to an exponential increase of knowledge which makes a global view of the human being impossible;
>
> Whereas, only a form of intelligence capable of grasping the cosmic dimension of the present conflicts is able to confront the complexity of our world and the present challenge of the spiritual and material self-destruction of the human species;
>
> Whereas, life on earth is seriously threatened by the triumph of a technoscience that obeys only the terrible logic of productivity for productivity's sake...[16]

Part of the beauty of transdisciplinary approaches is that they are broad and integral enough to tackle the trickiest of questions. Julie Thompson Klein writes, "Transdisciplinary approaches are far more comprehensive in scope and vision" than interdisciplinary approaches.[17] Transdisciplinary approaches exist in relation to a particular inquiry, just as a particular inquiry exists in relation to its complex context. In this way, they foster conceptual frameworks that transcend narrower disciplinary worldviews, allowing a researcher to focus on necessary data or ideas from different disciplines in pursuit of a real-world inquiry. Transdisciplinary approaches transcend disciplinary barriers.

Epiphanies about the importance of transdisciplinarity, related to epiphanies about the consequences of intellectual myopia, often lead to a knee-jerk reaction of disparaging disciplines. In the throes of reacting to the incalculable woes of treating complex subjects with solely reductionist lenses, scholars have said that with transdisciplinary approaches, disciplines become "irrelevant," "subordinate," or "instrumental to the larger framework."[18] While it is understandable to be alarmed by the damage done by the lack of transdisciplinarity in the social and environmental spheres, neither must we fall into the pitfall of some kind of strange desire to purge knowledge of disciplinarity, as abstract as it would be impossible. It is the articulation of both reductionism and synthesis, both simple and complex thinking, both disciplinarity and transdisciplinarity, that improves our understanding.

Eric Jantsch and Jean Piaget were founders of transdisciplinarity. While interdiscipinarity signifies the synthesis of two or more disciplines, establishing a new metalevel of discourse, transdisciplinarity signifies the interrelatedness of reality, transcending disciplinary limitations to conceptualize fuller dynamics. Jantsch thought that this notion of transdisciplinarity would always be beyond the complete reach of science, but that, nevertheless, it could guide the evolution of knowledge. His early view of transdisciplinarity is in line with philosophical interpretations of the complexity field, which also points to the profound intricacies and growth of reality and therefore, the limits to human knowledge. Complex, transdisciplinary thinking, even while paradoxically revealing these limitations of knowledge, also seem to offer the best way to advance knowledge as much as possible. Both are needed for Einstein's dictum to simplify as much as possible, but not more.

Ten years after de Freitas and colleagues published the *Charter of Transdisciplinarity*, two futures studies scholars, Roderick Lawrence and Carole Despres, revisited the meaning and the significance of the term, fruitfully linking transdisciplinarity and complexity. In distinguishing interdisciplinary from transdisciplinary research, they say, in the case of the latter, "the focus is on the organisation of knowledge around complex heterogeneous domains rather than the disciplines and subjects into which knowledge is commonly organised."[19] This perspective shows how complexity theories and transdisciplinary approaches share the radical capacity to reorganize inquiry around: not objects but subjects, not products but processes, and not order or disorder but rather the radical proposition throughout the material, the living, and social realms of self-organization.

Roderick and Despres make four further linkages that highlight the relationship of transdisciplinarity to complexity. First, they say, transdisciplinarity tackles complexity in knowledge, striving to overcome the fragmentation of knowledge. It deals with research inquiries that begin from a perspective of complexity and heterogeneity, and are thus characterized by hybridity, nonlinearity, and reflexivity, transcending academic disciplinary structures. Transdisciplinary research acknowledges the importance of uncertainty and of local contexts. Transdisciplinary knowledge arises from intersubjectivity; it includes the perspectives of individuals and freedoms and constraints of social, organizational and material contexts. And finally, transdisciplinary research is often action-oriented. It entails making linkages not only across disciplinary boundaries but also between methods and practices in pursuit of specific real-world goals.[20]

Transdisciplinary approaches allow us not only to deal with real-world topics, but also to contribute to their solutions. While transdisciplinarity has been associated with applied research, this narrow conception of it is restrictive and mistaken. Not only is there no inherent reason why theoretical development cannot be achieved by transdisicplinarity. On the contrary, the complexity framework shows how most social and environmental issues, especially highly complex ones, cannot be achieved without some recourse to transdisciplinary theory as well as transdisciplinary application.

The need for transdisciplinary analyses was often stated throughout the centuries. Rabelais said, "Science without conscience is but the ruin of the soul." When he uses this same phrase, Edgar Morin clarifies that he, Morin, is referring not just to moral conscience, but rather to conscience period. Conscience in this instance refers to the aptitude throughout the whole project of science and scholarship to provide analyses that conceive of the nature and directions of the ensemble of knowledge, the aptitude of science and scholarship to conceive of its socioecological context, and of itself.[21]

Transdisciplinary approaches in science and scholarship

Complexity theories provide a rich conceptual framework for transdisciplinary approaches, and appear to be necessary to the successful framings and analysis of many issues. Of course, transdisciplinary analysis is unnecessary for many kinds of issues, which are best addressed within disciplines. Yet, transdisciplinarity is necessary for social and environmental issues, and our current global crises are social and environmental. Regardless of its capacity, effectiveness, or utility with respect to any given issue, the complexity framework in Table 2.4 aims to include explicitly both wide scope and fine grain of analysis (within the bounds of our planet), and this provides a significant reference point for social and environmental issues.

Leading thinkers throughout the disciplines have increasingly called for both complexity and transdisciplinarity in the quest for sustainability. Dozens of hybrid disciplines have emerged to fill in where disciplinary blinders limit inquiries, as in the study of intertwined economic and environmental issues in ecological economics.

Strikingly, the trend toward transdisciplinary work appears to be more widespread and influential than is typically acknowledged in either academia or public discourse. Over the last few decades, the increasingly obvious need for a fuller, richer understanding of the social dynamics and rapid social and environmental change has been driving a major movement towards more transdisciplinary scholarship and discourse. There have been setbacks, but the general trend is clear. While the examples are indeed diverse, I focus on a few categories of today's transdisciplinary research, looking at how each is leveraging complexity to produce richer analyses.

Five general transdisciplinary areas that have emerged in recent decades include: transdisciplinary complexity theories; work explicitly called interdisciplinary, multidisciplinary, or transdisciplinary; ecological and socioecological systems studies; science and technology studies, sociology of science, and the philosophy of science; and applied philosophy. I already touched upon some complexity science in Chapter 3, and scholarship in Chapter 4, looking at, respectively, how people are using interdisciplinary and transdisicplinary approaches to highlight the complexity of, respectively, natural and social systems.

In this chapter I look at how their work shows not just the complexity of natural and social affairs, but also the transdisciplinarity of complexity. In the next two chapters I look at some examples from the philosophy of science and applied philosophy.

While the subject is vast, my aim here is to assess these broad-based approaches to treating issues of greater complexity, and how they do or don't take up complexity theories. Generally speaking, I choose these as examples here because they take up transdisciplinary complexity explicitly, in a significant sense.

We can see these various transdisciplinary approaches as five approaches to the same global system with five different foci. This view highlights the convergences linking the different fields. All five of these quite large and multifaceted categories share the common thread of drawing upon the resources of complexity and transdisciplinarity. Rather than using the simplifying and prioritizing lenses of one or another disciplinary niche alone, these fields apply more pluralist lenses to conceptualize crosscutting and dynamical issues.

These five areas represent approaches to one complex reality from five points of view. Transdisciplinarity, interdisciplinarity or multidisciplinarity, ecology, and science and technology studies, philosophy of sociology, philosophy of science, and applied philosophy, are five approaches very broadly construed focusing on,

Table 5.1 Five transdisciplinary fields and major foci

Fields	Foci
Transdisciplinary complexity studies, philosophy of complexity	All relevant disciplinary perspectives
Interdisciplinary, multidisciplinary	Some critical disciplinary perspectives
Theoretical ecology, environmental studies, socioecological studies, etc.	Socioecological, focusing on environments
Sociology, science and technology studies, environmental politics, etc.	Socioecological, focusing on societies and technologies
Applied philosophy, applied ethics, e.g., environmental ethics, philosophy of science	The nature of complex systems and their general implications for science and policy

respectively: (1) all disciplinary perspectives necessary to a given issue, (2) a more restrained set of two or three disciplinary perspectives, sufficient to a given more restrained or specific issue, (3) socioecological study focusing on environmental issues, (4) socioecological study focusing on social issues, and (5) the influence of complexity to applied philosophy, e.g., applied ethics.

Transdisciplinary complexity theories – self-organization, emergence, and transdisciplinary methodologies

Edgar Morin has approached complexity from the start as transdisciplinary. He himself has transdisciplinary training; a prominent social theorist, at times calling himself a sociologist, he has considerable expertise in physics, biology, ecology, anthropology, political theory, philosophy of science, epistemology, ethics, film theory, and more.

His conceptual framework is based upon a re-organization of knowledge into a greater framework that both encompasses the disciplines and also shows their rich conjuncture, focusing on central concepts of self-organization and the subject. Thus, he focuses on the notion of organization as opposed to assembly, subject as opposed to object, and process as opposed to product. He explores issues previously described in at least partially static, at times mechanistic terms, and reinterprets them in light of the dynamic processes that belie the simplicity of static interpretations, common features of our world such as subjects, emergence, and self-organization.

Edgar Morin, perhaps more than the other scholars of complexity writ large, explores complexity as method, and method as transdisciplinary. Morin names his major life's work, *Method*, playing with words as he is wont to do, to establish a break with the Cartesian focus on the method based on pure forms of determinism, atomism, universalism, essentialism, and reductionism. In this sense, Morin views not just his content, but also his approach, as anti-Cartesian and anti-method. Morin's goal is to avoid Descartes' foundationalist approach, which he sees as reifying false truths and certainties from the outset. As such, he articulates reconciliation between various philosophical standpoints such as realist and constructivist views, showing how they are intrinsically interrelated. Pure reductionism and pure disciplinarity can never capture the significant partnership of realism and constructivism. Thus Morin's view is based on articulating within and between all disciplines and transdisciplines or hybrid disciplines.

Morin identifies three Cartesian modes of over-simplifying thought: (1) to idealize – to believe that reality can be reabsorbed in the idea, that the intelligible alone is real; (2) to rationalize – to want to enclose reality in the order and the coherence of a given system; to forbid reality to overflow the neat boundaries we conceive; to need to justify phenomena by conferring on them a patent of rationality, and (3) to normalize – to eliminate the strange, the irreducible, and the mysterious.

In contrast, Morin cites Nietzsche who said in the *Antichrist*, "The method comes at the end." This need not entail a vicious circle, says Morin, if we and our knowledge come back changed by the voyage. Thus Morin's vision of method is similar to that of the philosopher Bernard Lonergan who defines method as,

> a normative pattern of recurrent and related operations yielding cumulative and progressive results. Discovery and synthesis ensue, but neither discovery nor synthesis is at the beck and call of any set of rules. Both logical and non-logical aspects are at play; while the logical tend to consolidate what has been achieved, the non-logical keep all achievement open to further advance.[22]

Whereas Descartes sought knowledge that cohered with his initial premises, for Morin, as San Juan de la Cruz said, "To reach the point that you do not know, you must take the road that you do not know."[23]

The Cartesian method assumed solid foundations of knowledge at the base of individual disciplines, or a philosophy known as foundationalism. Foundationalism is a view about the structure of justification or knowledge. The foundationalist holds that all knowledge and belief rest ultimately on a foundation of non-inferential knowledge or justified belief.[24] This requires that there is some ultimate truth beneath our burgeoning knowledge. This is perhaps one of the most deeply engrained of modernist beliefs, behind our most common sense of the world. The vast majority of the propositions we know or justifiably believe have that status only because we think we know or justifiably believe other propositions.

Foundationalism has failed repeatedly – in every realm and every discipline, in science, social theory and in philosophy – and is now dead, says Morin. The implications of this are deep. Truth is not accreted, there is no absolute truth, and so there is no absolute basis at the bottom of any discipline. Giving up foundationalism implies a radical shifting towards an acknowledgement of the limits of disciplines. Disciplines are but indirect descriptors of reality, which – for many though not all kinds of study issues and questions – can only be more fully accessed through transdisciplinary synthesis and interpretation.

For societal and environmental issues, the death of foundationalism calls for a stronger transdisciplinary dimension to knowledge. Rather than accreting further truths, we must develop further inquiries. We must begin with the opposite approach from Descartes. We must proceed with analyses that always pose further questions. We must learn to keep our ideas and analyses "at the temperature of their own destruction." We can only achieve a more realistic, more complete view of life by acknowledging life's inherent lack of absolute truths or absolute certainties. Rather, most phenomena are pervaded by uncertainty, process, and change.

Moreover, Morin advances complexity as method through an exposition of complexity *as* transdisciplinary. He begins by spelling out an array of fundamental rules guiding the study of complexity or complex thinking. For instance, complexity is the base, the "foundation"; hence you cannot reduce the complication of developments to rules with a simple base. All knowledge takes place within a larger hierarchical system of phenomena and its knowledge. The advancement of disciplines, including the organization of science into disciplines, emerges from the sociology of sciences and knowledge, from a reflection internal to each discipline and from a reflection of knowledge external to that discipline.

This leads to Morin's view that in the great scheme of things, complex reality is inherently embedded in transdisciplinary phenomena and can only be more fully conceived via transdisciplinarity in epistemology and ontology. Some degree of transdisciplinary analysis is often necessary. For many social and environmental issues, one cannot know the issue solely from within a single discipline. A fuller understanding emerges from consideration of a study system within its next higher order of hierarchical organization. To limit analysis solely to singular disciplines obstructs the thinking needed to resolve social and environmental challenges.

Morin sees complexity as a generalized shift both in the way the world is and in the way we study and know the world, advancing core concepts in ontology and epistemology. Within this, Morin's primary conceptual framework consists in a tri-part schema, what he calls a "tetralogical loop" of organization, order, and disorder in mutual and constant interaction. At once simple and abstruse, the tetralogical loop points to the networks of feedback of feedbacks, operating in so many of the kinds of systems of everyday life and contemporary concern. Some philosophers may claim that Morin's tetralogical loop is merely order writ large. Rather, it speaks to the indissoluble interactivity between order and disorder inherent to self-organization. Significantly, while we learn a lot about self-organization in individual disciplines, e.g., work by Per Bak on self-organized criticality, nonetheless, the greater comprehension and contextual implications of self-organization at any scale can only be more fully grasped via a partially transdisciplinary view, as Stuart Kauffman and Morin have shown as they have explored emergence and self-organization in different kinds of systems.

Morin approaches the central facet of this theory, self-organization, as transdisicplinary: the profound auto-organizational dynamics that are central to all realms of reality – physical, biological, and social. Morin defines organization as interactions of order, disorder and organization in a circular or spiraling relation, or "tetralogical loop," in which no one particular force acts independently of the others.[25]

He defines self-organization as the ensemble of processes involving order, disorder and interactions in a complex dynamic system. These interrelated circulating causalities manifest in complex dynamic systems to create and maintain the entities we recognize and define throughout our world. Again, almost everything we initially saw as simple element we now see as organizational and indeed self-organizational – atoms, molecules, stars, lives, and societies. But we know almost nothing of the true meaning of this term – organization.[26]

Ultimately, at the heart of organization lies self-organization. In the case of complex dynamic systems, it appears that all organization is in fact involved in self-organization. There is some "radical self" at the heart of organizational processes that science has not yet adequately understood.[27] Indeed, one of the hardest problems of biology is the auto-regeneration of living systems. Leading biologists such as Nobel Laureate Jacques Monod have noted that this is one of the most difficult problems in biology.[28] A central tenet of complexity theories writ large is that the scientific method alone cannot in fact grasp this radical self; it's only possible to comprehend it more fully through a synthesis of transdisiciplinary, pluralistic methods.

Nonetheless, several things have been established about organization. First, it is not an ensemble of elements, as the term previously implied. Organization is comprised of both ordered and disordered dynamics – in physical, chemical, biological, and social systems. Organization seems to occur in mutual correlation and co-relation with diversity and complexity. Ecologists have studied, for instance, potential correlations between network structures, biodiversity, and human impact.

In fact, the core concepts involved in emergence and self-organization are considered to be amongst the harder problems within the various disciplines they touch. This in part explains why some of the transdisciplinary complexity theorists may at times sound abstruse. Morin, for instance, defines organization through an elaborate discussion of related process concepts with which organization is intimately related, e.g., order, disorder, and interactions. The at times circular quality of Morin's work is in part due to the difficulty of the questions he studies. However, we only understand a text in relation to the worldview, paradigm, discourse, and theoretical lens with which we view it. Seen with modernist, disciplinary lenses, descriptions of self-organization at times appear impenetrable. However, viewed with a transdisciplinary, complex lens, self-organization begins to emerge more clearly. Indeed, transdisciplinary complexity scholars are making significant advances in physics, biology, ecology, sociology, ethics, and more.

Many scientists and scholars working on complexity principles argue for the significance and the challenging nature of self-organization. Theoretical ecologist and network researcher Albert-Lázslo Barabási describes the relationship between complexity, the need for synthetic as well as reductionist analysis, transdisciplinary work, and the significance of the ineluctable self-organization. To Barabási, networks are as much about reconnecting the disparate disciplines, as they are about reconceptualizing a system's interrelations. He says,

> Reductionism was the driving force behind much of the twentieth century's scientific research. To comprehend nature, we first must decipher its components. The assumption is that once we understand the parts, it will be easy to grasp the whole.... [Yet] we are as far as we have ever been from understanding nature as a whole. Indeed the reassembly turned out to be much harder than scientists anticipated. The reason is simple: Pursuing reductionism, we run into the hard wall of complexity.... In complex systems the components can fit in so many different ways that it would take billions of years for us to try them all. Yet nature assembles the pieces with a grace and

precision honed over millions of years. It does so by exploiting the all-encompassing laws of self-organization, *whose roots are still largely a mystery to us.*[29] (My italics)

Morin's principle tetralogical loop of complexity – again, organization, order, and disorder in mutual and constant interaction – appears to be central to all complex systems dynamics. One can find examples from every discipline, including: stars and vortices in physics, fractals in chemistry, the formation and maintenance of living organisms in biology, the evolution of patterns that make up ecological systems, and dynamics found in social institutions, human psychology, cognition, and ethics.

Like the tetralogical loop, Morin explores the meta-concepts of complex systems systematically: emergence, self-organization, eco-organization, and the relationship between self-organization and eco-organization. For the term emergence alone, Morin explores the definitions distinctly and conjointly amongst all the disciplines, showing its great necessity and polyvalence.[30] To try to reduce emergence to less than this would be disastrously distortional.

Beyond the oeuvre of Morin, and the works of many transdisciplinary thinkers such as Robert Rosen and Kurt Richardson, there are many other contributions that have been made under slightly different labels. Again, at this moment of paradigmatic shift, and given the transdisicplinary nature of this shift, it is natural that work has evolved under different labels and in different arenas. It behooves us to weave some of these great works together.

Transdisciplinary perspectives: a complexity index

The physicist Steven Jay Kline used the term multidisciplinary in a way that is synonymous with the transdisciplinary perspective I outline here. His last book, *Conceptual Foundations for Multidisciplinary Thinking* (1995), is a major contribution to transdisciplinary complexity.

Kline's great insight in this book is the significance of a transdisciplinary approach to social and environmental issues. Kline argued that transdisciplinary approaches are necessary in order to address emergent processes, and that since emergent processes are ubiquitous, transdisciplinarity is highly significant. He created a complexity index, in an attempt to more viscerally describe the degree of differences between various realms of reality – physical, environmental, and social systems – and thus how different our approach to these must be. Kline, a physicist, utilizes complexity to demonstrate the need for transdisicplinarity, by showing the ways in which, at least in one significant fashion, physical systems are vastly less complex than environmental and social systems.

There are two ways to look at this, going back to the distinction between overall and fundamental complexity in the introduction. On the one hand, everything the early scientists thought was a simple entity – atoms, stars, cells, etc. – we now know to be complex and self-organizing. In this sense, all of physics is complex, perhaps complex beyond our wildest imagination. On the other hand, if we look at a system in terms of the aspects of complexity dynamics, biological systems are vastly more complex than physical systems in significant ways.

Kline creates an index, a way of giving a general reference number to indicate degrees of complexity in various systems. The basic premise is intriguing and useful for getting across a sense of the relatively extremely high complexity involved in socioecological issues. Of course his approach is not beyond philosophical critique. One could certainly take issue, from a Weberian viewpoint, with the primacy of quantitative rationalism in this analysis, just as one could take issue, from a physicist's viewpoint, with the validity of this particular quantitative analysis. Nevertheless, Kline's analysis portrays a compelling and significant aspect of the role of transdisciplinary complexity theories for global social and environmental change.

I refer the readers to Kline's book for a more detailed description of the index. In brief, Kline's complexity index is based upon the number of independent variables needed to describe the state of the system (V); the number of independent parameters needed to distinguish the systems from other systems in the same class (P); and the number of control feedback loops both within the system and connecting the system to the surroundings (L).[31] Using various rules and procedures, Kline builds his analysis with this basic heuristic, the amount and interactions of variables, parameters and feedback loops, V, P, and L. Using these criteria, we see that "typical systems analyzed in classes in physics, chemistry and in analytical problems in beginning engineering classes have no control feedback loops; so $L = 0$". For these systems, typically $V = 1, 2,$ or 3, and thus we can say: $C_A < 5$. Class A systems include, "the motion of pieces of matter under prescribed forces; the properties of chemical solutions," etc. Such physical and chemical systems have a complexity index, capturing variables, parameters and feedbacks, of less than five.

In contrast, Class B is human-designed hardware. For say, cars, airplanes, or a computer, P may be in the 1,000s, 10,000s or even 100,000s, and we can estimate: $C_B < 10^6$. Whereas, in calculating the complexity index number for a single human being, enter: the human brain. The number of neurons in a normal adult human brain is between 10^{10} and 10^{12}. Calculating for just the brain alone, and not even counting the rest of the dynamics within a human body, the complexity index for a single human would be about $C_C > 10^9$.

Kline's elaborate method for how to (begin to fathom how to) calculate the complexity index for human social systems is interesting. Again, to get across some sense of this, he focuses on human brains:

Let us assume for discussion purposes that each of the 10^9 programmable neurons can be connected to any of the 1,000 neurons within the nearest 10 percent of the volume of the human brain; a fact that we now believe is roughly correct. With this assumption, the possible number of configurations of all possible human brains becomes of the order of $10^{8,000}$, a number so enormous that it is hard to imagine or even write out in the ordinary arithmetic form. "There are perhaps one hundred billion neurons, or nerve cells, in the brain, and the number of possible connections between these cells *is greater than the number of atoms in the universe*".... However, if we are concerned with human social systems, $10^{8,000}$ is too large ... because it describes the states of neurons and not the smaller number of emergent properties human use when they interact with each other. However, we can make an estimate for C_D in a different way. Let's suppose we have 100 or more humans in the system, the V for the collection of humans will be at least 100 times 10^9; hence we can write for typical human social systems: $C_D > 10^{11}$.

Thus, Class E, ecologies containing humans, must be at least this large, obviously larger, $C_E > 10^{11}$.

Sociotechnical systems are systems of coupled social and technical parts within ecosystems. Kline gives a few examples: manufacturing enterprises (Boeing, General Electric, etc.), use systems (airplane transport, newspapers, TV networks, households, marching bands, etc.), distribution systems (Sears, Takashima, Harrods), and research and development systems for creating new or modified sociotechnical systems. His focus on large corporations highlights some of the dynamics underlying current struggles for and against corporate control of societies and environments. See, for instance, Pulitzer Prize winning journalist David Cay Johnston's work on the economic and tax systems, and resultant economic feedback loops, of the wealthiest corporations like General Electric.

In 1990, Kline writes, many large sociotechnical systems involved thousands of humans, very complex hardware of many kinds, and feedback loops circling the planet. "It is difficult to make accurate estimates of the value of C for such systems." Indeed! Suffice to underestimate, decides Kline. Since sociotechnical systems involve not only many humans but also complex hardware with many feedback loops both within the systems and the greater world, Kline arrives at the "underestimate" of: $C_F > 10^{13}$.

Kline's complexity index bridges an often avoided, but crucial gap between disciplinary cultural and knowledge systems, and thus our way of comprehending and addressing contemporary issues as complex issues. While the complexity index may be questionable, to my mind it serves its aim; no matter how you look at it, socioecological systems are complex beyond our powers of imagination. And this has serious implications for how we act. Kline himself arrives at the conclusion that this immense complexity of enmeshed social, technical, and ecological systems leads to the imperative of multi- or transdisciplinarity, as well as the great significance of ethics.

While Kline was a physicist, in this last work he positions himself as a transdisciplinary scholar, and in so doing, helps to articulate the gap between physics and social theory, in a way that allows for mutual understanding between these groups. By focusing on complexity principles that are important in both physical and social spheres, and acknowledging and articulating the differences between them, he clarifies both the role of disciplinary and transdisciplinary knowledge, as well as new links between these realms.

For instance, in order to show the significance of emergent processes, Kline distinguishes between emergence in physical systems and emergence in more complex socioecological systems, underscoring the importance of the latter. He begins by looking at the feedbacks in complex dynamic processes, and by sketching a simple typology of feedbacks in different types of systems, from physical to social systems. Table 5.2 is an adapted version of Kline's hierarchy of systems classified by the complexity of their feedback modes.[32]

Kline's discussion of differences between physical and social systems is a fascinating starting point for any physicists exploring how and why social dynamics and issues of sustainability could never be based in or reduced to physics alone, and in fact that to approach sustainability with such a focus would be distortional and dangerous. In other words, his argument demonstrates the need for an approach to sustainability to be transdisciplinary from the start, and deeply focused in ethics.

Along with the many of the scholars mentioned in earlier chapters – Carolyn Merchant, Richard Norgaard, and others – scholars like Edgar Morin and Steven Jay Kline view complexity as a new perspective, and more specifically as the result of the tremendous shift away from the underlying assumptions of early classical science to that of emerging contemporary knowledge of complex systems. The shift from the mechanical universe of Kepler, Galileo, Copernicus,

Table 5.2 A hierarchy of systems classified by the complexity of feedback modes

Type of system	Feedback modes and source of goals	Examples
1. Inert, naturally-occurring	No feedback of any kind; no goals	Rocks
2. Human-made inert – without controls	None, but with purposes designed in by humans	Tools, rifles, pianos, furniture
3. Human-made inert – with controls	Autonomic control mode usually of a few variables	Air conditioner/furnace with thermostat; automobile motor; target-seeking missile; electric motor with speed control
4. Learning	Human control mode. Humans in system can learn and improve operations; systems can themselves change set points since they contain humans	Automobile with driver, chess set and players, piano with player, plane and pilot, tractor and driver, lathe and operator
5. Self-restructuring	Human design mode. Humans can look at system and decide to restructure both social and hardware elements via designs	Human social systems & human socio-technical systems: household, rock band, manufacturing plant, corporation, army

Newton, and Laplace – a universe of celestial spheres, perpetual order, and equilibrium – to a radically new acentric and polycentric universe, opened up to quantum mechanics, systems biology, and the great complexity of humans and societies.

Granted, this "new perspective" is not that new anymore. Yet, it is more important than ever, precisely because this perspective has not been articulated fully and systemically enough, indeed it has not even been conceived of very clearly or fully, and has not permeated contemporary thinking deeply or widely. Complexity theories contribute to the necessary fuller articulation.

The old view fought for clarity and certainty, laws and consistency, while the new view is more accepting of ubiquitous change and the emergence of novel, unpredictable states and effects. The old view was built on foundationalism, trying to reify and build upon knowledge, while the new view accepts the branching, dispersion and complexification of knowledge, and finds it necessary to de-reify knowledge, construing phenomena – the material, biological, virtual, and noological – as entities in perpetual process, decomposition, and genesis. The old view was based upon disciplinarity, dispersed and isolated domains of knowledge, with an ideological view of physics as the sole substrate, while the new view acknowledges the rise of transdisciplinarity as well, and the consequent need for pluralistic and integral methodologies to synthesize knowledge of the physical realm, with the realms of biology, ecology, societies, emotions, psychology, ideas and meaning. The old view celebrated basic science as a basis of building civilized democracies, while the new view celebrates the need for new visions to reorient societies towards sustainability.

It is ironic that we should be discovering this quality of our world at the moment when we appear to be shifting into a highly chaotic phase in both social and environmental affairs. In previous eras, intellectuals enjoyed the luxury of optimistic speculation about knowledge and the future. Today, we are faced with the specter of surviving, as well as thriving, in a chaotic world. Transdisciplinarity opens many possibilities for furthering sustainability.

Transdisciplinary complexity in environmental science and social theory

In recent years, a great number of researchers in academia and beyond in pursuit of addressing the environmental crisis, are exploring inter-, multi- and transdisciplinary approaches. Literature in this arena is often palpably exciting and engaging. While there have been many rich and successful interdisciplinary and multidisciplinary approaches, most of them fall into one of the categories that I describe below, and I include them here. Ulimately, disciplinarity and interdisciplinarity require that we also employ transdisciplinarity. As this approach evokes important social issues more trenchantly, the literature on social and environmental change has taken on a great vibrancy.

Conservation biologists and other scientists driven to applied science for sustainability have drawn upon complexity theories, including feedbacks, networks, vulnerability and resilience, as I noted earlier. Here I focus on how this growing area of science for sustainability has drawn on, legitimated and advanced transdisciplinarity, and highlighted the links between complexity and transdisciplinarity.

Environment and ecology: the example of resilience

The concept of resilience, and the work of the group the Resilience Alliance, are good examples of the role and significance of interdisciplinary and transdisciplinary work for sustainability.[33] My focus here is on the ways in which this research utilizes not just disciplinary, but also interdisciplinary and even to a small degree transdisciplinary complexity theories, and how this combination adds considerably to the effectiveness and strength of their contributions to sustainability.

Ecology was popularized by Rachel Carson's 1962 book *Silent Spring*, which showed the crucial interrelations of politics, business and economic interests, and health and ecological impacts. Throughout the sixties, many systems thinkers and environmentalists were struck by the fact that ecology appeared to be the systems science par excellence. Ecology treated living systems, small and large, automatically delineating concepts of systems within systems – networks and hierarchies. It is no surprise that theoretical ecologists have in many ways taken the lead in adopting complexity frameworks for approaching socioecological issues.

A number of prominent theoretical ecologists have shifted their focus increasingly to articulate both basic and applied science for sustainability. Ecologists, along with a few colleagues from social science disciplines such as economics, demography, and sociology, and a sprinkling of social theorists, have reorganized their work in the last two decades around transdisicplinary approaches, in order to capture adequately the complexity principles that appear to be central to their theoretical and applied aims regarding sustainability. Leaders throughout many disciplines and transdisciplines examining rapid social and environmental change have come to reorganize their work as at least in part, inter-, multi-, and transdisciplinary, or a combination of these. It has manifested in many kinds of related frameworks, of which a few have emerged as dominant inter-, multi-, and transdisciplinary conceptual frameworks, including: socioecological systems (SES), coupled human-environmental systems, and human-natural systems.

Leading, interdisciplinary groups are calling for a transdisciplinary framing of rapid global change and science for sustainability. These thinkers laud the complexity framework as necessary and central for these efforts to proceed. For instance, in a 2006 paper in the journal *Global Environmental Change*, a panoply of leading thinkers including Nobel Laureate Elinor Ostrom and *Panarchy* contributor Gilberto Gallopin, argue that "globalization is a central feature of coupled human–environment systems or, as we call them, socio-ecological systems (SESs)." Their focus is "the effects of globalization on the resilience, vulnerability, and adaptability of these systems." Utilizing the already transdisciplinary terms of social, economic and political globalization, and transdisicplinary framework for social and environmental sustainability, allows them to advance their discussion.

They discuss how "socio-economic resilience regularly substitutes for biophysical resilience in SESs, with consequences that are often unforeseen." Pinpointing a group of analytical dimensions of globalization – rising connectedness, increased speed, spatial stretching, and declining diversity – the authors argue that "each of these phenomena can cut both ways in terms of impacts on the resilience and vulnerability of SESs," and that, "The fact that SESs are reflexive can lead either to initiatives aimed at avoiding or mitigating the dangers of globalization or to positive feedback processes that intensify the impacts of globalization." Highlighting the centrality of these processes to global environmental change leads the authors to argue for the importance of studying complexity principles. This field is broad and sprawling, throughout much of environmental and sociological studies today.

The Resilience Alliance has been particularly influential in this area. These interdisciplinary ecologists and their social science colleagues have responded to mounting environmental crises by focusing on the complexity principle of resilience. They suggest that the study of complex systems and their characteristics may help to answer such questions as: How are self-organized patterns created and sustained in ecosystems and on landscapes at different scales, from meters to months to thousands of kilometers and millennia? How do such patterns, the processes that produce them, and species' adaptation, sustain critical ecological functions across those scales? How can we understand the role of diversity in allowing and modulating adaptability in a wide range of settings, from biodiversity to evolution to the diversity of ideas and its influence on human adaptability to changing circumstances?[34]

The resilience scientists are based primarily in the interdisciplinary environmental sciences. For instance, they developed the concept of the "panarchy," which is the basic adaptive cycle in natural systems based upon an iterative and infinite set of feedback loops including: events, adaptation, learning, strategy or evolution, change and subsequent events and adaptation. The panarchy, or feedback, helps to articulate the rest of ecosystem functioning. To these primarily interdisciplinary researchers, complexity theories have the flexibility and breadth to articulate the way in which feedbacks contribute to the self-organizing processes that create and maintain societies and environments. Critical processes within this include the cycles of carbon, water, nitrogen and other substances that play a key role in ecosystem functioning, or ecosystems "services," the somewhat anemic, anthropogenic term that nonetheless highlights our human dependence on ecosystems.

The resilience research has focused, for instance, on adaptive environmental cycles, while introducing consideration of basic components of the related social processes involved. For living systems dynamics, adaptive cycles are significant and useful framing devices. Ecosystems are neither controllable nor predictable. In such systems, individuals develop extensive adaptations to variability. One example is the lifestyle of elephants living in African deserts, traveling some 50 miles per day in search of less frequent and more diverse food sources, such as the nutritive roots of grasses ignored by elephants in more abundant ecosystems. Some living systems however exhibit variability over some scales, showing the full cycle of four phases of adaptation – growth, rigidity, collapse, and reorganization. Examples are both ecological and social, e.g., both productive temperate ecosystems and large bureaucratic social organizations.[35]

Some resilience scholars make contributions from the social sciences, and a few from social theory. Gilberto Gallopin, for instance, frames complexity for sustainability quite broadly in terms of the widespread philosophical implications of the complexity field – including its role in transforming our thinking in terms of ontology, epistemology, and applied philosophy. Generally speaking, complexity can be seen to be increasing in terms of both the interactions of systems and the creation of new ecological problems. Gallopin points out three facets of complexity that represent a broad view of the field: ontological, epistemological and political, or decision-making. For Gallopin, the complexity of the interactions and problems in human and ecological processes is increasing for reasons associated with each of these facets of how we can understand complexity itself. For instance, we are impacting the ontological complexity of the world – human-induced changes in the nature of the real world are proceeding at unprecedented rates, resulting in growing connectedness and interdependence at many levels. Carbon from fossil fuel burning mixes with carbon from deforestation, and join together to force global climate change. The ontological and epistemological implications of complexity are intertwined. This ontological shift of our major human impact requires shifts in our epistemological and political approaches.

A second way many scientists, e.g., in the Resilience Alliance, are taking up complexity and interdisciplinarity or transdisciplinarity is in the incorporation of uncertainty, unpredictability, and surprise. Using more complex concepts and models, they show how uncertainty and consequent unpredictability and surprise is common to reality at all scales, e.g., shown by scientific principles like Heisenberg's uncertainty principle, but also abundantly illustrated in questions of global socio-natural changes and challenges.[36]

While these approaches provide scientific advances, they say, of course they pay a price in having to grapple more with the challenges of uncertainty, unpredictability and surprise in the dynamics of complex ecological and socio-economic systems. Yet, it also clarifies the ways in which our ability to anticipate and change the future depends largely on our ability to comprehend and integrate complexity. Both ecological and social systems share complexity characteristics such as the absence of a global controller, a hierarchical organization, dispersed interactions, and the ongoing creation of novelty, selection, and adaptation.[37] Both ecological and social systems dynamics depend on history and lead to multiple possible outcomes. Thus, of fundamental importance is the degree to which system properties are environmentally determined versus the degree to which they are self-organized.[38] This is to say, the degree to which they are inevitable, versus the degree to which these processes are open, resilient, and adaptive.

A third way scientists are taking up complexity is the integration of nonlinear and linear analyses. In ecology, and in much interdisciplinary socioecological systems (SES) analysis that omits social theory, linear tools continue to domi-nate in empirical research and have to be adequately challenged, interpreted, and contextualized. Linear methods often prove superior to nonlinear ones for some practical analysis and policy implementation. Yet, increasingly, this must be understood against the background of evidence of important nonlinearities in alternate states of ecosystems,[39] spatial patterning of ecosystems,[40] and clumped or discontinuous size structure of ecological communities.[41]

Current ideas on SES analysis seem to fall into two clusters, calling for more or less integration of nonlinear modeling: one consisting in gradual reversible change described by adaptations of linear methods; the other embracing surprises, hystere-sis, and irreversibilities that imply fundamental nonlinearities. Increasingly, say the resilience authors, scientists should be asking when the weight of evidence indi-cates that complexity-based approaches add significant value for understanding or forecasting the system. Policy analysts should be asking when plausible nonlinear-ities create risks and opportunities significant enough to include in analysis. That's to say, one must integrate nonlinearity much of the time, since, even when the probabilities of sharp nonlinear changes may be low, they are usually nontrivial.[42] In this way, they are supporting the general trend towards incorporating nonlinear-ity and rapid change, as exemplified in the Introduction by the work of Jerome Ravetz and Silvio Funtowicz on postnormal science, or how to craft science and knowledge more generally in the instance of both high uncertainty and high stakes, qualities common to most issues of rapid global change.

Generally speaking, collaboratively, the resilience researchers work appears to support the incorporation of the entire transdisciplinary complexity frame-work, and subsequent necessity of interdisciplinary environmental sciences, integrated with some insights from the social sciences, especially the cluster of the framework concepts regarding learning, adaptation, and resilience.

Self-organization in physical systems may have similar properties and qualit-ies to self-organization in living and social systems, but of course the ramifica-tions for issues of global change are quite varied. The self-organized criticality of Per Bak's sandpile dynamics alone may not be obviously relevant for social issues, except in dodging rainstorms and debris flows. While, in living and social systems the adaptive cycle of self-organization, including learning, adaptation, and change, becomes central. Once we introduce the various threads of complex dynamics inherent to social issues, such as the examples of social movements from Chapter 4, then the adaptive cycle with its key component of learning, adaptation and change, is crucial. The resilience scientists' interdisciplinary approach and adaptive cycle framework presents one source for applications of the greater transdisciplinary approach and complexity framework.

Transdisciplinary studies of global change: The example of Science and Technology Studies (STS)

Whereas the Resilience Alliance focuses more fully on the ecological side of socioecological change, the Science and Technology Studies (STS) scholars focus more on the social side, while also working on socioecological issues. STS is perhaps the biggest of various proliferating interdisciplinary and transdisciplinary fields in the last two decades, based in social theory and examining the social dimensions of rapid global change. STS encompasses or mostly overlaps with related hybrid disciplines such as the sociology of science, and the social studies of science (SSS), also referred to simply as "science studies." STS is a burgeoning field boasting several journals, which has drawn together a great number of academics in dispersed fields of the humanities and social theory that identify with the field's topics and tactics.

In a recent overview of the field, Mario Biagioli said that while on the face of it the definition of science studies would appear to be a simple matter, in reality, "practitioners are dispersed over the widest range of departments and programs."[43] This great disciplinary fracturing and dispersion is sometimes seen as indicating a weakness of the field. On the contrary, it is precisely the escape from the confines of purely disciplinary approaches that has made these hybridizing fields grow so quickly and gain such prominence in academia. Far from diluting the field, it's precisely the space for transdisciplinary approaches employed to capture greater complexity that has made these new fields so quickly indispensable in most research universities and policy institutes.

Science and technology studies embrace inter- and transdisciplinary frameworks, as well as disciplinary scholarship, as a necessary way to incorporate crucial multi-sector dynamics at play in rapid, coevolving, social, technological, and global environmental change today. Biagioli notes how the field of science studies has demonstrated the nature of both reality and knowledge as complex and complexifying, increasing and growing in complexity, a concept from Nicolas Rescher that I describe further in the next chapter. Complexification, I argue, is the source of the both interrelated and yet partially disunified general nature of knowledge.

> As science studies produces more empirical work, it further "disunifies" itself methodologically while producing increasingly complex and "disunified" pictures of science, a double trend toward disunity that dissolves neither the field nor its subject matter.[44]

The central premise of STS is that in the wake of certain failings and dangers inherited from the project of modern science and technology production, we must study these fields and how and why they produce risks, harms, and at times collapses, in order to develop ways to better guide our societies. Scholars are finding that in order to adequately understand major trends in science, technology, knowledge production, and rapid global change, only theories that break the boundaries of traditional disciplines are capable of grasping the necessary variables and dynamics.

Science studies scholars, alarmed by our risk society and ensuing social and environmental crises, explore, for instance, how the failed assumptions of modernism are still largely operative in some ways and some degrees within our science, scholarship and technology production, as well as our economic and political theory and especially, of course, ideology; how this may contribute to our problems; and how to address this. Even while scientists, engineers, and technological experts have developed and integrated more complexity in their analyses, they have not always adequately rooted out or revised their overly modernist assumptions or methods. The stealthy continuation of modernist assumptions influences the processes of science and knowledge creation, technology, and thus rapid social and environmental change.

Science remains, these scholars argue, still much too broadly construed as the purview only of elites who need be trained solely in their respective scientific disciplines, entrenched in the modernist worldview of certainty and controllability, which rationalizes the divide between the creators of science and technology and their impacts on societies and environments.

However, the insights of complexity principles developed in these fields are increasingly breaking down the rationale and bases for these flawed modernist myths and traditions. Increasingly, scientists, corporations, and technocrats are called to task for the risks and harms associated with their results and products. The buildup of risks, harms, and counterproductivity must be increasingly accounted for and those involved held responsible for the collective consequences of their work.

Science, while in certain ways immune to it, is still greatly influenced by its context, enmeshed as it is in economic and political power dynamics, ideologies and outdated worldviews, and guided by biases and values at each phase in any enterprise – in the choice of systems studied, the framing and worldview of scientists overlaid on the formulation and procedure of study, and the response to results, including omitting and ignoring them. Ultimately, science often finds itself directly influenced by economic, political and cultural special interests, and only rarely free to focus on applications truly for the common good. Indeed, without a sufficiently transdisciplinary framing, there is no way that disciplinary-based even applied scientists may effectively gauge and guide how their work may or may not be ethically viable, contributing or not to degrading the commons, and serving, or not, the common good.

Science studies, with their broad focus, shed light on various complexity principles in late industrial societies, such as coproduction, coevolution, and constructivism. Knowledge production is central to the evolution of any society. What you study and why will shape and form ideas and practices and vice versa. Science studies force us to grapple with the greater context of our knowledge production and spotlight the continuous feedback loops whereby science, technologies, and societies coproduce each other and coevolve.

STS scholars draw commonly on complexity theories in their epistemology, framings and aims. For instance, epistemologically, STS scholars situate themselves as revisionists of the classical framework. In philosophy and thus social theory, "Classical epistemology has been concerned with the pursuit of truth. How can an individual engage in cognitive activity so as to arrive at true belief and avoid false belief?"[45] Descartes is recognized as one of the primary founders of this approach. In contrast, STS scholars, commonly assert some form of social constructivism. Weak social constructivism, generally speaking, is "the view that human *representations* of reality – either linguistic or mental representations – are social constructs." Whereas strong social constructivism holds not only that representations are socially constructed, but "that the *entities themselves* to which these representations refer are socially constructed."[46] In other words, not only are scientific representations of certain biochemical substances socially constructed, but also the substances themselves are socially constructed.

To most thinkers, the latter formulation is anathema if not absurd. However, once we contextualize the appropriately nuanced form of weak constructivism within the complexity concepts of coevolution and coproduction, as well as nested hierarchies and network causality, it becomes quite comprehensible. Moreover, much recent research, from physics to sociology to ecology, shows that observers and context can interact in surprisingly deep ways. Not only are there interactions in nature of various kinds, but also, observers are capable of deeply impacting their context in myriad ways. There are many examples, by which humans in close quarters impact each other. Science is unearthing the ways, for instance, that peoples' physiologies, emotions, heartbeats, brainwaves, menstrual cycles, and energy fields can influence each other.

Generally speaking, STS scholars speak of the significance of the ways that science is constructed by human ideas, values decisions, interpretations, and manipulations. More or less helpful data, ideas, and aims are favored over others, directed through a series of increasingly complex value choices. Increasing complexity of choices and changes require a concordant increase in the strength and effectiveness of democracy, as well as humility, ethics, and a focus on the common good. A constructivist epistemology acknowledges that science may be abstract in method, but nonetheless is entirely embedded within and continuously impacts and coevolves with real social and environmental systems. Science may seem isolated, but in fact necessarily is based in and interacts with social, economic, political and ethical contexts. Science is a transdisciplinary activity in disciplinary disguises, a wolf in sheep's clothing.

This is not to portray either scientists or scientific disciplines in a negative light – the work of competent scientists in their individual scientific disciplines, for instance on sustainability, is utterly essential. In addition, it is essential to admit and account for the realities of the way that science is enmeshed in and impacts upon our complex and multidimensional world. Disciplinary and interdisciplinary work provides the scaffolding upon which to develop the transdisciplinary perspective essential to shifting towards sustainability.

As discussed in Chapter 4, Ulrich Beck's 1992, *Risk Society*, an STS classic, showed that the concept of certainty, a cornerstone of nineteenth-century science, was overturned by the increasing significance of ubiquitous uncertainty. As high degrees of uncertainty become internalized as inherent to science, this necessitated a shift in the focus of policymakers, from uncertainty to risk. Following on this, Funtowicz and Ravetz's model of postnormal science – both high uncertainties and high stakes – characterizes most of humanity's pressing social and environmental issues; in issues of sustainability, uncertainty is orthogonal to significance.

Where significance of socioecological issues is high, some degree of transdisciplinary interpretation is necessary. This "postnormal" quality by which high uncertainty and high stakes characterize many contemporary social and environmental issues requires contextualizing them within the larger encompassing contexts and dynamics, necessitating trandisciplinarity. Transdisciplinary analysis is necessary to incorporate issues of cross-systems nonlinearity, feedbacks, networks, and hierarchies. In any multi-disciplinary systems – as in any issue of environmental sustainability – transdisciplinarity becomes crucial.

Interdisciplinary and transdisciplinary scholarship and "sustainability"

It is revealing to consider the two last categories together: on the one hand, natural science-based approaches to interdisciplinary environmental issues, and on the other hand, social theory-based approaches to the same issues. Disciplinary, interdisciplinary, and transdisciplinary approaches are all necessary to addressing and resolving issues of socioecological change.

An example is the way that different groups define and understand central terms. I look here at the example of how two groups of thinkers define a term central to this book, sustainability. A gap has formed between the connotations used by interdisciplinary environmental scientists versus interdisciplinary environmental social theorists. A transdisciplinary scholar is in a unique position to see how and why the views merged, and how and why to synthesize them.

The use of key terms is significant as it influences the whole discussion about responses, in the form of scientific, social, and political discourses and movements such as those based on resilience, degrowth, ecosocialist, or other growing intellectual and social movements. It is even more important because responses to environmental crises also come in less savory forms such as greenwashing, reactionary politics, Malthusianism, racism, and overly technocratic or managerial approaches.

One of the lessons of these burgeoning fields of socioecological studies is that in any inter-, multi-, or transdsiciplinary research, it's helpful to clarify what people in a particular context mean by interdisciplinary. One should assess what dominant disciplinary discourse, primary disciplinary methods, assumptions, theoretical frameworks and ideologies researchers are situated in; what research or literature they are familiar and unfamiliar with, include and exclude; what key terms they use and how they define them; and how these issues impact their research and analysis.

Mapping the discourses of sustainability through various disciplines, it becomes evident that interdisciplinary science and scholarship provides invaluable bridges and connections between critical areas of the science and scholarship of global change. In addition, some transdisciplinary work is necessary to bridge those bridges!

Evidently, natural scientists focus more on natural systems and the social theorists more on social systems. Of course, both groups are integrating some insights from "both sides." What is striking in our current era when, as Eliot early remarked, there is so much information, is that it is not always easy to get the fuller picture that we need for addressing certain issues. In the case of highly transdisciplinary subjects like sustainability, even for the most brilliant thinkers it is challenging to move beyond great science and scholarship, to a wise perspective. It seems to require periodically taking an extra step, to get an eagle's eye, transdisciplinary perspective.

For the sake of discussion, I have defined sustainability as "improving the quality of human life while living within the carrying capacity of supporting ecosystems."[47] While both natural scientists and social theorists tend to include both the natural and social dimensions, they still usually diverge in their framing, interpretation and analysis. According to Holling, Gunderson, and Peterson, "Sustainability is the capacity to create, test, and maintain adaptive capability."[48] This includes the social capacity to create, test, and maintain social and natural adaptive capability. As such it provides the basis for shifting from analysis of scientific issues to socioecological issues.

In contrast, science and technology scholars put a greater emphasis on various deeper social dimensions of sustainability. They often define sustainability similarly to the definition I use above. Yet, they tend to bring in more intricacies of the dynamics of human agency, human nature, subjectivity, power dynamics, and related philosophical issues.

These two sets of connotations bring to bear on the term "sustainable development." The average dictionary definition of development says something like "the act or process of developing; growth; progress."[49] While the most common definition is from the report *Our Common Future*, also known as the Brundtland Report, "Sustainable development is development that meets the needs of the present without compromising the ability of future generations to meet their own needs."[50]

A large group of international relations workers at the United Nations and elsewhere still work under this banner. Many people still take the term literally, and see it, regardless of politics, as a moral, social, and environmental imperative. Based in part on this, many interdisciplinary scientists adopt the general English connotation and see the pragmatic value of having some reference for the general development of society over time as sustainable, or specifically economic development as sustainable.

Whereas, many social theorists associate the term development with what are considered two major failures of the twentieth century – the failure of global economic development under institutions like the World Bank and the IMF, and the failure of societies to advance and implement the ideals of sustainable development born at Rio in 1992. In both instances, policies and outcomes have often promoted largely the opposite of the original goals. As a result, social theorists and those involved in that discourse such as the current generation of young environmental activists, tend to eschew the terms sustainability and sustainable development altogether. In their place, they have begun to opt for degrowth, resilience, alterglobalization, environmental justice, and other perspectives.

Certainly in agreement with many of these critiques, I use the term sustainability in a specific sense: as the opposite of collapse. By including the term directly in the complexity framework, I am using it as a crucial reference point with respect to both the dynamics of complex systems and to the specter of collapse. This view is very compatible with and can and should be integrated with particular theories and movements, e.g., resilience, lower-carbon economies, and environmental justice movements. In order to navigate through the transdisciplinary jungle of global social and environmental change, we need a reference to a flourishing state of being for the societies and environments that we care about, and that we must sustain.

Conclusion

Like complexity, transdisciplinarity is not yet another issue significant to sustainability. Rather, like complexity, transdisciplinary is a central, organizational issue. To understand ecocide and to articulate networked, multi-scale aspects of sustainability issues, requires a significant transdsiciplinary component to our entire project of knowledge making. Just as complexity theories cannot represent a separate branch of knowledge and be effective for sustainability, likewise, transdisciplinarity cannot be understood as yet another branch of knowledge. On the contrary, complexity and transdisciplinarity must be integrated into the very way that we understand, reorganize and advance human knowledge.

In our highly complex societies – or as Steven J. Klein would say $C_E > 10^{8,000}$ societies – we need increasingly rich lenses and interpretations. If we wish to address our global crises and Eliot's questions – "Where is the life we have lost in living, the wisdom we have lost in knowledge, and the knowledge we have lost in information?" – transdisciplinarity, like complexity, is not just a necessary part, but rather informs the very basis of adequate responses. Transdisciplinarity, like complexity, is an ever-present context at the moment that we frame, comprehend, and approach our research, policies, and practices. Disciplinary work is of course necessary, but it must be complemented continuously with some degree of both interdisciplinary and transdisciplinary methods and vision.

A number of leading scientists and scholars working on questions of sustainability have adopted this approach. Researchers have taken this up, not just in a handful of important disciplines, but it appears, across all of the disciplines related to sustainability. Ironically, thinkers throughout the disciplines are manifesting transdisciplinary approaches and complexity principles in attempting to conceptualize sustainability. Pioneering scientists and scholars in the last few decades have been developing increasingly powerful approaches with which to confront these issues head on. As extinctions, climate change, natural resource depletion, and social and economic crises continue, leading thinkers across the spectrum have gravitated towards transdisciplinarity – for a perspective that lets us better understand, strategize, and act at this epic moment.

As the first transdsiciplinary complexity scholars themselves put it, "Whereas, only a form of intelligence capable of grasping the cosmic dimension of the present conflicts is able to confront the complexity of our world and the present challenge of the spiritual and material self-destruction of the human species."[51]

6 Complexity in philosophy
Complexification and the limits to knowledge

> From this point forward, we are aware that unconsciousness of the limits of knowledge has been the biggest limit to knowledge.
>
> Edgar Morin[1]

> Neither science nor rationality are universal measures of excellence. They are particular traditions, unaware of their historical grounding. Yet it is possible to evaluate standards of rationality and to improve them. The principles of improvement are neither above tradition nor beyond change and it is possible to nail them down.
>
> Paul Feyeraband[2]

> The illusion … of putting two incompatible phenomena on the same level, is strictly analogous to what Kant called "transcendental illusion," the illusion of being able to use the same language for phenomena which are mutually untranslatable and can be grasped only in a kind of parallax view, constantly shifting perspective between two points between which no synthesis or mediation is possible. Thus there is no rapport between the two levels, no shared space—although they are closely connected, even identical in a way, they are, as it were, on the opposed sides of a Moebius strip.
>
> Slavoj Zizek[3]

Complexity and philosophy

Complexity theories have begun to illuminate a broad constellation of philosophical debates. In scratching the surface of these debates, I hope to give a few insights into the greater potential implications for twenty-first-century knowledge. In the paradigmatic shift from the worldview of the Scientific Revolution and modernity to a worldview of complexity, a coevolution has begun taking place as complexity theories infuse philosophy, and philosophy helps to understand complexity theories.

Specifically I make three arguments. First, complexification, as defined by Nicolas Rescher, becomes central in this coevolving shift. Second, the six complexity principles help to illuminate and explain complexification. Specifically I look at the way that three of the complexity principles – reflexivity (feedbacks), emergence, and self-organization – help to support and explain Rescher's thesis of complexification. Third, I examine how complexification leads to a few game-changing implications: the limits to science, the limits to knowledge, the acknowledgment of much unknowability, the need for integral methodologies, and thus an infusion of both humility and hope in human affairs.

The shift from a stable, mechanistic, deterministic, foundationalist universe, to a dynamic, emerging, self-organizing, foundationless, complexifying universe, brings a ripple of insights throughout philosophy – ontology, epistemology, logic, phenomenology, and ethics. I focus on a few examples to show how the shift from determinism to complexification is paralleled by the shift from the accretion of absolute truth to the philosophical implications of reflexivity (or feedbacks), emergence, self-organization, and complexification.

We have seen that complexity is transdisciplinary, and that transdisciplinary approaches help to advance our understanding of complexity throughout all realms of reality – physical, biological, social, and the realm of ideas and experience. No one domain has a claim on complexity; complexity has arisen throughout all the disciplines, including philosophy. Morin argues that in the modern era, complexity arose first in philosophy – in Kant, Nietzsche and others – and later in physics, chemistry, and biology.

I'll extend this perspective, and extend my argument in Chapter 4 on the widespread uptake of complexity throughout social theory. In Chapter 4, I noted that without using the same terminology, discussions about complexity have been widespread in the postmodern era throughout social theory, in the broad sense of the term, spurring considerable literature on other complexity principles such as risk and collapse, resilience and sustainability.

In a similar vein, in this chapter I take the position that complexity, in the general sense of the complexity framework outlined in Chapter 2, has been significant to various arguments and discussions in philosophy since at least Kant. Thinkers in every major philosophical school have come upon and grappled with complexity. This is particularly true of continental philosophy, which more fully eschews primarily reductionist approaches and aims for broader interpretations, but one finds debates based upon complexity principles and their implications throughout all camps of philosophy.

Complexification

As complexity theories overturn various central tenets of modernism, an underlying truth that emerges is the philosophical principle of complexification. Foundationalism held that all ideas are built on previous knowledge, and that science was a process of building from certain foundations towards the accretion of absolute truth. Mechanism held that the world was like a great machine, orderly, and controllable. While pure determinism held that all reality in all time was predetermined, from the past through the future. Founders of modern science believed that we continuously accrete Truth, and thus, eventually, we would come to understand everything. As Pierre Laplace put it optimistically,

An intelligence which for one instant could comprehend all the forces by which nature is animated ... would embrace in the same formula both the movements of the largest bodies in the universe and those of the lightest atom; to it nothing would be uncertain, and the future as the past would be present to its eyes.

Simply put, complexification is the process by which reality develops increasing degrees of complexity.[4] An essential philosophical premise that flows from complexity theories is that reality is not accreted, determined or mechanistic. Rather, reality complexifies. Through myriad processes such as emergence, self-organization, and consciousness, reality continues to develop novel properties over time. Thus, there is no Truth; instead, reality possesses a general tendency to become increasingly complex. In the history of the Earth, this has been punctuated by periods of rapid declines and collapses of life's complexity, only to slowly complexify once again.

The luminaries of the Scientific Revolution strove to overcome the ignorance, irrationality, and charlatanism of earlier eras. With the goal of developing more rational, reliable ways of knowing, order and truth, in the process they eschewed the realities of interactions, dynamics, and complexification. Today, however, a more radical shift may occur, as we integrate the best of modern knowledge while more thoroughly eradicating the falsehoods and myths of modernism that continue to distort and diminish knowledge. Complexity theories present a shift away from the early modern principles of foundationalism, mechanism, and determinism, helping us to see how knowledge has been distorted by oversimplification throughout the history of ideas.

Many modern thinkers, despite their affinity for absolute truths and grand narratives, also noted various aspects of complexity. Moreover, myriad thinkers throughout the disciplines in the last two centuries have given us poignant insights into complexity and complexification. The theologian Pierre de Chardin's book *The Future of Man*, first published in French in 1959, and then in English in 1964, grappled with a "scale of complexity," and increasing "degrees of complexity."

The more complex a being is, so our Scale of Complexity tells us, the more it is centered upon itself and therefore the more *aware* does it become. In other words, the higher the degree of complexity in a living creature, the higher its consciousness; and vice versa. The two properties vary in parallel and simultaneously. If we depict them in diagrammatic form, they are equivalent and interchangeable.[5]

Complexity visionary Kenneth Boulding was unique in having been president of the academic associations of five different disciplines, including the American Economics Association. Boulding noted that one similar quality of physical, biological and societal evolution is that all three "involve movement toward complexity of structure." For instance, "What happens in the evolution of chemical elements from hydrogen to uranium is increasing complexity of structure."[6] Similarly, in genetics there is an increasing complexity of genetic structures, and in societal evolution, an increasing complexity of knowledge structures.[7] Many others, without necessarily mentioning either complex dynamic systems or complexification, evoked some of their intriguing implications, as in Alvin Toffler best seller *Future Shock*.

Our current understanding of complexification comes from Nicolas Rescher, one of the most prolific American philosophers, having written over 100 books and 400 articles. Rescher was the only graduate of the Princeton philosophy department ever to have received a PhD by the age of 22.

Rescher published a seminal work on the philosophy of complexity, *Complexity: A philosophical overview*, in 1998, followed by several related books based on its implications. While other scholars have previously and poignantly noted the principle of increasing complexity in systems, Rescher defined and spelled out the term "complexification" and some of its wide-ranging philosophical meaning and implications.

Rescher defines complexity as the quantity and variety of a system's constituent elements and the interrelated elaborateness of their organizational and operational make-up.[8] He notes several important dimensions of complexity. First, he argues that complexity is itself a complex notion that combines compositional, structural and functional elements. Second, it is also a profound characteristic feature of the real. The world we live in is an enormously complex system – so much so that nature's complexity is literally inexhaustible. In the end, the descriptive, explanatory project of natural science is something that cannot be completed in a world that develops and evolves. Third, complexity is the inherent force in its own elaboration, as all complex dynamic systems tend towards self-maintenance and increasing complexification. These premises touch upon, respectively, complexification, emergence, and self-organization.

This leads to the insight that humans and societies, having emerged from the biological and physical, also tend to complexify through time. Human societies, organizations, institutions, science, and technologies also tend towards complexification. As we saw in Boserup's work on agricultural systems and Tainter's work more generally on human societies, complexification is a central feature of human societies, and one with major implications for the well-being, development, and successes of societies.

As life complexifies, and humans and their societies complexify over time, the practice of science itself complexifies over time. Progress in scientific research complexifies, as many have noted, including Rescher, which is to say that as science develops it acquires a growth in technical sophistication that renders science itself increasingly complex. In the course of scientific and technological progress we find ever-expanding complexity. This helps to explain the origins and fallacies of the modern Progress Myth. Complexification means that layers of additional complexity transform past layers of natural, societal, institutional, scientific, and technological complexity, which does not proceed in a simple or accretive fashion. Rather, each new layer of complexity transforms human ideas and societies. Networks, nested hierarchies, feedbacks, emergences and ongoing self-organization are such that networked, unintended consequences proliferate and interact, causing reverberating changes throughout systems. As Beck's concept of world risk society illuminates, these changes represent not only progress, but rather multifaceted and in part nefarious changes. The development of science and technology is inherently neither good nor neutral. From our perspective, and from the perspective of life on earth, our science and technologies are polyvalent, and just as prone to disaster as they are prone to improving the human condition.

While many scholars have critiqued progress and pointed to unintended consequences, Rescher's work has further implications – through explanation of the limitations of progress and the intrinsic inclusion of unintended consequences, due to the inherent clash between our singular introductions and experiments, and the consequent networked effects and impacts. Our singular actions are introduced into a world that is profoundly characteristically complex, a world that is at once compositionally, structurally, and functionally complex. An action may be simple, but its manifestation in the world is always polyvalent and never "neutral." Indeed, the very concepts of non-impact and neutrality become the abstract vestiges of a deterministic worldview.

Ongoing complexification makes for increasing sophistication, diversification, and ultimately, may in some ways undermine the enterprise of science itself. The ongoing development of natural science, Rescher points out, requires technological escalation – an ascent to ever-higher levels of sophistication and power. In turn, this escalation is achieved only by means of vast and ever-increasing effort and cost in the generation and processing of information. There are limits to our cognitive capacities, limits to the capacities of computers or biological robots, and limits to the costs we can pay for research.

Moreover, complexification or increasing complexity permeates all the dimensions of our lives; it is a ubiquitous to all realms of reality. Via all different projects characteristic of the human condition – specifically including the cognitive, social, technological, and cultural – we embark on a journey of increasing degrees of complexity, or complexification.

We must integrate the philosophical lessons of complexification with a deeper analysis of collapse and sustainability. As sustainability scholars, we are aware of this phenomenon of complexification. Evidently, one lesson for our future is that life tends toward complexification up to a point, the point at which we reach limits and constraints that undermine the process of complexification. Through extensive literature, we have seen how increasing complexification leads to types and degrees of societal collapses. Understanding this more fully gives us the power to act preventatively and proactively towards a better future scenario.

Rescher's view of complexification, supports the arguments of Ivan Illich, Joseph Tainter, and others discussed in Chapter 4. Rescher, like Illich and Tainter, argues that phases of degrees of complexification exhibit certain patterns throughout social affairs. In the first phase, greater complexity increases diversification and specialization, and increases learning and improvement of design, leading to many benefits. In a latter phase, there may be ongoing benefits, but these are often accompanied by unintended consequences, counterproductivity, increasing costs and marginal returns. For instance, as machines increase efficiency in some ways, they also create unintended consequences and costs in other ways.

Eventually, as societies become highly complex, Rescher argues, they utilize greater amounts of energy, they increasingly sap their own forces, and this tends to undermine and debilitate further progress. Despite the seemingly endless direction of choices, the individual must make delimiting decisions. While the realm of ideas and meaning may seem infinite, clearly, material resources are finite with respect to, for instance, labor, and energy. These limitations indicate the significance of personal choice in guiding values and priorities in an increasingly complex operating environment.[9] Over time, knowledge, technologies, institutions, legal codes, and other diverse aspects of human societies, tend to complexify.

Reflexivity (feedbacks), emergence, and self-organization

In 1985, British philosopher Hilary Lawson published a book called *Reflexivity: the post-modern predicament.* Lawson surely is not an "insider"; he quickly left academic philosophy. He may have left the academy, but not philosophy. Not only has Lawson made impressive contributions to philosophy, but also, he has done more to bring philosophy into the public sphere than many besides Simone de Beauvoir, Peter Singer, or Cornell West. After leaving Oxford, he went on to a major career in documentary film and in-depth TV shows, as well as developing a technique called video painting, and more recently he founded a major arts and philosophy institute, including a weeklong summer festival, highlighting conversations by some of the world's leading philosophers.

Lawson's first major philosophical book argued that reflexivity, or self-reference, is central to contemporary philosophy. Drawing upon Nietzsche, Heidegger and Derrida as examples, he sought to show that reflexivity was a primary motor in their work. The work upset some analytic philosophers, as Lawson implicitly argued that his theory of reflexivity should also be applied to analytic philosophy.

Lawson's book focused on one major complexity principle, feedbacks, and on their ramifications for individual lives and society. Lawson's argument can be extended to incorporate other aspects of the complexity framework. Lawson focuses on the narrow slice – rich with implications – of reflexivity in human life. Yet, we can extend his argument to focus on many other facets of complexity, and show how each of these has shown up throughout philosophy, particularly in the Continental philosophers who have had as their aim a more comprehensive synthetic understanding of contemporary societies.

Drawing on these three philosophers, one sees how reflexivity is interconnected with all six complexity principles, and how especially the principles of emergence and self-organization carry profound implications for such issues as the human subject, identity, meaning, subjectivity, autonomy, social life, and the intricacies of the human experience.

As they have with reflexivity, philosophers have long inquired into the qualities of emergence and self-organization, even if they had not yet conceptualized these processes in the way we now are beginning to think of them. The lively and with retrospect humorous debates of the Pre-Socratics examined elemental forms of these concepts as they explored how reality seems to exhibit both sameness and stability and also flux, change, and evolution. As our perspective on these aspects of complex dynamic systems develop, we must explore more seriously how they may influence debates in ontology, epistemology, phenomenology, and ethics.

Since Heraclitus at least, philosophers have been grappling with the problems of emergence and self-organization – problems that seem to be as difficult in philosophy as they are in biology. The philosopher of science Paul Durbin asked in 1968, how radical is emergence? He drew on Whitehead to argue for the significance of uncertainty, continuous change, emergence, and self-organization, based in Whitehead's philosophy of process and organicism. "The whole process of the modern doctrine is the evolution of the complex organisms from antecedent states of less complex organisms. The doctrine thus cries aloud for a conception of the organism as fundamental for nature."[10]

Erol Harris, a student of Whitehead, later noted the enigma and importance of self-organization, when he wrote,

> What was before merely a complex and polyphasic system of chemical reactions, becomes an auturgic, self-adjusting, and self-maintaining, living organism.... So that the organism maintains itself against the destructive tendencies of thermodynamics, against the strains and stresses imposed upon it by its environment.

Drawing on the complexity principles of feedback, network, and hierarchy, without using these terms, he suggests the significance of nested hierarchies to living systems. A cell is a part of a protozoa, and the protozoa itself a self-contained unit within a metazoa. "The philosopher cannot afford to ignore all this in the effort to understand the general nature of things."[11]

How radical is emergence? Philosopher Paul Durbin concludes,

> ...it is easy and natural to assume that contemporary dynamic interaction theories – from particle physics to the development of astrophysical system and even of the universe as a whole, to the unquestioned cohesiveness of biological evolution – point to an ontological structure of process and unfolding. At the very least such philosophers would be able to demonstrate the untenability of a static view of the universe, on the ontological level, in light of present scientific knowledge.[12]

Feedbacks or reflexivity show ways in which complexity theories carry much broader implications of emergence and self-organization for such issues as the human subject and the human experience.

The issues that will make or break our future as a species are based in ethics, politics, class, ideologies, institutions, cultures, mores – in short, every way in which social issues are embedded in the nested hierarchical contexts of not just physical, biological, and planetary (e.g., climatological, hydrological, and natural resources), but crucially also, social, political and ethical systems, theories, narratives, ideologies, and paradigms.

The limits of science and the limits of knowledge

The difference between science and scholarship that accretes knowledge versus that which complexifies knowledge is substantial. Various implications flow from this. Perhaps the most significant is that there are limits to science, truth, and knowledge. Ironically, there is now a substantial and growing body of knowledge on the limits to knowledge!

Complexity theories generally, and complexification specifically, further confirm the power and necessity of science, while also shedding light on the limits of science. Complexification, explaining the seemingly endless branching of knowledge, shows how these two realities interrelate. Even while complexity shows the need for scientific approaches of empiricism, quantification and modeling in the face of partial uncertainties, at the same time, the expansive quality of complexification highlights the limits to science and the problems of scientism. Philosophy of science John Dupre defines scientism as, "an exaggerated and often distorted conception of what science can be expected to do or to explain for us."[13] One should not throw out the baby with the bathwater. Both the lack of appreciation of the significance and role of science and its over-emphasis in scientism are flawed views.

Complexity, showing the dynamic links within and between the different realms of reality, necessitates both quantitative and qualitative, scientific and philosophical methods. Thus it is well placed to clarify the significance and limits of science.

When examining complex topics likes humans and environments, focusing solely on either science or philosophy may become distortional. Conjoining them helps us to show the spectacle of a complexifying universe that will not be fully reduced or comprehended in any kind of absolute truths. As such, complexity theories appear to be significant to debates regarding the present and ultimate limits or limitlessness of science, in terms of assessing uncertainty versus unknowability and in terms of the future potential of human knowledge.

According to philosopher of science John Barrow, science with complexity is still accumulative, it just isn't determinist: we accumulate more facts, broader theories, better measurements and advances in the creation of ever more powerful machines. But because the overall nature of knowledge is not determinist, the rate of growth is limited by the increasing costs. Nicolas Rescher distinguishes between the classical view of knowledge accumulation versus Barrow's notion of it. It's not just that there is knowledge that remains "veiled." It's that the very direction of science is not one of accumulation, in this critical sense, at all.

Through the development of science, knowledge is not accumulating more truth, but rather it is just accumulating more knowledge, more questions, and more falsifactions of past theories.

As a reference, it is useful to recall various claims to simplicity that have been successively overturned from the early scientific period until today. Early on, a fundamental wedge was levied beneath the cornerstone of simplicity, the early classical view that the universe is composed of simple elements. Founding fathers of early classical science – Leibniz, Descartes, Locke, and Hume – thought of three elements as simple: colors, elemental particles, and numbers. Since they thought these elements were simple, therefore they thought that the simple must be regarded as an ontological category. So they held that understanding that which is simple also must be simple, because it is easily recognizable. Therefore, simplicity was seen to describe two categories – the ontological and the cognitive. However, a colorless nature is not nature. Nature is not colorless when not perceived of in interaction with minds. Therefore, color is not a simple element. Rather, it is at once, a chemical interaction, an experience, and an aspect of our experience of nature. It does not exist as a simple entity in any way.[14] Similarly, of course it is now known that the atom is neither elemental nor simple, but rather highly complex, and that numbers are but abstractions for complexity.

Not only has science proven that simplicity does not exist, but moreover, according to Rescher the history of science is "an endlessly repetitive story of simple theories giving way to more complicated and sophisticated ones." Of course, we constantly seek to simplify science, striving for an ever-smaller basis of evermore-powerful explanatory principles. But through simplicity we discover complexity. In fact, complexity theories present the attempt to do this at the next greater level of detail and sophistication. This is one way to explain that complexity in no way replaces science or the scientific process, but is merely a new, transformative, accretion of this process.

In the course of this endeavor, the attempt to simplify, we invariably complicate the structure of science itself, says Rescher. And I would add, it is through this process of simplifying scientific studies that we also complicate the nature and structure of knowledge itself – create the need for ever more finely spliced disciplines, ever more information, and even means of storing and transmitting information. So, we do secure greater power, e.g., functional simplicity, but at the price of greater structural complexity. As Rescher says, with some humor I believe, by the time the physicists discover their "grand unified theory" what they will have will be so complex as to be likely far beyond comprehension. The math gets ever more powerful and elaborate, the training time necessary to developing the expertise is prolonged, and the computer power necessary increases. So despite its quest for greater operational simplicity (economy of principles) science itself is becoming ever more complex (in its substantive content, its reasoning, its machinery, etc.). Therefore, simplicity of process is more than offset by complexity of product, and so this ongoing complexification exacts a price of diminishing returns:

The Greeks had four elements; in the 19th century Mendeleev had some sixty; by the 1900s this had gone to eighty, and nowadays we have a vast series of elemental stability states. Aristotle's cosmos had only spheres; Ptolemy's added epicycles; ours has a virtually endless proliferation of complex orbits that only supercomputers can approximate. Greek science was contained on a single shelf of books; that of the Newtonian age required a roomful; ours requires vast storage structures filled not only with books and journals but with photographs, tapes, floppy disks, and so on. Of the quantities currently recognized as the fundamental constants of physics, only one was contemplated in Newton's physics: the universal gravitational constant. A second was added in the 19th century, Abogadro's constant. The remaining six are all creatures of twentieth century physics: the speed of light (the velocity of electromagnetic radiation in free space), the elementary charge, the rest mass of the electron, the rest mass of the proton, Planck's constant, and Botzmann's constant.[15]

Therefore, the course of scientific progress is not one of increasing simplicity. In fact, just the reverse is true. Scientific progress is a meter of complexification because overly simple theories invariably prove untenable in a complex world. The natural process of scientific inquiry impels researchers to ever more complex, ever more sophisticated descriptions. Our methodological commitment to simplicity and systematicity is necessary, but it is ontologically unavailing. Science over the last 300 years may have proceeded by simplification, but it has resulted in complexification. We should not let the method blind us to the ever more complex ontological picture that science has presented us with, the substantive discovery of complexity.

It would seem that the vast complexification of science should in fact be obvious by now. After all, in every discipline, scientists and social theorists alike are aware of the ongoing splintering and subdividing of disciplines; the ongoing escalation of jargon and incomprehensibility between even the closest scientific niches; the massive accumulation not just of quantity of information, but of its increasingly disparate, unarticulated nature. Every area of human lives becomes more complex with the concurrent development of science and technology.

Take the case of transportation. First there was the wheel and simple wooden cart, both produced locally through metal-smithing and carpentry. Then the wagon, made of wood, metal, leather, and cloth, which could have been produced locally, but perhaps pieces would be made more efficiently in disparate small factories. For the steam engine you need large factories to produce great quantities of mechanical parts such as pistons. For cars and airplanes, huge factories are needed, along with trucks to transport great quantities of materials, and gas stations to haul the trucks long distances. Moreover, the myriad components of subsequent generations of cars and planes increasingly have depended on goods and materials imported from and distributed across numerous countries, requiring electircial grids and dispersed power stations. As such the very creation and development of transportation technologies increasingly spurred the creation and dependence upon increasing amounts of energy and a proliferating network of additional goods and technologies. A similar pattern of increasingly intensive demand for energy and goods can be found for the lineage of other technologies and industries.

As mechanistic technologies are employed in living and social systems, the substantive differences between them come to light. While reductionist analysis helps us to understand various aspects of all of these systems, it can fully capture the dynamics of mechanical systems, but it only captures certain aspects of self-organizing and evolutionary dynamics. The former can be studied as ahistorical, while the latter cannot be studied without accounting for historical and future capacity for novel qualitative changes. Table 6.1 is modified from Paul Allen's work on systematic knowledge of the limits of knowledge.[16]

Physical, living, and social systems all complexify over time, whereas mechanical or engineered systems do not. Acknowledging and accounting for the qualitative differences of novelty, change and evolution inherent to living and social systems in particular, in contrast with mechanical systems, provides a more realistic general framework with which to grasp some of the epistemological intricacies of knowledge production.

To account for these qualitative differences across different types of systems, the methodological differences they necessitate, and the limits to science and knowledge they reveal provides a more successful basis upon which to prioritize and guide knowledge production for aims of sustainability. This perspective provides clear reasons to exercise precaution, regulation, speculation, and skepticism with regards to some aspects of science and technology research and development. It gives explicit rationale for the continued integration of ethics and science as a basis for future research and development funding.

Acknowledging complexification is a great boon. At first we may focus on the restrictions of the limits to knowledge. However, we benefit in myriad ways from developing this more realistic perspective, such as a fuller recognition of the nature, strength, beauty, and potential of the knowledge we do possess. Complexity theories in every realm bring to light the intricacies of human lives and experiences, showcasing the tremendous beauty of humans, societies, and the natural world. This perspective may contribute to diminishing hubris in human thinking and worldviews, reducing alienation, and contributing to a revival of wonder, awe, and the sense of enchantment.

Acknowledging the limits to science reinforces the value of both the science and the ethics within our grasp. In the context of considerable global change, it may alter the way we look at evaluating priorities in basic and applied sciences, and it may militate for greater appreciation and support for correlated work in the humanities and social theory. If complexification helps to explain the limits to knowledge, ironically this complements an exciting, extraordinary nonlinear growth of knowledge in recent years.

Moreover, the limits of science are just one facet of certain kinds of "limits" inherent to existing in the universe. We often think of the word "limits" in a very simplistic sense. In fact, limits may be double-edged, multifaceted. In fact the

Table 6.1 Systematic knowledge concerning the limits to systematic knowledge

Assumptions and type of model	Equilibrium	Nonlinear dynamics (including chaos)	Self-organizing	Evolutionary
Type of system	Fixed	Fixed	Can change its configuration and connectivity	Can change structurally
Composition	Yes	Yes	Can lead to new, emergent properties	Can change qualitatively
History	Irrelevant	Irrelevant	Important at the system level	Important at all levels of description
Prediction	Yes	Yes	Probabilistic	Very limited; high inherent uncertainty
Intervention and prediction	Yes	Yes	Probabilistic	Very limited; high inherent uncertainty

concept of a lack of limits is a total delusion of simple thinking, an abstract idea and impossibility.

In this broader sense, if seeming unsettling, in fact, both "limits" and "possibilities" actually provide a more realistic, comforting and inspiring view of life, in contrast to modern delusions of stability and simplicity. In the broader, philosophical sense of the term, "limits" do not just limit, they also permit, and make possible. As Barrows points out, while Newtonian laws still work to run our mechanical systems such as airplanes, it is because and not despite, the limits to the speed of light. Before Einstein, the Newtonian picture of the world placed no limit to the speed at which light or any other information could travel. In reality, such lack of limitations was impossible. A world that had no speed limit would have no humans. A world too simple to accommodate light would be too simple to accommodate humans. The recognition of the limits to the speed of light makes the consistency of the laws of Nature possible.[17]

Over the course of the last three hundred years, science has proven to have one great strength according to Nicolas Rescher: Science is "an endlessly versatile intellectual instrument capable of accommodating itself to ever-changing cognitive circumstances."[18]

At the same time, science has a number of limitations. In Table 6.2 I summarize and synthesize a list of the limitations of knowledge from the works of four philosophers, Nicolas Rescher,[19] John Barrow,[20] Kurt Richardson,[21] and Edgar Morin.[22]

I have chosen to focus on complexification, which seems sufficient for this chapter. I have discussed many of the other limits briefly and I lack space to do each of them justice. Complexification is a helpful central concept for our purposes. First, it shows a significant break, not only from early classical scientific assumptions – sole determinism, sole reductionism, and sole disjunction – but the evident residue and holdover of many of these assumptions even amongst scientists working almost entirely within the realm of complex systems. Second, complexification is the core source of many, or perhaps even all, of the other major categories of the limits of science and knowledge on this list. For instance, complexification results directly in such challenges as human limits, technological limits, informational limits, practical limits, financial limits, and experimental limits.

Generally, one major result of perceiving the pervasive complexifying process of the development of knowledge is that science does not describe successive truths, but rather successive destabilization of "truths" or theories. While there is always interest, value and purpose in pursuing knowledge in diverse domains, it comes at a cost: the increasing resource requirement of digging into ever-increasing complexity. Successive triumphs in many areas of science and scholarship are often gained at an increasingly greater price in time, materials and costs. Grappling with ever-greater bodies of information in the construction of an ever-growing study of our world appears to be an unavoidable requisite of continuing scientific and scholarly progress.[23]

Table 6.2 The limits to science and the limits to knowledge

From Nicolas Rescher:
- Fallibilism
- Instability
- Inability to arrive at anything ultimate or definitive
- The pragmatic dimensions of progress
- The obstacle of the escalation of complexity

From John Barrow:
- Even correct theories are limited
- Knowing process has an inevitable by-product of ever unveiling limits
- Understanding more leads to understanding more about limitations of previous understanding
- Human limits – arise from nature of our humanity and evolutionary inheritance
- Technological limits – rooted in our biological nature
- Limits on information – limits on human time, energy, resources
- Limits on speed of transmitting information
- Practical limits – we are surrounded by a host of practical problems
- Experimental limits – on what we can test
- Limit on the scope of questions – there is only so much we can approach in terms of major philosophical questions

From Kurt Richardson:
- Qualitatively different behaviors and scale independence
- Chaos versus anti-chaos
- Incompressibility
- Bottom-up limitations
- Top-down limitations
- Differences in the ontological status of behaviors
- The issue of emerging domains
- That of evolutionary phase spaces
- Cellular automata
- The position of the observer

From Edgar Morin:
Uncertainties inherent to cognition:
- Our incapacity to know other than by computation or signs and symbols, which render uncertain the profound nature of reality (we can determine the objectivity of the known reality, not the reality of that reality)
- Risks of errors linked to communication. In conformity with Shannon's theory all communication includes the risk of degradation of the message under the effect of noise – which is to say the risk of uncertainty or of error
- Uncertainties arising from the environment, e.g., uncertain events, disorders, ambiguities for an observer, and it is difficult or impossible to decide if a chance phenoena obeys or not a hidden determinism and if a deterministic phenomena arises or not from a chance origin.

Uncertainties linked to the cerebral nature of knowledge
- The relative closure of the cognitive apparatus
- Our sensory limits
- Multiplicity of inter-communications
- Nature of representation
- Subtractions and additions – that effectuate the perception with respect to sensory messages
- The hallucinatory component of perception
- The hysterical component of representation
- The unity of real and imaginary in one representation
- Selective attention and rationalizations of cultural origin in any one representation
- Infidelities, forgotten elements, deformations of memory

The implications of complexity, complexification, and the limits to knowledge for methodology: reductionism, constructivism, and integral methodologies

> Knowledge is not about trying to dissect the mystery of things, but rather, on the contrary, to reveal that mystery.
>
> Edgar Morin[24]

Most of the complexity of philosophy and philosophy of complexity is largely uncharted terrain. The last half-century has been marked by some helpful pioneers. Yet, as Melanie Mitchell argued about the lack of consensus around complexity definitions at the Santa Fe Institute, paradigmatic shifts require a substantial phase of pioneering and experimenting, during which even the very basic definitions and concepts may be unclear. As she pointed out, Newton was not comfortable with definitions of the term "force." Likewise, the philosophy of complexity is new territory.

Exploring transdisciplinary complexity requires articulating comprehension from multiple disciplines, including science and philosophy. This appears to provide opportunities for exploring and perhaps better articulating or reconciling differing viewpoints in the philosophy of science in the last century. For instance, complexity theories illuminate debates about epistemological realism, reductionism, and constructivism. On one extreme end, the early classical scientific viewpoint, based in determinism and foundationalism, denied any constructivism. On the other extreme, a few contemporary social theorists have gone off the deep end, expressing totalizing holism, or a kind of pure constructivism, seemingly abstracted from material reality.

Complexity theories help to articulate an intermediary position, where constraints intermingle with emergences, and realism, reductionism, and constructivism all work in consort. Reductionism is a necessary approach, but only within a context of the appreciation of constructivism. Realism, reductionism, and constructivism coexist and must be integrated to form a richer perspective.

If we take seriously the shift from a solely determinist world to a world comprised of both determinism and contingency, order and disorder, and if we take into account reflexivity, networks, hierarchies, emergence, and self-organization, what does this imply for the way that we understand and approach science and scholarship? In particular, what does it say about the diverse epistemologies and methodologies that we use to conceptualize different realms of reality?

The endless branching and novelty inherent to complexification shows the illogicality of absolute truths, and highlights the ongoing succession of Popperian refutations. As physicists know, new paradigms in physics are never total revolutions; they never "fully" refute the old paradigm, but rather they complexify the old paradigm, by adding game-changing new laws and thus a richer, fuller perspective. Mathematics, the language of nature in this powerful sense, has been an incredibly incisive tool with which to understand some underlying "truths" of our natural world.

Yet, differences in the nature of shifting paradigms in physical, biological and social realms must be accounted for. Even in the relatively lawlike physical realm, our knowledge is transformed by paradigmatic shifts. Quantum mechanics and string theories appear to represent substantial shifts in perspective. The biological and social realms are less lawlike and more highly complex and contingent. Given the role of mathematics in "unveiling" and "describing" those laws, physicists often see mathematics as the only true language of nature. Yet, in social systems mathematics will only get you so far, and alternative methodologies become more powerful, even if necessarily less precise or logical.

To draw on a metaphor from Chapter 3, these differences reveal a kind of Möbius strip phenomenon, whereby seemingly contradictory realities are both somehow true. One side of the Möbius strip shows that mathematics is the language of nature, and that to describe physical systems, mathematical reductionism works best. The other side of the Möbius strip shows that methodological pluralism is a more complete approach to highly complex living and social systems. Methodological pluralism, incorporating quantitative and qualitative approaches, becomes increasingly necessary for comprehending socioecological systems.

With respect to the goal of sustainability, most issues necessitate quantitative analyses, but also a shift in gaze to the fully transdisciplinary view of the Möbius strip, requiring more pluralist, integral methodologies. If we accept that complexity theories have a compelling transdisciplinary nature, and that our aim is social and environmental sustainability, then it becomes crucial to integrate the insights from both purely quantitative and more integral quantitative and qualitative approaches to complexity, or as Morin puts it, both "restrained," and "generalized" complexity.

It is against this backdrop that we must understand the philosophical insights and implications of complexity theories. And it is in light of this that we must see how to more effectively integrate the complexity sciences with philosophical understanding in pursuit of sustainability.

Reductionism

From the natural sciences, to social theory, to philosophy, complexity theorists are grappling with issues of reductionism, such as when an analysis is suffiently, but not overly, reductionist.

In her excellent overview of the Santa Fe Institute's complexity sciences, Melanie Mitchell starts out by positioning the Santa Fe Institute in opposition to reductionism. The very first word of the book is the word "reductionism." She quotes Douglas Hofstadter.

> Reductionism is the most natural thing in the world to grasp. It's simply the belief that "a whole can be understood completely if you understand its parts, and the nature of their 'sum.'" No one in her left brain could reject reductionism.
>
> (Douglas Hofstadter, Godel, Escher, Bach: an Eternal Golden Braid)[25]

Mitchell then begins the book by explaining how she is using the term,

> Reductionism has been the dominant approach to science since the 1600s. Rene Descartes, one of reductionism's earliest proponents, described his own scientific method thus: "to divide all the difficulties under examination into as many parts as possible, and as many as were required to solve them in the best way" and "to conduct my thoughts in a given order, beginning with the simplest and most easily understood objects, and gradually ascending, as it were step by step, to the knowledge of the most *complex*."[26]

The issue is rather complicated, as there are multiple definitions and facets of the term reductionism, of which scientists are often referring to one significant aspect, the aim and perspective that focuses on parts or whole and includes more or less interactions and dynamics.

At the same time, people often omit other significant connotations of the term reductionism. For instance, there is also methodological reductionism, the use of a certain epistemological lens and methodological approach at the exclusion of others. This is often appropriate, but nonetheless can delimit just how fully we comprehend particular issues.

Reductionism in the broad sense is a necessary aspect of complexity science. Yet "pure reductionism" is not. Therefore, Mitchell's rebuttal of totalizing reductionism brings quantitative and qualitative complexity theorists a step closer to advancing complexity with an epistemologically pluralist unified vision.

The successes of the complexity sciences are rich and numerous, as I outlined in Chapter 3, including the irreducible unpredictability of weather and climate, the complex dynamic processes involved in heartbeats, insect colonies, neuronal networks, the immune system, and the World Wide Web. The successes of the social theorists and transdisciplinary scholars are evident as well, as I outlined in Chapters 4 and 5, as they alone, with their philosophical, macrosopic, and transdisciplinary lenses, are able to intelligibly frame issues of postmodernity, risk, collapse, and socioecological resilience.

To some degree and in some ways, all of the above, scientists and scholars alike, are practicing reductionism. In the broadest sense, reductionism is simply focusing on isolating some study issues from some background issues, and looking at some causes and factors, to the neglect of others, also known as analysis, an inherent aspect of intelligible thinking. Any method involving quantification, modeling, or simulation is in this sense reductionist. And within the complexity perspective – where evidently determinism and contingency, order and disorder are intimately entangled – both more quantitative and methodologically reductionist and more synthetic, methodologically plural lenses appear to be necessary to conceptualizing complex dynamics.

Yet, as we shift away from the easier or more familiar confines of modernist framing, and towards an appreciation of complexification, we begin to see issues of methodological differences throughout the disciplines in a better light. To adequately grasp just what methodologies should be applied in a complex world, it's imperative to cut through the heavy evaluative judgments or connotations of reductionism, synthesis, constructivism, and other now trenchantly emotional and divisive buzzwords of the philosophical wars underlying the current paradigmatic shift.

Mitchell argues that the "new sciences such as chaos, systems biology, evolutionary economics, and network theory move beyond reductionism to explain how complex behavior can arise from large collections of simpler components." Here she is invoking the connotation of reductionism related to the scope and nature of the content. She is shifting beyond a narrower scope of analysis to include fuller dynamics.

Most complexity scientists are usefully shifting their gaze from more reductionist explanations, to more interconnected, interacting phenomena. However, they often do this within inherently reductionist quantitative methods. So they are exercising a fuller, more interdisciplinary focus, but doing so within certain restraints of an intrinsically reductionist methodology. Though, some complexity science also employs either pluralistic or synthetic methodologies, or more transdisciplinary collaboration and perspectives. Of course, quantitative methods simply are the most powerful for revealing what they do. Reductionist quantitative methods simply do produce much of the great successes we have seen throughout the complexity sciences. Nevertheless, for some issues, such as socioecological issues, a more pluralist epistemology and methodology is needed in order to contextualize and comprehend more aspects and dimensions of complex social and environmental dynamics.

Henri Atlan, mathematician, philosopher and founder of complexity theories in France, is both a rigorous, quantitative scientist of great caliber, and also a philosopher of science, and thus well placed to provide deeper insights into these puzzles. According to Atlan, the work at SFI is in this significant sense, "more reductionist than regular, non-complexity science."[27] Actually, he says by applying mathematical methods to complex subjects, the SFI scientists are bringing a reductionist lens to complex phenomena; in this way, he says, SFI science is more reductionist than non-complexity science! A scientist himself, he shares in these same methods with the same successful results.

So Mitchell is correct that she and her colleagues are not as reductionist as other scientists, in the sense that they are more conscious of and focused on the role of interactions, dynamics, and other aspects and qualities of complex phenomena. And yet, Atlan also is correct in pointing out that just because complexity scientists are conscious of and focused on complex phenomena, that does not change the partially reductionist nature of quantitative methodologies.

Atlan himself has conducted quantitative scientific study of biological emergence and self-organization since the 1960s. In his work as both biologist and philosopher, he produced both quantitative research and qualitative interpretations of it. In this way, his work brings in both sides of this Möbius strip view of reality, whereby both quantitative and qualitative interpretation are necessary to grasping the implications of complex dynamics more fully.

Atlan notes that, long before the Santa Fe Institute, biologists like Bertalanffy, economists like the Chicago School, and leading complexity scientists like Ross Ashby and Hienz von Foerster had as their objective to scientifically model phenomena of emergence and self-organization. These seminal works have been central to developing the whole field of complexity, both quantitative and qualitative, restrained and generalized perspectives.

> We explain emergence and self-organization by mechanisms – purely local, descriptive mechanisms. This nonlinear reductionism used in complexity science is an even stronger reductionism than linear reductionism.... Network causality permits us to predict the unpredictable, in the sense that it allows us to begin to understand how novel events can take place – from constraints themselves. (Hence), it's even richer, but it is not less mechanistic! Mechanism opens a richness that in the past we could attribute only to mystery.[28]

Complexity theories, by their transdisciplinary nature, shed light on a perspective that incorporates both reductionism and constructivism together. According to Atlan and Morin, it is possible to compensate for partial portrayal of complex realities achieved with partially quantitative reductionist work via more qualitative, transdisciplinary collaboration and theorizing. It is possible to reconcile and correlate the results derived from plural methodologies into a composite picture of complex phenomena.

The success of the reductionist part of the methodology depends upon the adequacy of the method to the issue. In the case of social and environmental realms, with their highly complex social and environmental issues, many thinkers reject the use of reductionist methodologies more fully. Although even here, methodological reductionism still produces some valuable results. The biosphere is a closed system, relative to the universe, and thus various methodologically reductionist approaches are more powerful when predicting trends at the scale of the biosphere, even if they are not as powerful for predicting how the trends will play out in particular regions. This is the case in climate change research, and helps to explain how climate scientists may have a very high certainty about the probability of overall planetary dynamics – general trends of increasing moisture and energy in the atmosphere, intensifying storms, etc. While at the same time, they may have a low degree of certainty about just how and when these dynamics play out at particular regional locations.

Part of the problematic here is scientism, defined by Dupre as the exaggeration of what science can explain.[29] Leading complexity theorist, physicist and philosopher Kurt Richardson has argued that vestiges of scientism, such as an ideological view of the primacy of methodological reductionism for all realms of study, have impeded our understanding of and explanations of complexity. He has discussed the philosophical ramifications of this ideology of methodological reductionism with respect to certain kinds of studies.

The limits to understanding complex systems come not only from our inability to bootstrap from one level to another in either direction, but also from the fact that the only complete description ... must be constructed from absolutely the bottom-up (i.e., from universal superstrings upwards) rather than from the top, or middle, down. This does not deny the possibility of developing useful and relatively robust knowledge from starting points other than the consideration of everything. In a simple, cellular automata experiment, for which perfect compositional knowledge is known, the future development can only be determined fully if the model itself is run. If we start with limited knowledge of some future development we can never be sure that a model obtained by working backwards will be accurate; we must have complete knowledge to build a complete model – a theoretical as well as a practical absurdity.... To dream that scientists might bootstrap from superstring to cells or social system is nothing more than that – a dream ...

Yaneer Bar-Yam, founder and president of the New England Complex Systems Institute, has shown some nuance on these issues. As a physicist, Bar-Yam is far more optimistic about our ability to understand human civilization than most experts in social theory and the humanities. Yet, he has come to admit the inherent limits of quantitative methodologies with respect to various study issues, parsing the limits of complexity science.

It should be understood that a mathematical model that is used to capture a particular aspect of two systems does not necessarily capture other aspects. Similar to qualitative analogies, the relevance of mathematical models to describing a system is limited. This is particularly true when we consider the modeling of complex systems where by their very nature simplified mathematical models cannot capture the full description or complexity of the system being modeled.[30]

Richardson explains further just what kinds of systems can be modeled and how much.

Contrary to popular belief, science is not capable of considering all phenomena. In fact, it is quite inflexible in its requirements.... Scientific methods require that an object is stable, i.e., boundaries or patterns that delimit the object from the background (the objects complement) must be stable and assumed to be real. This stability allows repetitive examinations.... Scientific knowledge can only be obtained for contexts which are incredibly stable.[31]

Thus a reductionist approach is necessary for many, many issues, including much complexity science, such as Atlan's description of "nonlinear reductionism." Reductionist methods work very well for developing cars, computers, and buildings, for instance, which are "incredibly stable," and behave in qualitatively the same way in many contexts. It is also necessary in getting a sense of the mechanisms of complex systems. Yet alone, it is not sufficient for many issues we want to better comprehend.

> Boundaries, patterns describe such systems continue to change and emerge such that the extraction of uniformities is far from a trivial matter. By their very nature, the context changes and repetitive examinations are at worst impossible, at best highly problematic. To apply reductionist science to such systems you have to fake stability. Of course this is what we really do when we look at any system – atom or ecology – but for some reason, our reductions seem to be more harmful when considering ecologies...[32]

Richardson has shown the potential for effectively modeling complex systems, as well as the limits of doing so. The best we can hope for, he suggests, are methods that allow researchers "to identify the causal loops that are primarily responsible for enabling complex behavior, for a particular study system only, during a particular period of time." From this, one can identify ways in which the system can be seen to be complicated or complex, and how it can and cannot be manipulated. But it is important to bear in mind that such models only fully work for "idealized and well-described systems."[33] While such modeling is clearly necessary with respect to many physical and biological systems – e.g., much of climate science as described by Schneider in the Introduction to this book – it becomes much harder with respect to highly complex issues, especially socioecological issues.

Yaneer Bar-Yam has noted the general principle whereby applying complexity principles to more highly complex systems will yield increasingly significant results. As he puts it, while the more highly complex systems, e.g., human civilization, pose the greatest challenge to complexity theories, this also implies that the more highly complex study systems are, the more that complexity analyses of these systems may find their greatest opportunity for contributing to our understanding.

> It is precisely the application of general principles of complex systems that can teach us about human civilization.... Rather than rejecting the qualitative analogies between human civilization [and other highly complex systems such as environmental systems] and other [simpler] complex systems, the theory of complex systems may reveal both their validity and their limitations.[34]

Analogies should not be dismissed out of hand; neither should they be taken beyond their realm of validity. In this respect, he is in accord with the transdisciplinary complexity scholars such as Edgar Morin, Stephen Jay Kline, and Kurt Richardson. Just as philosophers untrained in physics miss the depth of that field, physicists untrained in philosophy may not quite grasp why such aims are so ambitious. These kinds of gaps in understanding may be overcome as more scientists and scholars alike are more fully exposed to each others' methodologies and worldviews.

Complexification and methodological pluralism

Complexity theories for our broadest, most trandisciplinary issues seem to suggest the imperative of plural or integral methodologies. If we accept the critiques of Mitchell, Atlan, Richardson, and others about how reductionist methods can and cannot be effectively used with respect to different issues, and if we accept that natural science is still necessary to effectively exploring highly complex social and environmental issues, we must evaluate the appropriate methodologies.

By overturning the idea of a solely deterministic universe, complexity shows that another aspect of reality is constructivism. If life complexifies, if deterministic processes are conjoined with nonlinearity, feedbacks, and novel emergence, then life is not just determined but also coevolves within physical, biological and social realms, and especially in the realm of ideas, which is to say, it is in part constructed.

Jean-Louis Le Moigne, complexity theorist and collaborator of Edgar Morin, supports this constructivist view. Given Rescher's notion of complexification, and what it implies in philosophy, science, social theory and other analyses, one major result, says Le Moigne, is the centrality of constructivism to highly complex spheres of the world – social and environmental affairs. If reality is becoming more complex, branching, evolving, and emerging into novel shapes and forms, then determinism is only part of the puzzle. Determinism becomes distortional if we start to overlay it on the whole puzzle. In other words, there are non-deterministic or partially deterministic processes involved in emergence, self-organization, and the evolution and complexification of life, and constructivism helps to captures this.

In some cases, this perspective on the conjoining of reductionism and constructivism can be understood directly via analysis of major complexity principles. Pure linearity gives way to both nonlinearity and recursivity or feedbacks. Pure atomism gives way to nested hierarchies and networked causalities. In the modern worldview, singular words or ideas could be seen as iconic, a simple model of richer, greater complexity. Whereas within the complex perspective, as Derrida famously noted, words are understood not as iconic, but as symbolic, acknowledging that they are but partial, reductionist, and thus partially incomplete representations of a more polyvalent, continuously co-constructed realm of ideas.

As Jean-Louis Le Moigne has argued, the constructivist aspect of complexity carries certain epistemological and methodological consequences. Table 6.1 adapts and expands upon a similar table by Le Moigne.[35] To more fully grasp complex dynamic systems, a purely analytical process, or purely reductionist breakdown of subjects into isolated pieces, even complex pieces, must be replaced by methodologies and viewpoints that are both analytical and synthetic or dialectical. Similarly, reductionism, the study of parts, must be conjoined with

Table 6.3 Epistemological foundations and methodological consequences of constructivism

Simplifying concepts	Complexifying concepts
Linear	Recursive
Atomism	Networked causalities
Iconic	Symbolic
Analytical	Dialectical
Reductionism	Interactionism
Positivism	Constructivism
Determinism	Complexification
Ontology	Epistemology, phenomenology
Explication	Comprehension

interactionism, or the study of interactions. In this way, pure positivism gives way to a view of positivism articulated with partial constructivism; similarly, pure determinism gives way to partial determinism and the partial novelties and change inherent to complexification; and ontology is expanded by understanding it in continuous interplay with epistemology and phenomenology. Ultimately, the more ambitious, reductive aim of explication must be replaced with the humbler, more synthetic aim of comprehension.

Generally speaking, much of the early systems theories were seen to retain too much of the simplifying modernist assumptions, while complexity theories are seen to incorporate more of the latter, complex concepts. Of course the division is somewhat arbitrary, as much of the early system theories did incorporate complexity, and were important bases upon which to develop complexity theories, and much of today's complexity theories of course fall short in some ways. Ludwig von Bertalanffy for instance, included much of this perspective on philosophical complexity in his work in the 1940s. Nonetheless the arbitrary general distinction is helpful.

In the first wave of cybernetics, researchers focused on conceiving of artifacts that could "self-replicate" via mechanistic feedbacks. Psychiatrist Ross Ashby invented a self-regulating feedback-driven homeostat; mathematician John von Neumann conceived of abstract, mathematical, non-biological, self-replicating systems, culminating in his self-replicator model based on cellular automata; and Claude Shannon developed such ingeniously "self-replicating machines" as chess games and mechanical rats. These seminal works were essential to the later development of complexity theories.

Nonetheless, thinkers in science studies, philosophy of science, and philosophy of complexity, have commented on the philosophical underpinnings and dangers of extrapolating from some of the overly reductionist concepts of first-wave of cybernetics and systems theories to complex living systems, arguing that much of these theories maintained and reified the modernist principles, even while examining complex systems.

Lily Kay spelled out some of the problems associated with misconstruing different connotations of terms like information, based upon different epistemological premises and methodological treatments. Likewise, DNA on its own is not a key to life; isolated from its context, DNA is nothing but inert matter.[36] As Richard Lewontin and others have argued, one cannot replicate strands of DNA in abstraction, but only within an appropriate, protected environment, with the presence of a wide variety of complex molecular precursors, a set of protein enzymes, and a supply of chemical energy. Denying claims that DNA is the key to life, Lewontin concluded that DNA "is not self-reproducing, it makes nothing, and organisms are not determined by it."[37] DNA is just one element of the complex, dynamic processes that reproduce life.

One major point in the shift in understanding from mechanistic feedbacks to the complex feedbacks of self-organizing properties, and more generally from systems theories to complexity theories, was thanks to a frog. In a classic article on a frog's visual system, three central Macy's group researchers, Warren McCulloch, Walter Pitts, and Jerry Lettvin showed that a frog's visual system does not so much represent reality as construct it. By inference, the same appears to hold true for the human visual system. In other words, the human neural system is not uniquely formed such as to show the world as it "really" is; but rather it creates or constructs a view of reality.

While some of the authors themselves remained wedded to classical more purely realist, purely non-constructivist epistemology, the work revealed radical new implications. The young neurophysiologist Humberto Maturana, on the same research team of the frog paper, and his collaborator, Francisco Varela, used the research as a catapult us to a deeper exploration of self-organizing processes in living systems. Whereas the first wave of cybernetics focused on the more myopic concept of feedbacks and reflexivity in machines, the introduction of constructivism allowed researchers to envision the deeper principles, regarding the way that feedbacks are related to the processes of self-organization. The researchers wired the frog's brain to measure the strength of neural responses to various stimuli. The wired-up frog's brain reacted weakly to large, slow-moving objects, and strongly to fast, small, erratically moving objects, e.g., flies. In other words, through evolution the brain adapted to distinguish flies from the background environment of water, rocks, and leaves. As Hayles writes, "The results implied that the frog's perceptual system does not so much register reality as *construct* it."[38] As the original researchers noted, their work "shows that the [frog's] eye speaks to the brain in a language already highly organized and interpreted instead of transmitting some more or less accurate copy of the distribution of light upon the receptors."[39] Maturana drew upon these results to formulate the maxim central to a constructivist epistemology, "Everything said is said by an observer."[40]

The scientists involved did not themselves necessarily embrace the radical implications. According to Hayles, McCullough appears to have remained wedded to a strong or naïve realist epistemology.[41] I emphasize the degree of realism, since, again, the epistemology emerging from complexity studies is not anti-realist, but rather brings to light an epistemological position that conjoins realism and constructivism.

This conjoining of the realist and constructivist positions, with the concurrent intertwining of objectivity and subjectivity, becomes even more poignant in a later article in which Maturana and Varela break clearly with the prevailing assumptions of scientific objectivity. Researching color vision in other animals, including birds and primates, Maturana found that they could not map the visible world of color onto the activity of the nervous system. "There was no one-to-one correlation between perception and the world. They could, however, correlate activity in an animals' retina with its *experience* of color."[42] In other words, the sense receptors internal to the eyeball were self-organizing to construct perceptions based on light patterns. Thus, via input from the external world, sight was actually constructed via self-organization within the eyeball. Therefore, Maturana had found one more proof of Kant's position. As Maturana put it, "No description of absolute reality is possible."[43]

There are numerous implications to this philosophical shift. Among others, it argues against any version of pure teleology, as Hayles points out. This is worth citing at length:

> Information, coding and teleology are likewise inferences drawn by an observer rather than qualities intrinsic to autopoietic processes. In the autopoeitic account [of Maturana and Varela], there are no messages circulating in feedback loops, nor are there even any genetic codes. These are abstractions invented by the observe to explain what is seen; they exist in the observers' "domain of interaction" rather than in self-organization, or "autopoiesis" itself, "the genetic and nervous system are said to code information about the environment and to represent it in their functional organization. This is untenable, Maturana and Varela noted. "The genetic and nervous systems code processes that specify series of transformation from initial states, which can be decoded only through their actual implementation, not descriptions that the observer makes of an environment which lies exclusively in his cognitive domain. Similarly, "the notion of information only applies within his cognitive domain," The same applies to teleology. "A living system is not a goal-directed system; it is, like the nervous system, a stable state-determined and strictly deterministic system closed on itself and modulated by interactions not specified by its conduct. These modulations, however, are apparent as modulations only for the observer who beholds the organism or the nervous system externally, from his own conceptual (descriptive) perspective, as lying in an environment and as elements in his domain of interactions.
>
> (Hayles 1999, citing Maturana and Varela 1980)[44]

The epistemological shift here reveals the centrality of the observer and the context, and the significance of not just local dynamics, but also greater system-scale dynamics of emergence and self-organization. This philosophical stance is found not only with respect to physical and living systems, but also social systems, ideas, and meaning. The early systems theorists and cyberneticians used the terms feedbacks, recursion and reflexivity to refer to systems but not yet complex systems. Now, in the new era of complexity theories based in self-organization, I use the term reflexivity in the general sense, a synonym for complex dynamic feedbacks with significant parallels across the realms of knowledge. Moreover, reflexivity also engages with and brings in aspects of the other complexity principles – hierarchies, networks, and nonlinearity. It should be noted that reflexivity has become even more widely used in social theory than in philosophy. Of course, there is a fuzzy line between much of the literature categorized as social theory and philosophy; a great deal of social theory is devoted to the works of great philosophers, and most of today's great philosophers, especially Continental and constructivist philosophers, grapple with social issues. In understanding the reach of complexity concepts and their transdisicplinary links, these intersections and resonances are worth exploring.

Narratives

Timothy F. H. Allen, theoretical ecologist and founder of ecological hierarchy theory, has put forward one perspective on methods for conceptualizing socio-ecological issues: the narrative. A narrative is a theoretical context within which more reductionist views can be interpreted. According to Allen, a narrative is a set of elaborate scaling operations that make things of different sizes commensurate – earthquake, pestilence, and drought. You can make them commensurate by turning them into events. Thus, generally speaking, the point of science is to improve the quality of the narratives it tells. It uses models to do this, but it also uses narratives. Ultimately, science tells stories. In this perspective, Allen appears to take us a step forward in showing an intrinsic interrelationship between quantitative and qualitative methods. It's not just that we need them both, but also, that they are in many ways already intertwined, and we benefit from making this more explicit.

Allen's recent work develops complexity principles such as hierarchies and feedbacks, as well as overall complexity theories regarding socio-environmental issues. Allen draws upon Robert Rosen's definition of complexity: a system is complex when it cannot be modeled. In other words, you cannot "fully" model it; of course you can model it, but you will inevitably lose some of the complexity in the modeling. Simply put, all models are attempting to model some aspect of complex systems, yet none can capture the full complexity of the system without being so elaborate as to copy the system, which is impossible. It is in this sense that Rosen and Allen argue that complexity is that which cannot be modeled. Paul Cilliers concurs in his groundbreaking *Complexity and Postmodernism*. While he states that complexity is that which can be modeled, he follows with the caveat that no complex system can be *fully* modeled, due to the extent, degree and rate of change of complexity in most systems.[45]

A system cannot be modeled, says Allen, when:

• individual parts have multiple identities – e.g., the labels of both "citizens" and "terrorists"

- units of measurement are incommensurate
- scale changes become so large as to have qualitative implications – as in gas liquification
- adequate description demands more than one level of analysis – with the vast majority of systems, only by including an upper level, constraining context, can we give a full description of the lower level, and, generally speaking,
- the adequate description of a system demands multiple levels of analysis.[46]

While reductionism and models are fundamental components of knowledge production, in fact, argues Allen, in the instance of highly complex issues, one may require lots of reductionism and models, but in order to interpret that data, one must also and primarily contextualize those models, through the use of narratives.

Kurt Richardson discusses this view, noting how surprising this perspective can initially be to scientists whose training is steeped in the primacy of quantification. As Richardson says,

> To suggest that science, particularly physics, is metaphorical in nature would be verging on blasphemous to some scientists who wish to distinguish their efforts from the "soft" ways of social science, or the humanities. Maybe this is because "[m]etaphors are often construed to be 'as-if' devices and hence to have no place in a proper scientific description of the world which pretends to tell things as they are."[47]
>
> I personally know a number of natural scientists that would be deeply offended at the accusation that science is no more than metaphor. But they need not be so defensive. Science is obviously one of the most successful metaphors ever constructed.[48]

Explaining both scientific and literary methods in terms of narrative, which carry with them metaphors and analogies, indicates the commensurability between scientific and literary methods. One could say in this sense, that a model is a synonym for a narrative, or more specifically that a model is a scientific form of narrative, and a persuasive essay is a literary form of a model. Addressing what they see as the fuzzy line between models in the natural sciences and social theory, many transdisciplinary theorists such as science and technology scholars have shown that no scientific process is devoid of the biases, worldviews, and values of the scientist, which may skew the choice, procedure and delineation of her scientific research. And great novelists also embed models in their stories and narratives. This may be less evident to scientists for whom the study at hand appears to be entirely separate from the observer or the context, as in much of physics. Yet, even in physics, there are instances in which the observer influences the observed.

To some degree then, issues revolving around the observer in the system and commensurability are significant in all of the disciplines. In a sense, the natural and social sciences as well as the humanities are all ultimately engaged in the same process and ultimately limited and falsified to some degree by the constraints between our observations, perceptions, and interpretations, and the much greater complexity of the real world. Thus, quantitative and qualitative, mathematical formulae and language, all three realms of knowledge involve narrative.

For Allen, the role of models and narratives is multifold. Models improve the quality of narratives, such as the structural quality, give quantified precision to narratives, provide unequivocal constraints, explicate boundary conditions, define dynamical qualities, emerge from alternatives, and challenge the narratives on which they are based.

True narratives for science must be compatible with what we know or suspect happens. But that does not make a story true. A full chronicle would not only be impossible to capture, it would also no longer be a narrative. It would be a precise copy, which is abstract and impossible to model or narrate. If no decisions for a narrator exist, then there is no story! Thus, narratives are not about objective or absolute truth. They are about conveying interpretation and experience. What narratives do is to develop commensurate experience, not of an external observed object, but of unified observer-observation complexes. Narratives link incommensurate situations. Modeling without a narrative is dangerous. Complex thinking links narratives to models, so as to find trans-disciplines to address our highly dynamic, postmodern world.

In this way, Allen highlights another quite significant role of complexity theories – they have the capacity to link narratives to models. That is to say, they provide a way of communicating and coordinating between the quantitative and qualitative methodologies. Allen's work illuminates ways in which science and philosophy are inextricably intertwined, and must be understood as such. In this way, the concept of narratives may provide clues about how to surpass the culture gap between the natural and social realms.

Richard Norgaard and Paul Baer make a similar argument in their article, "Collectively Seeing Complex Systems: The nature of the problem."[49] They argue that reductionism cannot account for essential aspects of biological and social systems, therefore a more adequate grasp of highly complex systems must come from collective and collaborative efforts between large groups of scholars from many disciplines. Norgaard for instance participated in the use of collaboration and the integration of plural epistemologies and transdisicplinary knowledge, collaborative efforts to better "see complex systems" in his work on the Millennium Ecosystem Assessment.

In the end, scientists and scholars of all disciplines are needed to engage in a kind of complexity thinking wherein science interpreted in narratives is applicable to compelling social issues. Complexity is a new frontier, wherein humanity must be bold enough to break with the past, and dare to imagine beyond simple, if complicated, analyses. Complexity matters, claims Allen, for the survival of the most important human enterprises, and a mastery of it may even be required for a continued civilized existence.

Many complexity scientists have made advances in seeing how the very underlying implications of complexity theories may help us to reconcile the seemingly yawning two cultures gap. This appears to be very useful, not necessarily simple. As Morin, Hayles, Allen, and others have indicated, the implications of revealing the complexity of humans and societies is an ambitious enterprise that requires a thorough refutation and overturning of many modernist assumptions.

As Yaneer Bar-Yam noted, "It should be emphasized ... that there is a realm beyond which science cannot go." According to eminent molecular biologist Richard Strohman of the University of California at Berkeley, "So great is the complexity of a single cell, that science cannot even fully understand it.... How could that science ever 'understand' issues that are vastly more complex in natural and social systems?"[50] Complexification provides sufficient grounds to illustrate the many constraints and limits of human knowledge. Along with the philosopher Nelson Goodman, we might ask, "How do you go about reducing ... James Joyce's world-view to physics?"[51]

Conclusion

Complexification sheds light on the seeming paradox that super computers can now cope with highly sophisticated models, and yet at the same time, as our societies and knowledge become increasingly complex, we become more aware of various limits to knowledge.

Complexification has various ramifications. In brief, where there are limits to science and limits to knowledge, there are degrees of inevitable and perpetual uncertainties, ignorance, error and unknowability. While it may not at first appear so, acknowledging unknowability may be less of a bane than a boon, as it supports the need for complexity theories and complex thinking. Complexification appears to highlight, validate, and further a complex worldview that overcomes scientism, technocratic, and bureaucratic thinking, and promotes the advancement of ethics and responsibility.

I have argued that complexification provides sufficient grounds to argue that complexity theories have significant repercussions throughout many debates in philosophy. Complexity theories are important not just to the substance of major debates in philosophy, but to their articulation and development. While I have lacked the space to explore this deeply here, I hope that this brief overview offers a few insights into the potential implications of complexity to philosophy, and philosophy to complexity.

7   Complexity in ethics

When justice perishes, human life on Earth has lost its meaning.

Immanuel Kant

Injustice anywhere is a threat to justice everywhere. We are caught in an inescapable network of mutuality, tied in a single garment of destiny. Whatever affects one directly, affects all indirectly.

Martin Luther King Jr., Letter from Birmingham Jail, 1963

We are losing the moral foundation on which this country and our democracy were built.

Robert Reich, Former US Labor Secretary, Mario Savio Memorial Lecture given to Occupy UC Berkeley, November 15, 2011

Given the positive feedbacks associated with commerce, it is no accident that mercantile ethics have now displaced almost all other ethical systems in the industrial world.

Timothy F. H. Allen, Joseph Tainter, and Thomas Hoekstra[1]

Ethics is the search for the common good.

Aristotle

Complexity advances ethics. After all, if we concur that, generally speaking, both our societies and our knowledge of the world are complexifying through continuous processes of feedbacks, emergence, self-organization, and multifaceted coproduction and coevolution, then it would seem that we should integrate these realities into the ethical and political realms. Given that complexity theories apply throughout all reality and thus all disciplines; given that in doing so they provide needed transdisciplinary insights; given that they appear to move beyond the classical paradigm of knowledge, acknowledging and adjusting for the fact that knowledge is not "being completed," but rather complexifying; given, in short, that science, social theory and philosophy all are adapting to more fully incorporate complexity; and finally, given that resolving the greatest challenges of our era requires this new perspective; should it not be the case that a similar shift to this new framework must occur in the realm of ethics?

While complexity appears to be relevant for all the realms of ethical theory –
meta ethics, normative, and applied ethics – in this chapter I focus on applied
ethics for sustainability. I explore the way the complexity framework may
advance ethics; how disparate complexity principles are already being articulated in various prominent contemporary ethical theories; and finally, how conjoining multiple complexity principles often strengthens ethical theory.

My aim is not to look at all the ways that complexity informs ethics, or a full
critique of some the causes of environmental crises. Rather, my aim is to focus
on how my one framing of complexity principles for sustainability summarized
in Table 2.4 has already contributed to applied environmental ethics.

Obviously, complexity is not the only aspect of applied ethics for sustainability.
Various perennial issues of human behavior drive our current global crises, including fear, greed, exploitation, domination, violence, usurpation, deceit, wishful thinking, insanity, and evil, to name a few. There may be little connections between the
complexity principles I focus on in this book, and these other common drivers of
our global crises. However, replacing modernist simplifications with a richer view
can help to acknowledge threads of overly simplistic thinking, such as myths,
assumptions, ideologies, and simple ignorance of unknowns, and how these impact
social narratives. These may also feed into challenges of the human experience such
as fear, greed, and oppression.

Complexity ethics

A very few scholars have touched very briefly on the notion of how complexity
might inform ethics. Even fewer have touched on the way that transdisciplinary
or generalized complexity more systemically illuminates ethics.[2]

The complexity framework provides one perspective to applied ethics, which
appears to be especially valuable to issues of social and environmental global
change. These principles already have been important to ethical theory, and
merit more comprehensive and explicit study. I do not venture here into any
grand project of developing complexity ethics. Asking about a "new ethics"
seems to be the wrong question.

What we need is a continued synthesis and advancement of the existing canon
of applied ethical theories. I show here how complexity has been utilized successfully in existing ethical theories, showing patterns and possibilities for synthesis and advancement.

Clearly, the exponential increase in societal complexification in the last
century has contributed to our current, largely novel set of global crises. This
novelty is often stated as a reason to develop a "new" ethics. Various change
processes – the acceleration of scientific, technological, and organizational
change in contemporary societies, as well as corporate globalization, and rapid
resource depletion – bring up novel challenges to ethics. Yet, as I hope to show
in this chapter, we already have a rich trove of ethics with which to proceed.

If the planet is composed of highly complex enmeshed social and ecological
systems and processes, then ethics for global sustainability must be rich enough

Table 7.1 Complexity framework for ethics (same as *Table 2.4*. Complexity and sustainability framework)

Complexity Principles I: Complex dynamic systems	Complexity Principles II: General for many issues including sustainability	Complexity Principles III: Particularly for social and environmental sustainability
Nonlinearity	Rate, unpredictability, rapid change, surprise, thresholds, tipping points	Irreversibility, nonrenewability, cradle to grave accounting, long-term thinking
Feedbacks	Dynamic processes, uncertainty, unknowability, degrees of risk, probability	Social and environmental thresholds, tipping points, rapid change, and abrupt change
Networks	Network causality, networked consequences, coevolution, coproduction, unintended consequences, counterproductivity, interactions, interdependence	Environmental and social interdependence, myriad coevolving social and environmental crises, full systems accounting, synergistic approaches
Hierarchy	Observers, contexts, disciplinarity, interdisciplinarity and transdisciplinarity, systems boundaries, degrees of openness/closure, scale, grain	Physical, environmental and social contexts, levels, and transdisciplinarity
Emergence	Complexification, coherence, novelty, codes, constraints, evolution, species differentiation, human individuation, identity, autonomy, culture, meaning	Human learning, adaptation, strategy, and change, e.g., changes in human impact on societies and environments
Self-organization	Life, reproduction, dynamic disequilibrium, vulnerability, subjects, subjectivities, identity, autonomy, creativity, vision, epistemological and methodological pluralism of both quantitative and qualitative, reductionism, constructivism and narratives, precaution, proaction, crisis, opportunity, and wisdom	Collapse, resilience, and sustainability in social and environmental systems, limits to growth, degrowth, and regrowth, limits to natural resource depletion, and learning and self-organization for changes in ideas, policies, lifestyles, worldview and current and future societal visions

to capture and represent this. If our goal is an ethics capable of biospheric issues, then we need a framework realistic for all scales, from local to planetary, and for this the complexity framework provides a rich reference. And if our aim is sustainability, and we are seeking simple ethical principles, then we must seek these within a realistically complex context of human and environmental affairs.

Applied ethical theories and complexity principles

Environmental ethics of the past and present, indigenous environmental norms, cooperation and the commons

Needless to say, indigenous societies have practiced environmental ethics with considerable success many times and places, throughout human history. While indigenous peoples did conduct much hunting to extinction, and anthropologists have debunked the myth of the "noble savage," nevertheless numerous examples of successful and sophisticated local, indigenous environmental management inform our efforts today. Examples include detailed specific indigenous knowledge of ethnobotany in the rainforests, and intricacies regarding, for instance, utilizing sparse resources for curing meats and hides in the Arctic regions. Increasingly, interdisciplinary environmental scientists and scholars are drawing on such sophisticated indigenous knowledge developed over millennia, which may inspire us into the future.

The literature on indigenous knowledge informs various areas of contemporary applied ethics and interdisciplinary study of environmental change. We might see other areas of sustainability literature as extensions in various ways upon the wisdom of indigenous knowledge and norms. For instance, one example is the interdisciplinary applied focus of Elinor Ostrom's work on commons pool resources (CPR) management.

Garrett Hardin famously argued that people inevitably tend to destroy commons resources and therefore must be coerced into compliance. Ostrom and others' recent work on local community self-organizing and self-governance shows that thinkers like Thomas Hobbes, Thomas Malthus, and Garrett Hardin were wrong about ethics and governance on two counts. They were wrong to construe human interactions as inherently or dominantly cruel, and wrong to thus conclude that coercion is necessary. What Hobbes, Malthus, Hardin, and many other economists and political scientists leave out is one of the central and most gratifying lessons of complexity theories – the human capacities to learn, understand, adapt, and to create new ideas, worldviews, and strategies. This opens up a promising ethical perspective, one of expected and ongoing community cooperation, proven by a long history of such successes.

Ostrom extracts general theories and specific models of cooperative strategies, and shows how they repeatedly debunk the inevitability and determinism embedded in Hardin's tragedy of the commons theory. Ostrom refutes Hardin by showing that people in fact often resolve common pool resource struggles successfully. In fact, successful environmental ethics has often been the norm.[3]

Specifically, Elinor Ostrom created several frameworks and typologies of the ways in the tragedy of the commons in fact does not occur, and explores role models of successful strategies from which we can discern models and principles for constructive, cooperative self-governance. She looked, for instance, at specific case studies of CPR management by communal tenure in meadows and forests, water rights like irrigation, and fisheries, all occurring in different types of societies around the world. She focused on small-scale communities, of 5,000 to 50,000. When local communities have the freedom and capacity, they often tend towards an ethics of cooperation and common efforts in resource management.

A major challenge comes in when articulating extrapolations from past local successes to potential larger-scale regional and planetary successes today. Yet, even at the planetary scale there have been major successes of CPR management, based in successful environmental ethics. One could point to a few recent international treaties that have been, up until now, largely effective in protecting even planetary commons spaces. The Montreal Protocol successfully and swiftly allowed for international action to reduce ozone in the atmosphere.

Local and larger scale legal efforts are both necessary. The International Treaty of the Seas was signed in 1982 and effective in 1994. If we could effectively adjudicate the commons of the seas, then it is possible to successfully adjudicate, cooperate and change our habits with respect to other global commons, for instance, the atmosphere. Yet, while in 1994 we succeeded to create an international law of the oceans, on paper, in practice, by 2011 scientists announced that we may soon be losing most of the life of the oceans. International efforts require compliance based in both local and global ethics.

Land ethics, ecocentric ethics, deep ecology

Aldo Leopold's essay "The Land Ethic" (1949), lays out the basis for developing an ethics of complex human and natural systems.[4] The land ethic is based on the story of one mountain ecosystem. Characters in the story include the plants, trees, small animals, large animals – wolves, deer, hunters – and people enjoying nature for reasons of scientific research, recreation, and aesthetic enjoyment. Yale Professor Stephen Kellert would later expand on the benefits of nature to humans, including: biophilia, sense of place, spiritual enjoyment, psychological health, and other factors.

As such, Leopold's starting point is framing ethics on complex dynamic systems themselves, focusing on integrating issues of dynamics within and across networks and hierarchies; cognizant and inclusive of plural interdependent subjects; and aware of the core issues of sustainability, such as reversibility and renewability, and the need for humility in the face of complex "cogs and wheels," of which we are faced with considerable uncertainties and unknowns. The microscopic and macroscopic complexity lenses bring the truly profound complexity of what Leopold called in 1949 the "cogs and wheels" into greater relief. From subatomic protons, to quarks, leptons, and wave particles, to the magnitude of unknown universal dark matter, we are increasingly clear about the degree of uncertainties and unknowns.

The central ethical principle of the Land Ethic holds that: "A thing is right when it tends to preserve the integrity, stability and beauty of the biotic community. It is wrong when it tends otherwise." Four excerpts from Leopold's Land Ethic help to explain this further.

> [A] land ethic changes the role of Homo sapiens from conqueror of the land-community to plain member and citizen of it. It implies respect for his fellow-members, and also respect for the community as such.[5]

> The ordinary citizen today assumes that science knows what makes the community clock tick; the scientist is equally sure that he does not. He knows that *the biotic mechanism is so complex that its workings may never be fully understood*[6] (my italics).

> Perhaps the most serious obstacle impeding the evolution of a land ethic is that our educational and economic system is headed away from, rather than toward, *an intense consciousness of land*. Your true modern is separated from the land by many middlemen, and by innumerable physical gadgets. He has no vital relation to it; to him it is the space between cities on which crops grow...[7]

> Wilderness is a resource, which *can shrink but not grow*. Invasions can be arrested or modified in a manner to keep an area usable either for recreation, or for science, or for wildlife, *but the creation of new wilderness in the full sense of the word is impossible*.[8]

In each of these citations, Leopold evokes the shift from modernist to complex thinking. Interwoven in these passages, one finds many of the implications of the complexity framework identified in this book: the shifting relationship of authority between the science and ethics; issues of highly complex systems, uncertainty, and unknowability; the nature of dovetailing, coevolving forces of complexification and the ideology of modernism have led increasingly into a sense of alienation, isolation, and confusion; the limits of the natural world, non-renewability, irreversibility and restoration; the ways in which industrialization and complexification breed alienation that obscures our dependence on natural processes; and the significance of these principles for the relationship between people and nature, and for the potential for collapse or for sustainability.

Finally, in the fourth chapter, Leopold foresees the critiques of the slow growth, zero growth, and sustainable development movements to emerge 30 years later; wilderness can shrink, but it cannot grow. Indeed, he forewarned that spending billions on the Biosphere projects was a flagrant waste; humankind cannot understand the complex mechanisms of single organisms, so much less can we "create wilderness." And indeed, why bother, since the version we have is quite beautiful?

Aldo Leopold has had a tremendous influence on contemporary environmental ethics. The French philosopher Catherine Larrère explains the evolution of environmental ethics from the 1970s through the 1990s, with two early branches: biocentrism and ecocentrism. The prior acknowledged the intrinsic value of all biological beings. The latter, following Leopold's example, expanded upon this to acknowledge the instrinsic value in the greater biotic community, and the ethical principle that follows form this, that we have obligations to all other members of the community.[9] And we must underscore, to value the greater biotic community is to value complexity, including the complexity that we cannot grasp of our most fundamental needs – all the myriad processes of self-organization, emergence and being, which we do not fully comprehend.

In this way, Larrère reveals and describes the incorporation of greater complexity at the heart of ecocentrism. By placing the focus on the entire environment, ethical theory must move beyond the atomistic, individualist moves of earlier ethical theories. By treating the larger scale of environments, ecologies and humans included, we are forced to frame ethics so as to address not just singular entities or relationships, but the entire web of interrelationships, with all the networks of realities that this entails.

By shifting the basis of ethical concern from parts and partial relationships to wholes and all relationships, ecocentrism shifts from interdictions to harming individual parts, to principles for maintaining wholes, argues Larrère. As she puts it,

> In contrast to the deontological biocentric ethics, which primarily put forth interdictions (what one could call a "don't touch" principle), ecocentric ethics is an ethics of good practices, of good habits for human conduct in the natural world: those that Aldo Leopold presents in the essays in *A Sand County Almanac*. Ecocentric ethics permits links between respect for community members and the entire community, along with responsibility of those within it. What then, can ecocentric ethics bring to ethics, more anthropocentric, or more pragmatic, with respect to responsibility? Essentially, this brings us the capacity to situate ourselves in the natural world of which we are a part and to represent nature to ourselves. Yet, contrary to how it is often presented, ecological problems or environmental protection do not pose a conflict between humanity and nature (e.g., people against wolves, bears, etc....) but poses the question of knowing in what nature we want to live.[10]

Larrère considers the context of the evolution of environmental ethics in the United States, which has flourished in response to the human genocide and ecological devastation of what was a vast and rich wilderness, Native Americans included, at the time of conquest.

Regardless of the ways in which the coevolving techno-natural world of cities is more or less complex than wilderness areas, one can understand Leopold's development of ecocentrism as a prescient early response to the massive changes with the spread of complexifying and intensifying population, science, techno-logy, and development from 1945 to today.

At this dawn of great change, in the wake of prior critiques of modernism such as the Frankfurt School which Leopold may have been aware of, Leopold hit upon the way in which coevolving systems of population, industrialization, technology, and other human systems interact with environmental systems. He saw that social networks were increasingly inextricably ensconced in a growing web of techno-urban networks. As Thoreau had proclaimed in the last century, changes in the landscape provoked seemingly irrevocable changes not only in ecosystem biodiversity and integrity, but also in the way people feel, think, and live. It was in this sense, as well, that Thoreau proclaimed that in wilderness is the salvation of the world.

In short, ecocentric ethical theory may serve sustainability better than, for instance, the biocentric alternative, by encompassing the full realities of the greater scale the theory underscores: the complexity of human and natural inter-actions and potential outlines of a more viable and adequate environmental ethics, including multiple stakeholders, healthy ecosystems, and the issues of irreversibility, vulnerability, resilience and continuous evolution, adaptation and strategy for change.

Ethical extensionism, ethics of globalization

Ethical extensionism refers to the shift in ethics from narrower to broader foci, or less complex to more complex foci. As expressed by Leopold and later developed by ethicists like Peter Singer, it is an effective way to incorporate greater complexity in ethical analyses. Leopold cuts past constraints of former ethical theories by focusing not on choices solely between people, or even socie-ties, but rather on all of the interrelationships involved in a certain area of land.

> All ethics so far evolved rest upon a single premise: that *the individual is a member of a community of interdependent parts.* His instincts prompt him to compete for his place in the community, but his ethics prompt him also to cooperate (perhaps in order that there may be a place to compete for.) The land ethic simply *enlarges the boundaries of the community to include soils, waters, plants, and animals, or collectively: the land*[11] (my italics).

The decades in which environment ethics has developed have been especially marked by the striking increase in both global population and global intercon-nectedness. Alongside and in relation to the concepts emerging from ecocen-trism, as well as parallel scholarly fields such as conservation biology (begun in the 1980s), a wave of ethicists have framed their work in terms of increasingly large-scale environmental conservation.

Yale School of Forestry and Environmental Studies professors William R. Burch and Tim Clark, for instance, have focused on the whole constellation of conflicts within a certain area of environmental conservation efforts. Clark focused on analyzing all the major stakeholders in the highly contested and often deadly battles over land management in places like rural and wilderness areas in Montana and the Rockies. While Burch focused on entire urban areas through Long-term Ecological Research Sites, such as the area of Baltimore Maryland defined by natural rather than political boundaries, e.g., the watershed. In this way Burch implemented Leopold's land ethic, revealing the necessary and intricate process of developing management strategies for communities and ecosystems within, not abstract jurisdictions, but actual, fully complex, socioecological places.

Likewise, Australian ethicist Robert Elliot articulated the nebulous and intensely conflict-ridden nature of environmental ethics on the ground, based on case studies of conservation battle sites. His essay "Environmental Ethics," discusses the ethical questions involved in the fight over Kakadu National Park in Australia's Northern Territory.[12] He starts by listing multiple interests found there, which I add to[13]:

- Important environmental landscapes – woodlands, swamps, waterways
- Saving endangered species – Hooded Parrot, Pig-nosed Turtle
- Ecosystem services – e.g., water, food, topsoil, etc.
- Recreational opportunities
- Research opportunities
- Great beauty and aesthetic enjoyment
- Spiritual significance to the Jawoyn aboriginals
- Mining interests – gold, platinum, palladium, and uranium

Kakadu National Forest has several advantages that make successful environmental management more feasible there than in many similar natural battle zones around the world. It is jointly managed by aboriginal indigenous peoples and the Australian Director of National Parks, and it is a UNESCO heritage site. Nonetheless, issues like mining, exotic species, and climate change make even this relatively protected place a site of intense battles.

Elliot hypothesizes, for instance, about the types of harm that will occur if mining were permitted in Kakadu National Park. The list encapsulates the major environmental issues of concern at the global scale, showing the network causalities and global commonalities by which each environmental struggle is significant in the greater goal of biospheric sustainability. Mining diminishes some crucial ecosystem functions and destroys others. Over the necessary long-term rates and scales, mining spurs vicious cycles of social and environmental degradation. While financial and social gains are short-term, over the long-term, mining contributes to biodiversity loss and species extinctions, which lead to further degradation of the environment, which leads to increases in endangered species, foreshadowing further extinctions. Various opportunities for advancement in local communities and the international community are reduced, compromised, or destroyed. Spiritual significance to one stakeholder group is destroyed, and in the end, the mining profits only a small group of individuals and not the community at large.

He concludes with a list of possible harms if mining were to be permitted in Kakadu Park, which again, I adapt and add to[14]:

- Important landscapes will be degraded or destroyed; it will pollute rivers, poison wildlife, and endanger more species
- Species will become extinct; biodiversity will decrease
- Ecosystem services will be disrupted, degraded, diminished, or destroyed
- Naturalness of the place will be compromised
- Recreation opportunities will be reduced
- Research opportunities will be reduced
- Aesthetic opportunities will be reduced; beauty will be lessened
- Spiritual significance to the Jawoyn aboriginals will be disrespected
- Mining will profit some individuals, and probably only incur losses for locals.

Next, Elliot denominates the steps in the process of ethical analysis. One must first determine validity of at times competing or contested empirical facts regarding causes and results. Arguments regarding the facts will then only make sense against a certain kind of background. The differences in this background give rise to different assessments of what should be done. What constitute this background are such things as: desires, preferences, aims, goals and principles, including moral principles. This step reveals how much of the complication of resolving environmental management derives from the complexity of humans, with conflicting values, aims, and desires fueling conflict in most cases of conservation management.

One must sort through the various profound if rhetorical and self-evident ethical questions that result from this method of roping out an area of complex dynamic natural systems, focusing on what kinds of principles in operation may offer moral guidance in our treatment and relationship with wilderness areas.

1   Would it matter if actions caused species to become extinct?
2   Would it matter if actions caused individual animals to perish?
3   Would it matter if actions caused widespread erosion in Kakadu?
4   Would it matter if the mining turned the South Alligator River into a watercourse devoid of all life?
5   Is it better to protect Kakadu or to generate increased material wealth which might improve the lives of some people, and may harm others?
6   Is the extinction of a species alright in order to increase employment?[15]

The rhetoric highlights obvious flaws in our current economic, legal, and political systems, fostering what are – at the scale of the planet – ecocidal activities. This calls for a variety of competing, including partially overlapping, environmental ethical theories. These include: human-centered, animal-centered, life-centered, biotic and abiotic together, ecological holism, and a combination of more than one of these.[16]

Following my thesis here that an integration of key complexity principles from multiple ethical theories may be most adequate to large-scale environmental issues, consider the way in which Elliot's work is strengthened by conjoining ecocentric and human rights-centered ethics. This is essentially the ethical theory with which conservationists have now framed fights between indigenous occupants and external environmentalists in recent years. Eliot succeeds by considering and reconciling multiple interests: the interests of ecosystems, other species and the humans living within and outside of various lands. Where these conflict – for example in the common case in which people's rights or lifestyles can only be saved by degrading an ecosystem – then some kind of tradeoff or balancing is required. One should always start by seeking win–win solutions, even if sometimes these "wins" are relative, and attempts to reconcile them reveal the need for further ethics, as the obvious general case of reducing the overall human ecological footprint, particularly the very large ecological impact of elites.

In the end, while Elliot does not offer prescriptions for Kakadu National Forest, he provides one rationale for complexity-based ethics. He writes,

> If it is organizational complexity per se that makes something morally considerable then some non-living things will be morally considerable; e.g., the bodies which make up the solar system, patterns of weathering on a cliff and a snowflake. The property of having a diversity of parts constituted by complexity, constituted in a more complex, richer fashion – this may be the best criteria for moral consideration...
>
> Understanding the rainforest is a complex system with interrelationships leads us to value it as a whole more than we otherwise might. Knowing how the parts work in concert to maintain the whole might assist us in seeing it as a thing of beauty. Counting these kinds of reasons as reasons for avoiding environmental despoliation provides the basis for an environmental ethic, which reaches beyond either a human or animal centered one and possibly beyond a life-centered one as well.[17]

Finally, while he does not articulate it, he implies that there is a clear policy choice to be made in the case of Kakadu, because the harms outweigh the benefits. He states,

> It may not be correct to say that human should always come first or that preserving an ecosystem is always more important that protecting any set of human interests. Nevertheless there will be cases, such as Kakadu, where the morally appropriate policy is clear enough.[18]

Elliot follows the classic approach of the ethicist – empirical data, background analysis, specific ethical principles, and considerations about how to weigh them. He demonstrates throughout the difficulty and intricacy of the issues involved. And yet, perhaps, the proceeding analysis is detailed enough to keep from going too far awry. This is of course the nature of ethics. Ethics, like science, has limits, and resolves these limits through both rational analysis and evaluative judgment. Ethicists have always grappled with deep uncertainty; they have never had the same motivations to presume or pursue truth and certainty in the way that some natural scientists have. Rather it is presumed that in highly complex situations there may be no certainty, no way to conduct a "complete" ethical analysis, and no ultimate ethical "truths." Yet, when the survival of our societies and our species is at stake, oftentimes "the morally appropriate policy is clear enough."

Pragmatist ethics

Another approach to effective incorporation of complexity is to give more weight to pragmatism than to theory. I think of this humorously as the applied branch of applied ethics. These thinkers are primarily philosophers and ethicists by training. Andrew Light, Eric Katz, and Anthony Weston are some of the leaders of environmental pragmatism. The pragmatist school of environmental ethics developed in response to the inefficacy of two decades of environmental ethics deemed to be overly theoretical and incapable of its intended goal, saving the environment. As Light said,

> The intramural debates of environmental philosophers, though interesting, proactive, and complex, seem to have no real impact on the deliberations of environmental scientists, activists and policymakers.... It is imperative that an environmental philosophy as a discipline, address [the environmental] crisis – its meaning, its causes, and its possible resolution. [For this to occur] the fruits of this philosophical enterprise must be directed towards the practical resolution of environmental problems. Ethics cannot remain mired in long-running theoretical debates in an attempt to achieve philosophical certainty.[19]

Like scientists and social theorists, philosophers must also be explicit about the newfound logic by which complexity shifts the conversation from uncertainty to degrees of risk. In a world where uncertainty, unknowability, and complexification are the norm, ethics, like science and social theory, must, frame analyses in terms of probability in order to seek "clear enough morally appropriate policy." Through the 1970s and 1980s many applied environmental ethicists tried in vain to resolve certainty in theoretical debates. Again and again, they hit one of Morin's three walls of seeking simplicity in complex systems: the wall of uncertainty. Rather than frame for uncertainty as if it were an anomaly, we must normalize uncertainty, and thus frame for risk. Rather than denying the ubiquity of uncertainty, we must normalize policy based on the probability of risk.

The more we elaborate arguments for certainty in complex systems the more we run into the walls of both uncertainty and unknowability. However, we might refer to the typology of kinds of complexity, ascending from mechanical and physical systems as the least complex at least in relation to the human scale, through more complex biological systems, and finally the hyper-complex realms of human ideas, meaning, and emotions. Large-scale socioecological perspectives show that ethics encompasses all of the above, attempting to assess and deliberate within hyper-complex contexts of socioecological change – and in this basic sense, it is the most complex realm of knowledge. While they arrived their via different methods, this is the conclusion of, for instance, physicists and complexogists Stephen Jay Kline and Yaneer Bar-Yam.[20]

The pragmatist ethicists' move is to acknowledge that ethics shares this quality of uncertainty – and, we must add, unknowability and complexification – with science, and that this renders ethics both more significant than previously realized, even as it imbues it with more uncertainties. After all, the subject and aim of ethics, especially applied ethics, involves the most complex social and environmental processes. Again, the argument is even stronger in light of the complexity framework, which shows that ethical subjects and debates are necessarily comprised of processes that are not only imbued with uncertainties, but also highly mutable, evolving, often nonlinear processes, involving emergent, novel factors, within the context of nested hierarchies of networks, thus typically characterized by unintended consequences, as well as ripple effects, positive feedbacks, and waves of changes throughout the greater networks of societies and environments.

The shift towards complexity and the uncertainties it unearths heightens our appreciation of the interdependence and complementary roles of all of the knowledge disciplines. Complexity theories may help to reduce uncertainties where possible, but also best help to mitigate and navigate the necessary uncertainties. In this way, complexity theories highlight the solidarity between the disciplines, e.g., science and ethics. While both science and ethics necessarily are imbued with degrees of uncertainties, nonetheless we use the tool of science to know and the tool of ethics to act. In spite of its own uncertainties, ethics is one of the tools we need to grapple with scientific uncertainties in the name of policy.

Thus complexity is useful to pragmatic ethicists, whose goal is to bypass interminable uncertainty in the name of short-term action. For, after all, when are humans inactive? Complexity highlights that the world is generally highly and continuously dynamic – little in human and environmental realities is static. And the Anthropocene highlights that humans are important agents in those global dynamics. Pure precaution does not work well in our age, when human inaction is an oxymoron.

> The pragmatist goal is to find workable solutions now. Pragmatists cannot tolerate theoretical delays to the contribution that philosophy may make to environmental questions.[21]

Environmental pragmatism is the open-ended inquiry into the specific real-life problems of humanity's relationship with the environment. The new position ranges from arguments for an environmental philosophy informed by the legacy of classical American pragmatist philosophy, to the formulation of a new basis for the reassessment of our practice through a more general pragmatist methodology.[22]

Within pragmatism, one finds justifications, motivations, and goals outlined by many of the crosscutting analyses in social theory mentioned earlier in the book. In this case, many of the critiques on which the pragmatists base their work are interrelated with the growing transdisciplinary domains we have discussed, such as science and technology studies (STS), ecological economics, conservation biology, and the philosophy of science, as well as with past social theorists' critiques of modernity. For instance, some pragmatists draw upon the Frankfurt School's early critiques of the Enlightenment and modernism. Pragmatists presume such issues as the non-duality of humans and nature, the intrinsic value of all natural things, and the necessity of ecosystem services. Drawing from these lessons of the past, they aim to focus more effectively on proactive policies.

Philosophers Sandra B. Rosenthal and Rogene A. Buchholz argue that philosophical pragmatism is a critique of the modern scientific worldview, which objectifies and separates humanity and nature. Like complexity theories, pragmatism offers a "radical correction of modernity." Likewise, Bryan Norton contrasts applied and practical (or pragmatic) philosophy, appearing to reinforce my view that pragmatic ethics is the applied branch of applied ethics. In his distinction, applied philosophy tests a valid theoretical principle in a specific situation, and thus requires a commitment to theory before application. Whereas, pragmatic philosophy arises within a specific problem situation, deriving theories as needed from the context of the problem itself. The role of the pragmatic philosopher goes a step farther than most applied philosophers in addressing and resolving practical problems.

It is no surprise then that key aspects of pragmatism mirror the policy called for by many leading bodies of environmental scientists and thinkers. Key aspects of pragmatism include: the call for moral pluralism, the decreasing importance of theoretical debates, and the placing of practical issues of policy consensus in the foreground of concern. This takes on a variety of forms, such as (1) the articulation of practical strategies for bridging gaps between environmental theorists, policy analysts, activists, and the public, and (2) developing general arguments for theoretical and meta-theoretical moral pluralism in environmental normative theory.[23]

So not only do the pragmatists draw from the same sources and the same general theories as many of the transdisciplinary groups mentioned previously – science and technology studies, the theoretical ecologists, philosophy of science, etc., as well as the policy conclusions of the IPCC and the MEA to be explored in the next chapter – but they also seem to arrive at the same conclusions. The lists of criteria with respect to bridging gaps, including and negotiating between multiple stakeholders, and developing and applying theoretical pluralism, echoes the calls of these various groups – STS scholars and IPCC scientists. Ultimately, says Light, environmental pragmatism is a new strategy for approaching environmental philosophy and environmental issues. It is not a single theory or view, but rather "a cluster of related and overlapping concepts."[24]

In order to work on problem solving, Light says, one must strive for meta-theoretical compatibility between opposing theories. Here, the centrality of pluralist methodologies to complexity is rightly placed front and center in pragmatist ethics. In any multitiered, transdisciplinary ethical issues, meta-theory will need to articulate and integrate multiple theories. The commitment to solving environmental problems becomes not only the precondition for any workable and democratic political theory, but also a regulative ideal "emanating from practice" – both from environmental activism and from the development of political and normative theories. In an example of this, Light strives to reconcile ontological schools of environmental ethics, like Arne Naess' deep ecology, with materialist schools, such as Murray Bookchin's social ecology.[25] Ultimately, these are neither mutually exclusive nor incompatible; they simply require a broader, more pluralistic framework of ethical theory. For this reason, pragmatist environmental ethics strives for a "metaphysical tolerance of a multiplicity of approaches." In this way, the pragmatists hope to render environmental ethics "a relevant participant in the search for *workable* solutions to environmental problems into the next century."[26]

Light's analysis of the broader framework encompassing ontological and materialist schools of environmental ethics is a perfect example of the benefits of complexity ethics – an ethics which acknowledges that at times the broader, more complex framework facilitates a more realistic account, this involves all aspects of large-scale systems, e.g., ontological as well as materialist, and in large-scale issues, this pluralist integration becomes paramount.

In some cases, this may just indicate that there will be a certain degree of ignorance in the modeling and analysis, and this should lend caution and humility to the work. Similarly, natural scientists working on highly complex issues like climate change must seek "workable" results, while keeping in mind that there is an inherent degree of limitations to science that is greater in the case of highly complex systems. Though again, climate scientists can rely on the advantage that, relative to human and environmental affairs, the global scale is a closed system, whereas regional scales are open systems.[27] It is this degree of openness and closure that renders predictions stronger or weaker. This is why IPCC assessments can give very accurate general predictions about climate change globally, while somewhat weaker predictions about exactly how it will play out in specific places.

Thus ethics and science work in concert; where science has an advantage so does ethics. In this case, the ethics of regional climate change might be somewhat more complicated, but the ethics of global climate change is crystal clear – climate change is wreaking havoc, the planetary climate stabilization system is passing critical tipping points, and greenhouse gas emissions must be reduced. This feeds back to the regional scale. Acknowledging that global emissions must be reduced should induce everyone to do so.

Pragmatist environmental philosophers such as Light seem to have caught on to something very important – if science is plagued by uncertainty, so is ethics.

Yet that does not render either of them less significant. Quite the contrary, it renders them both all the more significant. As environmental ethicist Mark Sagoff has written:

> We have to get along without certainty; we have to solve practical, not theoretical, problems; and we must adjust the ends we pursue to the means available to accomplish them. Otherwise, method becomes an obstacle to morality, dogma the foe of deliberation, and the ideal society we aspire to in theory will become a formidable enemy of the good society we can achieve in fact.[28]

Responsibility, complexification, counterproductivity, and catastrophe ethics

A major current of thought has developed around the notion of responsibility. In recent years these thinkers have dealt increasingly with the responsibility not just to preserve the natural world, but also to prevent the catastrophe of its destruction. This work builds upon extensive ethical theories and a rich literary history addressing the central place of morality in the face of the Promethean power of human impact, such as anthropogenic climate change.

Hans Jonas' elaborate ethics of responsibility proposed a reformulation of ethics around the core concept of responsibility in all of its facets, debunking notions of utopia and absolute progress, and developing a more realistic, forward-looking perspective. His work touched upon many questions that remain central to ethics today, such as this passage that sends shivers up the spine (1979).

> Yet the combustion of fossil fuels, beyond simply causing local air pollution, also presents the problem of global warming that may enter into a strange competition with the depletion of reserves. This is the "greenhouse gas effect" that remains after the carbon dioxide that has formed during combustion accumulates at the global scale in the atmosphere and acts as the glass cover of a greenhouse, which is to say it allows solar radiation to enter, but it prevents thermic radiation from leaving the earth. A worldwide temperature elevation set off and maintained by us (beyond a certain degree of saturation this will continue even in the absence of supplementary combustion) may put in motion long-term consequences for the climate and for life, which nobody would want – all the way to the extreme possibility of the catastrophic melting of the polar ice caps, the elevation of Oceans, the immersion of great swaths of lowlands ... as such the frivolous and joyous party that humankind enjoyed during a few industrial centuries may be paid for by millennia of a transformed terrestrial world.[29]

In terms of complexity, what is striking is Jonas' acute sense of the vulnerability of the world, conjoined with a full awareness of climate change, rare in his day.

Student of Husserl, Heidegger, Bultmann, witness to both world wars, contemporary of Sartre, Arendt, and other post-World War II intellectuals, and of course writing this after the view of the Earth from the moon and the first Earth Day, Jonas was especially well placed to appreciate the fragility of both human civilization and the natural world. Additionally notable, is the way in which negotiators today still mostly use the term catastrophic only when referring to the future, while Jonas and anyone in 1979 surely qualified the melting of polar ice caps and rising of oceans – already well underway today – as catastrophic. Climate change has been so nonlinear since 1979 that our calibration of the ethical terms used to describe it is lagging increasingly far behind.

One or two generations after the rising critiques against the progress, modernity, and the lost hopes for utopia, and a generation before Ulrich Beck was to describe societies in the 1990s as crisis-ridden "risk societies," Ivan Illich described some of the peculiar ways in which progress could be unpacked. Notably, he explained the concept that directly stems from the complexification of societies, which he called "counterproductivity": the accumulation over time of unintended, nefarious consequences.

In complexity terms, Illich had touched upon the key principle of unintended consequences. Illich saw how unintended consequences become aggravated over time producing new sets of problems. He noted that as modern societies developed technologies, human lifestyles and landscapes coevolved, and this coevolution interwove in ways that were at times beneficial, but often unfortunate.

Obviously, many modern technologies were immensely beneficial, saving lives, prolonging lives, and generally improving the quality of life like nothing before in human history. But as modernity evolved, the benefits became increasingly mired in the accumulation of unintended consequences. The nature of change slowly became distinguished from the myth of absolute progress. It is increasingly evident that many innovations, once introduced into the complex context of human lives, display degrees of dysfunctionality; the intended benefits undermined by myriad intersecting consequences, some of them negative. In every domain there is a unique term for it: in medicine – side effects; in the military – collateral damage; in scholarship – contingencies. Illich studied the large-scale, global manifestations, unintended consequences and their accumulation over time, which he called, "counterproductivity."

> ...[T]he Illichienne critique throws into doubt the stronghold that the logic of detour exerts on our thinking. He who is animated by the logic of detour may fall prey to its own trap; he can forget that the detour is, precisely, only a detour. He who retrenches the better to spring forward keeps his eyes fixed on the obstacle that he wishes to surpass. If he stands back while looking in the opposite direction, he risks forgetting his objective, and mistaking his regression for progress, taking the means for the ends.[30]

As technologies, in context, have this characteristic of counterproductivity, so does our thinking suffer from counterproductivity. In the 1970s, Illich and

Jean-Pierre Dupuy conducted a study in France of people who spent more than four hours per day in a car, of which the average speed came to an astounding seven kilometers per hour. This is faster than a person walking on foot, but notably slower than a cyclist. Yet, the car owner spends a good deal of office time simply paying for the costs of the car, gas, and upkeep.[31]

> The mathematical result [of our research] implies the following: The average French person, deprived of his car, and, let's suppose, freed from the necessity of working long hours to pay for it, would spend less of his "overall time" dedicated to transport if he made all of his trips by bicycle – and we do mean, all of his trips, not only those daily trips he makes between the house and the office, but also the weekend, going to his distant country house, and at the holidays, travelling to a distant seaside. This alternative scenario would be judged absurd, impossible. Nevertheless, it would economize time, energy and nonrenewable resources, and it would amount to a lesser impact on what we call the environment. Where is the difference then which makes it that in one case, the absurdity is patent, whereas it is obscured in the other? Since, in the end, isn't it more comical to work a great deal of one's life just in order to pay for the means of transport to go to that job?[32]

Once again, reacting effectively to the environmental crisis seems to require a certain inversion of what seems logical in our everyday worlds, enmeshed in highly complex and complexifying systems. In the case of the precautionary principle, this amounts to reversing the burden of proof, reversing the order of time, and reversing assumptions about progress. In the case of ethics, one has to shift rationality from linear to nonlinear, calm to chaotic, and predictable to uncertain and prone to surprises.

In contemplating how counterproductivity can lead to catastrophe, Dupuy developed an ethical theory that turns on an inversion of time. An adequate environmental ethic entails a projection in the future in order to act as if the worst tragedy would occur, so as to prevent it. Like the authors of the prescient Club of Rome report, one has to assume the worst-case scenario in order to motivate society to perhaps not take that route.

In his book *For an Enlightened Catastrophism* Dupuy argues that we must reverse the logic of the place of the observer in time with respect to the harm or catastrophe. When the observer is in the present speculating about future harm, one utilizes wisdom, and is confronted with the difficult issue of how to cope with the probability of harm. When the observer is in the distant future – assuming harm in the near future – one also will turn to wisdom, in the sense of the need to balance conflicting ethical claims on the best way to proceed in many complex cases; however, one has a stronger rationality upon which to act than mere precaution. Once one assumes that the worst will occur, the rational choice is to take the fullest actions possible to prevent it, supposing that the ratio of probability to harm is sufficiently alarming. Here is an ethical principle designed to address the extreme events that Brian O'Neill lamented so inevitably fell out of the IPCC reports. Here is an ethical principle for climate change.

Ethics of care

The ethics of care emerged in the wake of Carol Gilligan's influential book *In Another Voice* (1982). In brief, this school of ethics holds that besides reason, duty, rationality, and responsibility, there is another driver of everyday ethical action: the natural desire to care. Ethicists aimed to develop this, expanding upon the motivation from the local to the global, from small everyday social groups and environments, to change human behaviors in larger social and environmental spheres. This is an inherent human tendency that is so obvious and yet so largely omitted from intellectual discourse. And yet, perhaps this inbuilt human tendency contributes to effectively operationalizing some of the previously mentioned ethical theories, such as ethical extensionism and Ostrom's focus on self-governance – extending care from parenthood and local community building, to our interactions with wider and wider groups of peoples and their environments.

While the ethics of care has evolved from Gilligan's original thesis about gender difference, care ethicists have developed Gilligan's idea that care is a trait upon which much of the real ethics of everyday life is based, and thus a promising basis for ethical theory. One of the key questions, for Gilligan, is how care is then linked with responsibility.[33]

Care-based ethics reflects the complexity framework in various ways. First of all, care places the full observer back into the system. By focusing on care – rather than one rational criteria or another – we immediately include the full apparatus of the human as observer and subject in the complex systems context towards which the ethical theory is aimed. There are a number of strengths in this approach. It seems to reflect some of the truth about ethics that lay dormant during the modern era when many leading ethicists attempted to base or frame ethics in rationality. As noted by philosophers throughout history, and recently by Bernard Williams, the exercise of first utilizing rationality in order to then express caring is not really how we operate, nor how we should. As Williams points out, if his wife and a stranger were both drowning, he should not have to stop to rationalize his actions, before plunging in to save first his wife and only then the stranger.

Care theory gets past such issues by recognizing that the basis of much of real life ethics involves the instinct and desire to care. The concept of care has been extended to the environment, for example in the notion of biophilia developed by Stephen Kellert and E. O. Wilson who contend that human and other creatures tend to have feelings of affection and care for other living things, across many species boundaries. Humans care about nature. While there are innumerable reasons to care for nature to a certain extent they are irrelevant, because we innately just do care about nature; we have inbuilt feelings and tendencies of love and stewardship for nature.

Second, care-based ethics is contextual. The metaphysical theory of contextuality constitutes an alternative model for moral theory. The philosopher Joan

Toronto argues that care-based ethics is one of what is called a set of "contextual" ethical theories, which eschew abstraction and require the incorporation of real actors and a real society.[34] According to Toronto, these theories are founded on certain ideas about the nature of morality that differ from the meta-ethics inspired by Kant. In any contextual moral theory, one must situate ethical questions in a concrete context, which is to say regarding particular actors in particular societies. The simple enumeration of principles is not sufficient for understanding the theory. It thus also reincorporates Aristotelian virtue theory, as the contextual ethical theory "concentrates its attention not on the morality of certain acts but on the greater moral capacity of the actors."[35] Moreover, morality cannot be determined by posing hypothetical moral dilemmas or by affirming moral principles. Rather than being based in the hypothetical, care theory is based in the moral imaginary, the character, and the capacity of each person to respond to the complexity of a given situation. Toronto considers contextual ethical theories to include: Aristotle's moral theory, and the theory of moral sentiments of the Scottish enlightenment philosophers David Hume and Adam Smith. Due to the initial interest in character, any contextual ethical theory must incorporate a portrait of the complexity of the subject.[36]

According to Toronto, modern a-contextual ethical theories utilize rational tests to verify egoistic tendencies. Hence, modern ethicists falsely identified morality with rationality. In contrast, the contextual ethicists hold that moral sensibility and moral imagination are determining factors for the ethical life. Rather than creating the ideal of being the rational actor, moral contextualism explores the individual's capacity or incapacity for moral development, based in the capacity of caring for others. The ethics of care is a framework capable of articulating the reconciliation between one's own needs and the needs of others; balancing between forces of competition and cooperation; and maintaining the network of social relations in which one is placed.[37]

Beyond the initial feminist founders of the ethics of care, other major philosophers have since taken interest. American philosopher Harry Frankfurt developed a theory of care on a greater scale than previously attempted by the original feminist authors, a veritable "metaphysics of care." In his 1988 book *The Importance of What We Care About*, Frankfurt gives the concept of care an architectonic position that largely surpasses the scope of other care ethics.

Frankfurt saw the flaws in the classical, modernist views that tried to mimic the hyper-rationality and empiricism of science in ethics. He saw the fatal pitfalls of trying to base ethics on the same rationality that had shored up the sciences. Moral philosophy had long sought to justify the oppositional objectives of good and bad, making these reference points the principle recourse, the very definition of a human and a responsible life.

In opposition to this, Frankfurt held that a metaphysics of care could allow for a major reframing, shifting away from the rationality of good and bad towards a new basis of human motivation. Frankfurt is motivated by the desire to rid morality of the primacy of various fallacious modern tenets, such as the axis of good and evil. He found in care ethics a means to avoid the pitfalls of numerous modern ethical theories: the fallacies inherent to an overreliance on rationalism, the glossing of Kantian universalism, the incommensurability inherent to utilitarian calculi, and the anemic Manicheanism that emerges from the axes of good to bad and right to wrong.

The repeated attempt in the history of philosophy to develop the axis of good and bad has simply failed, argues Frankfurt, not in a contingent way, but, rather in a more categorical way, based in moral and rationalist presuppositions that were completely unaligned with the deeper complexity of real human lives as they are concretely lived, in their diverse forms.[38]

Partnership ethics

So far I have looked at the land ethic, extensionist ethics, e.g., globalization and planetary ethics, responsibility, care, and pragmatist ethics. To borrow terms from complexity theories, each of these groups has called for a shift from more "restrained" to more "generalized" ethics. Each of these groups of ethicists is calling for an ethics that incorporates more wide-ranging complexity, with a more integral, multi-dimensional approach.

Carolyn Merchant's ethics derives from and integrates rich sources including eco-centric ethics, homocentric ethics, social ecology, deep ecology, feminist ethics, ethics of care, radical ecology, and various spiritual traditions. Most fundamentally, it synthesizes ecocentric and homocentric ethics, and in so doing debunks the false premise of egocentric ethics, the notion that "what is good for the individual is good for the society." Merchant thus disbands with the pretense of rationalization, given the tendency toward human domination and exploitation of both peoples and environments. As she wrote in 1988:

> The partnership ethic I propose for consideration is a synthesis of the eco-centric approach based on moral consideration for all living and nonliving things, and the homocentric approach, based on the social good and the fulfillment of basic human needs. All humans have needs for food, clothing, shelter, and energy, but nature also has an equal need to survive. The new ethic questions the notion of the unregulated market, eliminating the idea of the egocentric ethic, and instead proposes a partnership between nonhuman nature and the human community.[39]

In an early article on partnership ethics, Merchant notes the nexus of the process of technological complexification, the process of capitalist intensification and expansion, and the correlative increase in unsustainable extraction of natural resources and human impact on the environment. While settlers up until the 1850s merely used gill nets on the Columbia River below Portland, from the 1850s through the 1860s they added purse seines, traps, and squaw nets, catching and exploiting ever-greater quantities of fish and in the process altering ecosystem dynamics. By 1879 they had added fish wheels on the Columbia River – "like ferris wheels with movable buckets," which "operated day and night scooping fish out of the river and dumping them down shoots into large bins on the shore to be packed and slated." By 1899 she notes, there were 76 fish wheels on both sides of the river. Simultaneously, there was an increase in canning facilities, also intensifying the business. "In 1866, the canning industry began operating on the banks of the Columbia near Eagle Cliff, Washington," and by 1883, there were 39 canaries shipping to New York, St. Louis, Chicago, and New Orleans."[40]

As societies complexified, so did their societal stories and narratives. The indigenous tribe of the Pacific Northwest around the Columbia River, the Yakima, "believed there were sacred bundles of magical objects given to an individual by a guardian spirit, defined, not as rights and privileges as in the Western system, but as relationships and obligations to other human beings, to the tribe, to nature, and to the spirit world." In contrast, as most societies developed greater complexity and social hierarchies, the concepts of money and property arose and developed.

As in many places throughout the world, older systems of reciprocity, sharing and mutually binding responsibilities, care and the resulting partnership ethics, were replaced by abstract systems of money and ownership that allowed power to accumulate and fuel the expansion of empires. Likewise in the Pacific Northwest Region of the Columbia River, under laissez-faire capitalism, a mercantilist and profit-based ethic replaced the older indigenous belief system for managing the commons.

Fisheries from 1823 to the 1880s in the Pacific Northwest operated under a laissez-faire capitalist logic rooted in an egocentric ethics, based almost entirely on individualist motives. From the 1880s to the early 1900s, the fisheries employed a homocentric ethic, based more fully on social motives, and exemplified by the idea of the maximum sustainable yield. Fish wheels were outlawed and fishing times curtailed. In 1877, Washington closed the fisheries from March through August to give fish time to reproduce. Oregon followed suit in 1878. The states began to regulate the gear that could be used, the size of the nets, and the area of the river that could be fished. In 1917, purse seines were outlawed. In 1948, size regulations were imposed limiting catchable fish to those above 26 inches in length.

Yet all of these good measures were no match for the technology that would emerge next. In the 1930s, homocentric ethics called for hydropower and flood control, and thus it was thought wise to introduce dams. The limitations of homocentrism were put to the test, as the technology proved to be disastrous to one of the local people's most important food sources and natural resources: fish. In 1937, George Red Hawk of the Cayuse Indians observed, "White man's dams mean no more salmon," to which the Chief Engineer of the Bonneville Dam retorted, "We do not intend to play nursemaid to the fish." By 1940, the catch of Coho salmon was reduced from 1890 levels by 90 percent.[41]

Societal and scientific complexification spurs technologies that, introduced into the complex socioecological world, produce unintended consequences, and in Illich's term, counterproductivity. Merchant's analysis points once again to acknowledging the possible need for a medium degree of societal complexfica-tion, to achieve a reorganization of society in various realms that would help us to advance human and natural sustainability. Utilizing the key complexity prin-ciple of organization, we can begin to envision what this may look like. As Merchant writes:

> "A partnership ethic would bring humans and nonhuman nature into a dynamically balanced, more nearly equal relationship with each other.... We would instead organize our economic and political forces to fulfill people's vital needs for food, clothing, shelter, and energy, and to provide security for health, jobs, education, children and old age. Such forms of security would rapidly reduce population growth rates since a major means of providing security would not depend on having large numbers of children..."

Academic philosophy

Thus far, I have not said too much about "ethics," as in the work in most univer-sity philosophy departments. There is a consensus amongst contemporary envir-onmental ethicists that the great modern opuses on ethics are inadequate to the kinds of problems that the globalized world requires today. Nonetheless, a number of contemporary philosophers have taken up promising approaches. I mention just one here, amongst many examples.

I lack space to do justice to Thomas Scanlon's substantial work, *What We Owe to Each Other*. However, in keeping with the argument here, I wish only to signal that this is another example of a leading contemporary ethicist chipping away at the edifice of modernism and revealing the more complex face of ethics beneath. In this case, Scanlon delineates a new contractualist theory, based on more of the details and nuances of specific everyday personal choices. Scanlon focuses, for instance, on the difficulty of making ethical choices with multifac-eted causes and effects, as complex persons enmeshed in very complex social systems. As such, he frames his ethics on the intricacies of human interactions, involving, without using these terms, the principles of networks, network causal-ity, and networked complex societies. Likewise he focuses on humans as complex subjects, observers also necessarily interacting within complex dynamic systems, coping with multifaceted uncertain, unknowable, and complexifying consequences. As such, in contrast with past contractualist ethicists, Scanlon's work reveals more pluralistic and finer-grain details involved in questions of interpersonal interactions in today's highly complex globalized societies.

In a sense, although I suppose that he may never refer to it in this fashion, Scanlon's theory provides a major step towards developing what Carolyn Mer-chant has called for in partnership ethics. As she mentioned over 20 years ago in her article *Fish First!*:

> We might come back to the notion that Barbara Leibhardt-Wester proposed in her comparison of native and European Americans – the idea of the

"sacred bundle." Like the Native American sacred bundle of relationships and obligations, a partnership ethic is grounded in the notions of relation and mutual obligation.[42]

Integrating applied ethical theories for sustainability

I have explored eight of the leading areas of applied ethics today, all of which are replete with the complexity principles. In each area, we can see these theories implicitly taking up complexity principles. Yet, looking back at these theories in their greater ensemble, this becomes all the more apparent.

A pattern appears across these eight theories aimed at environmental sustainability. Each in its own way, these theories speak to the need to include complexity theories as an essential starting point. Conjoining multiple complexity principles has often strengthened applied ethical theories. Indigenous knowledge systems were built upon direct experience of ecological systems. The land ethic, ecocentrism, and the commons pool resources management literature are all based on taking account of nature and people as sets of interdependent complex dynamic systems. Extensionism, pragmatism, responsibility, care and partnership ethics,

Table 7.2 Theories of applied ethics and complexity principles they are based upon

Ethical theory	Complexity principles
Indigenous knowledge, commons pool resources management	Entire framework in knowing ecosystems; self-organization and self-governance at social scale, community norms, strategy, agency, learning, adaptation
Land ethic, ecocentrism	Entire framework: complex dynamic systems, unknowability, complexification, limits to economic growth, limits to environmental depletion, conservation, humility, wisdom
Extensionism	Networks, hierarchies, dynamics, interdependence, frame as conjoined socioecological systems (SES), weighing probabilities of risk, proaction
Pragmatism	Uncertainty, unknowability, proaction, pluralist theories and methodologies, hierarchies and networks require integral theories and meta-theories, agency
Responsibility	Vulnerability, risk, unintended consequences, counter-productivity, extreme events, proaction
Care	Contextual, observer and context, moral capacity of subjects/actors, caring inherent to interdependence and beingness
Partnership	Complex dynamics systems, integral and pluralist theories, societal self-organization for sustainability
Contractualism	Networks and network causality in complex societies, observers in complex societies, pluralism, subjectivity and agency

and contractualism each present a slightly different angle, each based on the principle of ethical consideration encompassing human and natural interactions. And each of these theories draws primarily on complexity principles in articulating its major premises and arguments.

From this one can extrapolate various general principles of how we might look at ethics, and therefore at policy approaches. The land ethic, commons pool resources and other ecocentric ethics are based in considering land areas with all their animal and human inhabitants as interdependent ensembles. According to all of the above theories, taking into account whole systems seems to be a necessary starting point for addressing sustainability.

In turn, each of the theories picks up on different complexity principles in different ways, highlighting the need for various key approaches for sustainability. Elliott for example, employing extensionist ethics, looks at types, rates, scales, and probabilities involved in weighing and understanding environmental harms over time, and how interrelated environmental issues lead to multifaceted vicious cycles of environmental and social harms. As such he highlights the many-sided impacts, network causality, and the significance of vicious versus virtuous cycles of change. By looking not just at economic or political implications, but at myriad mutually influential ecological, social, and cultural implications, the results come into clearer focus.

One could in turn examine each of the ethical theories in this light, bringing to bear on the many ways in which complexity principles serve to elucidate both the applied approach and the intended results. A list of the ways in which complexity principles then inform ethical and policy approaches appears in Table 7.3.

The power of complexity theories for ethics is multifold. Complexity theories offer us various ways to highlight and draw upon the strengths of applied ethics. They help us to move beyond classical, modernist approaches that have been obstacles to progress in ethics. Aldo Leopold saw in the land ethic a way in which to move beyond the constraints of framing ethics merely in terms of rights and duties. Carolyn Merchant saw in partnership ethics a way to move beyond the impasse of more individualistic, atomistic models. Similarly, Harry Frankfurt saw in care ethics a way to incorporate our experience as interdependent actors in a shared reality, breaking free of oversimplified rationalist ideals of the classical mindset. Seeing the threads of complexity theories running through such ethics fosters advance.

Successful implementation requires a consistent effort in moving beyond overly classical thinking, and incorporating some of the deeper lessons of complexity theories, so as not to repeat the errors of the past. We must look at the issues of environmental ethics and justice, not with the modernist perspective that teaches us to isolate, analyze, and understand, but rather with complex thinking that teaches us to conjoin comprehension of complex systems dynamics with pragmatism, understanding as much as possible, for both precaution and proaction. In the case of climate ethics, as in other areas, we may have a tendency to frame our analyses in the modernist fashion, attempting to isolate, analyze, and understand every nuance of every ethical question so that – and

Table 7.3 Complexity principles and implications for ethics and policy approaches

Complexity principles	Ethics and policy approaches
Complex dynamic systems	The complexity framework provides a good base reference for developing ethics and policy
Observer in the system; significance of context, nested hierarchies	Multi-scalar and multi-grain analyses; transdisciplinary framework analysis at least iteratively
Interdependence	Symbiotic solutions, virtuous cycles, win-win-win, problematization
Network causality	Network analysis
Feedbacks	Incorporate extreme events
Uncertainty, unknowability	Probability of harm, weighing of evidence
Dynamic, changing, evolving	Iterative, expect uncertainty
Pluralistic methodologies and approaches	Broad ethics and policy frameworks based in the complexity framework
Unintended consequences, counterproductivity	Precaution and proaction, self-organization for common good, self-governance of commons
Nonlinear change, thresholds, tipping points	Inclusion of low probability, high impact events
Resilience, vulnerability, sustainability, potential collapse	The complexity framework is a basis for developing broad-based perspectives and wisdom

there is the false logical leap – knowing all of these particularities will somehow enable us to address all of them in their ensemble and on the global scale.

Rather, complexity principles demonstrate that we need to pay attention to how processes are operating at all scales, including the larger scales. Highly logical approaches to ethics will not build up from the smaller to larger scales. Contemplating common utilitarian thought experiments about which trolley switch to pull or not to pull, or how many Indians it may be morally correct to kill in order to save other Indians may be informative in some ways. But they do not build up to an understanding of the dynamics of global change. For large-scale global issues, for sustainability, ethics necessitates an acknowledgment of our role and impact as actors in innumerable networks and hierarchies of inter-dependent complex, dynamic systems.

The expansion of ethics, the limits to ethics, and the increased need for ethics

Looking at these eight theories together highlights the importance of interde-pendence, pluralism, and the increasing recognition of network causality and interrelated, interdependent ethical and policy solutions. Moreover, the interre-lated nature of both environmental and social problems and solutions shows the importance of care, dialogue and partnership, and construing issues in terms of commons pool resources and the common good, for environmental ethics and policy. As Catherine Larrere said,

> The choice is not between humans and nature, but between a uniform world modeled solely on economic interests, and a diverse world that leaves space for the plurality of human aspirations, lifestyles and approaches to be seen within the context of a plurality of living beings. From this point of view, ecocentric ethics, which has the ambition of integrating human activities within the natural environment, can provide models of action.[43]

In the case of climate change, for instance, in just the last decade, this centrality of socioecological systems, complexity, pluralism and participatory structures of democracy, in ethics and politics, has moved from scattered and marginalized to central, the consensus view. Construing environmental issues in terms of complex dynamic systems and interactions, and coupled socioecological systems, has become the consensus view not only amongst ethicists and most social and political theorists, but also amongst scientists, policymakers, the IPCC, and other organizations most implicated in global environmental change. In science and technology studies, Harvard professor Sheila Jasanoff defends it; in biology and ecology, C. S. Holling and Timothy F. H. Allen support it; in climate science, F. Stuart (Terry) Chapin and James Hansen argue for it; and in ethics and philosophy, leading thinkers like Thomas Scanlon in academic philosophy and Andrew Light in pragmatist philosophy, all support this emerging view. Indeed, across the disciplines working on sustainability and ethics, increasing numbers rally around these views. Thus, even while the central terms like complexity theories and complex thinking have not yet been widely employed, the details and implications of complexity theories for ethics have had a major influence on academia, policy circles, and an array of social institutions.

This position, which recognizes complexity and supports pluralistic views and participation in ethical theory, is challenging. As noted, acknowledging complexity and complexification requires a recognition that there are limits to science. Upon further examination, it also reveals that there are limits to ethics. Indeed, the more we examine complexity in every realm of human knowledge, the more we see how all realms of knowledge are riddled with uncertainty and unknowability, and how each one has limits.

However, this does not dilute the power of ethics. A curious kind of see-sawing takes place, in which at first it seems that science cedes power to ethics, and then it seems that ethics cedes power back to science, as we alternately run up against the limits in either system. In the end, a new vision is emerging in which science is revalidated, but with serious caveats as to a new framing in which the limits of science may militate against spending any amount of resources on its endless expansion. In turn, just as we see that ethics does have limits, we also reaffirm its power, and its essential relationship to science and technology. In many situations, especially highly complex socioecological situations, despite its limits, ethics nonetheless takes on new power and validation.

In the case of highly uncertain and complex global change, ethics becomes all the more essential.

Ethics is not a choice but an aspect of our reality. All of our actions will have impacts, and failure to choose is itself a choice. In a complexifying world, with a multilayered tangle of social, environmental, economic, and technological problems, all action and inaction is ethical. In a world of networked, interlocking, interdependent hierarchies of socio-environmental realities, the wise choices are choices for the common good in a world in which we are all fatefully intertwined. In 2011 we saw the biggest wave of social uprising in decades, a great opportunity for democracy. As Martin Luther King Jr. stated so eloquently at another great moment of social uprising:

> We are now faced with the fact that tomorrow is today. In this unfolding conundrum of life and history there is such a thing as being too late. Procrastination is still the thief of time. Life often leaves us bear, naked and dejected, with lost opportunity. The tide in the affairs of humanity does not remain at the flood, it ebbs. We may cry out desperately for time to pause in her passage, but time is deaf to every plea and rushes on. Over the bleached bones and jumbled residues of numerous civilizations are written the pathetic words, "too late." We still have a choice today, nonviolent coexistence or violent coannihilation. This may well be humankind's last chance to choose between chaos and community.
>
> (Dr. Martin Luther King, Jr., February 1968)[44]

Conclusion

I set out to describe the implications of complexity theories for ethics, and by extension for policy, focusing on the case of applied ethics for sustainability. I explored eight contemporary ethical theories, showing how each one is developed and explained by the complexity principles. Indigenous environmental ethics and contemporary focus on commons pool resources, land ethics, deep ecology, and ecocentrism all find great strength in the complex dynamic systems framework.

Each in its own way, ethical extensionism, pragmatism, care, partnership, and contractualism all strive to surpass the confines of the previous modernist framings. Each draws in important ways from complexity theories to achieve this newer, richer perspective. Finally, there are ethical theories built on the complexity principles of complexification, responsibility, counterproductivity, and collapse.

It's possible to integrate some of these theories together to conjoin their strengths. Likewise, it's fruitful to look at the ways in which the principles they elicit each shed light on principles and guidelines for ethics and policy in the aim of sustainability.

Issues of uncertainty, unknowability, and ignorance pervade ethics just as they do science. Yet, increasingly, as scientists and scholars alike focus on the greater puzzle of socioecological systems, it is by acknowledging and accepting the inherent degrees of uncertainty and unknowns that both science and ethics become all the more significant. Seeing humans as powerful agents in vulnerable environmental systems, it is clear that ethics is not an abstraction or a choice, but, rather, a central facet of our world.

8   Earth in the Anthropocene

At least we are winning one war, the war on the environment.

Anonymous

Everyone in the world depends completely on Earth's ecosystems and the services they provide, such as food, water, disease management, [and] climate regulation.... Over the past 50 years, humans have changed these ecosystems more rapidly and extensively than in any comparable period of time in human history...

Millennium Ecosystem Assessment[1]

A Great Transition to a future of enriched lives, human solidarity, and environmental sustainability is possible.

The Great Transition initiative[2]

The age of humans

In 2008, amidst headlines of the financial crash, Mumbai terrorists, Somalian pirates, and a divorce that cost Paul McCartney some 48 million, the world's media barely noticed one quiet pronouncement. In a rare turnaround for a scientific society of highly conservative standards, the Stratigraphy Commission of the Geological Society of London accepted a proposal that the Holocene, the geological era we have been living in for 12,000 years, had just ended, and we have begun a new geological era, the Anthropocene, or the age of humans.

The new era is characterized by a few striking facts. Human population, which at the start of the Industrial Revolution in 1750 was 790 million, by 1999 had reached six billion, by 2008 6.5 billion, and only four years later in 2011, it reached seven billion. In the 11,000 millennia leading up to 1750, energy use was limited mostly to human muscles and firewood. By 2008, we were using 85,000 barrels of oil per day, or 31,025,000 barrels of oil per year.[3] Humans have caused erosion, denudation of lands, and sedimentation of rivers at a rate that surpasses natural levels by an order of magnitude.[4] While humans have caused extinctions since the Pleistocene, in the last few decades the rate has been increasing rapidly so that the rate of extinctions is now estimated at 100 to 1,000 times the normal background rate. Already in 1997, scientists warned that humans have transformed between one-third and one-half of all land surfaces on the planet, replacing vast areas of vegetation largely with agricultural monocultures; humans fix more atmospheric nitrogen than all other natural terrestrial sources combined; and humans use more than half of all accessible fresh water on the planet.[5] On June 20, 2011, the world's leading oceanographers warned that due to a cocktail of issues including warming, acidification, and anoxia the world's ocean is at high risk of entering a phase of widespread marine species' extinctions.[6]

By 2005, carbon dioxide levels were at 379 ppm, over a third higher than in pre-industrial times, and higher than any time in the last 0.9 million years.[7] In June 2008 scientists first published evidence of the positive feedback loop of warming permafrost releasing methane in Siberia and other northern regions, at a rate "considerably more rapid than those associated with glacial-interglacial transitions."[8]

Nobel laureate in chemistry Paul Crutzen first proposed the new geological era of the Anthropocene, a symbolic marker to break with modern delusions of total stability. We have entered a phase in human history that with retrospect we might say began with the fossil fuel-based Industrial Revolution, an era ironically, in which humans overcame many of our past vulnerabilities only to create various new ones. For millennia, nature's whims made us vulnerable. Now our lifestyle is making life on Earth vulnerable.

Yet, if we have the power to degrade and destroy, we also have the power to sustain and flourish. The power to choose a fossil fuel intensive economy presupposes the power to make other choices. By more fully acknowledging both environmental vulnerability and human agency, we might take a step towards a more realistic worldview more adequate to our era, to begin to live up to the name homo sapiens, or wise people.

The current era is marked not only by rapid social and environmental impact, degradation, risk and collapse. It is also marked by rapid developments in science, technology, humanities, culture, and the arts. New technologies throughout the sciences have produced a dazzling array of discoveries. Scientists are discovering: secrets of the brain and consciousness, microbiology and genetics, multifaceted aspects of intelligence and emotions, entirely new ecosystems, layers of archaeological sites revealing whole new episodes of human history, and much more. Via film, video, satellites, and the Internet this inspiring array is rapidly shared and assimilated. This great array of new knowledge is both greatly enriching our lives, and at times contributing to solutions to our environmental problems. At the same time, societal complexification and new technologies, as Nicholas Rescher, Ivan Illich and others have argued, may also become counterproductive at times creating new environmental problems, and distracting us from the present transformation of the water, foods, soils, climate, oceans, and web of life on which we depend.

Crutzens' idea of the Anthropocene is brilliant, though, to my taste, I wish it had come just a bit sooner. Over 250 years after the Industrial Revolution, and

30 years after the first Earth Day, our carbon lifestyle and its impacts have been relentlessly intensifying.

The environment in the Anthropocene

In the calamitous first decade of the twenty-first century, the mainstream media also mostly overlooked a major response to the dawning Anthropocene, as leading scientists and scholars worldwide conducted the two largest scientific studies of the earth's environmental systems. I look at the Millennium Ecosystem Assessment (MEA) report in this chapter, and the most recent International Panel on Climate Change (IPCC) report in the next.

In this chapter and the next, I analyze the way that these assessments did and did not incorporate complexity theories in their analyses, methodologies, and synthesis; how complexity does and does not play into considerations for future such assessments; and what these two examples of major scientific assessments of our planet tell us about complexity theories as one framework for the study of highly complex global change.

There remain considerable challenges to studying phenomena of large-scale, socio-natural complexity. Complexity theories appear to provide one important conceptual toolbox. Various concepts and frameworks have been developed in recent decades, as global phenomena have increasingly taken center stage, and technologies such as computers, the Internet and highly complex modeling tools have facilitated the study of them.

My method was to evaluate the work that has been done in these two large-scale developments, looking at primary resources, the reports themselves, and the critiques written by the report writers themselves, as well as reviews and related literature by other scholars. Specifically, I looked at complexity principles from all of the previous chapters, and saw how some of these principles were and were not highlighted in the MEA report.

I found that some conclusions from each of these chapters were indeed significant to the MEA report. Complex dynamic systems were central in myriad respects, in both natural and social systems. Transdisciplinarity was central to many of the report's premises and conclusions. Integrated approaches were not buzzwords, but central to the approach and results of the MEA.

Additionally, I found that the work of the MEA extended upon these principles in highlighting major issues that flow from all of the above. A key principle that was especially important to the MEA report was the human capacity for learning. As we saw in Chapter 3, John Holland argued that a key characteristic of emergent processes is learning. Specifically, the MEA report highlighted the significance of learning to adaptation and resilience. Due to the transdisciplinarity of the research, the MEA was especially focused on integrated methods, pluralistic epistemologies, and highly collaborative approaches.

The Millennium Ecosystem Assessment (MEA) was begun in 2000 and completed in 2005, written by 1,360 scientists and scholars who convened in locales around the world. In their words, they undertook this massive research report:

...to assess the consequences of ecosystem change for human well-being and the scientific basis for actions needed to enhance the conservation and sustainable use of those systems and their contribution to human well-being.... [F]indings on the condition and trends of ecosystems, scenarios for the future, possible responses, and assessments at a sub-global level are set out in technical chapters grouped around these four main themes. In addition, a General Synthesis Report draws on these detailed studies to answer a series of core questions posed at the start of the MEA. The practical needs of specific groups of users, including the business community, are addressed in other synthesis reports.... Each part of the assessment has been scrutinized by governments, independent scientists and other experts to ensure the robustness of its findings.[9]

The MEA took on unprecedented degrees of complexity in their planetary scale study of socioecological change. Surely, many scholars and scientists have studied a multitude of aspects of socio-environmental change in the last half-century. Some precursors of these recent assessments focused more explicitly on how to grasp and evaluate change at the global scale and what it means for human societies and for environmental sustainability. Examples are the documents and studies stemming from the Club of Rome's report, "Limits to Growth," and the major international environmental conference, the Rio Summit in 1992. The MEA, which I analyze here, and IPCC reports of which I focus on the latest in the next chapter, are environmental studies of great scope and ambition. The MEA researchers covered multifaceted global ecological change, and at every step they were forced to frame this as socioecological change, recognizing widespread, interdependent social and ecological changes.

The Millennium Ecosystem Assessment

Just as Crutzen proposed the Anthropocene in the year 2000, his proposition was about to be tested in the form of the massive MEA study. In 2000 the MEA teams set out to organize this complicated task. By the time they were done in 2005, they had muddled through not only enormous quantities of data, but along the way also substantial, difficult, at times novel, and to many, unfamiliar, unanticipated, and pioneering, theory and philosophy. In the attempt to assess the health of the world's ecosystems, they came up repeatedly against the major theoretical challenges of epistemological, methodological, and conceptual pluralism, transdisciplinarity, and complexity.

In the Introduction to this book, I noted the conclusions of the report laid out by the MEA director Walter Reid. In the last 50 years humans have brought about massive transformations of every major life-support system on Earth. From 1954 to 2007 humans increased the CO_2 concentrations in the atmosphere from about 320 ppm to now over 390 ppm. Out of the 24 global ecosystem services that the MEA analyzed, we have enhanced four of these through such measures as reforesting of Northern woodlands and some technological improvements such as pollution absorption; we have created mixed patterns of degradation and improvement in five of these ecosystem services; and yet, overall, we have dangerously degraded 15 of the 24 ecosystem services.

Moreover, the MEA study pointed to various complex and crucial lessons, including the elephant in the room: both widespread poverty and corporate greed drive the degradation of ecosystems and the depletion of natural resources. Both intense deprivation and overconsumption must be transformed to develop sustainable societies. Inequity is a root problem.

One group of leading MEA scientists and scholars attempted to engage in what leading interdisciplinary scholar Brian O'Neill has called "learning about learning." These researchers reflected on the MEA experience of what they call "bridging scales and epistemologies."[10] The authors call for the need to "reason together" as Harvard professor and leading STS scholar Sheila Jasanoff says, engaging in, "intentional deliberation, exchange, and comparative evaluation and critique among epistemic frameworks."[11]

In their report, *Bridging Scales and Epistemologies*, the authors state that the MEA process highlighted that the need to incorporate and synthesize analysis from data at different scales and using different epistemologies is an essential part of global analyses, "particularly acute in global environmental governance."[12] They go on to consider strengths and weaknesses of the MEA in addressing the interdisciplinary and pluralist aspects of the MEA and to highlight the enormous challenges of global assessments. As philosopher Ian Hacking has said, adequately studying issues of multiple scales and multiple disciplines is complex, costly, and sometimes uncomfortable. This is true even amongst natural science disciplines, which already diverge greatly in preferences regarding models, instruments, methods, and styles of reasoning.[13]

Bridging scales and epistemologies is not simply a matter of increasing spatial or temporal resolution, but of "stitching together multiple knowledge systems that encompass divergent paradigms and operate from distinct assumptions and evidentiary standards, ideological commitments, and frames of meaning."[14] In this sense, they note, bridging scales becomes a special case of bridging epistemologies, as epistemic frameworks emerge as a key difference across scales.[15]

While this suggestion already has great implications for the difficult and extensive nature of global assessments, it is just one piece of a complexity framework I have discussed. The authors' analyses of lessons learned and improvements for future global assessments support this hypothesis. They suggest four challenges to overcome in future work, and five ways that global environmental assessments can in turn facilitate understanding of how "mutual learning occurs across scales and knowledge systems."[16] The four challenges include:

1   building capacity for critical policy reasoning
2   promoting epistemic tolerance and pluralism
3   enhancing reciprocal dialogue and exchange, and
4   restructuring scientific assessments to serve as deliberative spaces within

global governance, where this mutual learning amongst a plurality of scientists groups and disciplines can occur.

These suggestions may sound banal at first glance, but a closer examination reveals that with respect to the current state of academia, scientific discourse and norms, education systems, and public media and discourse, and insofar as these are serious intellectual goals, these challenges call for radical changes. This view calls for major reforms not only in academia, but also in the spheres of science and technology, the school systems, and throughout institutions and corporations. It would seem necessary to increase funding for all levels of education, especially in the areas of social theory and philosophy that facilitate transdisciplinary approaches, and implement serious regulation to protect universities from the encroachment of increasing economic pressures from industries and corporations. Yet, these suggestions seem indispensable.

The authors of *Bridging Scales and Epistemologies* also suggest that environmental assessments facilitate this learning by:

1   making differences across styles of reasoning explicit
2   structuring comparative evaluation of reasoning techniques
3   promoting dialogue about the appropriate application of methods and frameworks on global contexts
4   facilitating cross-cutting evaluation, and lastly,
5   communicating these deliberations broadly.[17]

Again, if the language sounds somewhat academic, the implications are far from ordinary. Most of these suggestions would require a serious acknowledgement and the incorporation and advancement of some currently underdeveloped and perhaps underestimated schools of epistemology. Thus, it would require the active engagement of leading philosophers. The last few suggestions require a great deal of dialogue and dispersal of ideas, which, to effectively take hold, would require major investment and years of development. With suggestion number five – communicating these deliberations broadly – the authors signal that pluralism is not just critical between scientists and scholars, but also between different parties and stakeholders of the public, confirming the position of science studies scholars that science and understanding of this complexity cannot be relegated to academia, but, rather, must be analyzed by a representative, educated, general public who embody the diverse sets of knowledge, and think critically, not just across disciplines, but across regions, ecosystems, cultures, and political and institutional groups. This is not a question of a few new grants and programs, but rather a systematic restructuring to integrate understanding from scientific, sociological, philosophical, and environmental groups. This would require new forms of cooperative insights across disciplines, territories, and cultural groups.

Indeed, looking at global non-governmental institutions in recent years, this is exactly what has been taking shape. Complexity, interdisciplinarity, transdisciplinarity, and integral approaches, such as integrated assessments, are not buzzwords, but the very basis of the bulk of research on global change. If the modernist lens often still mitigates the full integration of these approaches, there have nonetheless been remarkable advances in a short timespan. While these approaches mostly only emerged a few decades ago, they already are commonly construed as the primary approach for understanding rapid social and environmental change.

The authors' conclusion offers ideas on ways to build upon the successes and the methods of the MEA. First, subglobal assessments should not fall back into the easy comfort of old-style, place-based assessments. For complex global issues, local assessments of local concerns are insufficient. To drive home some of the main points of their conclusions, it's helpful to use more explicit complexity terms: you cannot ignore the nested hierarchies, the networked causes and consequences, the issues of positive feedbacks and thresholds, and the profound interrelatedness of various realms of human affairs and environmental realities.

Instead, as they say, the general approach must synthesize variations in causes and impacts of global environmental change. In practice this may be quite complicated. For instance, it would involve eliciting subglobal variations in frameworks of meaning and styles of reasoning for producing knowledge about global risks. Subglobal assessments should abandon fixation on geography as the sole defining organizational characteristic. The point of bridging scales and epistemologies is to find alternative ways to slice up global problems for analytical purposes, as many sub-global processes are not geographically confined. Any geographic outlines will be arbitrary with respect to the great entanglement of many of the major network causalities, which are inherently not local, but global. Acidification is not confined to any one coastline, and greenhouse gas emissions do not stop over any one particular city. The very concept of NIMBY, while significant with respect to many types of human impacts, dissolves with respect to others.

Interpreting the Millennium Ecosystem Assessment

The complexity framework, as a reference guide in considering policy options, may at first appear to open up a Pandora's box, or perhaps an Alice's wonderland. Yet, while the MEA's perspective on bridging scales and epistemologies at first may appear to be daunting, in fact it seems to represent an essential step forward in opening up our thinking to better, more realistic approaches to studying and acting on global change. The sooner we accept the more fully complex perspective they evoke, the sooner we can explore new ways to advance and implement their suggestions.

The MEA authors looked at several ways to achieve this. For instance, assessments must reach out in their deliberative mechanisms beyond the experts who participate in the assessment itself. If global environmental assessments are to help reduce ideological fissures in societies, then they must cease being isolated exercises of expert analysis and start becoming focal points by which whole communities and experts from diverse realms can begin to learn to reason together.[18] Many global issues necessitate the participation of groups and societies across the planet. Much more needs to be done to fully evaluate the implications both of reasoning together as an approach to democratizing international governance and of using more complex framings in our strategies for achieving this democratization.

The magnitude of these issues sheds light on the substantial challenges to improvement of global assessments of socio-environmental change. As such, at first glance, this brief report may be falsely seen as frantic arm waving about the enormity or even impossibility of the tasks at hand. Quite the contrary, the *Bridging Scales and Epistemologies* report supports my view that such analyses can be advanced with the concepts and lenses such as the complexity framework in several major ways. If it indicates some of the potential pitfalls and even weaknesses of or limits to utilizing a richer complexity framework for future global assessments, it also shines light on discernible, feasible paths forward to both global assessments and sustainability, rid of some of the major limitations of modernist antecedents.

Yet the analysis and final reports argue that the lessons extrapolated from the MEA should be used to advance future assessents. While many of these goals are laudatory and promising, as articulated in the report they are still nascent and largely abstract. The material, data, epistemologies, peoples, and ecosystems to be somehow synthesized reads more like a list than a set of ideas that might be "stitched together." Moreover, as natural scientists are already wary of the immense cost and challenge of effective global climate assessments, such additional challenges surely appear to some as overly costly. It is one thing to list challenging and novel institutional collaborations for all areas of scholarship; it is another to carry them out, finding ways to effectively synthesize plural methodologies, including quite different methods of modeling, experimentation, and theorization. If only a small cadre of scholars would have the requisite skills to conduct such syntheses, how then could a team of over a thousand MEA scientists and scholars live up to the task, not just of incorporating different disciplines, not just of developing correlative transdisciplinary analyses, but also effectively integrating the plural voices and ideas of the greater public?

Nevertheless, the MEA already made major advances in each of these areas. First, they actually brought together myriad communities of scientists and scholars with diverse groups of concerned parties. Second, they broke the outmoded scientific norm of the expert-novice divides in considerable ways, such as listening more deeply to indigenous perspectives and integrating these more seriously into their analyses. Third, they took major steps towards breaking down the culture gap of quantitative and qualitative spheres, by not just acknowledging, but rather giving a central place to the process of integrating the primary epistemologies that too often remain separated – quantitative science, qualitative social theory, philosophical perspectives, indigenous worldviews and practices, and more. As such they laid out some groundwork for advancing further trans-epistemological, transcultural, and transdisciplinary discussions.

As many leading successful studies have shown in recent years, advancing and integrating "pluralistic epistemological communities" is not just all the buzz, but also a realistic necessity. One can see it as an enormously challenging task. But one can also see it as a rich opportunity for the advancement to an exciting new phase of more sophisticated, systematized transdisciplinary science and ideas. It is possible and perhaps most rational to accept the theory of complexification, accept necessary degrees of both ignorance and unknowability, and therefore, consciously opt to use the best possible new conceptual tools to confront these challenges.

The MEA has undertaken a monumental task, and has succeeded in various ambitious, main goals – respectively, laying the groundwork for a fuller understanding of the need to act on rapid global social and environmental change, as well as a sufficient trove of scientific data upon which to gain further insights into both human environmental vulnerability and resilience. This is a major step, a basis upon which further to plan, to learn, to strategize, to adapt, and to change course.

On the one hand, this is already a powerful approach, and represents a substantial shift in many ways towards complex thinking. On the other hand, there is room to build on the MEA's success. While it was done largely implicitly and not explicitly, the MEA report drew extensively from the complexity framework. Elements of the framework were largely atomized and dispersed throughout the report. Nonetheless, examining the report in light of the complexity framework may contribute to advancing meta-assessments. Through a fuller consideration of the complexity framework, we make more evident and accessible a comprehensive resource from which to explain, justify and highlight the MEA authors' own conclusions, and take them further.

The complexity framework implicitly, though not explicitly, serves as a map for understanding some of the key findings of the MEA report. At the same time, those principles that haven't always been fully accounted for – dynamic interactions, nonlinearity, nested hierarchical contexts, emergence, self-organization, and more – could be incorporated more fully in the future, contributing to the advance of these crucial scientific reports.

Global environmental changes are issues of unprecedented societal complexity. Characteristics of today's global environmental change include: immense hierarchical scale and grain, highly transdisciplinary nature, and substantial, novel kinds and degrees of risk, uncertainty, and unknowability. This is not to say that these principles are always related or must always be explicit. Yet, some issues necessitate integrating complexity principles directly, as I explore in the rest of the book.

Complexity theories highlight the significance of transdisciplinary approaches and comprehension to global assessments. This is true both within and between the current realms of knowledge. As I argue in the preceding chapters, complexity theories and transdisciplinary approaches are intimately interconnected. The MEA concluded that this is crucial, but also that these approaches must be further advanced.

The MEA report furthers the shift from the dominance of the reductionist approaches of modern worldview, to a more synthetic approach that embraces rather than eschews the characteristics of complex system so common to socio-ecological issues. The MEA conclusions and analyses suggest that only with a complex and transdisciplinary lens can we adequately address issues like the buildup of wastes and toxins, economic and financial collapses, the effectively irreversible loss of crucial resources like topsoil and fresh water, and the questions of energy policies surrounding climate change. Any one of these issues is deeply entrenched in the disciplines of sociology, ethics, economics, ecology, politics, and culture, among others.

There is a great lesson to draw from this, which I explore in Chapter 11: the aim to transform interrelated crises with synergistic solutions. This can often be done without certain complexity principles per se. Generally, though, as we confront highly complex systems and interactions, the framework seems to become increasingly helpful to articulating the ways in which both problems and solutions stem from seeing the dynamics and interdependencies involved. Effective policy for major changes such as rapid changes to lands, agriculture, oceans, and the climate must take into account the many contributing and interrelated crises today.

This is challenging. However, from the modern worldview it appears as much more challenging, or impossible; whereas, from a complex worldview it appears as not just possible, but also much more evident. The more we explore and understand complex thinking, the more possible integral solutions may become.

Global environmental change is anything but a single issue. Clearly any approach that focuses on singular crises and singular solutions will miss the mark. Rather, if we look at the list of these crises, each one brings to bear rather strongly in the outcome of overall environmental policies. Myopic and simple thinking inherent to some of today's political and religious ideological discourse lessen our powers of resilience. Flawed economic, social, technological, and environmental models are problematic. However, a great deal of study on more successful models has been done over several decades, and many of these ideas could spread more widely and rapidly.

A great contribution of the MEA was its focus on the capacity, and necessity, for learning. The current global crises are opportunities, an extraordinary chance for learning, collaboration, and transformation. As the world confronts a set of interrelated crises, we are compelled to confront the problem of overly simple analyses and the challenge of complex thinking.

Applying complexity to sustainability in the Anthropocene

The complexity framework is open to many and diverse approaches. In what follows, I trace one conceptual thread, one series of central examples of complexity principles and their implications for sustainability in the Anthropocene. There are a great many important considerations I do not include here; the scope of issues is vast. I hope only to indicate some important points of reference.

Stability, instability, and punctuated disequilibrium

Every kind of social and environmental system can be described as having a range between stability and instability. It is possible to make significant distinctions between degrees of equilibrium or stability in various kinds of systems, from the physical to the political. Likewise, all systems undergo phases that can be described as having degrees of vulnerability, resilience, robustness, and sustainability. Precise measurement of particular instances is not always possible, but clearly, sufficient measurements of certain criteria show that a system is in a relatively vulnerable or resilient state with regard to certain impacting forces, and this is significant.

The modern concept of equilibrium was a source of fierce debates. Since Aristotle it had been widely accepted that the universe was composed of a hierarchically nested set of eternally stable, entirely orderly systems. Religious bodies, political parties and social groups sought stability and safety, wishing to rid society of disorder, chaos, uncertainty, and risk. Throughout history, the world was divided into unsafe places (e.g., wilderness and hell) seen as chaotic, uncertain, and dangerous, and safe places (e.g., the church and the court). Modern science set out to control chaos and uncertainty, and to establish stability, order, and controllability.

This myth of order and stability, devoid of disorder and instability, was copied throughout all the disciplines, and, unsurprisingly, ecologists also copied this motif. Frederic Clements laid out the modernist version of ecosystem states – ecosystems progressed along a clear, linear, chronological path of development toward long-term equilibrium. In 1926, Henry Gleason was an early detractor, opposing Clementsian concepts of linear ascension and equilibrium. Many uses of ecological equilibrium since have been debunked, although local applications are still useful. The predominant view in theoretical ecology is one of ongoing dynamic disequilibrium or non-equilibrium. It is not a matter of some fundamental state of being, but one of observations relative to an observer. It is a matter of a set of observations yielding or not to equilibrium, homeostasis, non-equilibirium or far-from-equilibrium.

Knowledge of ecosystem dynamics is increasing rapidly, yet many kinds of dynamics are still inherently partially uncertain or unknown. Not all uncertainty with respect to some scenarios of smaller or larger ecosystem collapses due to climate change can be fully clarified within the short time frame within which we must react to prevent worst-case scenarios. There are many necessary unknowns, as the problem is novel in terms of drivers, rates, degrees, and types of change throughout human history. Various hypotheses have not and cannot necessarily be cleared up by science in the short timeframe within which we must react to climate change. A one or two degree Celsius shift in net equatorial temperature possibly could precipitate the collapse of a rainforest. The perspective of systems in terms of states of non-equilibrium, thresholds, vulnerability and resilience, clarifies the need to integrate complex dynamics and extreme events in risk analysis.

Interdependence, networks, network causality, connectivity

Similarly, scientists and humanities scholars alike have been thrilled and mystified in recent years by the study of systems in terms of their interactions and interdependence. Interactions are partly mediated by networks, defined earlier as webs of nodes and links, or elements and interactions between them.

In the complexity perspective, causality is understood to have not just linear, singular, and direct, but also nonlinear, networked, manifold, and indirect manifestations. The concept of network causality, or processes of the interrelated causal interactions of multiple elements, provides a substantial change to analyses in many fields. This phenomenon is familiar to, for instance, doctors, lawyers, and environmental health practitioners fighting the tobacco industry, who have found that linking cancers back to original sources is highly difficult. While science doesn't prove things but proves things false, nonetheless there are ways to triangulate so as to improve our understanding, including pluralist, multiple methodologies.

Scientists studying Arctic climate change in the last 30 years have shifted increasingly from an appreciation of various isolated, single causes, towards analyses that incorporate an array of hydrological, biological, geological, and physical interconnections, feedbacks, and networked causality across hierarchical scales. At first, we discerned a few positive feedbacks operating in climate change, e.g., the poster child of Arctic feedbacks, the ice albedo effect, whereby as ice melts the surface cover shifts from snow to water, light to dark, increasingly absorbing more heat. Now, we see that it is just one of the many interconnected positive feedbacks in climate change.

Likewise in the humanities, there has long been a common sense understanding that if you pull one string, as the saying goes, you will eventually unravel the whole ball. This metaphor, like many, evokes complexity without adequately capturing it. After all, a ball of string is a very simple system, even relative to the kitten tangled in it. Yet, such common metaphors evoke our common-sense familiarity with network causality.

Interdependence refers to the degree of interconnectedness in a system, measured in various ways. Connectivity has long been defined as "the characteristic, or order, or degree, of being connected (in various senses)."[19] In ecology, connectivity is

> A measure of the degree to which units, sometimes landscape units, are linked to one another. Measures may be connectance, connectivity or strength of interaction. For example, hedges that have intact and frequent lateral branches have a high degree of connectivity.[20]

In contrast to linear connectivity or homogeneity, high connectivity in various networks implies a much greater degree of difficulty or impossibility in determining exact interrelationships of phenomena or causality.

In the basic sense, complex thinking highlights how inextricable various socio-ecological systems are from each other, and in many cases, how interdependent they are. With respect to sustainability, this view highlights our inherent dependence upon thriving natural systems.

Unintended consequences, irreversibility, and nonrenewability

Stemming in part from connectivity and network causality, we may begin to clarify the common characteristics of unintended consequences, irreversibility, and nonrenewability in various kinds of social and environmental systems. If causes exist in networks, then so do effects; if single causes bring about complex outcomes, then multiple causes bring about even more complex outcomes. This militates against singular "solutions," in complex systems; insofar as it's even possible, it rarely has the singular or clear impact initially sought, and usually brings about other unintended consequences.

Whereas classical scientific thinking construed actions as being isolated (not in networks), and having isolated results (on individual, desired outcomes), network causality highlights the impossibility of tracking causes and effects, unpredictability of networked and evolving effects, and thus uncertainties and unknowns regarding some of the impacts of our actions. Unintended consequences lead to impacts that will affect systems in ways that are at times irreversible and nonrenewable.

Complexity shows that we cannot track all the intricacies of complex causes and consequences, but that often we can discern key criteria and patterns that clarify how to strengthen resilience, reversibility and renewability. The less discernible some of the intricate effects may be, the more we are able to use the complexity principles to map, analyze and plan for change in highly complex systems. Rules and principles for better understanding and addressing network causality are being developed for all kinds of systems, natural and social.

Studying network causality reveals the importance of unintended consequences. Generally speaking, unintended consequences highlight the significance of vulnerability and resilience in natural and social systems. Specifically, knowledge of unintended consequences shows the significance of issues such as particular types and degrees of renewability and reversibility.

Another system-wide characteristic that was at times less legible within the classical reductionist outlook is the distinction between irreversibility and nonrenewability. Irreversibility refers specifically to trends that reach tipping points "of no return," such that the system enters a new phase and cannot return to the prior state in terms of some characteristics. In contrast, nonrenewability refers to the depletion of finite resources. This in turn can be divided into the category of substances that can be renewed but only at a time-scale much longer than that of current human demands versus substances that cannot necessarily be renewed at all.

With disruptions of ecosystems such as changes to the composition and characteristics of oceans, forests and other ecosystems, heavy metals, radioactive, and toxic wastes, and the still unknown effects of many technologies, humans are now altering long-term and large-scale planetary patterns, for better and worse.

Threshold, tipping point, and abrupt change

Threshold is a term with a long etymology, which has taken on renewed significance in recent years. Generally, a threshold is "a fixed value (such as the concentration of a particular pollutant) at which an abrupt change in the behavior of a system is observed,"[21] or "the minimum intensity of a stimulus that is necessary to initiate a response."[22]

Only in recent years have various new definitions of the term emerged, related more specifically to issues of social and ecological, local and global change. In the last 20 years, as use and definitions were increasingly being produced by the complexity scientists and scholars, these terms quickly became established in ecology. A recent review undertaken by twenty leading ecologists analyzed the meaning and significance of the term threshold in ecology. Echoing a question that I explore in this book – whether complexity theories may be on the one hand inapplicable and unnecessary for certain issues, and on the other hand, highly significant for many other issues – the article was entitled, "Ecological Thresholds: The Key to Successful Environmental Management or an Important Concept with No Practical Application?" The authors define and discuss the term ecological threshold:

> An ecological threshold is the point at which there is an abrupt change in an ecosystem quality, property or phenomenon, or where small changes in an environmental driver produce large responses in the ecosystem. Analysis of thresholds is complicated by nonlinear dynamics and by multiple factor controls that operate at diverse spatial and temporal scales. These complexities have challenged the use and utility of threshold concepts in environmental management despite great concern about preventing dramatic state changes in valued ecosystems, the need for determining critical pollutant loads and the ubiquity of other threshold-based environmental problems.[23]

However, the authors conclude by saying,

> We argue that the examples presented above suggest that we are poised for major advances in this area and that ecological thresholds will soon be commonly used in the analysis of environmental problems and will be important in improving the quality of environmental management and our ability to predict the behavior of ecosystems over the next 10–20 years.[24]

The terms threshold and tipping point are used loosely, sometimes as synonyms, sometimes with a distinction. It seems that either we create arbitrary but perhaps useful categories of more or less systemic changes, or else we admit that they are effectively synonyms. The distinction that is sometimes made is that they are the same thing but that somehow thresholds are less substantial, whereas tipping points are more substantial – either influencing more networks and more hierarchical scales, or else more influential within the networks and hierarchical scales they impact. According to the latter view, a tipping point is a type of threshold, but one that is rarer and more acute.

In a recent study related to climate change, edited by Harvard Professor and interdisciplinary sustainability scholar William C. Clark, the authors wrote that the term tipping point commonly refers to a critical threshold at which a tiny perturbation can qualitatively alter the state or development of a system.[25] In step with the ecologists' appraisal of thresholds, the authors of this study claim that the tipping point concept is invaluable for advancing climate science and policy. As they say,

> We critically evaluate potential policy-relevant tipping elements in the climate system under anthropogenic forcing, drawing on the pertinent literature and a recent international workshop to compile a short list, and we assess where their tipping points lie. An expert elicitation is used to help rank their sensitivity to global warming and the uncertainty about the underlying physical mechanisms. Then we explain how, in principle, early warning systems could be established to detect the proximity of some tipping points.[26]

It appears as yet unclear whether it is more useful to distinguish them as qualitatively different, or to understand them ultimately as synonyms. I explore this issue further in the next chapter, where I examine interrelated feedbacks and thresholds occurring throughout different hierarchical scales, producing emergent properties within many environmental systems.

The term abrupt change has evolved within the context of rapid global change, to connote a sudden, large-scale, highly systemic tipping point. The related term surprise is used in ecology and global change literature to refer to "the condition in which an event, process, or outcome is not known or expected."[27] So, in one sense, these two terms pose similar questions. In complex material and living systems, where there is much interdependence, we might ask how much all of these terms remain useful distinctions. Abrupt climate change implies an even more systemic or multi-systems change than either a threshold or a tipping point. Surprise might be seen as our perception of an inherent aspect of complex dynamics while still ensconced in a partially modern worldview, with its expectations of total truths, certainty, knowability, and stability. Once we accept the uncertainty, unknowability and complexification described in Chapter 6, a surprise is perhaps just a change that we could not fully comprehend or predict.

Catastrophe, collapse

In a similar vein, in recent decades there has been a rise in sociological and environmental literatures on fear, risk, and apocalypse, and the possibilities for catastrophe and collapse. In the complexity framework, the ultimate manifestation of degradation is collapse. A small event may trigger the tipping point to collapse, but the greater reason for the collapse may involve a much more involved and long-term process of degradation, and the subsequent loss of resilience.

Potential catastrophes can be due to either natural or human causes, however, these are often largely interconnected or coproduced. Most scenarios of catastrophes involve both natural and human causes, due to the connectivity of natural and social systems. Our current climate change may be induced mostly by human actions of burning and emitting greenhouse gases. Nonetheless, once the carbon is released, it sets into motion an intricate set of further environmental changes that must be taken into account as well.

Nonlinear changes are one cause or aspect of catastrophes; many catastrophes are threshold events that shift a set of systems into a new state. A devastating hurricane in one sense is a nonlinear process that proceeds from a stirring of warm air over water that culminates in heavy winds and rain. The intensification can be seen as a nonlinear buildup of air and water patterns, and the hurricane itself, as the climax and release of this process. We also refer to disease outbreaks, stock market crashes, and human genocide as catastrophes that sometimes bring about small or larger-scale collapses. Evidently, there is much subjective qualitative assessment here. The increase of vulnerability to disease of plants and animals due to global warming is another kind of nonlinear pattern set in motion. Likewise, a disease outbreak itself starts with a single infection, but can quickly spread to a pandemic. As the utilitarians have debated for decades, how do we distinguish between one death and one million deaths? Delineations between particular and systemic climate change tipping points are made from the perspective of the observer. There are hummingbirds that migrate from Mexico to as far north as Alaska. Yet some of their primary food sources are now blooming weeks earlier, due to global warming induced seasonally premature blooming. From the perspective of the hummingbird that flies nonstop 3,000 miles only to discover that she missed her food source by two weeks and dies, catastrophic climate change has already occurred.

Nonlinearity, feedbacks, and network causality are core aspects of vulnerability and collapse, as well as resilience and sustainability, in the case of both natural and human causes. Understanding how networked causalities lead to and trigger rapid changes has become crucial in the highly interconnected and crisis-ridden early twenty-first century. A small literature is now developing on so-called wicked problems, Gordian knots, and synergistic solutions, to examine how complexity principles may shed light on interactions of multiple disasters, network causality and interconnections amongst disasters. An obvious example is the overall intersection of economic crises, climate change, depletion of natural resources, renewable energies, and green jobs.

Complexity theories may help to illustrate not only human vulnerability with respect to collapse, and not only our responsibility in this regard, but also the precise ways in which we possess substantial degrees of free will, agency, and the capacity to learn, adapt, and change. Understanding of interconnected, networked crises, related to approaches to interlinked solutions, can spur important critical and creative thinking on developing and fostering appropriate ethics, politics, and policy.

Vulnerability, resilience, and sustainability

The mounting environmental crises – climate change, depletions of nonrenewable quantities of topsoil, fresh water, and natural resources, deforestation, ocean acidification, and other threats – make us increasingly aware of issues of ecological and social vulnerability, resilience and sustainability. Simply put vulnerability is the susceptibility of a system to collapse, and resilience is the capacity of a system to rebound from stresses and sustain itself. Awareness of social or ecological vulnerability alone is insufficient without an understanding based first in their mutual interrelation. Social and ecological vulnerability and resilience can exacerbate each other or mutually enhance each other. Defining either in isolation of the other misses some key features.

On a smaller scale or within a narrower range, a specific example of vulnerability is the susceptibility of a whirlpool to the kinds of disturbances that may disrupt, alter, or destroy its structure. On a larger scale, vulnerability leads to the degradation and collapse of entire ecosystems, such as forests, lakes, and rivers, and of ecosystem functions or services, such as production of topsoil, agricultural land, water purification, etc. The parallel that I am drawing between systems like whirlpools and rainforests is the degree of weakness or vulnerability in the face of disturbance. Natural scientists define weakness as a lack of resistance, and vulnerability as a lack of resilience. Lack of resistance is fragility, as in the susceptibility of glass to breaking. Lack of resilience leads to collapse, making it central to sustainability. Ecologists define resilience as "the capacity of a system to absorb disturbance and reorganize while undergoing change so as to still retain essentially the same function, structure, identity, and feedbacks."[28]

Largely independently of one another, thinkers across the disciplines have seized upon these terms as central to their aims. From ecology, biology, and climate science, to psychology, sociology, and philosophy, the last two decades has seen a rapid rise in literature on vulnerability and resilience, as well as related topics in postmodernity, risk, fear, apocalypse, collapse, environmental philosophy, and more.

As we have seen, sustainability is a term that is so broad and incorporates within it so much complexity, that, like the words nature and complexity, it proves difficult to define adequately. The different discourses, assumptions, biases, and worldviews in different disciplines are such that small differences in wording or connotations sometimes underlie substantial differences in viewpoints and understanding.

In brief, I have defined sustainability as "improving the quality of human life while living within the carrying capacity of supporting eco-systems,"[29] while also considering that the term is based in such a multifaceted reality that only a definition based in transdisciplinary collaboration and ongoing, iterative, creative, and critical thinking will do it justice.

Sustainability, like vulnerability, must be defined in a broad, transdisciplinary fashion. The slightly more adequate definition I have explored in this book states, "Sustainability is improving the quality of human life while living within the carrying capacity of supporting eco-systems."[30] While this begins to capture ideas like quality of life, social solidarity, the vulnerability of ecosystems, and the interdependence of natural and social factors, it does not yet articulate the values, evaluative judgment, economics or politics underlying these crucial aspects of sustainability. It does not yet say sustainability by whom, for whom, how, why, and at what cost? The world today is facing serious social and environmental crises, while also coping with the most intense gaps in class, wealth, and power since the Gilded Age. Moreover, terms like "carrying capacity," while useful points of reference, are also elusive, partially subjective, and anthropogenic. Like complexity, sustainability is a term that is hard to adequately define, but still a crucial point of reference. It must reiteratively be problematized, critiqued, and contextualized.

While sustainability is not typically framed as a complexity term, I claim that not only is sustainability a key element of the complexity framework, but that explicitly defining and describing it as such is an invaluable step toward clarifying the links between the fields of complexity and social and environmental sustainability and thriving.

The link between the two is intrinsic and inherent. First, by construing complexity within a framework that includes the axis of collapse to sustainability, we highlight the way in which planning for sustainability requires a vision that incorporates all of the many variables found throughout not just physical and environmental, but social, political and ethical systems. Defining sustainability as a key reference point in the complexity framework centers and guides the necessary transdisciplinarity.

Framed within the context of complexity theories, in a general sense, sustainability within each of the disciplines is a cross-disciplinary synonym for an ongoing phase state, or ongoing non-equilibrium. While at the same time, it is a transdisicplinary term referring to ideas regarding humanity's survival and thriving. In a physical system like a whirlpool or eddy in a stream, maintaining a phase state implies maintaining the form and function of the whirlpool. Today's societies are extraordinarily complex, making comprehension of sustainability all the more challenging. Yet, broad patterns can be discerned. As Elinor Ostrom's work has shown, highlighted in the Introduction, we can discern key models of more and less sustainable socioecological systems. Our current unfettered, neoliberal global capitalist system has tended towards massive extraction, production, consumption, and waste of natural resources. Yet, sustainable social and environmental systems are not only possible, but myriad examples are practiced successfully today throughout many corners of the globe.

While complexity highlights the vastness and nebulousness of the term sustainability, nevertheless it also provides some of the specific variables necessary to considerations of sustainable practices.

Towards a great transition in the Anthropocene

Over recent decades many academic and social movements have formed around the concept of changing course, and steering humanity towards a more sustainable future. Some groups have called this the great transition, or the great transformation. As the full complexities and challenges of "sustainability," become increasingly clear, numerous splinter groups develop interests in how societies might learn, adapt and strategize for the future.

The unprecedented changes of the last 200 years, and increasingly rapidly in the last half-century, are based in a mix of social, scientific, industrial, technological, economic, and demographic revolutions, or emergences, as described by Harold Morowitz in Chapter 3. They have manifested not only unprecedented social and ecological changes, but novel human impact that has increased by orders of magnitude, to the point of dominating usage of the majority of the Earth's biomass, natural resources, and ecosystem services.

It is stunning to think of the diverse and novel ways in which so many social and technological innovations of the last 100 years have changed societies and the Earth. Increasingly, we see that we must understand particular instances of change, but also the nature of the interrelated, interacting ensemble. We have to synthesize and articulate between disciplinary foci. A core requirement is collaboration. For instance, no one movie can capture all the facets of global change. The BBC documentary *Planet Earth* makes visible the spectacular living world we rarely see from our largely urban outposts. In the movie *Manufactured Landscapes*, Edward Byrtynsky gives another important view of global change, showing the human conditions and experiences of poverty and exploitation, and the ravages of intensive industries on diverse peoples and landscapes. While Chris Marker's stunning *Sunless* gives a more philosophical perspective on the complexities of this socio-ecolgical change. Extrapolating from multiple such perspectives gives a fuller picture of the nature of our moment in history. Likewise the MEA work began as a great collaboration, and the process only reinforced the significance of further transdisciplinary and collaborative approaches.

Complexity principles were found to be central to the MEA work. Comprehending the world in terms of complex dynamic systems, and complexity more generally, more fully reveals our vulnerabilities, but also our potential for learning, strategy and change, in ideas, behaviors and even our worldview. In acknowledging the prior we must focus on the latter. Insofar as complexity theories shed light on the functions and dynamics of systems vulnerability, risks, thresholds and collapse, they also highlight robustness, resilience, adaptation, and agency for change. While the modern perspective has trouble articulating such dynamics, the complexity perspective provides some important keys to changing course.

Conclusion

The 1,360 scientists and scholars involved in the Millennium Ecosystem Assessment, the largest environmental study of all times, set out on an in-depth study of the state of Earth at the dawn of the Anthropocene, to assess the health of the world's ecosystems. They focused on many interrelated environmental systems – water, air, soils, biodiversity, climate change, and more. And they looked at how these are inextricably enmeshed in greater, interlocking challenges – economic, social, cultural, political, and more – involving substantial and rapid changes in societies and ecosystems.

Their modus operandi, discoveries, and interpretations and policy suggestions, are much aligned with perspectives and lessons to be drawn from complexity theories. The MEA *Bridging Scales and Epistemologies* report supports my view that such analyses can be advanced with concepts and lenses such as the complexity framework in several major ways. If it indicates some of the potential pitfalls and even weaknesses of or limits to utilizing the complexity framework for future global assessments, it also shines light on discernible, feasible steps to both global assessments and sustainability.

As the MEA team toiled through this task, they came up repeatedly against the major theoretical challenges of epistemological, methodological, and conceptual pluralism, transdisciplinarity, and complexity. Various lessons from the MEA report are articulated and advanced by complexity theories. The report showed the significance of transdsiciplinarity, for instance, to comprehend the links between extreme poverty, extreme wealth, and environmental decline. They looked at complex, integral approaches, not just as buzzwords, but as central aspects of their work. The MEA showed, implicitly, the significance of the central property of emergence noted by John Holland: learning. The report, in process, results and conclusions, also supported the need for pluralist epistemologies needed to bridge hierarchical scales and different fields of studies, and thus the significance of scholarly collaboration.

The report showed how, through complex thinking, transdisciplinarity, and collaboration, we can work towards more sustainable outcomes. At the same time, the report clearly warned that the majority of current socioecological trends are now negative, with humans degrading 60 percent of the planetary ecosystem services upon which we depend.

Yet, if we have the power to degrade and destroy, we also have the power to sustain and flourish. The power to choose a fossil fuel intensive economy presupposes the power to make other choices. By more fully acknowledging both environmental vulnerability and human agency, we take a step towards a worldview more adequate to the Anthropocene.

9 Complexity and climate change

If carbon dioxide continues to increase, the study group finds no reason to doubt that climate changes will result and no reason to believe that these changes will be negligible.[1]

National Academy of Sciences, first official report on climate change, 1979

The fifteen warmest years on record (from 1850) were: 2005, 2010, 1998, 2003, 2002, 2006, 2009, 2007, 2004, 2001, 2008, 1997, 1999. 1995, and 2000.[2]

National Oceanic and Atmospheric Association, National Climate Data Center, 2011

The rise of extreme weather

In 1988, atmospheric scientists Hugh Willoughby, Jeff Masters, and their crew flew a small National Oceanic and Atmospheric Administration plane right through what was then the strongest hurricane ever observed in the Atlantic, Hurricane Gilbert. The flight was filmed for a PBS documentary called, "Hurricane!"[3] As they approach Gilbert, the young Masters assesses the risks.

> If we go at 5,000 ft., we should miss that heavy cell there. ... It might be big enough to orbit if we had to. We could climb to 10,000 ft. orbiting the eye, if we did get a bad pass at 5,000 feet...

The head scientist Willoughby cheerfully replies, "Well, like I say [Hurricane] Allan was like that, and we spent the whole day at 5,000 ft. with [only] one good bump." To which Masters says, "Yeah, it should be a pussycat." And they fly off into the record-setting Gilbert.

After flying into Hurricane Hugo the next year proved even more intense, Masters quit Hurricane Hunters and went on to get a doctorate and co-found the Weather Underground. Unwittingly, he now had front row seats for a drama far beyond Hurricanes Gilbert and Hugo. The adventurous work of Hurricane Hunters was good training for the wild ride of data he would blog about in the last few years as Director of Meteorology for the Weather Underground.

In 2012 we look back at a decade of perhaps the weirdest weather in recorded history. In the last few years extreme weather has increased, and scientists have documented unprecedented events across a wide range of weather categories: rainstorms, floods, droughts, hurricanes, snowstorms, cyclones, typhoons, and more.[4] Throughout the years there have been occasional singular weather events. In 1816, Mount Tambora's volcanic eruption was the largest in 1,600 years blackening the skies during the "year without a summer."[5] In contrast, the current changes are more systemic. The entire atmosphere has warmed, which has increased overall energy and moisture, intensifying myriad types of weather events. The last few years has seen an exponential increase in record breaking weather events around the planet.

Globally, extreme weather is playing out very closely to what climate scientists have predicted for the last four decades. The increase in extreme weather in the last decade, and especially the last few years, have been predicated for years by climate scientists, and therefore validate the scientific consensus on climate change in the last two decades. What has taken most scientists by surprise is the rapid rate of change.

2010 and 2011 both set general global extreme weather records. Nineteen countries set all-time heat records in 2010, an area that constitutes over 20 percent of the Earth's surface area. Canada had its warmest, driest year on record. Back-to-back snowstorms pounded the US for months, including the blizzard Snowmageddon, which dropped two feet of snow on Baltimore and Philadelphia. Rains flooded one-fifth of Pakistan, the Russian heat wave killed 55,000 and cut the country's wheat crop by 40 percent. Australia had the most rainfall in 111 years of record keeping, flooding a region larger than France, and costing an estimated 30 billion.[6]

Weather became more extreme in 2011, breaking records in heat waves, snowstorms, spring floods, and hurricane flooding around the globe, and hitting hard in every weather category in the United States. From January to August in the United States alone ten weather disasters set new records, each inflicting more than one billion dollars of damage, but cumulatively, reaching an estimated total damage of closer to $53 billion.[7]

Complexity and climate change

In this chapter I examine how several specific principles from the complexity framework explored in Chapter 2 are especially helpful in articulating the nature and implications of anthropogenic climate change, namely: feedbacks, thresholds, vulnerability, and uncertainty. The whole complexity framework sheds light on various aspects of climate change. I focus on the ways in which these specific principles are especially significant to climate change, and also tend to reinforce our understanding in terms of the full complexity framework. As such, both these specific principles and the full framework directly inform considerations of resilience, strategy, risk assessment, ethics, and policy.

The complexity principles, and particularly feedbacks, thresholds, vulnerability, uncertainty, and resilience, have been central in all areas of climate literature – scientific, greater academic, and popular literature. Of course, these principles are closely interrelated with many of the others in the framework. Resilience is the degree of a system's effective response to vulnerability; nonlinearity is a quality of feedbacks, which lead to thresholds and tipping points; and the term abrupt climate change is specifically used to describe a hypothetical global-scale climatic tipping point.

Further, other aspects of complexity explored in previous chapters also are significant to climate change, such as: unknowability, unanticipated consequences, and transdisciplinarity. Nicholas Rescher's concept of complexification and Ivan Illich's concept of counterproductivity help to explain unintended consequences. As we increasingly need transdisciplinarity, so we need multidisciplinary and interdisciplinary approaches, and these are employed as an organizing principle by almost every environmental studies agency, department, and organization. These transdisciplinary approaches in turn shed light on the nature of uncertainty. Beyond uncertainty one finds the newer but not less significant term discussed in Chapter 6, unknowability.

One of the challenges of this area of study is that when not properly contextualized within the fuller complexity framework with its broader implications, philosophical as well as scientific and social, the complexity principles may be misused and misinterpreted. Uncertainty, particularly, has been used as a weapon in the wars between the well-funded lobbyists and pseudo-scientists working for wealthy energy corporations, and the majority of the population who wish to more accurately understand and act on the realities of climate change. In this chapter, as I hope to show, when we focus on uncertainty solely within the lingering modernist worldview, the complexity principles are easily manipulated. When, however, we succeed in framing climate change more fully within a complexity worldview and complex thinking, the validity of climate science and urgency of the current climate crisis become clearer.

That the terms feedbacks, thresholds, vulnerability and many others are found throughout climate change literature does not alone prove my point. In what follows I analyze just how these terms are significant to comprehending climate change. Tables 9.1 and 9.2 catalogue these terms and some examples of the ways in which these terms are central to understanding climate change. All the terms in Table 9.1 are from the IPCC report, Climate Change 2007.[8]

Feedbacks: singular, multiple, and interconnected

My aim in this section is to explore just how relevant feedbacks are to climate change, how complex thinking sheds light on these feedbacks, and in turn on climate change.

Just as the complexity principles are all inherently interconnected, so are the dynamics occurring within any one of these categories, such that feedbacks in many interrelated types of dynamics are interdependent. In analyzing the case of highly complex socioecological issues like climate change, the complexity principles cannot be fully conceived in isolation, but must always be understood in terms of their interactions.

Table 9.1 Complexity principles and their expression in the climate change literature

Complexity term	Climate change term
Adaptive	**Adaptive Capacity** The ability of a system to adjust to climate change (including climate variability and extremes) to moderate potential damages, to take advantage of opportunities, or to cope with the consequences.
Vulnerability	**Vulnerability** The degree to which a system is susceptible to or unable to cope with adverse effects of climate change, including climate variability and extremes. Vulnerability is a function of the character, magnitude, and rate of climate change, the variation to which a system is exposed, its sensitivity, and its adaptive capacity.
Diversity	**Biodiversity** Myriad life forms sustaining and sustained by climate and more or less vulnerable or resilient in the face of climate change.
Uncertainty	**Likelihood and confidence language (probabilities)** Virtually certain >99% probability of occurrence Extremely likely >95% Very likely >90% Likely >66% More likely than not >50% Very unlikely <10% Extremely unlikely <5% Very high confidence – a 9 out of 10 chance of being correct High confidence – an 8 out of 10 chance Medium confidence – a 5 out of 10 chance Low confidence – a 2 out of 10 chance Very low confidence – less than a 1 out of 10 chance
System state or phase state	**Sustainability** Maintaining global environmental systems, e.g., climate systems, within relatively stable states.
Nonlinearity, surprises	**Surprises** Unpredicted, sudden shifts in climate regime.
Irreversibility	**Irreversibility** A phase change in which an ecosystem undergoes changes that cannot be reversed subsequently, e.g., rainforest becomes savannah or savannah becomes desert.

Once again we find that the complexity processes are interconnected; nonlinear feedbacks lead to thresholds at which system states change and previously robust ecological systems may become more vulnerable, and may even collapse. Cumulatively, multiple positive feedbacks can lead to more systemic tipping points, at which a greater quantity or expanse of interrelated complex systems –

Table 9.2 Comparison of mainstream and complexity conceptual frameworks

Mainstream analysis of climate change	Complexity analysis of climate change
Usually constructed from the point of view of one discipline, with the accompanying somewhat constrained epistemology and methodology.	Utilizing any or all of the knowledge disciplines applicable to a given area of study, as necessary; integrating various necessary epistemologies and methodologies.
Synthesis consists in disciplinary and interdisciplinary practices, primarily those singular in methods, assumptions and epistemological perspectives.	Synthesis consists in studying and determining which of the many disciplines, epistemologies, and methodologies involved, in what combination, are most appropriate to the particular study at hand.
Contextualized primarily in one knowledge discipline, and thus within the context of its literature, assumptions, perspectives, and methods.	Contextualized in multiple knowledge disciplines; with the potential of references to vast, often disparate though actually interrelated bodies of literature; with multiple counteracting assumptions, perhaps rendered more visible or reconciled through this process.
The policymaker must reintegrate the unidisciplinary result of a study back into its transdisciplinary milieu. This process is usually more prone to inadequate previsions, unnoticed errors, and nefarious, unintended consequences.	The policymaker reintegrates the transdisciplinary result of a study back into its transdisciplinary world. Methodologically transdisciplinary research is often more challenging and prone to other kinds of errors. However, this process permits a better grasp of highly complex phenomena, with less errors with respect to overall systems-level dynamics.

ecosystems and societies – transform into system states in which more aspects of societies or ecosystems are degraded, diminished, or destroyed.

In Chapter 3 I defined feedback as the process by which the output of a system is passed back (or fed back) to the input. I defined positive feedback as a force that affects its environment such that the initial force is then increased. While, a negative feedback is a force that affects its environment thereby causing the initial force to diminish or to remain equal.

The National Academy of Sciences (NAS) has defined two drivers of climate change – feedbacks and forcings. Feedbacks are "processes in the climate system that can either amplify or damp the system's response to changed forcings."[9] An example of a positive feedback is the greenhouse effect itself, by which an increase in greenhouse gas (GHG) emissions increases atmospheric temperature, which increases the quantity of atmospheric water vapor, which then amplifies the warming.[10] A climate forcing is an energy imbalance imposed on the climate system by human activities or other forces. Examples include changes in solar energy output, volcanic emissions, deliberate land modification, or anthropogenic emissions of greenhouse gases, aerosols, and their precursors. A climate feedback is an internal climate process that amplifies or dampens the climate response to a specific forcing.

Various positive feedbacks have already been proven to be among the most significant and influential to the process of climate change at the planetary scale. Other positive feedbacks have been identified as drivers of previous rapid climate changes, reason to expect that they could be or become drivers in current climate change. Furthermore, there may be major feedbacks that no scientists have as yet identified. Or course there are also negative feedbacks that counteract positive feedbacks. In 2001 scientists warned, "A substantial part of the uncertainty in projections of future climates is attributed to inadequate understanding of feedback processes internal to the natural climate system."[11] Therefore, it is crucial to understand, model, and monitor climate feedback processes.[12]

Yet, much of the uncertainty is not known. For instance scientists have pinpointed that cloud feedbacks are one big source of uncertainty, but that that uncertainty is reasonably well characterized. Through increasingly complex climate models, scientists have shifted this subject from an unknown unknown to a known unknown. They are well aware that this is a significant area, and so are able to calculate that known unknown to a degree into their interpretations.

According to some estimates generated by climate models, feedback mechanisms internal to the climate system will bring about over half of the warming expected in response to human activities.[13] Scientists are exploring such climate feedbacks as, for example: cloud, water vapor, and lapse rate feedbacks; sea-ice feedbacks; ocean heat uptake and ocean circulation feedbacks; and land hydrology and vegetation feedbacks.[14] Feedbacks already occurring in climate change processes include the albedo effect, glacier fissures, sudden coral reef collapses, and Arctic methane release due to rapid permafrost melting. Worrisome potential feedbacks include cloud feedback, water vapor feedback, lapse rate, carbon cycle responses, and more. Some are positive feedbacks, like water vapor, some negative, like lapse rate, and some could be either, like cloud feedback. Such feedbacks and others might trigger events like the halting of the oceanic North-Atlantic thermohaline circulation (THC) belt, the acceleration of Amazon rainforest conversion into savannah, collapses of tropical forests, and various other kinds of sudden releases of methane, e.g., giant methane bubbles emerging from the ocean.

Generally speaking, the global carbon and sulfur cycles contain the potential for numerous important feedback processes. This includes carbon uptake by the land and ocean, such as atmospheric, biospheric, and oceanic processes that influence the abundance of CO_2 in the atmosphere. In other words, the entire surface of the globe can be seen as a potential source of carbon sinks or leaks. This leaves plenty of room for other feedbacks, positive and negative.

The Polar Regions of course are seeing some of the most rapid and extensive climate change. The average temperature of the Arctic has risen more than 4 degrees Fahrenheit (2.2 degrees Celcius) in recent years, in comparison with the approximately one degree average for the globe. In the past few years, Arctic sea ice has been melting much faster than most scientists had predicted. While climate feedbacks are turning out to be incredibly complex, scientists have been able to pinpoint some significant patterns of feedbacks. This begs the question when, in highly complex situations, complexity theories are useful or just another complication.

The ice albedo effect

The poster child of positive climate change feedbacks is the albedo effect. The albedo effect occurs when increased melting of ice leads to a larger surface area that is not light (ice and snow) but dark (ocean waters), thus absorbing more solar radiation and increasing the rate of ice melt.

One of the first feedbacks to be widely reported and discussed, from the 1980s through the 1990s, it was the token example of a climate feedback. While scientists have been exploring issues like water vapor and cloud feedbacks from early on, often in the popular press the ice albedo effect was taken as central. In recent years, study of complex systems and study of the complex dynamics of climate change have coevolved to give a truer picture of the significance of multiple interacting feedbacks.

Climate models give some estimates of ice albedo feedback and forcing in the Arctic. Perhaps a clearer measurement is the amount of sea ice decline – 17 percent over the last 25 years, as measured in 2007[15] Since 2007 the rate of melting has continued to increase. Over the 1990s and early 2000s, as scientists noted such data they increasingly saw how multiple feedbacks were to blame. Arctic scientists Roland Lindsay and Jinlun Zhang of the Polar Science Center at the University of Washington explain further:

> There appears to be a feedback at work in the sense that increased open water and thin ice in summer absorb more solar energy during clear skies or produce more low cloud and increased long-wave absorption, leading to less ice growth the following winter. It has been proposed that the Arctic may be near a "tipping point," a new equilibrium state between increased radiative absorption in the ocean during the summer and the amount of first-year sea ice that can grow during the following winter.[16]

Thus, the authors note the ice albedo effect, as well as cloud and water vapor feedbacks.

Of particular note is the large reduction in summer ice from 2002–2005.[17] Scientists began to investigate what seemed to be the ice albedo effect due to a string of hot summers in the 1990s. Some suggested that the increased Arctic temperatures created observed shifts in wind fields, causing higher winds in turn blowing hotter air over the Fram Straight region. Thus, decreased ice thickness in the Fram Straight has been blamed on the high temperatures of the 1990s, which caused "a large volume of thick multiyear ice ... to have departed from the Fram Straight ... leaving the Arctic with more thin, first-year ice more prone to melt in summer."[18]

Yet, the more scientists looked for feedbacks, the more they seemed to find. Just as the albedo effect may have triggered shifts in wind patterns so myriad other systems have been shifting, such as: changes in cloud cover, vapor, and terrestrial ecosystem emissions. Over the last ten years it has become evident that the cumulative feedbacks between these numerous feedbacks are significant. Increasingly, we must speak of cumulative network causality of interacting feedbacks, in which multiple smaller-scale feedbacks feed back into each other, potentially amplifying the amplification.

An example of this is "dynamical ice melting." This term has been used to describe the way that ice itself melts in the Arctic, regardless of other factors like wind. It came as a surprise to climate scientists in the early 2000s that massive glaciers do not just melt from the top down, but, rather, also due to feedbacks within the glacier itself. For instance, fissures form, capable of rapidly creating channels that suck water from the top down to the bottom of glaciers. Pools then form under glaciers, spreading, and so facilitating the growth of further fissures. This dual process is self-enhancing and soon there is a network of rivers and pools forming throughout the glacier, adding to the speed of melting.

To some, such analyses of snowballing feedbacks smack of alarmism; at least, they are unfamiliar. Scientists continue to look for empirical evidence of the impact of these effects individually and cumulatively. Generally, studies about networks of local feedbacks interacting within the Arctic region raise more questions than they answer. Finnish Arctic researcher Bruce Forbes and colleagues studied geographic variations in anthropogenic drivers throughout the Arctic, looking at how they influence vulnerability and resilience of socioecological systems.[19] Forbes makes many optimistic projections. He notes hopefully that over long periods of the Tertiary and Quaternary, ecosystems displayed significant resilience to small degrees of climate change, for instance, elements of the boreal and Arctic tundra biota adapted to high variability in climate and other factors. In the end analysis though, "Despite this record of resilience and the capacity to buffer against change, northern ecosystems have traditionally held a reputation for being 'fragile' and therefore vulnerable to immediate, long lasting and perhaps irreversible change."[20] For the near future, concerns include interactions between myriads types of changes in the Arctic. Warming permafrost not only releases methane, but interacts with other dynamics – acceleration of cryogenic processes such as thermokarst and solifluction, affecting the structure and function of forest and tundra ecosystems, land use, social and economic upheaval, and accelerating disturbance regimes such as fire and insect outbreaks.[21]

Studies that are able to rely on past evidence of specific, large-scale thresholds manage to give a somewhat clearer sense of urgency. Several scientists have postulated on the major causes of the Marinoan climate warming, occurring about 635 million years ago. One theory holds massive methane release from equatorial permafrost as the greatest trigger in this global meltdown.[22] Past major climate events give ominous clues about the significance of current changes. The massive climate change that ended the Eocene happened more slowly than today's climate change.

Indeed, other research focusing on equatorial changes in past climate changes also attempts to pinpoint relatively specific causality, e.g., global scale impacts, which may obscure which initial drivers were significant in bringing about the later, larger drivers. While policymakers prefer the apparent clarity that the focus on the greater past drivers provides, analysis of such acontextual focus that also acknowledges the significance of context thus reveals an alarming degree of the limits to knowledge in such cases. After all, of primary concern to policymakers today is not the ultimate result of biospheric change, but the initial set of drivers that if altered by current policy could substantially change or even altogether avoid that final result.

In Chapter 6 I noted the limits to science and to knowledge, and the normalization of unknowability and ignorance. One major aspect of the limits to knowledge in the case of climate science is the limitations in assessing systems dynamics beyond a certain degree of complexity, such as the complexity of feedback dynamics over time. This militates against too much focus on the classical science methods and goals geared towards absolute precision, predictability, and truth. Moreover, it forces natural scientists to abandon the hope of full knowledge of various climate change dynamics and instead accept the necessity of uncertainty language, including uncertainty bands and statistical probabilities. This means that societies will have to make risk management choices under conditions of partial uncertainty.

> The Amazon rainforest is not an ephemeral feature of South America; rather it developed during the Cretaceous and has been a permanent feature of this continent for at least the last 55 million years. However, it seems that due to human activity the Amazon rainforest is entering a period with unprecedented disruption and climatic condition with no analogue in the past. Some modeled results suggest that a significant portion of the Amazon rainforest may turn to savanna by the mid to late Twenty-first century.
>
> (e.g., White *et al.* 1999; Cox *et al.* 2000)[23]

This and other recent studies show a non-negligible probability that multiple feedbacks will push entire rainforests to major tipping points, e.g., transformation into savanna or desert. Rainforests have high biodiversity and thus high complexity; the variables and factors involved in assessing the impact both of climate change on rainforests and of deforestation on climate change are numerous.[24] Indeed the Amazon rainforest alone contains one-half of all biodiversity on Earth.[25]

As appears to be the case with the considerable variables in positive feedbacks driving climate change, the variables in the rainforest suggest that prediction is highly difficult. Additionally, it may be that the more interacting variables there are, the more potential drivers there are, the more potential for triggers of new positive feedbacks, the greater the degree of network causality amongst feedbacks, and thus, the greater the potential to reach climate thresholds. The implications of a rainforest collapse are mind-boggling. Rainforest ecologists agree that prediction about feedbacks from human impact and climate change endangering large rainforests remain among the most difficult, but that that difficulty renders a rainforest collapse no less probable.

An example of a positive feedback born of innumerable other positive feedbacks is polar permafrost methane release. As I was writing my dissertation on complexity and climate change in June 2008 a potentially serious climate positive feedback became a reality. Scientists in the Arctic observed the release of methane from below the Siberian tundra in the form of numerous columns of rapidly rising methane gas.[26] As I was finishing this book, in December 2011, this Siberian methane release had increased exponentially.[27] Yet, scientists are still unclear about whether or not there may be mitigating factors.

Methane contributes 25 times more than carbon dioxide to global warming. While carbon dioxide remains in the atmosphere for centuries, methane only remains for a decade. Yet its presence during the decade is no less forceful in driving accelerating feedbacks, and thus contributing to long-term irreversible climate change. Evidence of large quantities of methane is present in data on past major global warming events. For instance, evidence seems to show that a methane release was one of the causes of the Permian-Triassic extinction event, 252 million years ago, the Earth's most severe extinction event, which wiped out up to 96 percent of all marine species and 70 percent of terrestrial vertebrates. Moreover, it is the only known mass extinction of insects; 57 percent of all families and 83 percent of all genera perished.

Many atmospheric feedbacks seem to be, on the face of it, quite simple. The albedo effect, in isolation, appears simple. Dark surfaces absorb more heat, and thus create a vicious circle of increasing warming. However, this assertion belies the lessons that the complex systems framework reasserts over and again. In fact, the more that the Arctic is studied, the more complex it appears to be. A series of simple feedbacks does not equal a large set of simple feedbacks, but, rather, an immensely, perhaps impossibly, complex puzzle.

At the same time, as with many highly complex puzzles, the results may be relatively simple with respect to how we must respond. When a house is on fire, we do not stop to calculate all the complexities of wind, temperature, causality, and potential consequences. It might be helpful to do so, but we prioritize putting out the fire. In the case addressing climate change, we need to make complex value judgments, but it's clear that we must reduce major causes such as deforestation and carbon emissions.

Greater understanding of the complexities of climate change, e.g., of multiple intersecting climate feedbacks, may help in answering the question: at what point do we have enough information to act? Once we clarify major drivers, trends, and scenarios, how many additional details do we need? Can we put out the fire? How many details do we need to know about risks of collapsing ecosystems, and when do we know enough about enough actual and potential feedbacks to make reasonable judgments?

Complexity principles like feedbacks and thresholds shed light on uncertainty, unknowability, and above all, the complex nature of human impact. One main lesson to draw from this is the concomitant potential of human learning, agency, intelligence, ingenuity, and strategy, and therefore the great potential to change course and to rethink and reconceptualize our strategies for sustainability.

Multiple intersecting feedbacks in climate change

I have mentioned two conceptual categories of climate feedbacks – isolated positive feedbacks like the ice albedo effect, and more complex sets of feedbacks, such as those driving dynamical ice melting in the arctic.

Climate change involves an ensemble of multiple-type, multiple-scale, intersecting positive and negative feedbacks. Recent studies emphasize the complexity of Arctic amplification and the multiplicity of processes that contribute to it. Princeton atmospheric scientist Michael Winton has argued that the ice albedo effect popularized by the media is perhaps insignificant relative to other constellations of networked climate feedbacks, and perhaps even insignificant to global warming generally.

> The analysis of forcings and feedbacks performed in this paper shows that the Arctic amplification arises from a balance of significant differences in all forcings and feedbacks between the Arctic and the globe. The direct CO_2 forcing and non-SAF [(surface albedo feedback)] shortwave feedbacks inhibit Arctic amplification while the net TOA flux forcing, SAF, and longwave feedback favor it. The SAF, while important, is a lesser factor than the net TOA flux forcing and the longwave feedback in promoting Arctic amplification. Comparing the Arctic and sub-Arctic regions (Table 2), SAF is a negligible influence on the substantially greater temperature change in the Arctic. Multiple factors also contribute to the model differences in Arctic amplification with the non-SAF shortwave feedback seemingly the most important.[28]

After attempting to estimate the role of albedo feedback with respect to the surprisingly rapid melting in the Arctic, Winton concluded that actually the role of albedo is only one of many factors in accelerating arctic warming. More significant perhaps is Arctic-global, long-wave feedback difference originating from cloud, water vapor, and temperature feedbacks.

Michael Winton thus suggests that "combining these feedbacks might lead to either an under- or overestimation of the relative role of SAF (surface albedo feedback)," but that, "a clearer picture of the mechanisms of Arctic amplification in the models will require application of more refined feedback analysis techniques."[29] Other climate scientists agree about the significance of multiple hydrological feedbacks.[30] The feedbacks he points to, such as cloud, water vapor, and temperature feedbacks, remain among the most difficult to calculate.[31]

What seems to emerge from the flurry of studies on Arctic melting in the last decade is that cases of innumerable intertwined causal networks are perhaps the most significant, but also among the most challenging to capture empirically. It can become difficult to discern the degree to which each cause is contributing to the overall effect, and thus which are the areas of priority for further research and policy.

Furthermore, multiple interacting feedbacks are not the only driver of Arctic melting. Other causes are not necessarily feedbacks per se, but simply contributing factors adding to the overall dynamic. According to James Hansen and colleagues, another perhaps significant contribution to Arctic melting is the pollution emitted from nearby industrialized countries, which exacerbates the albedo effect. Soot, according to this theory, increases warming because snow retains aerosols, darkening the surface more in the late winter and spring when the sun is high in the sky and most effective, thus increasing absorption and lengthening the melt season. Hansen says the problem is perhaps more difficult than scientists thought at first, explaining, "Although laboratory experiments show that fine BC (black carbon) particles can escape with meltwater more readily than larger aerosols, there is a tendency for even the finest aerosols to be retained and enhance absorption in the melting season."[32] This example is one among many that signify that unanticipated interactions between the human-driven environmental problems are significant during the current era of unprecedented change.

Facing such challenges of highly complex dynamics, some scientists are directly employing complexity theories in order to address feedbacks more effectively. For instance, ecologists Lisa Belyea and Andrew Baird of the University of London have studied interwoven feedbacks within peat bogs. Because methane is a much more powerful greenhouse agent than carbon, and because much of the Northern permafrost covers such ecosystems, peat bogs could play a significant role in climate change. In this area, Belyea and Baird created a general complex adaptive systems (CAS) model based upon Simon Levin's CAS criteria and Timothy Allen's hierarchy principles.[33]

Belyea and Baird's complex adaptive systems model and analysis were significant to the success of their research. The authors linked peat land properties to what they call four general properties of complex adaptive systems (CAS): spatial heterogeneity, localized flows, self-organizing structure, and nonlinearity. They also present a framework for modeling peatlands in terms of CAS.

> In this framework, the system is disaggregated, both vertically and horizontally, into a set of components that interact locally through flows of energy and resources. Both internal dynamics and external forcing drive changes in hydrological conditions and microhabitat pattern, and these autogenic and allogenic changes in peatland structure affect hydrological processes, which, in turn, constrain peatland development and carbon cycling.[34]

Thus the authors link local dynamics regarding a common source of methane emissions with greater hydrological processes, and track how these hydrological processes in turn constrain peatland development and carbon cycling. Their work contributes to those researching larger hydrological patterns, such as Inez Fung and Michael Winton, and thus is an example of a local-scale CAS model benefitting larger-scale research.

Yet it raises the question of how well and whether in fact such a small-scale study on peat bogs can be magnified to look at larger regions of such ecosystems. Further, while this particular line of research may be promising, what happens in adding up innumerable such small-scale research projects? Does it lead to more clarity on macro-scale patterns such as global hydrological and carbon cycles? It leads back to a question raised by many climate thinkers – scientists, philosophers, and social theorists alike – which is the question of the limits of capacity and utility in aggregating immense amounts of data that ultimately will maintain some degree of uncertainty or unknowability with respect to the multiple interactions of a networked causality that one cannot possibly track completely. If one were to include most of the regional and global feedbacks involved in Arctic ice melting in a single model, the number and types of feedbacks and their interactions seems astronomical, an overwhelming task. It would require highly costly, complex models, begging further questions such as: At what point is the pursuit of precision in modeling unnecessary, uneconomical or unfeasible? When does further precision offer greater insight into the risks faced or the risk management options available?

Moreover, the answer to this puzzle necessarily cannot rely on reductionist modeling techniques alone. As Henri Atlan commented humorously,

> It's so very complex that, above all else, one must not use a reductionist method. In order to appreciate the nefarious effects, and one must integrate these, this necessarily requires a complex (methodological) approach. One must model climate change effects, integrated with economics, ecosystems – who wants to model all of that! There is only one solution. We must increase research budgets![35]

To follow the example of peat bogs and potential methane release further, beneath the Arctic permafrost lie large expanses of methane. While it is impossible to measure precisely, records of past climatic changes beg the question of whether there is enough methane to make the precise quantity a moot point.

Thresholds

Climate feedbacks are clarified in relation to another term in both the complexity and climate change literature, thresholds. Just as we see feedbacks throughout the climate change literature, and complex thinking helps to illuminate the nature of climate feedbacks, the same is true of thresholds.

Positive feedbacks lead toward thresholds, and at times toward major thresholds known as tipping points or in the case of climate change, large-scale abrupt climate changes. It's important to note that not all tipping points are abrupt climatic changes, and not all abrupt climatic changes come about through nonlinear feedback and consequent tipping points. Linear changes can also lead to a species' extinction.

There are both smaller-scale and larger-scale, and both social and ecological tipping points involved in climate change. Examples of smaller-scale tipping points include human use of a natural resource to the point of depletion, or deforestation to the point of a shift to a new phase state, e.g., savannah or desert. A tipping point in one system may drive tipping points in multiple other systems. Overuse of coal plants leads to various tipping points such as coral reef bleaching, ocean acidification, ocean carbon dioxide levels, and the collapse of ecosystems. Conjoined climate change tipping points at the global scale is called abrupt climate change.

Another common term used to describe such thresholds is "surprise." Generally speaking, the nonlinearities inherent in the hierarchy of the many systems making up the global climate system lead to changes that humans, in an effort to predict, plan, and understand, do not grasp. Such unanticipated consequences are termed "surprises." According to Stephen Schneider,

> Strictly speaking, a surprise is an unanticipated outcome; by definition it is an unexpected event. Potential climate change, and more broadly, global environmental change, is replete with this kind of truly unexpected surprise because of the enormous complexities of the processes and interrelationships involved (such as coupled ocean, atmosphere, and terrestrial systems) and our insufficient understanding of them. The IPCC (1996) defines surprises as "rapid, non-linear responses of the climatic system to anthropogenic forcing (e.g., greenhouse gas increases), such as the collapse of the 'conveyor belt' circulation in the North Atlantic Ocean or rapid deglaciation of polar ice sheets."[36]

Schneider distinguished between somewhat anticipated and truly unexpected surprises. This reveals a sensibility that is increasingly born out as climate scientists see that on the one hand, many feedbacks and thresholds they correctly anticipated have come to pass, while others they did not anticipate have also arisen. Due to complexification, the limits of knowledge, and unknowability, there are more or less "surprising" surprises.

Thresholds are thus ubiquitous in the climate change literature as well, but under many labels: surprise, tipping point, abrupt climate change, catastrophic climate change, sensitivity of system to disturbance, resilience of system to thresholds, vulnerability of system to thresholds, and more.

While local thresholds are significant in the case of climate change scientists focus increasingly on abrupt or catastrophic change for the obvious reason of significance to the aim of preventing collapses. This brings about a certain tension, the seeming paradox that if the analyses are ultimately too complex to carry out, once there is a certain degree of complexity – with its accompanying certain degree of intertwining of feedbacks, unintended, unforeseeable consequences, and surprises – then it seems to lead to insurmountable obstacles in the traditional research model. Scientists are then forced to adopt a research method that is more tenable for highly complex systems.

In discussing thresholds, the lesson of the past decade has been to incorporate nonlinearity – all of nonlinearity, meaning the tail end distributions or extreme events. Scientists have long included nonlinearity in analyses of climate change, but from Arrhenius to today, scientists often have underestimated it. Arrhenius' predictions of the amounts of carbon dioxide to accumulate in the atmosphere were extraordinarily accurate back in the 1890s. What he omitted was the possibility of nonlinearity, with the ensuing abrupt change it could bring about. So Arrhenius was correct in the amount of greenhouse gas emissions to accumulate in the atmosphere, but he inaccurately suggested that the climatic effects, e.g., melting of the Arctic sea ice, would not be seen for another 3,000 years.

As recently as 2006 and thereafter, climate scientists often have spoken in careful hypotheticals. In 2007, Richard Kerr wrote in *Science*,

> A few years ago, researchers modeling the fate of Arctic sea ice under global warming saw a good chance that the ice could disappear, in summertime at least, by the end of the 21st century. Then talk swung to summer ice not making it past mid-century. Now, after watching Arctic sea ice shrink back last month to a startling record-low area, scientists are worried that 2050 may be overoptimistic.[37]

In 2007, Kerr quoted John Walsh of the University of Alaska, Fairbanks, a polar researcher, "This year has been such a quantum leap downward, it has surprised many scientists. This ice is more vulnerable than we thought." And that vulnerability seems to be growing from year to year, inspiring concern that Arctic ice could be in an abrupt, irreversible decline. "Maybe we are reaching the tipping point."[38]

In an article entitled, "The Thinning of Arctic Sea Ice, 1988–2003: Have We Passed a Tipping Point?" climate scientists Ronald Lindsay and Jinlun Zhang argue that we have already passed a critical threshold in global climate change.[39] They cite the satellite data showing the record or near-record lows for ice extent in 2002–2005. Models of the melting have shown that since 1988 the thickness of the simulated basin-wide ice thinned by 1.31 meters or 43 percent, greatest along the coast from the Chukchi Sea to the Beaufort Sea to Greenland. According to Lindsay and Zhang, thinning since 1988 is due to:

> …preconditioning, a trigger, and positive feedbacks: (1) the fall, winter, and spring air temperatures over the Arctic Ocean have gradually increased over the last 50 years, leading to reduced thickness of first-year ice at the start of summer; (2) a temporary shift, starting in 1989, of two principal climate indexes (the Arctic Oscillation and Pacific Decadal Oscillation) caused a flushing of some of the older, thicker ice out of the basin and an increase in the summer open water extent; and (3) the increasing amounts of summer open water allow for increasing absorption of solar radiation, which melts the ice, warms the water, and promotes creation of thinner first-year ice, ice that often entirely melts by the end of the subsequent summer.[40]

The IPPC scientists have been increasingly aware of the problems of not including greater potential nonlinearity in their models. With respect to the general climate models (GCMs) at the core of early IPCC reports, Stephen Schneider and economist and climate scholar Christian Azar noted in 2001,

> Although these highly aggregated models are not intended to provide high confidence quantitative projections of coupled socio-natural system behaviors, we believe that the bulk of integrated assessment models used to date for climate policy analysis – and which do not include any such abrupt nonlinear processes – will not be able to alert the policymaking community to the importance of abrupt nonlinear behaviors.[41]

Climate scientists must manage to include risks of catastrophes in cost-benefit analysis, or find better forms of analysis. Schneider and Azar wrote that the complexity of the climate implies, "that surprises and catastrophic effects could well unfold as the climate system is forced to change, and that the larger the forcing, the more likely there will be large and unforeseen responses."[42]

Some theories about past major climate changes in Earth's history now hinge on an abrupt shift in which multiple thresholds were triggered. One theory is that abrupt climate change triggered volcanoes, which in turn blocked sunlight, in turn provoking major species losses, creating cascades of extinctions, and exacerbating conditions for all species. In an example of a cascade of tipping points, climate change itself, as well as seismic activity, can trigger volcanic eruptions, inducing further climate change.

> Abrupt climate change can trigger volcanic collapses, phenomena that cause the destruction of the entire sector of a volcano, including its summit. During the past 30 ka, major volcanic collapses occurred just after main glacial peaks that ended with rapid deglaciation. Glacial debuttressing, load discharge and fluid circulation coupled with the post-glacial increase of humidity and heavy rains can activate the failure of unstable edifices. Furthermore, significant global warming can be responsible for the collapse of ice-capped unstable volcanoes, an unpredictable hazard that in a few minutes can bury inhabited areas.[43]

By seeing the various facets of the complexity framework in their mutual interaction, at times the complexity framework seems to redefine itself. One grasps the terms individually, and then as an ensemble, upon which one sees the interconnections between them, which ultimately leads to a renewed understanding of each of the original terms, and so on. In this instance, we understand the causal links between these three terms – feedbacks cause thresholds that cause surprises. However, if we were looking for surprises in the first place, we may call them by a different name. As Schneider puts it,

Events that are not truly unexpected are better defined as imaginable abrupt events. For other events – true surprises – although the outcome may be unknown, it may be possible to identify imaginable conditions for surprise. For example, if rate of change of CO_2 concentrations is one imaginable condition for surprise (i.e., more rapid forcing increases the chances for surprises), the system would be less rapidly forced if decision-makers chose as a matter of policy to slow down the rate at which human activities modify the atmosphere. To deal with such questions, the policy community needs to understand both the potential for surprises and how difficult it is for integrated assessment models, or IAMs (and other models as well) to credibly evaluate the probabilities of currently imaginable "surprises," let alone those not currently envisioned...

A common view of the climate system and ecosystem structure and function is that of path independence (no memory of previous conditions). However, the multiple stable equilibria for both THC and for atmosphere-biosphere interactions in West Africa suggest a more complex reality. In such systems, the equilibrium state reached is dependent on the initial conditions of the system. Crossing thresholds can lead to unpredictable or irreversible changes. Furthermore, such complex processes have an implication for effective policymaking. Incorporating possibly damaging effects of changes in THC into modelling of climate change policy, for example, can significantly alter policy recommendations and lead to discovery of emergent properties of the coupled social-natural system.[44]

Positive feedbacks and thresholds are clearly central to climate change science, and thus to climate policy, ethics, and conceptions of our societies and our common future. See also, for instance, P. Higgins et al 2002, "Dynamics of Climate and Ecosystem Coupling: Abrupt changes and multiple equilibria."

Vulnerability, resilience, and strategy

Since primary causes of climate change are anthropogenic we have considerable power to change policy now and into the future. Feedbacks and thresholds help to clarify overall understanding of human and natural vulnerability and resilience, emphasizing the role of strategy and proaction on climate change.

Given that numerous interdependent feedbacks and network causalities involve degrees of ignorance, unknowns and surprises, highly complex issues like climate change require a shift in focus from studying primarily individual drivers, towards studying both individual drivers and systemic, cumulative effects. Increasingly complex models have been developed to strive to pinpoint major drivers and forcings that are playing out at multiple hierarchical levels in the global systems influencing climate change.

In the case of highly complex environmental change, it becomes less important and often impossible to fully clarify individual feedbacks, and increasingly important to act on what is clear, such as the need to: reduce carbon dioxide emissions, promote net reforestation, and alleviate poverty. Whatever the precise means by which multiple feedbacks lead to accelerating climate change, it is evident that past a certain threshold there is an increasingly high probability of catastrophic consequences. Moreover, many of these consequences play out in terms of networked interactions and consequences. The complexity principles of network causality and unanticipated consequences support the need for increased proaction to reduce climate change, while these same principles also forewarn of the risks of geoengineering.

Clearly we must reduce activities causing unnecessary carbon emissions, leading to the challenge of democratic decisions about values and priorities. Complexity theories also help to clarify the nature of social and environmental interdependence, vulnerability and resilience. Increasing awareness of the links between interdependence and resilience may facilitate discussions of common values with respect to policies, strategies, and visions for the future.

The major empirical evidence of climate change in the last decade is sufficient to merit great policy changes to mitigate against further climate change. The modernist belief in absolute truths has been shattered. Dynamic, complexifying systems call for action in the face of partial ignorance and uncertainties, given the strength of what we do know.

In fact, we have always based the majority of actions and policies on a large degree of uncertainties and unknowns. We have held assumptions that science produces certainties but we have lived lives of uncertainties, unknowns, vulnerability and resilience. Just as in everyday life, so in the case of climate change we must act on the best evidence, and not some kind of impossible "absolute" evidence.

As University of California at Berkeley biologists Margaret Torn and John Harte report,

> Experimental and modeling evidence is accumulating that terrestrial ecosystems could form positive feedbacks with global warming in the next century through changes in, for example, primary productivity, soil carbon storage, and methane emissions due to the influence of climate on, for example, length of growing season, soil moisture, and permafrost, respectively. All ten simulations in the recent coupled climate carbon cycle model intercomparison (CAMIP) show positive feedback by 2100 due to ecosystems.[45]

Torn and Harte argue that scientists should pursue better understanding of the feedbacks. But their principal message here was to state that the nature and significance of interacting feedbacks must bring about a greater sense of urgency in climate policy. Once the nature of feedbacks is understood and more accurately included in climate scenarios it becomes more obvious that the stakes are quite high, militating for rapid emissions reductions.

Schneider contextualized discussion of thresholds with other major complexity principles – equilibriums, emergent properties, and irreversibility:

Most global systems are inherently complex, consisting of multiple interacting sub-units. Scientists frequently attempt to model these complex systems in isolation often along distinct disciplinary lines, producing internally stable and predictable behavior. However, real world coupling between subsystems can cause the set of interacting systems to exhibit new collective behaviors – called "emergent properties" – that are not clearly demonstrable by models that do not also include such coupling. Furthermore, responses of the coupled systems to external forcing can become quite complicated. For example, one emergent property increasingly evident in climate and biological systems is that of irreversibility or hysteresis – changes that persist in the new post-disturbance state even when the original forcing is restored. This irreversibility can be a consequence of multiple stable equilibria in the coupled system – that is, the same forcing might produce different responses depending on the pathway followed by the system. Therefore, anomalies can push the coupled system from one equilibrium to another, each of which has very different sensitivity to disturbances (i.e., each equilibrium may be self-sustaining within certain limits).

The foregoing discussion is primarily about model-induced behaviors, but hysteresis has also been observed in nature (e.g., Rahmstorf, 1996). Exponential increases in computational power have encouraged scientists to turn their attention to broadly focused projects that couple multiple disciplinary models. General Circulation Models (GCMs) of the atmosphere and oceans, for example, now allow exploration of emergent properties in the climate system resulting from interactions between the atmospheric, oceanic, biospheric, and cryogenic components.[46]

Schneider wrote this in 2003. By 2008 James Hansen and other climate scientists declared that we had passed critical global climate change tipping points.

Leading climate scientists discussed in this chapter have shifted their analysis to incorporate greater complexity. Some mainstream interpretations have also begun to shift, but more adequate complex framing of climate change remains to be done. Table 9.2 notes some of the issues involved in this shift. It also highlights the centrality of transdisciplinarity to complexity, and both to issues of rapid global change.

The Intergovernmental Panel on Climate Change Fourth Assessment Report: uncertainty, irreversibility, and effective risk management

The Intergovernmental Panel on Climate Change is the primary international scientific organization that has reported on climate change since 1988. Inquiring into their utilization of complexity principles, I reviewed the most recent comprehensive IPPC report, *Climate Change 2007*, published in three parts in the winter and spring of 2007, with an additional synthesis report published in November 2007.[47] The main activity of the IPCC is to provide in regular intervals assessment reports (AR) of the state of knowledge on climate change. The IPCC will release the fifth assessment report in 2013. Experts from more than 130 countries contributed to the fourth report, representing six years of work. More than 450 lead authors received input from more than 800 contributing authors, and an additional 2,500 experts reviewed the draft documents. The total involvement and consensus comprises over 3,700 of the world's leading scientists.[48]

In the IPCC reports since 1988, and increasingly by 2007, many complexity principles play a central role. Along with feedbacks, thresholds, and vulnerability, resilience and strategy, several other terms are clearly central in the IPCC report on climate change. Central among these are uncertainty, adaptive capacity, interdisciplinarity, and transdisciplinarity. Uncertainty has increasingly led to grappling with what is knowable and not knowable, and how to construe and cope with risk and risk assessment for policy. The focus of climate science on degrees of uncertainty, risk, and irreversibility, is coevolving with the further complexity principles of agency, strategy, and proaction.

Uncertainty has become a dominant theme in the science and discourse of climate change. In various ways, feedbacks, thresholds, vulnerability, and sustainability lead us back time and again to the issue of uncertainty, its meaning and significance, what it signifies about our scientific method, beliefs, and frameworks, how it influences our methods, interpretation, and goals. Subsequently, this indicates the need to shift from framings of uncertainty to framings centered on risks and strategy for risk management.

Over the past ten years, several prominent climate scientists and scholars have begun to reveal in more depth the significance of uncertainties in climate change and how uncertainty is part and parcel of complex, dynamic systems. As Stephen Schneider and Chrisitan Azar wrote in 2001,

> Uncertainty surrounds every corner of the climate debate. Moreover, because of the complexity of the climate system, surprises can be expected (e.g., IPCC, 1996a, p. 7; IPCC, 201b, Chapter 1). Low probability and catastrophic events, as well as evidence of multiple equilibria in climate system are of key concern in the climate debate.[49]

Likewise, as Schneider wrote in a 2002 paper, significant uncertainties plague projections of climate change and its consequences.[50] Yet, climate science in the last two decades has clarified two points about uncertainty. First, it only further validates the significance of science, with which we at least have very good models of probabilities and risks. Second, as Schneider used to say, "uncertainty cuts both ways." We are uncertain about negative outcomes, but also about potentially positive ones.

Similarly, adaptation and mitigation, which are directly dependent on highly complex socioecological interactions, introduce various types of uncertainties, many of them great. As Katherine Vincent, climate change social theorist writes,

> Assessing adaptation is fraught with uncertainties, as it requires future projections of whether adaptive capacity assets will be drawn upon in times of

need. Instead the potential for a unit of analysis to adapt, or its adaptive capacity, tends to be considered, even though assessing this is still uncertain. The capacity to adapt to climate change is dependent on a wide variety of social, political, economic, technological and institutional factors. The specific interaction of these factors differs depending on the scale of analysis: from the level of the country down to the individual. Adaptive capacity is multidimensional: it is determined by complex inter-relationships of a number of factors at different scales.[51]

These uncertainties carry over into the study and evaluation of adaptations. Vincent writes, "Although controversial, the use of indicators and indices is one means of quantifying adaptive capacity for the use of policymakers. However, the process of identifying and deriving accurate indicators is [also] fraught with uncertainties." In the typology of uncertainties, three of these include: a normative selection of driving forces, the choice of an appropriate indicator of that driving force, and a determination of the direction of the relationship between indicator and driver.[52]

Indeed, as researchers have been confronted with increasing focus on highly complex systems in recent decades, they have developed a new sense of uncertainty, the understanding that complex systems, and particularly highly complex socioecological systems, have the inherent characteristic of uncertainty. In examining the extent and depth of uncertainties in climate change, many scientists have remarked on the ubiquity of uncertainties in other large, socioecological phenomena. As Suraje Dessai and colleagues, another group of social science climate scholars, wrote:

> Uncertainty, then, is pervasive in the climate change debate, but uncertainty is not unique to climate change. There is uncertainty associated with other global phenomena – the economy, geopolitics, and health – whether in relation to economic crises, terrorism, or influenzas and pandemics. In fact, uncertainty is a multi-dimensional concept that is omnipresent in our society.[53]

Indeed, uncertainty also is an inherent aspect of the scientific enterprise, as philosophers such as Karl Popper, Paul Feyeraband, and Nicholas Rescher have pointed out. It is in this sense that climate scientist Stephen Schneider notes that uncertainty, and more specifically, the level of certainty needed to reach a firm conclusion, is a perennial issue in all science for policy as in all knowledge.

Uncertainty, like complexity, while ever-present, did not interfere much with the progression of science and technology throughout most of the modern age. Like complexity, uncertainty is ubiquitous, and yet human scientists, technologists, and other social leaders did not have to confront it directly all the time, or at least managed to ignore it consistently. But as Westernization and globalization progressed, human societies usurped more of the earth's total biomass, land-surface, and natural resources. As the impacts of human actions have intensified, extending human impact in both reach and in networked causalities, complexity principles like uncertainty – along with all the related complexity principles like risk, harm, vulnerability, unintended consequences, and thresholds – has come increasingly to the fore. No longer are fire or theft insurance the only areas in which uncertainty is dealt with in a rational, probabilistic, manner. As Schneider notes, "the difficulties of explaining uncertainty have become increasingly salient as society seeks policy advice to deal with global environmental change."[54]

Although mainstream climate change scientific community has widely acknowledged of the problem of uncertainty and made major advances in incorporating these uncertainties, nonetheless, incorporation of certain aspects of uncertainty into analyses was still partly lacking in the IPCC 2007 assessment reports. Historically, IPCC assessment reports like other climate assessments made the mainstream mistake of mostly omitting events considered to be low-probability but high consequence. As Stephen Schneider has suggested of climate change literature more generally, for the most part, up through the Fourth Assessment Report, the IPCC reports primarily considered scenarios that attempted to "bracket the uncertainty" rather than explicitly integrate unlikely events from the "tails of the distribution."

Moreover, interactions between social and ecological systems, which are numerous, rapid, and carry significant impacts in contemporary times, are largely omitted. Schneider wrote, "Not even considered in the standard analytical works are structural changes in political or economic systems or regime shifts such as a change in public consciousness regarding environmental values."[55] These can work both to exacerbate and to correct for climate change. So the science also must incorporate human responses to climate change.

Critics have found that the IPCC reports omit too much by way of networked feedbacks, nonlinear change, and thresholds. Although researchers may recognize the wide range of uncertainty surrounding global climate change, and although they include much consideration of feedbacks, their analyses typically have been surprise-free – an omission that amounts to a monumental policy failure. As Schneider said,

> Decision-makers reading the "standard" literature will rarely appreciate the full range of possible outcomes, and thus might be more willing to risk adapting to prospective changes rather than attempting to avoid them through abatement, than if they were aware that some potentially unpleasant surprises could be lurking (pleasant ones might occur as well, but many policymakers tend to insure against negative outcomes preferentially).[56]

Brian O'Neill, a futurist who Simon Levin has called, "one of the brightest young scientists out there," is one of the youngest scientists in the IPCC network, "trying to reformulate climate change projections that can cope better with uncertainty by accounting for 'future learning.'"[57] O'Neill works on improving what he sees as major shortcomings in the IPCC work and hopes to improve upon the IPCC failure to adequately account for complexity, uncertainty, and tipping points. According to O'Neill, researchers desperately need a strategy for tackling climate uncertainties.[58]

O'Neill is pointing to an epistemological failure, the way that uncertainty is studied, framed, and thus approached. This issue has always been part of our lives, and we have dealt with it well in other instances. We have always used probabilistic methods to assess and allocate insurance in the case of fire, theft, and other unpredictable, rare or extreme events – always possible but in any given moment uncertain. We must extend this logic to climate policy, by similarly taking extreme events seriously.

After noting the challenge of uncertainty in climate prediction for example, climate social scientist Suraje Dessai and colleagues argued for policy and action in the face of uncertainty. They found for instance that given "deep uncertainties" involved in climate prediction and the prediction of climate impacts, and given that climate is usually only one factor in decisions aimed at climate adaptation, therefore, the "'predict and provide' approach to science" in support of climate change adaptation is significantly flawed.[59]

Campaigns against climate science have used seventeenth-century notions of scientific processes to argue that full certainties are prerequisites to action. In fact, complexity shows that uncertainty, unknowability, probabilities, and risks, are just inherent characteristics of highly complex systems. Collapses are also inherent risks in complex systems. Increasing the complexity of models and analysis has helped scientists to demonstrate that risks and probabilities are logical bases of adaptation and mitigation policies. In the face of high stakes situations with the potential for irreversible, networked consequences, it is foolish and irresponsible to fail to learn and adapt. Inaction, just like proaction, is a choice.

Suraje Dessai and colleagues conclude, for instance:

> We suggest that decision makers systematically examine the performance of their adaptation strategies/policies/activities over a wide range of plausible futures driven by uncertainty about the future state of climate and many other economic, political and cultural factors. They should choose a strategy that they find sufficiently robust across these alternative futures. Such an approach can identify successful adaptation strategies without accurate and precise predictions of future climate.[60]

Similarly, in a coauthored chapter on research methods for the Fourth Assessment Report, Brian O'Neill echoed the epistemological concerns, such as those of Dessai and Schneider mentioned above, that IPCC assessment reports primarily consider scenarios that attempt to "bracket the uncertainty," rather than explicitly integrate unlikely events from the "tails of the distribution." Bracketing the uncertainty may appear as the next logical step for those trained in mainstream policy methods involving certainty and clear delineations between outcomes. However, embracing the perspective of complex systems and inherent degrees of uncertainty in social and environmental systems, requires embracing the related approaches of probabilities and risk management.

Bracketing the uncertainty is like Cuba deciding at the beginning of a hurricane season not to prepare for a level five hurricane at all, because there is less than a 50 percent change of a level five event. Obviously, with a 10 percent chance of a level five hurricane, residents will be willing to pay for major preparations. It is because we explicitly integrate extreme events in such examples we have always lived with, that Cubans and others in hurricane-prone areas usually prepare well for a level five event, even with only a one percent chance. With this same logic we must work to reduce the risks of climate change. We have always included tails of distribution for the probability of flooding in flood plains. Why would we not include tails of distribution for a *cause* of potential flooding: climate change!

In writing the IPCC chapter, O'Neill saw that in the effort to create consensus, important complexity analyses fell out of the final drafts. He warned that when scientists lack knowledge of how accurately to describe probabilities of such unlikely but catastrophic events, they simply omitted them or wrote them in very vague terms. Granted, any large group writing effort is plagued by the need for compromise. And there does need to be consensus for climate scientists to be taken seriously and to send clear messages to policymakers. O'Neill acknowledges that it is important for climate scientists to speak with a powerful, united voice. However, he says, this is counterproductive if it results in a misrepresentation and minimization of the most serious risks. "The extreme scenarios that tend to fall out of the IPCC process may be exactly the ones we should most worry about."[61]

To address this problem, O'Neill has been organizing interdisciplinary groups to work on the issues of feedbacks, thresholds and uncertainty in the assessment process. For instance, he assembled a team of a half-dozen demographers, economists, statisticians and physical scientists to try to sharpen the models to better account for uncertainty and thresholds. Early in 2008 he organized a meeting of top climate scientists, economists, and demographers to think about how they generate knowledge. What emerged as the most significant issue was how IPCC scientists have been failing to adequately incorporate what they called the "Wile E. Coyote effect" – the moment when the cartoon coyote doesn't realize that he is falling off of a cliff until he looks down, too late to turn back. The Wile E. Coyote moment is a climate change threshold.

In particular, scientists wish to clarify knowledge about climate thresholds such as an abrupt change to the ocean's "conveyer-belt" system, or thermohaline circulation (THC) belt. O'Neill warns that while scientists need to know more about the natural variability of the oceanic THC, they still don't even know "how precise your measurements have to be" or how large an area must be studied before uncertainty could be sufficiently reduced to spot "the edge of the cliff."[62]

Climate scientist Michael Schlesinger points to another example. Only a decade ago, climate scientists predicted a much slower melting rate of Arctic ice.

Each year since, we have learned that polar ice sheets are melting "faster than anticipated."[63] "Things are happening right now [2006] with the ice sheets that were not predicted to happen until 2100," said Schlesinger. "My worry is that we may have passed the window of opportunity where learning is still useful."[64] Climate feedbacks are taking place in largely interconnected, interacting systems, but there are also many unknown and uncertain drivers and forcings working within them. Uncertainty cuts both ways; in highly complex systems there may be welcome surprises.

We have to be cautious of classical thinking that sees change as monolithic, black and white, inevitable success or inevitable failure. Yet we have to be equally cautious of the classical thinking that dissociates science from ethics, and fails to see issues of rate, nonlinearity, and the potential for irreversible collapses.

Certainly, scientists in and outside the IPCC have made much progress in grasping and incorporating the role of uncertainty in scientific assessments. It has been a step-by-step process as climate science and complex thinking coevolve. The IPCC reports have increasingly included plenty of data on nonlinear change and thresholds, such as the ubiquitous nonlinear graph popularly called "hockey-stick charts," a long straight line followed by a sharp exponential curve upwards, a threshold. A famously large hockey stick chart in the movie *An Inconvenient Truth* included such a steep threshold that to show it to the audience Al Gore had to climb a tall ladder.

IPCC reports regularly include graphs of potential thresholds and tipping points. However, since more and more experts' views must get incorporated with each round of more general summaries, the most nonlinear events tend to be included in the detailed reports, and then excluded from the concluding summaries. Amidst the writing of the Fourth Assessment Report, some IPCC scholars made the following remarks about how the IPCC improved their uptake of uncertainty from 1990 to 2007.[65] They noted that different disciplines use different methods to study conditions of uncertainty. Thus, any hope of a universal approach to uncertainty management has been debunked; it is necessary to embrace a plurality of methodological approaches to uncertainty throughout the myriad disciplines that bear upon climate change. Finally, scientists must learn to capture key uncertainties without oversimplifying the way different kinds of uncertainty appear at different scales. As Einstein said, they must simplify as much as possible, but not more.

> Looking back over three and a half Assessment Reports, we see that the Intergovernmental Panel on Climate Change (IPCC) has given increasing attention to the management and reporting of uncertainties, but coordination across working groups (WGs) has remained an issue. We argue that there are good reasons for WGs to use different methods to assess uncertainty, thus it is better that WGs agree to disagree rather than seek one universal approach to uncertainty management. In the IPCC First and Second Assessment Reports, uncertainty was not addressed systematically across WGs.

Uncertainty statements were not centrally coordinated, but left at the authors' discretion.

In 1990, the WG I executive summary started with what the authors were certain of and what they were confident about, thus taking a subjective perspective. They used strong words like "predict", a term which would nowadays rightly be avoided. For WG II (Impacts) and WG III (Response Strategies), the review procedures were not very rigorous yet and uncertainties were not a major topic of debate.[66]

Transdisciplinary science studies commentators noted some of the flaws of these approaches. As climate change opponents and detractors began using uncertainty against the IPCC scientists, these scholars aimed to cut through the confusion surrounding uncertainty. Analyzing an IPCC report in 1996, leading STS scholars Simon Shackley and Brian Wynne suggested that the potentially damaging effects of uncertainty in scientific knowledge could be limited if certainty about uncertainty could be achieved. Attempts at clarification or "auditing" of uncertainty is common in scientific reviews and assessments and plays a role in the process of achieving consensus around scientific knowledge claims. As Sir John Houghton, chairman of the scientific assessment Working Group (WGI) of the IPCC, stated, at the IPCC,

> [C]lear distinctions have been drawn between what is likely to occur (with appropriate ranges of uncertainty given) and changes which are much less likely and more speculative.... This clarity of approach very considerably aided the wide acceptance of the IPCC's finding by policymakers and the signing by nearly all countries of the Climate Convention.[67]

While Houghton said, "the [quantitative] estimation of uncertainty is at the heart of the scientific method ... [e]ven when the uncertainties are large."[68]

Seeking to bridge the concerns of policymakers and scientists, Shackley and Wynne analyzed the conundrum of sufficient certainty about uncertainty. They discussed the difficult navigation between the goal of objectivity and the false routes of positivism and relativism, following Kristin Shrader-Frechette's advice to not "throw out the baby of objectivity with the bathwater of positivism."[69] While supporting the authority of the IPCC scientists, they aimed to show how, to date, the IPCC was falling short of sufficiently articulating climate change uncertainties. It is worth quoting at some length.

> Although scientific uncertainty appears to be well articulated in such representations [as the IPCC's second assessment report], closer inspection suggests that climate scientists are unable to demarcate clearly or fully the extent and type of all forms of uncertainty by the methods and practices of climatology. For example, nowhere in the IPCC's reports of 1990 and 1992 is there a systematic discussion of what is meant by uncertainty in different contexts, of the different meanings of uncertainty, or of methods of analyzing it. In the

absence of further explanation, therefore, it appears paradoxical that the IPCC reports rely so heavily on qualitative indications of certainty. It is also beguiling that while scientists apparently favor quantitative uncertainty ranges, Houghton (1994) reports that scientists have a difficult time agreeing on exactly what the ranges mean.

For example, in assessment for policymakers, climate scientists usually give a range of estimate for the temperate response at the earth's surface to a doubling of carbon dioxide (CO_2), sometimes called the "climate sensitivity." This range of $1.5°$ to $4.5°$ Celsius is arrived at by using deterministic climate models and is not a probability range. The most sophisticated models adopt fundamental laws, such as Newtonian laws of motion and the gas law, to simulate the circulation of the atmosphere and ocean at grid points in a three-dimensional space. These general circulation models (GCMs) have been developed from weather forecasting models and have a large computational requirement. They can be "run into the future" with a sudden or gradual increase in the prescribed atmospheric concentration of CO_2 as a means of exploring climatic changes. One of the scientists involved in preparing the IPCC's 1990 report commented in an interview:

[W]hat they were very keen for us to do at IPCC, and modelers refused and we didn't do it, was to say we've got this range $1.5–4.5°$, what are the probability limits of that? You can't do it. It's not the same as experimental error. The range has nothing to do with probability – it is not a normal distribution or a skewed distribution. *Who knows what it is?* (emphasis added)[70]

Such limitations in the articulation – and understanding – of uncertainty, as judged by climate scientists' own expressed standards, only emerge from more detailed enquiry and would not be apparent to most policymakers. Climate scientists, however, do understand such limitations of the analysis of uncertainty even if they do not always articulate them fully. Accordingly, most scientists can be satisfied about the validity of representations such as those in the IPCC reports even when the limitations are not made fully explicit. Policymakers can also accept this discourse of the management of uncertainty because it is sufficiently ambiguous not to threaten their authority as decision makers (e.g., accounting for uncertainty can be seen as a useful "service function" of science for policy).[71]

In the end, climate science has prevailed. Even while grappling with the increasingly clearly central issues of complexity and uncertainty, climate science has been vindicated, as, globally, predictions have played out with remarkable accuracy. The critical global trends of climate change we see today were all thoroughly understood and predicted by climate scientists for the last few decades. The crucial take-home message is that climate science has succeeded. Even while particular understanding of uncertainty, nonlinearity, and risk assessment have developed in conjunction over the last few decades, the science of global climate change has been highly accurate.

Just as our certainty about uncertainty has increased, the empirical evidence has born out precisely the general predictions that climate scientists had made, only faster. In other words, it's clear that specific predictions about when, where, and to what degree particular events would play out – which ice shelves would break, precisely when and where droughts, floods, and hurricanes would take place, etc. – is impossible. However, scientists' general global predictions about climate change have been highly accurate. In this sense, climate scientists have become more certain about both uncertainty and about the validity and strength of their increasingly complex models and scenarios.

Warmer air means three precise, highly predictable trends: more water in the oceans, and more energy and moisture in the atmosphere. At the global scale these three trends are very predictable. At the scale of particular regions, much about how these will play out over time is predictable – e.g., most of Bangladesh, two-thirds of Florida, and much of New York, London, and Venice will be underwater. Generally speaking, more energy and more moisture in the air means that some regions will have heavier flooding, and some heavier droughts. In this sense, climate science predictions have been highly successful.

Perhaps the major weakness of climate science in the last few decades was to omit or underestimate the significance of feedbacks, nonlinearity and therefore potential thresholds.

In the summer of 2005 Arctic sea ice underwent very rapid and sudden melting. Climate scientists were surprised not by the events, but by how fast they were happening. Chunks of sea ice the size of US states began falling off glaciers into the sea. Such events spurred erstwhile reluctant scientists to take the questions of uncertainty and thresholds more seriously. At the same time, these events validated both complexity science and climate science, and demonstrated the need to continue to link the two.

Meanwhile, interdisciplinary teams of IPCC scientists had become increasingly aware that initial, more classical scientific approaches, more fully reductionist and more based on absolute certainties, was unattainable. In its place, methodological and epistemological pluralism amongst different disciplines involved in climate science had become imperative. This is the thesis of the IPCC scientists in the article subtitled "Agreeing to Disagree."[72] As scientists worked on ensuing IPCC reports, talk shifted from prediction to projection and from uncertainty to degrees or scales of uncertainty. This implied that uncertainty should be framed not as an inconvenience to be overcome, but as an inherent aspect of complex global systems that had to be understood in terms of degrees and scales. They wrote,

In the Second Assessment Report (1996), WG I dropped the usage of uncertainty terms in its main policy messages, but added a special section on uncertainties. Efforts were made to reach consensus on appropriate formulations for uncertainty-laden statements. The key formulation "the balance of evidence suggests" was coined during the plenary meeting jointly by IPCC delegates and lead authors. "Predicting" was replaced by "projecting" climatic changes on the basis of a set of scenarios. In its concluding chapter "Advancing the understanding," WG I mentions the need for a more formal and consistent approach to uncertainties in the future. WG II, which covered scientific–technical analyses of impacts, adaptations and mitigation of climate change, assigned low, medium or high levels of confidence to the major findings of the chapters in the executive summaries, following again the subjective approach. Explicit reporting of uncertainties was not a key focus in the WG III assessment on the economic and social dimensions of climate change. They were captured through reporting of ranges from the literature and scenario-based what-if analyses of costs of response action. In preparation for the Third Assessment Report (2001), a strong demand for a more systematic approach to uncertainties was identified—as recommended by WG I in the Second Assessment Report.[73]

A more systematic approach to the uncertainties came in 2000 in the form of a crosscutting guidance paper on uncertainties by leading climate scientists Richard Moss and Stephen Schneider.[74] The paper summarized the relevant literature and built upon the Second Assessment Report's lessons. The team which prepared the book in which Moss and Schneider's report was found discussed the idea of organizing the guidelines on uncertainty around a general scale ranging from totally true, certain, or known, to totally unknowable. The known to unknown scale was seen as attractive from the perspective of the need for simplicity. But the writers decided it would be overly simplistic. In the end, they came upon a "two-dimensional, qualitative" way to qualify key findings based on two factors: first, the amount of evidence – the number of sources of information – and second, the degree of the agreement – how much the different sources point in the same direction. It was left up to individual author teams to calibrate the two scales – the amount of evidence and the degree of agreement.

Thus, the scientists found themselves in the position of an exercise that many of them had not been well trained for, the epistemological question of how to discern qualitative measures for uncertainty. They were forced to become more transdisciplinary thinkers, or to listen more carefully to the more transdisciplinary climate scientists. The relationship between evidence and belief varies a lot between disciplines, according to Moss and Schneider. Presumably, a single available case study would score low on the first scale, while seven or more independent controlled experiments would score high. If seven or more experimenters' results were similar, they'd score high on both scales. Thus, the guidance paper proposed:

1   A pluralist methodology (recommended steps for assessing uncertainty)
2   A common vocabulary to express quantitative levels of confidence, and
3   Terms describing qualitative levels of understanding, based on both the available amount of evidence and the degree of consensus among experts.[75]

This is one example of IPCC efforts to better incorporate uncertainty and extreme events. Many scientists have reflected on appropriate ways to approach, capture, and describe uncertainties. Uncertainty is more present in the IPCC's Fourth Assessment Report. As O'Neill points out, however, it still seems to omit what may be the most important data of all, the more large-scale, more abrupt changes.

Such concerns are not new, just increasingly evident. Questions of inherent uncertainty and risk have been addressed for a long time and increasingly since the 1970s. The complexification of knowledge after Rescher, along with the partial ignorance and unknowability it brings to light, help to explain two key lessons for the science, ethics and policy of climate change. First, the main complexity principle regarding the significance of observers and contexts shows that science is always imbued with partial uncertainties and unknowabilities with respect to all knowledge, but especially in the case of large, highly complex systems. Second, the principle of nested hierarchies shows that in large complex systems one requires the full cadre of disciplinary, interdisciplinary and transdisciplinary knowledge. At the same time, while transdisciplinarity improves knowledge of highly complex systems, it also further demonstrates that any one observer or discipline is always limited with respect to transdisicplinary problems. This perspective makes very clear the need for what is now called collaborative scholarly communities and epistemological communities, which is recognized as central to the work of both the MEA and the IPCC.

Understanding that climate systems are complex and transdisciplinary and accepting the implications of this, can help society to make more informed and beneficial risk management choices.

Conclusion

The Intergovernmental Panel on Climate Change and the Millennium Ecosystem Assessment have responded to issues of extraordinary social and environmental complexity by developing and advancing the major complexity principles involved, such as feedbacks, thresholds, and uncertainties. All of these issues have improved our understanding of the related issues of vulnerability and resilience. As they address issues that are both highly complex and significant such as climate change, scientists and scholars have naturally been driven to exploring and advancing complexity principles, to harness their power in understanding global change.

The applied aims of climate science for policy necessitates generalized complexity theories. Complexity theories writ large help us to frame and to comprehend many of the key complexity principles at the heart of climate change – feedbacks, thresholds, transdisciplinarity, uncertainty, risk, vulnerability, and proaction. In the climate science literature, for instance, these issues are often boiled down to a few key issues for policy, such as the uncertainty of outcomes, the potential for high consequence outcomes, and the potential for irreversible outcomes. Put simply: uncertainty, risk, and irreversibility.

Rapid global change has pushed thinkers in all disciplines onto a fast track of learning about complexity. We need nothing less; the current global crises require urgent action, and complexity shows us the need for and basis of a deep and radical rethinking. One of the great lessons of the two large environmental assessments in the last decade, the MEA and the IPCC reports, is the profound importance of transdisciplinary collaboration and thinking.

The complexity framework can assist in developing this collaboration. First, complexity can help to articulate and operationalize concepts about which there is general consensus, but not yet much advanced elaboration. One hears much talk, for instance, of the need for plurality in methods and analyses, or "epistemological pluralism," but little concrete details on how to achieve this given the vastness of data. Often throughout these global assessments the authors point to the need for synthesis between diverse disciplines, epistemologies, methods, and scales. However, in the past, researchers have often not carried it through very far, failed to state or underrated many of the implications of this work, and omitted or underemphasized insights or results of epistemological pluralism or integration that become clearer within the context of more complex parameters including: unknowability, the limits of certain scientific methodologies to certain issues, irreversibility in ecosystems, network causality in socioecological systems, and the nature of systems state changes across scales, e.g., cascade effects and abrupt change.

Moreover, assessment authors at times speak to the complexity of the problems, but do so in a way that remains partially mired within the classical science framework, and thus fails to achieve adequate understanding of either the degree of challenge or possible ways to view or to approach it. For instance, in the 2007 WGI scientists use the term "dynamical ice loss" in a way that may be read as banal or fully inconclusive. Within the complexity framework we see that it is usually not so inconclusive, but, rather, a clear sign of feedbacks, thresholds, and the risk of nonlinear changes. In the summary for policymakers, the authors fail to note the acceleration in the speed of sea ice loss in the summers of 2005 and 2006. Instead, they say,

> Dynamical processes related to ice flow not included in current models, but suggested by recent observations could increase the vulnerability of the ice sheets to warming, increasing future sea level rise. Understanding of these processes is limited and there is no consensus on their magnitude.[76]

Thus, while some crucial ideas trickle down to summary reports, the essential messages of speed, irreversibility, tipping points, and cascade effects often do not make it into the summary reports.

Similarly, the authors note that,

> The resilience of many ecosystems is likely to be exceeded this century by an unprecedented combination of climate change, associated disturbances (e.g., flooding, drought, wildfire, insects, ocean acidification), and other global change drivers (e.g., land use change, pollution, over-exploitation of resources).[77]

And that, "Over the course of this century net carbon uptake by terrestrial eco-systems is likely to peak before mid-century and then weaken or even reverse."[78] But this is left without clearly stating that this would imply a nonlinear increase in climate change. Abrupt climate change is mentioned, but the sense of its true significance often falls out.

One must not oversimplify, but still extract some of the key policy lessons of complex thinking. Non-abrupt changes could be catastrophic and abrupt changes could be beneficial. Nonetheless, nonlinearity, high stakes and rapid change must all be increasingly integrated in our understanding of global change.

The omissions of such elements in the final summaries often results in strangely vague, understated conclusions:

> The large ranges of SCC are due in the large part to differences in assumptions regarding climate sensitivity, response lags, the treatment of risk and equity, economic and non-economic impacts, the inclusion of potentially catastrophic losses and discount rates. It is very likely that globally aggregated figures underestimate the damage costs because they cannot include many non-quantifiable impacts. Taken as a whole, the range of published evidence indicates that the net damage costs of climate change are likely to be significant and to increase over time.[79]

Furthermore, the summaries have tended to underrate what scientists now understand to be significant interactions between various biophysical systems. They have been missing a greater integration of the complexity principles of multiple intersecting feedbacks, networks, hierarchies, and the greater emergent properties of large-scale socioecological systems Thus far, the assessments include little analysis of the interactions between different large-scale ecological issues, and potential compounding or cascading consequences. Factors that influence climate change are often omitted or insufficiently analyzed, including: pollution, human encroachment on ecosystems, human depletion of natural resources and subsequent biodiversity loss, feedbacks between biodiversity loss and climate change, and the like. The current rate of biodiversity loss and extinctions is unprecedented in human history and interacts with climate change. The omission of interactions and feedbacks between other drivers of biodiversity loss, extinctions and climate change is significant. IPCC summary authors report that these cross-cutting, biophysical interactions exist and should be analyzed, but that no one has done this as of yet.[80]

If we were to further integrate the multiple drivers of climate change including extinctions, the carbon footprint of poverty, the carbon footprint of luxury, and the like, we would come a step closer to helpful futures scenarios. Complex thinking may be challenging, but the only real obstacle thus far is that it has remained too unarticulated and unfamiliar. The more we develop complex thinking, the less classical thinking will seem easier; rather, it seems increasingly more backwards and barbaric. Scientific reports like the IPCC and the MEA can advance by not only speaking about complexity principles, but also by more fully overcoming the classical mindset that keeps people from actually integrating complexity more fully into their thinking, framing, analyses and conclusions.

For instance, these drawbacks carry over into the IPCC's work on adaptation and mitigation as well. In one positive observation the IPCC authors note that, "There is a growing understanding of the possibilities to choose and implement mitigation options in several sectors to realize synergies and avoid conflicts with other dimensions of sustainable development (high agreement, much evidence)."[81] Yet, they do not discuss the complexities of this statement or how one might determine, address, or implement such synergies. The complexity principles of network causality and consequences, hierarchy, and interdependencies, may all help to take the IPCC analyses to the next level. We must shift beyond talk of interconnection, to the realities of interdependence. We have to examine ways in which purposely or unwittingly we are supporting interdependent problems or interdependent solutions.

Generally, early meta-assessments have stated the importance of complexity, but have done so largely from within the classical scientific framework. Thus, in the consensus process in writing synthesis reports, the authors end up deleting substantial claims such as "Unmitigated climate change would, in the long term, be likely to exceed the capacity of natural, managed and human systems to adapt."[82] By the summary of the same report, this statement was watered down to, "The resilience of many ecosystems is likely to be exceeded this century by an unprecedented combination of climate change, associated disturbances (e.g., flooding, drought, wildfire, insects, ocean acidification), and other global change drivers (e.g., land use change, pollution, over-exploitation of resources).[83] Reading between the lines, the specter for collapse seeps through. To state this more explicitly would allow for more advanced articulations of multiple intersecting and in some cases causally interacting problems, paving the way towards more adequate urgency and actions.

One of the weaknesses in the past IPCC reports, as in much of the science and scholarship of global change, is the lack of sufficiently transdisciplinary analysis. Thus far, a disconnect remains between climate science, and the interwoven social, economic, political, and ethical issues that this science necessarily implies. At this point the need for climate change adaptation and mitigation is a monumental ethical, social, and political reality. The WGII authors of the Fourth Assessment Report touched lightly on such significant issues as to who will pay for mitigation and adaptation.[84] Effective articulation of these issues has come from vibrant international environmental justice groups. Clearly, in addressing climate change, we must comprehend and approach these central issues collaboratively.

The IPCC, like the MEA, has undertaken bold and cutting edge work, and has succeeded remarkably well in its main goals – respectively, creating a legitimate basis for acting upon climate change, and creating a comprehensive analysis of the vulnerability and resilience of our planetary ecosystems. To appreciate the significance of this chapter and the hypothesis regarding thresholds, one should consider the reports of polar ice melt not only from the period of 2002–2005, but also that of 2005 to today. A striking aspect of this is captured by Julienne Stroeve, a research scientist who has observed sea ice loss over recent years, whose has penned repeated articles bearing approximately the same title repeatedly: Arctic sea ice decline is faster than previously forecasted.[85]

In the last few years, a series of dynamical ice melt events has dazzled the global scientific community – dynamical ice melting, fissuring, fracturing and collapsing of glaciers, ice shelves and icebergs across the Polar Regions. In 2008, an Antarctic ice bridge ruptured sending forth a gigantic iceberg. What was initially understood simply as dynamical ice melting, which the 2007 IPCC report writers admitted was largely omitted because it is "little understood," has fractured into a hundred aspects of dynamical ice melting. Meanwhile, in early April 2009, the BBC reported that another iceberg which they first reported on in 2002 as the largest iceberg ever recorded, had collided with glaciers in Antarctica, presumably causing a massive impact. Such impacts may lead to further fissures and cracking, exposing more glacial surface area to warming water and further melting. As the IPCC authors stated, it is little understood. However, within the conceptual framework of hierarchies, networks and nonlinearity, one does understand a little better.

Complexity may help to illuminate too much, more than we wish to know. But it also illuminates much of what we need to know to more realistically cope with the growing climate crisis. As we face the many consequences of industrialization, we can appreciate even more deeply one of the beautiful cries of the dawn of the industrial era.

> The world is too much with us; late and soon,
> Getting and spending, we lay waste our powers;
> Little we see in Nature that is ours;
> We have given our hearts away, a sordid boon!
> This Sea that bares her bosom to the moon,
> The winds that will be howling at all hours,
> And are up-gathered now like sleeping flowers,
>
> For this, for everything, we are out of tune;
> It moves us not – Great God! I'd rather be
> A Pagan suckled in a creed outworn; (1)
> So might I, standing on this pleasant lea, (2)
> Have glimpses that would make me less forlorn;
> Have sight of Proteus (3) rising from the sea;
> Or hear old Triton (4) blow his wreathed horn.[86]
>
> (William Wordsworth,
> *The World is Too Much With Us*, 1806)

Writing of the transformation – social, environmental, political, cultural, spiritual – of factory towns in England at the dawn of the industrial era, William

Wordsworth's lament is doubly ironic today, as we now awaken to the fact that we have been laying waste not just to our own powers, but also to our world.

Complexity theories reveal human impact, but also human agency; vulnerability, but also resilience; and potential, but also responsibility. It is never too late to do all that we can for the planet's climate. In the Anthropocene, we must come to acknowledge our own powers. We had the power to create the climate crisis, and we have the power to change course.

10 American dreams, ecological nightmares, and new visions

Never say there's no hope; hope disappears only when you say there is none. So long as you come down with us, there is hope.

Asmaa Mahfouz, 26 year-old Egyptian revolutionary,
YouTube video, January 18, 2011

Martin Luther King Jr. had a dream. We have dreams. The Yemeni people have dreams.

Tawakkol Karman, Nobel Peace Prize Laureate, December 2011

Economists are understood
To study goods, if not the Good,
Although their goods, we often find,
Are pale abstractions of the mind.

Kenneth Boulding[1]

Will you be a living contradiction?
Or will you go forth with your mission?
The mission to re-adjust our vision...
Be a risk taker, not a move faker.
Don't be scared to care.

Ursula Rucker, Q & A

American dreams

In Spring 2007, in the Marais district of Paris, I knock on the door of Edgar Morin. I feel like Neo in the film the Matrix, going to see the Oracle. When I read the first volume of Morin's six-volume work on complexity theories in 2001, everything had changed. Reading *La Méthode* I felt like Neo taking the red pill; all coordinates shifted and I was thrown into a different vision.

A leading European intellectual, Morin is one of a great many complexity theorists today. Yet his work has provided a monumental contribution to our current understanding of complexity theories. In the course of five decades he has written some 2,000 pages on complexity theories, and over 1,000 pages more engaging with related implications. I had first met with Edgar Morin in 2001, and we have met several times since. This was the first day I'd met with him in his home office, and he had a certain air of purpose.

If I can joke about going to see the "oracle of complexity," it is only because the strength of Morin's work is precisely in his powerful refutation of such a possibility. Complexity theories require the conjoined insights of multitudes. In fact, Morin tirelessly attributes his ideas to the widest range of scholars, from predecessors going back to Heraclitus and Blaise Pascal to colleagues like Henri Atlan. If anything, his view of complexity reveals the great limits of any one thinker, and the need to advance knowledge collaboratively.

At the core, Morin's approach denies the accretion of truth, and speaks to the way in which knowledge proceeds by falsification, branching, and discovering further complexities. Just as one cannot know the method before the inquiry, refuting Cartesian absolute reductionism, rationalism, and certainties; just as one cannot know the universe from a point of abstraction, refuting Laplace's absolute determinism; just as no one angle of approach can explain everything, refuting a reliance solely on mathematics; so complexity theories do not determine truths, but, rather, open up ever more questions. Like Socrates, part of Morin's wisdom lies in his embrace of the unknown.

Edgar Morin opened the door to his apartment with a large, amiable smile. He was wearing a button-down sweater and loafers, and greeted me with the Parisian two kisses. I had amusedly expected something special; that his apartment would be filled with glowing lights or heavenly sounds. Instead, like Gloria Foster, his presence feels profoundly human. Unlike Gloria Foster, who led Neo into a kitchen where she sat smoking cigarettes and baking cookies, Morin led me into a small office filled with an encyclopedic library, true to his intellectual voyage of the last eight decades. On this day he sounded stern, as if to ensure my full attention: "The American dream has failed," he said. "The American way of life does not work. Consumption, competition, and wealth do not produce happiness…"

The United States is not the only or the first society to engage in great consumption, extravagant waste, imperial wars, neoliberal capitalism, or Manichean thinking; we are just the champions. It happens that the United States bears the greatest responsibility for climate change, both historically and currently, and we are still the highest per capita emitter in the world. China only recently became the greatest net emitter, not per capita, and is coping with far higher rates of poverty. While many other governments signed the Kyoto Protocol, created regional climate policies, and promoted greater mitigation, the US government has been a major obstructionist. Many American citizens have not stood up strongly enough on this issue of our times.

Americans are also highly adaptive, caring, creative, entrepreneurial, pioneering, and proactive peoples. We have piloted better dreams. Complexity perhaps may revitalize our vision, revealing some of the intertwined problems in the American way of life, and helping us to discern more synergistic, successful ways.

Of course Morin was preaching to the choir, as I have been lamenting the failures of the American Dream and way of life since I can remember. Yet, coming at this urgent moment in history the words spilled into the air like gems seared into my conscience – a call to action.

American intellectuals long have maligned the American way of life. Already in 1976, a leading social science institute, the Russell Sage Foundation, reported on the failures of American ways.

> If we take standard of living [wealth] as the crucial criterion of the quality of life, then the excellence of life in the United States in the 1970s surely has few parallels. This conclusion, alas, would be greeted with derision in many part of the world, and with a sense of despair by Americans themselves.[2]

Indeed, despite the "dazzling spiral of rising affluence" from 1945 to the 1970s, the vast majority of people back in 1976 felt that life in the United States was in fact getting worse, and that wealth was not a guarantee of happiness. "The bright promise of economic prosperity has proved illusory and the naïve faith that national affluence would produce national well-being has been severely shaken."[3]

Moreover, the report unearthed some of the deeply flawed classical approaches to the study of lived experience.

> …the measures of the objective conditions of life are taken as surrogates for the subjective experience of life. We take a measure of rooms per person as a substitute for the feeling of pleasure and satisfaction a person gets from his housing; we take a measure of occupational status as an indicator of the sense of fulfillment a person gets from his work; we take the crime rate in a neighborhood as a measure of the sense of insecurity the people who live there feel.
>
> These translations all appear eminently reasonable but the fact is that we do not know how well objective measures like these represent underlying psychological states or how well social indicators can be taken to represent the quality of life experience.[4]

Ecological nightmares

Dr. Igor Semiletoz of the Far Eastern branch of the Russian Academy of Sciences said he had never seen anything like it. In early December 2011, while hundreds of officials droned on at the climate conference in Durban, South Africa, Dr. Semiletoz and his research team gave a report to the American Geophysical Union in San Francisco.

Having monitored the East Siberian Arctic shelf region off Northern Russia for nearly 20 years, they were astonished. Columns of methane had first been detected seeping out of the Siberian region in June 2008. In three years, the quantity of methane rushing out of the Arctic seabed had grown exponentially. According to Dr. Semiletoz:

Earlier we found torch-like structures like this but they were only tens of metres in diameter. This is the first time that we've found continuous, powerful and impressive seeping structures, more than 1,000 metres in diameter. It's amazing. I was most impressed by the sheer scale and high density of the plumes. Over a relatively small area we found more than 100, but over a wider area there should be thousands of them.[5]

A few days later, the extended climate conference in Durban finally closed to the conclusion that no actions would be binding until at least 2020. Human politics and biospheric processes seemed to be at a greater disjuncture than ever.

However, like the ice albedo effect, the role and significance of permafrost methane release remains uncertain. Scientists debate the nature and impacts of the current permafrost methane releases. Some have suggested that the current methane release rates may not be such aberrations, as background rates may be higher than previously realized; or that bacteria may eat the released methane, counteracting the effects. According to French climate scientist Valerie Masson-Delmotte, permafrost degradation may enhance methane emissions in boreal wetlands, but large uncertainties exist regarding the magnitude, rate, and impact of the emissions.

Nevertheless, some ecological nightmares have already begun, such as Arctic melting, rising sea levels, and increasing extreme weather, sufficient evidence that dangerous climate change already has begun.

We see the ironic Gordian knot whereby the United States produces great climate science and ethics, great research on climate policy, and great political obstruction.

The American way of life today can be marked with some statistics:

- One-twentieth of the world population, Americans use one quarter of the world's fossil fuel energy. While China's emissions have doubled in the last decade, their per capita emissions are still less than one quarter that of Americans.[6]
- ExxonMobil Corporation raked in 30.5 billions ("excluding special items") in profits in 2010. This was up 57% from 2009.[7] Exxon spent 32.2 billions in 2010 on investments in "capital and exploration expenditures," including "growing unconventional gas production."[8]
- It is estimated that it would take at least one hundred human slaves working 24/7 in order to provide the total energy used by the average American.[9]
- For the many millions already being displaced or disenfranchised in the last decade through extreme flooding, hurricanes, tornados, droughts, and wildfires, climate change is already happening.
- Our economic system has driven the largely irreversible decimation and depletion of our ecosystems' integrity and services, such as: many wetlands, the Oglalla Aquifer, farmland topsoil, fisheries, and pollinator species of bees and bats.
- While the American Dream has never worked for many of the nation's poor, since 2007 millions more Americans have been thrown into poverty.

These trends of ecological, economic, and social dissolution are not coincidental, but rather are coextensive consequences of the same classical ideologies of limitless conquest, consumption, and growth. Just as we reached the geographical limits of the American frontier, so we seem to be crashing into economic, political, and ecological limits. Moreover, many now argue that the well being of the economic, politic, social, and ecological spheres can only be addressed together, integrally.

Complex thinking and new dreams

Throughout this book I have argued that transdisciplinary complex dynamic systems provide one useful framework for the aim of shifting to a more sustainable world. I have given numerous examples of the ways that complexity theories provide one rich source from which to inform a more adequate worldview for the twenty-first century.

In these last two chapters, I extrapolate from all of these individual areas, and explore ways in which complexity theories may support sustainability. Specifically, I examine how the complexity framework informs five ways of adjusting our vision: accounting for complexfication, uncertainty, and natural limits; acknowledging self-organization; considering how to transform vicious cycles into virtuous cycles; articulating issues from different hierarchically nested scales; and strenghtening solidarity in a world of networks and interdependence.

Our lives are composed of complex dynamic systems – social, economic, political, and much more. We do not need to use complexity theories explicitly all the time. Yet, incorporating the lessons of complexity theories and more generally, what Morin calls complex thinking, appears to be helpful in myriad ways, discussed throughout this book, to shift out of problematic ways of thinking and being in the world, to more successful approaches.

In this broad sense, complex thinking informs us in some ways about the failures of the American way of life, and about how to change course, and to develop better visions. For instance, the false myths of modernity – notions of pure linearity, pure determinism, pure progress, pure stability, controllability, and knowability – have all been involved in supporting numerous ways of thinking and being that have helped to get us off course, setting into motion various processes of nonlinear degradation, such as the negative trends in nine out of 15 crucial planetary ecosystem functions, as shown by the Millennium Ecosystem Assessment.

Modernist myths are not the only causes of planetary malaise. Other culprits include everyday greed, domination, violence, war, and existential angst. All of these struggles are central as well. Moreover, some problematic trends, such as the rapid consumption and waste of natural resources, may be partially driven by simple thinking, but also simply by a lack of thinking! Perhaps just as common as overly simplistic thinking is the absence of thinking, remaining ignorant or in denial, or being quite conscious of complexity and adopting unethical behaviors anyway for personal gain. So complex thinking is not the only cure; it is just one part of a greater toolbox.

Table 10.1 Complex thinking and sustainability

Complexity principles	Significance and role for sustainability
Complexification	Complexfication and limits are interrelated central aspects required to understand the nature of global socioecological change.
Self-organization	The self-organizing property inherent to complex dynamic systems, eschewed by classical thinking, is central to new visions.
Virtuous cycles	Understanding how complexification, feedbacks, networks and hierarchies may elucidate ways to transform vicious cycles into virtuous cycles.
Integral approaches	Grasping complex dynamics and our reactions to them requires a conjoining and articulation of both disciplinary and transdisciplinary approaches, and nested hierarchical levels.
Solidarity	The primacy of building solidarity in a world of networks and interdependence.

Yet, awareness of complexity helps our thinking on multiple levels and infuses our thinking with a richer perspective, as discussed throughout the book, and the increase of complex thinking is at least one part of addressing some of the most serious global challenges today.

The complexity framework laid out in Chapter 2, Table 2.4, provides a goldmine of ideas and insights for thinking about complexity for sustainability. All of the principles in Table 2.4 are useful in navigating and understanding the complex dynamic systems that make up our societies and environments.

To reiterate, in these last two chapters, I attempt to go a step further and focus on lessons that we can distill from the greater complexity framework, five keys lessons for adjusting our vision: accounting for complexfication, uncertainty, and natural limits; acknowledging self-organization; considering how to transform vicious cycles into virtuous cycles; articulating issues from different hierarchically nested scales; and strenghtening solidarity in a world of networks and interdependence.

Complexification in a world of limits

> Anyone who believes that there can be endless growth must be either a madman or an economist.
>
> (Kenneth Boulding)

One major thread running through the complexity framework for sustainability, and thus the approach to comprehending and envisioning a more workable way of life, is found in the triad of: societal complexification, societal and technological counterproductivity, and societal self-organization.

To recap, Ivan Illich introduced the concept of counterproductivity, referring to the way in which the direction of modern societies seemed to create a spiral of unintended nefarious consequences, such that eventually, new technologies would undermine their own effectiveness. Illich and Jean-Pierre Dupuy outlined examples, for instance the way in which use of cars over time led to gridlock, pollution, and higher fuel prices. After a certain point, the density of cars on the road leads people to spend more time in cars driving to work just to pay off the costs of repairs, gas, and insurance for those cars. For all of these reasons, after a certain threshold point, cars become less effective transportation than bicycles or trains.

In a general sense, counterproductivity is caused by injecting simple ideas, practices and technologies into complex socioecological systems and then watching the results ripple throughout the networks and hierarchies of socioecological systems. Generally, as societies complexify, gains began to be trumped by counterproductivity, and risks trumped by harms, as Ulrich Beck has argued. And counterproductivity can be usefully explained by both societal complexification and the problematic general nature of diminishing returns in overly complex systems, as Joseph Tainter has argued.

By reframing our thinking around self-organization, emergence, networks and hierarchies, we achieve multiple goals. We see the ways in which ideas, technologies and practices manifest throughout complex systems, highlighting network causality and network consequences. Seemingly innocuous or immutable technologies – anything from cell phones, to industrial farming practices, to nonviolent social protest movements – produce anything but simple consequences in complex systems. What Bruno Latour calls "immutable mobiles," or particular ideas or technologies introduced into our networked socioecological fabric, bring to light the challenges of the Anthropocene. In a world that is networked and hierarchically interrelated, we need to shift away from atomistic, short-term, and individualist planning, towards more full systems, cradle to grave, and long-term planning,

More broadly, an acknowledgement of the failures of modern thinking, planning and policies, like Latour's immutable mobiles, shows the urgency of implementing cross-sector, integral, virtuous cycles; and the broader mandate of effective organization for the common good at the scale of the planet.

This perspective has the advantage of moving us past dichotomous thinking whereby such issues have been framed, quite unrealistically and distortionally, in terms of: cosmopolitans versus luddites, luxuries versus subsistence goods, or rich versus poor. Clearly, the framework of complexification in a world of limits calls for new ways to consider and evaluate just what today's societies should even be striving for and how.

Such a framing moves us past the equally false ideas that we should give up solidarity, social security and humanitarian aims, or give up on the aim of washing machines, Macbook Airs, and lattes for all. Such a framing moves us past the idea that we can work only in a piecemeal fashion, rather than a networked fashion; either Maslow's basic needs for all, or the luxuries of elites, rather than a good quality of life for all.

However, to work towards this desirable world, we have to reorganize societal systems, such as energy systems, not just in an isolated fashion, but in a fashion that integrates socioecological affairs across multiple scales, disciplinary and transdisciplinary knowledge, individual systems and the greater web of hierarchically enmeshed systems. Recycling, gardening and local shopping are a good start. But they will not succeed without great transformations, not just of individuals, but also of the entities with the greatest environmental impact, such as: corporations, industries, social institutions, militaries, and governments.

People are demanding a better world not based on modernity's delusions of growth, progress, and control, and not based on fulfilling the luxuries of a few, bringing ecological nightmares to all. People are waking up to the reality that everybody counts on only one, entirely limited planet, with only one climate. The only viable path forward is based on the common good. As I write, I can hear the glaciers crashing into the ocean.

Self-organization for sustainability, or S.O.S.

The processes of self-organization appear to be a crucial aspect of reality. For instance, self-organization is found at all levels in the nested hierarchical structure of the human body, such as in: atoms, cells, organs, the nervous system, the circulatory system, and the mind. Stars and universes self-organize, chemicals exhibit self-organizing properties, and small-scale social entitities, like families and clans, self-organize.

As we look up the hierarchical scales, to networks bridging different types of hierarchies, self-organization is less apparent, though there are numerous examples even at the planetary scale. In other words, self-organization seems to be an essential feature of the emergent processes of physical and biological systems, and to a degree within social systems. On the other hand, when we look at the larger societal scales, it is much less apparent. In fact, at these scales it is unclear whether the term "self-organization," can be applied in the same fashion. For my purposes here, I will use the application of self-organization to the broadest societal processes as a very literal metaphor for self-governance, referring to governance and organization in all kinds of social systems.

While our bodies and environments are comprised of self-organizing processes, self-organization seems less evident at larger scales of complex social systems. Though, even in the era of globalization there are some attempts towards societal self-organizing at all scales. An example is the United Nations, an organization that strives towards self-governance not just of local communities, but, rather, self-governance of the entirety of humankind.

At the scale of societies, we must create it; we must understand the dynamics of our world, learn, adapt, strategize, create, and develop self-governance. Meanwhile, we must understand and strive to transform countervailing forces that undermine self-governance, forces of domination, social hierarchy, exploitation, and corruption – all of which undermine efforts for large-scale societal self-organization regarding issues like climate change.

Of course, there is also a long history of ongoing activism for social solidarity at all scales. In social movements, social institutions, and academic disciplines we possess a rich legacy of increasing social solidarity. Through ethical extensionism discussed in Chapter 7 – the gradual extension of ethical principles from the most intimate relationships of immediate families and clans towards increasingly greater social and natural systems – we have begun to apply the same humanist values that we practice to some degrees within families and communities, at greater social scales. This is the basis of the rich history of left progressive social movements – liberation movements, labor movements, civil rights movements, women's movements, decolonialization movements, and uprisings against dictatorships and oppression around the globe.

Self-organization, as the principle of complex systems that we are only beginning to explore more deeply, is not a term to be used too freely. However, just as I use the terms of complexity and sustainability as reference points despite their great complexity and thus ambiguity, similarly, "societal self-organization" also provides a kind of abstract reference point that may help in understanding some central challenges of our times. While he has many ways of referring to aspects of the social processes that permit and facilitate "sustainability" – solidarity, justice, community values, ethics, democracy, activism, etc. – ironically, it seems useful to have a similarly general term to refer to all of these efforts, albeit necessarily an equally complex and thus equally ambiguous and challenging term, such as "self-organization."

The social sciences, social theories and social movements show efforts to build in self-governance at the scale of families, communities, and societies. As many global environmental reports such as the MEA and IPCC have made clear, today we need to foster and develop rigorous planetary-scale societal solidarity and self-organization at the largest scale of humanity.

In the most general sense, of course, there is nothing new about this goal. It is as old as the history of ideas – the heart of all mystical traditions, it is thus found in all religions, and in our greatest social and philosophical theories. Our greatest aspiration has been "self-organization," in the general sense of the common good of all humanity. Aristotle called for this when he said that ethics is the search for the common good. Social movements throughout the ages have advanced this cause. Martin Luther King Jr. said the moral arc of history is long, but it tends towards justice. Societal self-organization is an idea at the heart of our aspirations for democracy, peace, justice, and solidarity. Throughout history, we see attempts to develop effective self-organization at the greater social scales – democratic constitutions, international institutions, laws, and treaties.

In a more specific sense, the call for greater societal self-organization for sustainability is not new either. Social luminaries long have called for multi-sector, multifaceted self-governance in response to the myriad crises facing humanity. One pioneer of "self-organization for sustainability" was Kenneth Boulding. Boulding was a polyglot, transdisciplinary visionary, Quaker, and pioneer of the evolutionary economics movement, coining the term "spaceship earth." He touched on societal complexification and environmental degradation in 1964 when he wrote the following.

> It may be that the solution of the material and physical problems is just around the corner. It will not be surprising if the next fifty years bring some major advances, both toward new and practically inexhaustible resources of energy and also toward anti-entropic modes of organizing the flow of materials into and out of the necessary physical components of our environment. The uncertainty in the movement toward stable, high-level technology, however, makes one all the more resentful of the waste of resources involved in the world war industry and in frivolous and useless consumption. It may be that humanity has only a slim chance of achieving a stable, high-level technology and that every gram of material or dyne of energy that we waste and that is not directed toward making the great transition is an appreciable diminution of the probability of making it. On the other hand, it is also possible that stable, high-level technology is within easy reach and we will attain this while we still have unused reserves of fuels and ores.
>
> The result of failure, however, would be so momentous from the point of view of humans and the evolution of this part of the universe that it would seem wise to make the most pessimistic assumptions possible, and for humanity at this stage to make a concerted and deliberate effort to avoid the waste of our exhaustible resources in war and luxury and to concentrate their use in expanding knowledge in the direction of achieving a closed-cycle, high-level system. Once the exhaustible resources are gone, however, it is very doubtful whether humans could ever break out of this medium-level economy, and as far as we are concerned, the evolutionary process would have to come to an end. We cannot afford to take even a small chance of a failure which would have consequences for millions of years in the future.[10]

Sadly, the 50 years of which he spoke, ending in 2014, have seen little progress and much regress at the kind of integral societal reorganization he was hoping for. Happily, however, Boulding and other visionaries did spur an immense body of scholarship on exactly the kinds of changes he was calling for. While we have had repeated political setbacks in a few areas – notably support for renewable energies and the transformation of various industrial processes – nonetheless, scientists, scholars, and leading thinkers in every domain have amassed a great volume of workable solutions, and implemented examples of them successfully across the entire planet.

Increasingly, in recent years, people from every sector – politicians, journalists, academics, institutional leaders, and activists – are calling for major change. More and more leaders are calling for major transformations for conjoined environmental and social security. In the 1960s activists and environmentalists were talking about global change. In the last decade, not just activists, but the German government, the Pentagon and the CIA have all conducted investigations of the national security implications of a multiply determined world crisis in the coming decades.

Increasingly, leaders say, the unprecedented types and scale of environmental, economic, and political change requires an unprecedented scale of social reorganization. The projects required to transform global energy systems, infrastructure, economies and institutions, would appear to make the New Deal, the Marshall Plan, and the Manhattan Project look like grade school projects.

The knowledge is there. What's missing has been a comprehensive, synthetic understanding and political will to take up this vast literature on potentially more sustainable institutions – soft energy pathways, permaculture and swidden farming, self-governed businesses, green jobs, democratic vitality, human health, community well-being, etc. – and integrate these at various scales. To integrate this literature with the complexity principles of feedbacks, networks, and hierarchies, might help, as the Chinese suggest, to turn a great crisis into a great opportunity.

The year 2011 showed that there is a strong will on behalf of the people of the world. Social movements erupted in the majority of countries around the world, including mass uprisings in the Middle East, China, Chile, the EU, and the US. Thinkers and leaders from many fields can draw on the lessons of complexity to frame our aims for a better world more systematically. Complexity theories can help to effectively operationalize and advance a half-century of comprehensive sustainable theory and praxis, shifting efforts from the largely piecemeal to the large-scale. As we've seen throughout this book, this entails the integration of all aspects of our enmeshed socioecological systems, including addressing some of the deepest challenges to increasing global social justice, equity, and democracy – poverty, oppression, overconsumption, and exploitation.

"We are now faced with the fact that tomorrow is today."[11] As we see in the case of the oceans, even while the International Law of the Seas was successful in creating binding international compliance to save the oceans, our economies and appetites for consumption nonetheless have driven our oceans to the brink of large-scale collapses. Even while protecting the oceans on paper, we have yet actually to save them in practice. It appears that to conserve the oceans we have to address the full ensemble of interacting global economic, political and social crises today.

Complex dynamic systems and wicked problems

Back in the nineteenth century, Bertha Benz could not have imagined the madness of LA's Route 110 four-level highway interchange at rush hour. On August 5, 1888, when the wife of Karl Benz took her husband's wonderful invention – the first fuel-driven motor car, like a leather couch on wheels – on the first long-distance motor car trip from Mannheim to Pforzheim Germany, she did not foresee that Mr. Olds and Mr. Ford would soon start up mass production. She did not predict that by 2007, there would be 600 million cars around the globe clogging roads, covering cities with smog, fostering alienation, and contributing to climate change. She did not imagine that per year, together, these 600 million plus cars would burn some 260 billion gallons of fossil fuel.

An invention that was readily seen as an emblem of inexorable progress in 1888 would gradually coevolve with societies, economies, cultures, and the climate. By 2012, while cars are still seen by people around the world as a mark of progress and prosperity, they have in fact become inextricably enmeshed in a set of what we call "wicked problems." Already beyond the "carrying capacity" of the planet, the burning of 260 billion gallons of fossil fuels annually is unsustainable, nevermind the myriad other problems involved in mass individualized transportation.

Wicked problems are those that are "complex and defy simple formulations and easy solutions."[12] Wickedness isn't a degree of difficulty. Wicked issues are different because traditional processes can't resolve them, says John Camillus, who traces the term to a 1973 article by Horst W. J. Rittel and Melvin M. Webber, professors of design and urban planning at the University of California at Berkeley. "A wicked problem has innumerable causes, is tough to describe, and doesn't have a right answer."[13] Classic examples, says Camillus, are poverty and environmental degradation. In contrast to, "hard but ordinary problems, which people can solve in a finite time period by applying standard techniques [, n]ot only do conventional processes fail to tackle wicked problems, but they may exacerbate situations by generating undesirable consequences."[14]

We are no longer living in 1888. We are living in a time of crisis; the catastrophic irreversible melting of the polar caps of which Hans Jonas warned in 1979 has already started. We are living in a world in which greenhouse gas emissions are measured in tons of emissions per person per year. Table 10.2 shows the per capita emissions in the year 2000, compared to what has been estimated as a sustainable world average.[15] In total, the United States is emitting some 25 times the sustainable rate.

We are living at time when it is frequently acknowledged that there are multiple crises in the economic, environmental, political, and social spheres, and that these often operate in vicious cycles. As the economist Richard Wolff said of the developing crisis in Europe in 2011, the economic system "isn't working," but we now have a "dysfunctional economic system coupled to a ... dysfunctional

Table 10.2 Per capita emissions in the year 2000

Country	Ton of CO_2 emissions per person in the year 2000
World sustainable average	1.0
India	1.9
China	3.9
UK	11.0
Germany	12.3
US	24.3

Table 10.3 Transitioning to sustainability: from vicious to virtuous cycles

Vicious cycles due to oversimplifying in complex systems dynamics	Virtuous cycles due to integral approaches to account for complex systems dynamics
Counterproductivity, diminishing returns, and increasing risks	Integrity, resilience of societies and environments
Unrestrained societal complexification	Planned partial degrowth, partial regrowth, for enlightened, mid-range societal complexification
Diminishing returns	Sustainable returns
Rush towards ecological collapses	Self-organizing for sustainability at all scales

political system" and instead of fixing each other, these two systems are compounding each other "in a kind of spiral downturn."[16] An optimistic thesis is that virtuous cycles at the scale of the planet and humanity may be created by integrating the extensive knowledge developed over the last half-century on individual instances of sustainable solutions throughout multiple sectors.

Transitioning to a more sustainable world requires us to confront and grapple with these aspects of our highly complex societies. Without yet finding the conclusions, I propose some hypotheses worth exploring. Rather than despairing over diminishing returns, we can utilize our knowledge of them as red flags for instances of needed policy reforms. Rather than being anxious about increasing risks and harms, we can utilize our knowledge of complexity to reduce risks and capitalize on learning and adaptation, increasing our social and environmental resilience. Rather than continue on a path towards multiple ecological and social collapses, as the authors of the MEA and IPCC reports have warned, we can utilize the information in these reports to transform the very societal systems that are driving our current environmental and social downward spirals. Rather than lament vicious cycles, we can explore new concepts and lenses with which perhaps to create virtuous cycles.

From classical myths to complexity narratives, the new Planetary Dream

> You are very strong.... You have to believe in your own power; if you don't believe in your own power, you couldn't change anything. You have to believe in yourself, because you are very, very strong.
>
> (Asmaa Mahfouz, Democracy Now, October 25, 2011)

"Natura non facit saltus," Latin for, "nature does not make jumps," so goes one principle of natural philosophy since the time of Aristotle. Yet, there have been times in history – the Renaissance, the Enlightenment, the French and American revolutions, the Civil Rights, women's, and environmental movements – when societies have made great leaps in practices, laws and norms, reorganizing societies in substantial ways. Complexity theories may help to facilitate, not only small steps, but also greater shifts forward in moral, economic, political, and organizational change.

While each of the complexity principles, in isolation, is a step forward with respect to one flawed, over-simplified assumption of early modern science, the complexity framework in its ensemble facilitates a shift, not just in singular assumptions and precepts, but, rather, in our broader way of thinking. It allows us to shift, not singular ideas, but general societal myths, stories, narratives, and ultimately our worldview.

More generally, complexity asks us to problematize, a step beyond critical thinking. To problematize, to explore an idea or theory critically from many angles, contextualizing and complexifying it in the process. Foucault once said that he would have a very hard time discerning his "discipline," somewhat ironically since he gave us a masterful critique of "discipline." Clearly he was not a philosopher in the typical sense, in that he was focused on transdisciplinary issues involved in understanding power dynamics, oppression, and the flourishing of the individual and the society. Rather, he said, if he had to describe his discipline he would call it "problematizing social theory."

In light of the significance of complex thinking, transdisciplinarity, integral approaches and focus on applied synergies, it is this manner of problematizing thinking that we must employ and develop. We need to apply this practice, problematizing social theory, with respect to the many facets of sustainability.

While this is a vast project, I will touch just on a couple of examples, outlined in Table 10.4. Complexity theories help us to advance Einstein's dictum of simplifying as much as possible, but not too much. We see that precaution or proaction, growth or degrowth, and restoration or resilience, are overly restrictive framings, highlighting the limits of dualisms, and the need to think in terms of complexity principles such as networks, feedbacks, and hierarchies.

Table 10.4 From modernity's myths to new planetary dreams

Modernity's myths	Twenty-first century narratives
Abstraction of simplifying ideas	Complex thinking, humility and hope, precaution and proaction
Nature versus society	Interrelated physical, living, and social complex dynamic systems
Infinite total growth versus poverty	Growth, degrowth, zero growth, and regrowth in different sectors
Life, liberty, and happiness found in materialism, status, and social hierarchies	Interdependence, common good, new planetary worldview, narratives, and dreams
Total individualism, total competition, nation states, war	Individual freedoms and interdependence; individual striving and mutual cooperation; social diversity and solidarity; complex cultural expression and the ethics of care, cooperation, and responsibility

We must continue to problematize our thinking at all scales, from individual ideas, to the greater scope of our social myths and narratives. At the same time, we must engage with the urgency that environmental pragmatists like Andrew Light have called for, because while knowledge is imbued with uncertainty, the poles are melting most certainly.

We must problematize the most fundamental terms of nature and society, perhaps two of the most problematic words in the English language. In our conceptions of them, we simplify too much. Nature and society are perceived as abstracted and disconnected, the backdrop of ecocide. As long as society and nature remain separate, and the interdependencies they contain obscured, then economists may cling to the delusional notions of infinite growth, infinite depletions of resources, and infinite accumulation of capital.

Likewise, growth is a highly oversimplified term, and those disturbed by the present social and ecological degradations of rampant global capitalism call for degrowth. Rather, the problem is not growth per se, but abstractions and oversimplifications. The coal, oil, and gas sectors must go through a rapid degrowth, at least in the short term. Yet plants need to grow, biodiversity in general must regrow, and habitats must regrow. Social solidarity, worn down by the logic of money and consumption, must regrow. As many have pointed out, it's both poverty and overconsumption, driving the decimation of both communities and nature. Social equity appears to be crucial to the social solidarity and environmental regulations needed for sustainability.

Ideals of life, liberty, and happiness must be problematized, as terms with rich meanings, continuously transformed by rapid global change. Delinking happiness from luxury, such as the correlation between CO_2 emissions and happiness, is a challenge. Yet, if anything, it appears that over a certain threshold of wealth and power, happiness does not increase. Great wealth leads to the bizarre and ironic situation in which the rich are willing to leave their very communities, if it allows them to shelter more of the wealth, even that which they will never in fact utilize. The ultra-rich in France, so it is said, have their suitcases packed and ready to move to Switzerland, if the left should win and raise taxes, all to protect an inheritance that is effectively too big to really use. Luxuries and happiness must be delinked. Great fortunes often do not produce more happiness, and often contribute to the degradation of democracies.

The philosopher Alain de Botton, for instance, has done work on the reasons for social and environmental irresponsibility of elites. He claims that materialism does not produce happiness, but, rather, even though it does not bring happiness, we live materialist lives in order to feel that we are not too low in the societal pecking order. In the nineteenth century, the 99 percent never expected to live like the aristocracy. In contrast, today while there is increasing rhetoric about and belief in economic equality, we are in fact plagued by increasingly deep socioeconomic inequalities.

The American Dream is a deep-rooted myth. The American Dream holds that if you just work hard, you can join the 1 percent. While in past societies the vast majority of the society might be called the "less fortunate," today, the poor are seen as lazy, incapable, and losers. It's understandable that Beck's song "Loser" was a hit. The 99 percent of Americans, working feverishly, are immersed in the rhetoric that if they only worked harder, they too would be rich, and if not, they are no longer "less fortunate"; they are simply losers. This reframing from the poor, working class, or disenfranchised to the "loser", is perhaps originally American, but like the American Dream, it has spread across the globe. At the root, we must see, says de Botton, that materialism, consumerism, and extravagant expenditure is linked to our deepest emotions. In a world of rampant rhetoric of equality, mixed with the decisive lack of real equality, we exacerbate feelings of envy, insecurity, and vulnerability.

> We are often told that we live in very materialistic times, that we are greedy people. I don't think that we are particularly materialistic. I think we live in a society, which has simply pegged certain emotional rewards to the acquisition of material goods. It's not the material goods we want, it's the rewards we want. And that's a new way of looking at luxury goods. The next time you see someone in a Ferrari, don't think this person who is greedy, think – this is somebody who is incredibly vulnerable and in need of love. Feel sympathy, rather than contempt.[17]

Sympathy – that might be a lot to ask of many onlookers, plagued by the social breakdowns of joblessness, family imprisonment, lack of health care, education, or a frayed social safety net. Sustainability requires nothing less than a radical ongoing problematization of the ensemble of issues driving our environmental crisis. We will not find all the clues we need by focusing solely on wealthy or middle-class problems. We will also find the clues to the deeper issues involved in synergistic solutions, at the daily struggles of our most impoverished and disenfranchised communities. Only in our prisons and our poorest communities can we more fully comprehend the shelled out remnants of the American Dream, and the source of new dreams.

Solidarity and Practicing Utopia now

> The main task today is to reinvent Utopia – the space of Utopia.... True utopia for me is not a matter of the future. It is something to be immediately enacted. When there is no other way. Utopia in this sense simply means: Do what appears within the given symbolic coordinates as impossible. Take the risk; change the very coordinates.... Even big well-known, even sometimes conservative acts, have this utopian dimension. Like, to take a ridiculous example, thirty years ago, remember, Richard Nixon's trip to China. There was almost a utopian dimension to it. Why? Because, He did what appeared as impossible. China was portrayed as the ultimate evil superpower.... That act changed the entire coordinates. He did the impossible. This is what we need more than ever today. Because ultimately, I claim, the true utopia today is not a different order. It's the idea that the existing order can function differently...

We should dare to enact the impossible. We should rediscover how to not imagine, but (to) enact utopia. The point again is not, again, about planning utopias; the point is about practicing them. And I think, this is not a question of, should we do it or should we simply persist in the existing coordinates. It's much more radical. It's a matter [of] survival. The future will be utopian or there will be none.

(Slavoj Zizek, *The Reality of the Virtual*, 2004)

Due to degrees of uncertainty, ignorance, error, and unknowability, "No one can ever know if and when it is too late."[18] Yet, through means presented in this chapter and the next, we can perhaps articulate and actualize the extraordinary science and scholarship of world change that has been produced over the last half-century. There is no need to reinvent wheels. In every discipline and for every sector, there is a treasure trove of sustainable solutions. We need to integrate and actualize these practices, which requires changes in almost every sector of society.

We must wrench ourselves awake from the seeming comforts of modernity's delusions – control, individualism, isolation, and oppression are delusions. Safety is not found in competition alone, but in a considerable degree of cooperation; not only in individualism, but in the acknowledgement of our interdependent lives; not only in luxuries, but in the truer happiness of connection, art, culture and lives of meaning, of humanitarian values, and of what transcends humanity. As Friedrich Schlegel said, "To attain our humanity, we must have a sense of that which is beyond humanity." Perhaps our environmental crises can become the catalyst for change.

Seeing the entire planet in terms of sets of interdependent, complex dynamic systems, we begin to see humanity as one global social network that must cooperate in a self-organizational capacity in order to transition towards sustainability.

No man is an island entire of itself; every man
is a piece of the continent, a part of the main;
if a clod be washed away by the sea, Europe
is the less, as well as if a promontory were, as
well as a manor of thy friends or of thine
own were; any man's death diminishes me,
because I am involved in mankind.
And therefore never send to know for whom
the bell tolls; it tolls for thee.
(John Donne, from *Devotions Upon Emergent
Occasions*, Meditation XVII, 1624)

11 Complexity and sustainability

Wicked problems, Gordian knots, and synergistic solutions

I went to San Francisco because I ... had been paralyzed by the conviction that writing was an irrelevant act, that the world as I had understood it no longer existed. If I was to work again at all, it would be necessary for me to come to terms with disorder.

Joan Didion, Preface to Slouching Towards Bethlehem.[1]

[The Somalian famine of 2011] was predicted long ago by people on the ground. [The multiple causes are] a combination of war, climate change and very bad policy, particularly an embrace of radical free market policies by regional governments that mean the withdrawal of support for pastoralists...

Christian Parenti, Tropic of Chaos: Climate Change and the New Geography of Violence, on Democracy Now

There is a growing understanding of the possibilities to choose and implement mitigation options in several sectors to realize synergies and avoid conflicts with other dimensions of sustainable development (high agreement, much evidence).[2]

IPCC 2007

If you like everyone in the room, the coalition isn't big enough.

Bernice Reagan Johnson

Things fall apart

To address issues like climate change in an adequately complex light requires the recognition that things sometimes do "fall apart," and to enquire into what makes systems collapse and what makes systems thrive, as people are doing in fields like risk, collapse, apocalypse, sustainability, well being, and resilience.

In the twentieth century, the social chaos of World War I was seared into the modern conscience in William Butler Yeats' poem, "The Second Coming," referred to in the title of Joan Didion's book, *Slouching Towards Bethlehem.* Societies at times transform in a manner that is more rapid and far-reaching than we seem to be conceptually prepared or emotionally eager to acknowledge. Generally, human thinking has tended to avoid uncertainty, risk, and collapse and to focus on order and that which we can control for many reasons, including not just the limits to knowledge, but other limits as well: cognitive, emotional, and psychological limits. In the early twentieth century, modernists eschewed disorder, seeking universal scientific order, but also seeking order in the social, cultural, class, and religious spheres.

> Turning and turning in the widening gyre
> The falcon cannot hear the falconer;
> Things fall apart; the centre cannot hold;
> Mere anarchy is loosed upon the world,
> The blood-dimmed tide is loosed, and everywhere
> The ceremony of innocence is drowned;
> The best lack all conviction, while the worst
> Are full of passionate intensity.
> Surely some revelation is at hand;
> Surely the Second Coming is at hand.
> The Second Coming! Hardly are those words out
> When a vast image out of Spiritus Mundi
> Troubles my sight: a waste of desert sand;
> A shape with lion body and the head of a man,
> A gaze blank and pitiless as the sun,
> Is moving its slow thighs, while all about it
> Wind shadows of the indignant desert birds.
> The darkness drops again but now I know
> That twenty centuries of stony sleep
> Were vexed to nightmare by a rocking cradle,
> And what rough beast, its hour come round at last,
> Slouches towards Bethlehem to be born?
>
> (William Butler Yeats,
> "The Second Coming," 1919)

On the eve of World War I, people were largely ensconced in the worldview of certainties, control, and order, about to witness great disorder, horror, and decimation. One hundred years later, tragically, we are still grappling with many of the same social ills and wars.

Perhaps in one way, however, we are at a distinct advantage to the moderns of the early twentieth century. Today our worldview has shifted beyond the rigid notions of control, stability and certainty, pure order and pure disorder, opening up new perspectives. The rapid growth of new knowledge and technologies make a transition to new lifestyles more obtainable. The phenomenon of emergent processes makes more evident our own drive to learn, adapt, strategize and change.

Interdependent problems, interdependent solutions

Generally speaking, complex thinking highlights interactions and interdependence. Several terms have come into use evoking the interdependence of many of today's social and environmental crises, terms like: wicked problems, Gordian knots, deadly cocktails, and hypercomplexities. Likewise, as interdependent problems coevolve, they are sometimes mutually reinforcing, creating what some call a downward spiral or vicious cycle.

The opposite of a vicious cycle is a "virtuous cycle," which occurs, in theory, when multiple systems interact in ways that are mutually propitious. Feedbacks in human thinking, learning, and action appear to be central to the understanding and maintenance of virtuous cycles. Feedbacks allow for monitoring and modifying important causes of change, in order to adjust and change course. Virtuous cycles are comprised of synergies, or parts or aspects of systems working together in mutually beneficial ways. Synergy derives from the Greek for "working together." R. Buckminster Fuller defined synergy as "the behavior of whole systems unpredicted by the behavior of their parts taken separately," concurrent with today's definitions of emergence.[3]

In this chapter, I explore the hypothesis that complexity theories shed light on socioecological issues like climate change, in ways that help us to pinpoint key issues, and influence those, so as to transform vicious cycles into virtuous cycles. Within today's context the study of virtuous cycles is a rich area for exploration. I will only scratch the surface of this project, and merely suggest that despite some major challenges, this is one promising area for exploration.

In the exploration of wicked problems, Gordian knots, and vicious cycles, and the hypothesis of the virtuous cycle, I explore three examples of propositions made for addressing climate change. Specifically, through these examples, I explore the thesis that complex dynamic systems analysis helps to reveal and articulate the patterns that contribute to vicious cycles, and therefore, may provide clues for addressing important drivers to transform vicious cycles to virtuous cycles.

We have found that silver bullet and monolithic approaches to policy in complex systems create unintended consequences and ripple effects that are often problematic. It is an increasingly popular proposition that for highly complex issues, we need to use interdependent approaches, to resolve issues in their interacting ensembles. Even, or perhaps especially, in the case of multidimensional, global issues like climate change, we may be able to pinpoint key drivers across highly complex systems, and achieve not just isolated, atomistic interventions, but multi-system, multi-scale transformation.

Moreover, social and environmental issues are transdisciplinary. When social and environmental problems are caused by intertwined ethical, political, economic, social, and environmental problems, we cannot succeed by just addressing one set of issues: just economic, just social or just environmental. Rather, we must tackle all of these issues together. By getting to a set of root problems and transforming these systemically, perhaps we may strategize to transform vicious cycles to virtuous ones.

Another way to view this, more broadly, is the hypothesis that we need to treat complex dynamic systems as such. We need to stop employing simplicity to treat complexity, and instead learn the language and dynamics with which to treat complexity with complexity.

Nicholas Rescher's principle of complexifcation may contribute to comprehending vicious cycles, and perhaps even to developing virtuous ones. Complexification helps to explain our world, and thus may contribute to understanding our current global crises. As argued by Rescher, Ivan Illich, and other philosophers and theorists, as the sciences, technologies, bureaucracies, and today's societies become more complex, principles like feedbacks, network causality, and unintended consequences help to articulate the ways in which some aspects of our lives may develop vicious cycles of greater and greater diminishing returns, stresses, speed, and counterproductivity. Complex problems belie silver bullet solutions. Yet, perhaps they may yield to synergistic and win–win strategies.

Proposals for addressing Gordian knots, wicked problems, vicious cycles, and hypercomplexity often take the form of so-called "win–win solutions," "synergies," or "virtuous cycles." In conflict resolution, a win–win strategy is one in which gains from cooperation result in making everyone better off than they would have been taking a non-cooperative approach. In environmental and sustainability discourse, win–win solutions call for the integration of multiple interdependent factors, such as economic, social, and ecological dynamics. Admitting the multidimensional aspects of socioecological issues like poverty and climate change, we might call these win–win–win strategies, highlighting the high degree of political challenge. A related concept is symbiosis, from the Latin root for "living together, companionship." Solidarity, community, and democracy all appear to be central to sustainability, thriving and envisioning the future.

Another category of analysis for complex or wicked problems falls under the label of "integral." One of the earliest proponents, the California Institute of Integral Studies (CIIS) in San Francisco, CA, holds "integral education" as its central mission. CIIS began by bringing Eastern wisdom traditions to the West, specifically focusing on enhancing knowledge and wisdom by exploring the linkages between the mind, body, and spirit. Founder Haridas Chaudhuri, who held a doctorate in Indian philosophy, and his wife Bina, crusaded to bring an integral perspective to the mainstream views on philosophy, science, and religion. Early president of the institute, Alan Watts, expanded on that vision by bringing the philosophy of Zen Buddhism to the Institute and to the West. CIIS continues to expand the notion of integral learning, to encompass "the study of traditions and experience from around the globe," including "all aspects of learning: the intellectual, the experiential and the applied."[4]

The Integral Institute is another educational institution aimed to foster integral education and thinking. According to the Integral Institute,

> Integral theory is an all-inclusive framework that draws on the key insights of the world's greatest knowledge traditions. The awareness gained from drawing on all truths and perspectives allows the Integral thinker to bring new depth, clarity and compassion to every level of human endeavor – from unlocking individual potential to finding new approaches to global-scale problems.[5]

Integral theories are related to complexity theories. In brief, an integral vision shares with complex thinking the aim of surpassing more purely simplistic and reductionist approaches. It seems that complexity theories provide some very useful concepts and frameworks for effective integral approaches.

Complex thinking and integral approaches can easily fall apart back into simplistic thinking, dualisms, assumptions, and ideologies. There are many ways to oversimplify. For instance, given the role of feedbacks and thresholds in climate change, it may be tempting to see just feedbacks, or just thresholds, or just uncertainty, as "the central issues" to climate change science and policy. In fact, I would argue, this view repeats the classical thinking that has gotten us into so much trouble, always looking for single culprits and silver bullets. Ultimately, myriad simplistic interventions and their consequences cascade through networks and come back to haunt us.

In today's societies, people sense an exponentially rising return of errors coming home to roost. Like Tippi Hedren in Hitchcock's *The Birds*, who sat nervously smoking a cigarette on a parkbench while a flock of killer birds slowly gathered behind her, so in the twenty-first century we nervously sense a mounting menace.

Complex thinking may shed some light on the fuller dynamics of our global situation. There are no singular evil forces from outside, driving our rapid global change. Rather, myriad forces within ourselves, our way of thinking and way of life are driving global change. We may be wired to find enemies outside ourselves. In our globalized society, there is no longer any "outside." We are finding that singular problematic ideas and behaviors may spur various systemic and multidimensional problems throughout highly complex societies.

This understanding of vicious cycles may be a positive development, insofar as it opens the way towards understanding how to transform them. As Latour has argued, to cut Gordian knots with classical knives only produces more Gordian knots. The only way to surpass the current crises is to stop producing them. Perhaps complex thinking may help us to pinpoint and stop producing some of these issues.

While these approaches may be promising, they are challenging. Win–win propositions often sound good on the face of it, but we must always ask, they involve wins: for whom, at what cost, to whom, within what larger nested matrix of interactions and trends? Many reforms masquerade as win–win proposals, but in fact are founded upon a structure that inherently exploits a losing party, often undermining an otherwise successful system. Many so-called win–win proposals and practices are in fact windfalls for the few at the expense of the many.

Synergies, integral approaches, and win–win have obvious appeal. Yet, history is filled with the failure of seemingly winning and synergistic approaches, which turned out to be only winning for some, and losing for others, ultimately spurring more problems. Numerous attempts at integral, broad, or pluralistic thinking fall prey to either a lack of rigor or an over-emphasis on holistic analyses, lacking sufficient complexity.

Wicked problems and complex thinking

Complex thinking provides some general premises that may help to reduce the tendencies towards oversimplifying reality, and open the way to seeing more of the complexity of Gordian knots and wicked problems.

For instance, as Illich, Rescher and others have argued, the general principle of complexification appears to help to explain issues like the marginal returns on increased costs, increased loopholes, tendencies towards increasing energy demands, and the degradation of democracies. Second, the principle of transdisciplinary methodologies helps us to move beyond myopically distortional perspectives in science and scholarship. Specifically, quantitative scientific models retain their power, but they are better contextualized, more fully understood to exist in conjunction with qualitative methodologies and more synthetic conceptual tools, such as broader philosophical and social theory, integral analyses, and framing in terms of greater narratives and stories. As Timothy Allen has argued, the purpose of science is to improve our narratives.[6] That is to say, for complex issues, the scientific method works in correlation and coproduction with greater historical and contextual explanations, and narratives, and ultimately, the greater worldview.

Generally, the complexity and transdsiciplinarity of global issues like climate change has come to center stage. Increasingly, the interdependency of the systems involved has also become a focus. As researchers grapple with highly complex interactions, they begin to use terms such as the convergence of issues, wicked problems, Gordian knots, and vicious cycles to describe them.

Steve Vanderheiden, professor of political science and environmental studies at the University of Colorado at Boulder, highlighted the imbrications of social and environmental interrelated factors in his edited volume *Political Theory and Global Climate Change*. Utilizing a rights-based focus, Vanderheiden notes that climate change involves converging multiple rights claims: the right to develop, the right to sustain a minimum per capita level of greenhouse gas emissions or, after Henry Shue, the right to "survival emissions," and the right to achieve climatic stability.[7] Vanderheiden shows the feedbacks between poverty, wealth and the environment, the highly multidisciplinary nature of climate change both within and between disciplines such as ethics, politics, and economics. Shue discusses the feedbacks and interdependence between extreme wealth and extreme poverty, arguing that these must be addressed and resolved together.

Similarly, climate ethicist Stephen Gardiner adopted a Gordian knot framing of climate ethics around what he calls the "perfect moral storm," involving three intertwined moral problems.[8] First, a "global storm" – the fact that climate change causes and effects are both widely dispersed, leading to a spatial fragmentation of agency that undermines global efforts to curb greenhouse gas emissions. Second, an "intergenerational storm" – due to time lags and delayed impacts, agency is temporally fragmented creating an intergenerational collective-action problem that defies straightforward solutions. Finally a "theoretical storm" – multiple intersecting problems are too complex for classical approaches in ethical theory, leading to "conceptual confusion."

Complexity principles underlie each of Gardiner's storms. Networked causality and networked consequences drive the global storm; issues of feedbacks, nonlinearities, and rate spur the intergenerational storm; and the greater ensemble of complex dynamic processes contribute to the "multiple intersecting problems" that "challenge conventional terms of ethical analysis," and challenge analysis of climate change period. The ensuing conceptual confusion may be framed as a surfeit of simple thinking or a lack of complex thinking.

Ecologist and interdisciplinary thinker, Peter Taylor, Director of the Creative and Critical Thinking Graduate Program at the University of Massachusetts, has advanced complex thinking to navigate environmental issues. In the book *Unruly Complexity*, he aimed, "to stimulate scientists to become more self-conscious and systematic about the ways in which they deal with the unruliness of complex situations." In the words of Raymond Williams, he wants to encourage others not to mentally draw back, but, rather, to make the effort of "looking in an active way, at the whole complex of social and natural relationships which is at once our product and our activity."[9] More generally, says Taylor,

> I argue that both the situations studied and the social situation of the researchers can be characterized in terms of unruly complexity or "intersecting processes" that cut across scales, involve heterogeneous components, and develop over time. These cannot be understood from an outside view; instead positions of engagement must be taken within the complexity. Knowledge production needs to be linked with planning for action and action itself in an ongoing process so that knowledge, plans, and action can be continually reassessed in response to developments – predicted and surprising alike.

Taylor suggests principles and practices that will help scientists to remain open and aware to the need to incorporate complexity into their approach to and understanding of the scientific process. The work includes "steps in the development of a framework ... that integrates conceptual, contextual, and reflexive angles on the practice of researchers."[10] Taylor comes to several conclusions both about the nature of complex systems, the ways in which we further wicked problems, and approaches to further understanding and promoting complex thinking. For instance, the framework he develops exposes the hidden complexity of the simplification that various fields use to focus attention on supposedly well-bounded systems.[11] Intriguingly, he notes that in ecology, "complexity begets instability."[12] This may inform how we understand the nature of complexification in natural and social systems, and how types or degrees of complexification may be ideal to human sustainability and flourishing, Moreover, complexity is better conceived, he says, not in terms of well-bounded systems, but, rather, in terms of intersecting processes.[13] Elucidating pitfalls of either avoiding systems or reifying systems, he points to ways to navigate complexity more effectively. "The full system consists not only of variables but also of their dynamic interrelations. Systems ecology, in my opinion, has been too ready to translate measurements of covarying variables into equations without elucidating the biological *dynamics*...''[14] We have to contextualize quantitative results within their qualitative contexts. As we have to navigate between being too myopic and too inclusive.

As an interdisciplinary thinker, he adds that this is generalizable, and must also apply to other fields, he says, e.g., economics and social theory. Their models and conceptual frameworks often also require explicit reference to variables that have dynamics of their own. There is a contrast between conceptual and practical commitments that render a complex situation "system-like," and those moves that help researchers to more fully represent and engage with "unruly complexity." Perhaps all these approaches are useful in different instances. But Taylor argues that for many issues of sustainability, adequate analyses must avoid the former and promote the latter. Like Einstein, we must simplify, but not too much. As Taylor puts it, we must strive for an account that has "intermediate complexity," it is neither highly reduced nor overwhelmingly detailed.[15] Of course, this is precisely what many scientists are already aiming for. A hope of many complexity theorists is that elucidating the complexity of their study subjects may advance this practice.

Complex thinking has been applied more broadly in conceiving general sustainability practices. One such approach is the transdisciplinary analysis of complexity and sustainability by Timothy Allen, Joseph Tainter, and Thomas Hoekstra in *Supply-Side Sustainability*.[16] Their general premise is that in order to conceptualize issues of sustainability it is necessary to frame them within the greater context of nested hierarchies and complexity theories. Western thinking and capitalist profit motives have facilitated linear, reductionist frameworks for planning, e.g., managing for outputs. Instead, the authors argue, we need to manage for contexts. For instance, rather than managing for how many fish we can extract, we must manage for how many fish an ecosystem can reasonably produce in a season. Rather than managing for how much food crops we want to produce, we should manage for what amount of crops the topsoil and aquifers can sustain over the long term.

One quickly runs into inescapably transdisciplinary issues. Environmental issues must be framed foremost as transdisciplinary if we are to take seriously the need to surpass nature-culture dichotomies. To manage for context one must know them, and to know them is to bring together transdisicplinary teams who cannot necessarily easily communicate their plural viewpoints. The philosopher of science Paul Feyerabend pointed out that not only can the holders of different viewpoints not communicate, but also, they may not even share the same perception of experiences.[17] As Allen, Tainter and Hoekstra noted wryly, a colloquium involving two ecologists and a social scientist, worked only when the three thinkers "negotiated to (relative) homogeneity." In other words, the varying perspectives may not be completely reconciled, but nonetheless, they must be navigated and conjoined as well as possible. The effort was made easier by the use of complexity theories such as hierarchy theories, since the abstract concepts of these approaches apply to systems of many kinds.[18] Nonetheless, they note that efforts to integrate social theory and ecological science do not occur "seamlessly." This kind of transdisciplinary research requires open minds and experimentation. They strove to adopt a "bee's eye view," a "multi-faceted view of contiguous planes. One accepts the fracturing of such a view, in order to gain the benefits of a multidisciplinary perspective."[19] Such perspectives become essential in the quest for sustainability. For sustainability, as environmental historian Stephen Pyne has said, "is not an ecological condition, so much as it is the interplay between a continuously evolving state of nature and a constantly changing state of mind."[20]

The principles of supply-side sustainability, simple on the face of it, are radical in their implications. We must manage, not for outputs or for material production, but, rather for productive natural systems, or as Carolyn Merchant has emphasized, reproductive natural systems. We must manage systems by managing, not for short-term profits, but rather for the long-term ability of systems to sustain themselves, and therefore for the long-term and broadest common good. Disproportionate private gains may not just be unfair; they may also irreversibly undermine the integrity of social and environmental systems.

To manage for long-term systems integrity requires us to identify what dysfunctional systems lack and to supply only that. We must support and restore, not human subsidies, but rather the underlying ecological processes that will subsidize our management efforts, and thus, indirectly, continue to "subsidize" societal needs and well being. But that means that we must stop doing the converse! We must stop subsidizing management efforts to "control" or "manage" ecological processes for disproportionate productivity and profit.[21] Finally, the complexification in systems requires us to incorporate in environmental management the principle of diminishing returns to problem solving, as discussed in Chapter 4.

This may sound hard, but managing for complexity is actually easier. One stops working against the grain. It seems to makes sense that insofar as it is more effective, it leads to virtuous cycles. Of course, it may lead to significant social strain during the transition, with reduction of marketable outputs. Yet, the current vicious cycles also are poised to create increasing social and environmental strains and degradation. In fact, various recent global environmental studies such as the MEA and IPCC reports indicate that some current vicious cycles may lead to further collapses, diminishing the very potential for long-term environmental integrity in various respects. Again, there are examples from throughout human history of sustainable, apparently synergistic ways of organizing societies and environments. As noted in the Preface, Elinor Ostrom's work on one small area of this won her the Nobel Prize. To collect and study such examples is a research priority, as successful examples may be adapted in various ways to our contemporary situations.

Cutting the Gordian knot of climate change policy

Many scholars who have developed promising climate change policy have drawn on the lessons found throughout this book. Like F. Stuart Chapin III and Stephen

Schneider, they have integrated more complexity both into their scientific models and their philosophical interpretation of these models. Like the Santa Fe Institute pioneers, they include complex parts of the puzzle – interactions, interdisciplinarity, and systemic patterns and processes. Like the social theorists and philosophers, they incorporate social and philosophical dimensions of the socioecological context. Like the transdisicplinarians they understand the need for epistemological pluralism and the deeply collaborative nature of effective climate policy. Though not stated explicitly, like all of these scientists and scholars, they express a need for what Morin has called complex thinking.

In what follows, I look at three examples, the work of leading interdisciplinary and transdisciplinary thinkers on climate science, ethics, and policy. These scientists and scholars have drawn on some of the best ideas from throughout this book. In addressing climate change, they began with solid science, explored and developed many relevant quantitative criteria and indicators, and have begun incorporating the multifaceted scientific, social, economic, ethical, and political principles necessary to decipher an adequate approach.

Climate science for policy

For the most part, we had sufficient climate science for policy by the late-1990s and sufficient climate ethics shortly thereafter, by the mid-2000s. In fact, as Hans Jonas' discussion of the greenhouse effect demonstrated already in 1979, we had sufficiently compelling science to merit a substantial shift in industrial societies over 30 years ago. By 2000 we had a global consensus of scientists, social theorists and ethicists. The science and ethics we already possess call for a major shift in social policies, a planetary-scale New Deal for climate stabilization. This requires transitioning to a lower-carbon economy.

There are at least three major ways to frame scientific criteria with regard to known risks, to estimate the degree of human impact that would likely avoid global catastrophic climate change. The three criteria are: tons of greenhouse gas (GHG) emissions per person per year, the total average global temperature increase in degrees, and net carbon emissions in parts per million of the atmosphere.

Regarding the first criterion, tons of greenhouse gas (GHG) emissions per year per person, the US level of GHG emissions has been rising from about seven tons per person per year, while the average of Western industrialized societies is more like five. Suggested goals for reductions range from three tons to as low as one-third of a ton.

Regarding the second criterion, average global temperature increase, from 1970 until about 2000, the global average was about eight-tenths of a degree. However, from 1990 the rate of change has been accelerating. The IPCC warns of perhaps a five to seven degree average global warming over the twenty-first century. With each incremental rise in net global temperature, the probability increases for a host of environmental impacts.

A third criterion is the measure of climate change in total carbon concentrations in parts per million of the atmosphere. According to the Global Carbon Project, in 1751 the pre-industrial background quantity of greenhouse gases in the atmosphere was 280 ppm. Between 1970 and 1979 atmospheric concentration of CO_2 rose by 1.3 ppm per year. Between 1980 and 1999 it was just over 1.5 ppm per year. From 2000 to 2007 CO_2 concentrations increased by 2.0 ppm per year, and by the time of the 2007 IPCC report, the total was >380 ppm. From 2007 to 2009 it increased by 2.2 ppm per year.[22] When Nicholas Stern came to the estimate of 450 ppm maximum using largely classical economic formulae, a backlash from leading scientists quickly pointed out the lack of feedbacks, non-linearity and abrupt change, and called for a more realistic threshold at 350 ppm.

With such rapid change, the scientific questions also changed quickly. The old, late-twentieth-century questions were: Is climate change real? Is it driven by human impact? Is it happening already? Due to positive feedbacks, network causality, and nonlinear change, by the first years of the twenty-first century, scientists were asking entirely new questions: Have we already passed dangerous climate thresholds? How much can we assess about the nature and trajectory of accelerating, interacting feedbacks and networked causality and consequences? Will there be one or more large sources of potential abrupt climate change in the near future?

Possible sources of abrupt climate change include a singular dramatic event such as a sudden methane release from the permafrost or from the ocean, a sudden collapse of the Amazon rainforest, or the halting of the ocean's conveyor belt. Or abrupt change could be driven by a combination of more anodyne local positive feedbacks creating a snowball effect of rapid change at the planetary scale.

Climate ethics

A few crucial ethical framings of climate change also provide a basis for action. These framings can be seen in terms of the degrees and types of complexities they omit or include. Climate ethics is inherently an extraordinarily complex puzzle. As Stephen Gardiner pointed out, it is highly global, dispersed, historical, geographically and contextually variegated, and thus necessitates a rich theoretical framework.

One framing for climate ethics is burden sharing. This view frames decreasing the use of fossil fuels as a burden that should be shared in an ethical manner. This approach captures the complexities of global burdens and struggles today, and can promote synergies between wealthy and poorer nations. On the other hand, relying strictly on a burden-sharing theory may obscure significant historical issues, such as: responsibility for greater or lesser creation of and benefit of the climate problem, colonialism, capitalist exploitation, wealth gaps and inequities, and fossil-fuel intensive wars. While evidently no one knows exactly how, clearly, we must learn to integrate these issues in our considerations, to achieve successful international negotiations and cooperation.

A second framing of climate ethics is resource sharing. This view incorporates many important contextual issues, such as successful self-governance of common pool resources and various types of tragedies of the commons. Yet again there are some potential drawbacks. For instance, focusing solely on resources may omit important potential influences such as technological innovations, e.g., the possible inventions and rapid uptake of new energy technologies, which might alter in some respect the course of future climate change.

Perhaps the most adequate and now predominant climate ethics framework is "allocation justice," referred to in ethics as distributive justice. Peter Singer uses the concept of an atmospheric pie.[23] There is one global atmosphere, and we should divvy up human impact on the atmosphere equally amongst all people; everyone should get a fair share of the pie of carbon emissions. In this view, parties that already have exceeded their share have obligations to parties that will therefore have less right to impact the atmosphere today and in the future.

This framing is open enough to incorporate various items for allocation, including fossil fuel use, emissions rights, costs, technologies, and trading rights, environmental rights, and the like. On the face of it, just allocation would seem to allow for strong ethical principles in key practical areas of climate change adaptation and mitigation. Analysts aim to derive some fair quantities in the categories of allocating rights for amounts of emissions, amounts of financial and technical assistance, rights for emissions trading schemes, and the like.

However, the flip side of this openness is that proposals that are very much at odds with each other co-exist under the name of allocation justice. For instance, during the Bush II Era, US negotiators called for emissions rights to be allocated with respect to a country's capacity to produce; essentially emissions rights should be proportional to GDP. The irony in this proposition is grotesque, as correlating emissions rights to GDP omits or negates a wide array of crucial contextual issues, such as historical responsibility for the net atmospheric GHG concentration. Similarly, the Kyoto Protocol, while better than what has followed, nonetheless was based in part on the elitist proposition of grandfathered allocation rights, whereby those who have most benefited from carbon intensive technologies for the last 100 years should be doubly rewarded by maintaining a better standard of living, even while, poorer nations bear the worst brunt of current climate change.

Much depends on the complexity of the framing and analysis. Allocation-based framings may also be based on concepts such as current per capita emission rights, promoting equity in standards of living. Some versions go beyond this, arguing not only for per person allocation rights, but also for principles of historical accountability, and even future accountability. Such framings promote an equitable leveling, incorporating issues such as socioeconomic class, history, and the qualitative differences between subsistence and luxury emissions.

The Greenhouse Development Rights Framework: climate policy synergies

In an article called, "Cutting the Gordian knot: Adequacy, Realism and Equity," Sivan Kartha, Paul Baer, and Deborah Cornland develop one climate policy framework designed to adequately incorporate the complexities of climate change.

> Despite the almost impossible complexity of the climate deadlock, it is possible to map its most profound contours. They range, unsurprisingly, outside the traditional domains of climate politics, across lands defined by post-Cold War geopolitics, the struggle for development, the challenges of sustainability. For all this, however, they define a tangle – a Gordian Knot – in which three principle strands may be clearly discerned: adequacy, realism, and equity.[24]

A focus on adequacy, realism and equity suggests that an adequate climate policy should include: an allocation justice system based on equitable per capita rights, incorporating issues of historical debts and responsibilities, and considerations of equity. This is the basis of a report by Paul Baer and his colleagues, "The Greenhouse Development Rights Framework: The right to develop in a climate constrained world," published in 2007, with an update in 2008.[25]

Their approach is to build up principles that extend human rights and humanitarian principles to everybody, while fairly distributing the costs and burdens of rapid deceleration of greenhouse gas emissions. The authors devise a few tools for this. First, they develop an indicator that captures both responsibility and capacity with respect to emissions reductions, based on treating all countries, rich and poor, according to the same formula. Next, they examine multiple, interdependent social, economic, ecological and ethical issues, striving for synergistic solutions.

> This paper argues that an emergency climate stabilization program is needed, that such a program is only possible if the international effort-sharing impasse is decisively broken, and that this impasse arises from a severe, but nevertheless surmountable, conflict between the climate crisis and the development crisis. It argues, further, that the best way to break the international climate impasse is, perhaps counter-intuitively, by expanding the climate protection agenda to include the protection of developmental equity, which can and should be specified in terms of the UNFCCC's notion of "common but differentiated responsibilities and respective capabilities." The Greenhouse Development Rights (GDRs) framework does exactly this, in the context of an extremely ambitious emission reduction pathways designed to hold global warming below 2°C. It defines national responsibility and capacity, and assesses national climate obligations, in a manner that relieves from the costs and constraints of the climate crisis those

individuals who are still striving for a decent standard of welfare – represented by a "development threshold" defined at an income level modestly above a global poverty line. Moreover, it takes intra-national income disparities formally into account, stepping beyond the usual practice of relying on national per-capita averages, which fail to capture either the true depth of a country's developmental need or the actual extent of its wealth.[26]

The second edition made major changes, both to adjust to greater complexity in data, and to mimic greater complexity in their methodology. Specifically, the authors adopted the International Energy Agency's 2007 World Energy Outlook reference projections as their new business as usual case. They estimated the no-regrets potential against the influential new McKinsey estimate, also based on the 2007 World Energy Outlook reference case.[27]

Furthermore, they worked to render their model more dynamic. Rather than calculating the key metric, the Responsibility and Capacity Indicator (RCI) on the basis of current national data (GDP, population, cumulative emissions), they calculated it on the basis of projections of these indicators, projections that were derived from the 2007 World Energy Outlook. While the World Energy Outlook is also imperfect, it has served to give them a more accurate analysis in light of major recent change, enabling the authors to reveal, as they say, "some intriguing and politically challenging results."[28] But while the results certainly appear to be politically challenging, they present a path forward that is scientifically sound, politically realistic, and reasonably fair.

Nowhere in the Greenhouse Development Rights paper do the authors discuss complex systems, complexity, complexity science, or complex thinking per se. Yet, in many ways, the basis, interpretation and implications of the report depend upon our understanding of complex dynamic systems as presented throughout this book. This includes the significance of accounting for feedbacks, thresholds, uncertainties, and nonlinear and abrupt events, as outlined in Chapter 9. Yet, it also includes other factors that complex systems help to more fully explain. It includes an integration of social theory, with such necessary dimensions as ethics, economics, culture, and politics. Furthermore, it includes an awareness that political, scientific, and economic changes only take place within the context of multidimensional social relations and interdependence, and therefore that developing global social solidarity is a necessary component of any international negotiations in our highly interconnected, globalized world.

If our world is indeed comprised of complex systems, as the scholarship described throughout the book indicates, and if climate change seems to hinge not on a mechanical worldview but on the mechanisms of the complex worldview, then it seems that the preservation and further development of the complexity framework is a means to accompany and perhaps to guide the advancement of climate ethics and policy.

The great energy transition: global 'self-organization' and synergistic solutions

> It is my belief that we humans are poised to become, from now on, the means by which Gaia will regulate at least some of its essential processes.
>
> (Tim Flannery[29])

At the heart of all complex dynamic systems are processes of self-organization. In contrast, at the scale of the planet, there do not appear to be inherent "self-organizing" properties between social groups or between societies and environments. In fact, as the Millennium Ecosystem Assessment made clear, human impact is largely degrading and undermining global environmental systems. Evidently, there are many causes, war, colonialism, globalized capitalism and more, all of which have to be addressed with policies for more sustainable societies, and I cannot cover all of that in detail here.

Complexity theories may contribute to a theory of "self-organizing" or reorganizing societies and environments sustainably. It would have to be sufficiently rid of the damning properties of classical, modernist, technocratic, and authoritarian thinking, permitting a more enlightened, humanist, ecological perspective.

The simple act of taking the notion of self-organization from its organic roots within singular organisms and systems, and trying to graft it onto much more complex multidimensional global societies and environments should raise alarm bells. It conjures up images of totalitarianism, authoritarianism, and other failed projects of modernity. Yet, a rich lineage of relevant social theory and political philosophy can inform this approach. And complexity terms such as resilience, regulation, and self-organization might help us to take on a more enlightened role in resolving twenty-first-century crises.

Tim Flannery has examined such issues with a rather broad lens, presenting one approach to some of the central dynamics of the climate change crisis, one of our most pressing environmental Gordian knots, and attempts to resolve it with win–win strategies. Flannery shows one strong approach to conceptualizing the multiple kinds of self-organization that we might want to consider in conceiving of sustainable societies.

Science has come a long way in understanding how many vital environmental systems function. Thanks to this science, we can now describe in some detail: how the Earth recycles minerals and nutrients; how atmospheric and oceanic chemistry is maintained; how the surface temperature of the planet is regulated; and how biodiversity is protected from external shocks. Such deep understanding of Earth's self-regulatory systems, says Flannery, is invariably empowering. Knowledge of carbon cycles directly informs how to promote effective regulation of the Earth's climate cycle. If the twentieth century was an era of technological triumph, the twenty-first will be even more significant, the century when "our knowledge of Earth's processes must be put to use."[30] There must be a feedback, wherein the knowledge we have gained gets put back into our understanding of how to monitor, modify, reorganize, and enhance human-environmental systems.

One of the lessons of this book is that there are both dangers and opportunities inherent to the complex worldview, and we must mitigate the dangers and build on the opportunities. There are dangers, as humans are prone to take any new knowledge as proof of our power over nature, as in the power to control, manage and regulate climate, e.g., through geoengineering. Yet, the complexity principles of complexification, the degree of unknowability and impossibility of tracking all feedbacks and networked effects, the issues of counterproductivity and nefarious consequences, and the ubiquity of uncertainties, vulnerability and potential collapses, militate against the pure hubris of past eras. Where consciousness of complexity does not succeed, the rapid environmental degradation in so many ecosystems functions, as outlined by the MEA, provides a backdrop of humility.

More specifically, Flannery frames climate policy around one central Gordian knot he calls the "coal conundrum." Flannery chooses a strong starting point by focusing on one major driver of climate change: coal. Simply put, the current situation looks to some like a win–lose–lose situation, while in a deeper sense it is also a lose–lose–lose situation. While a few corporate elites and their allies in media, business and politics, reap the profits of burning coal, the mass of humanity and the environment suffer the consequences, now and into the future. Corporations and elites gain short-term financial profits, for instance, while everyone loses viability of environmental systems to varying degrees in the shorter and longer term.

Flannery's solution is based in the recognition that in complex systems, humans are interdependent on each other and on nature, and therefore we simply must adopt cooperative strategies. Flannery points to how the switch from competitive to cooperative policies, is necessary to truly benefiting anyone in the near future. As a condition of funding the Australian coal industry, says Flannery, the Australian government should force it to give any intellectual property in clean coal technology it develops to Chinese power companies for domestic use. Australia's carbon trading scheme, in place by 2011, could also be effective in assisting China to deal with its energy desires, if the scheme involved a clean development mechanism similar to the one operating in Europe.[31]

True, it's bitterly unfair that further government subsidies should go to the very industry that has lied to the public for decades and has done more than anyone to create the climate crisis in the first place. It's unfair, says Flannery, but it works because it provides a way out of the current crisis. We need solutions that work for the developed world, for the large emerging economies, for the poorer developing countries and for the planet as a whole. While this may seem harsh, simply permitting current levels of coal plant emissions will be far worse. As Flannery says, our children and grandchildren will deliver a far harsher condemnation of today's coal burning than either our courts or our economies can today.[32]

There have been many win–win strategies to fixing the coal conundrum. In 2010, Denmark quickly developed a nation-wide, wind-powered electric car grid. Multiple systems work synergistically. For instance, the electric car battery grid can hold the electricity stored from wind turbines, making even intermittent wind a stable energy source for cars. The scale and monopoly of Denmark's new car grid make it directly competitive with big oil in that country; perhaps a true win–win solution.[33] Of course, in most cases, such a shift may mean a substantial short-term loss in profits for the transitioning industries, which is at the crux of the Gordian knot. Flannery's solution is to mitigate the losses, and aim to supply new wins for these industries.

A major topic in global climate change debates in the last few years has been REDD, the United Nations program "Reducing Emissions from Deforestation and Forest Degradation in Developing Countries," which many call a classic lose-lose policy, often masquerading as a win–win policy. In brief, REDD promises to reduce emissions by allowing Northerners to quantify and buy the ecosystem "services" or functions produced by Southern forests. In theory, locals will be paid to protect their forests, benefitting everyone.

In practice, this over-simplification falls apart, as the term "locals" is quickly exposed as a dangerous abstraction. Far from protecting the lives of all locals, it privileges a few elites while destroying the livelihoods of most locals. Under the program, Northerners pay a small number of elites in poorer tropical countries, who often evict indigenous groups dependent upon local forest ecosystems. Thus, small profits for third world elites at times create a generation of climate refugees forced to live unsustainably in growing city slums, and even the extent to which forests are ultimately protected under corrupt regional governing systems in socially and economically unstable areas remains seriously in doubt.

REDD is one example of myriad recent proposals via which neoliberal elites usurp land from poor peasants. A few select corporate and third world elites gain profits in the short term, but in the slightly longer term everyone loses environmental and climatic viability. When elites drive traditional pastoralists and forest dwellers off their lands, it's a clear example of a lose–lose scenario. Pastoralists and forest dwellers often lose everything – not just their lands, but also their homes, means of subsistence, cultural heritage, languages, and more. Poor throughout the world have been rapidly losing entire regions and cultural histories. In the process, their societies are losing socially stability, and ecologically sustainable, renewable sources of food, water, medicines, building materials, and climate. Elites in the industrialized world, as well as counterparts throughout the tropics, lose a vital opportunity to stabilize the earth's climate, as well as the future potential for social and economic stability and thriving. For almost everyone involved, certain "longer-term" consequences may now occur in our own lifetimes. Moreover, it's a truism that funds given to governments in the tropical, developing world rarely make their way down to the village level. Mass opposition has called out corporate usurpation of peasant lands and resources for its true lose-lose nature. As Flannery said, "That sort of profit-taking must surely be regarded as theft, regardless of the letter of the ... law."[34]

As in the case of further subsidies for big coal, some concessions will be needed to promote alternate propositions. By definition, everybody makes some gains in win–win scenarios. The question is how to allocate these so that the overall balance will tip towards human survival and thriving.

Flannery provides a creative approach to an alternative to the failed REDD proposal, one aiming to achieve a truer win–win outcome. First, bring the Internet into primary schools throughout forested tropical regions. Have NGOs sponsor widespread computer training programs in these regions. By utilizing Google Earth and other technologies, help locals to introduce themselves to the rich world, explaining how they plan to protect their existing forests or to reforest degraded grasslands. Utilizing an auction system like eBay, interested northerners can purchase climate security, by sponsoring local carbon sequestration projects in the tropics. Satellites can provide periodic surveillance. An auction system can update statistics on "seller" honesty and dishonesty. The publication of both vendor and purchaser reliability records can help to regulate the success of forest protection efforts over time. It's reasonable to assume that, Flannery concludes, "within a few years, five gigatonnes of carbon could be drawn down from the atmosphere each year. This represents 2.5 percent of the historic debt of carbon that has built up in the atmosphere since 1800."[35] In the absence of such a program to draw down carbon in some fashion, scientific consensus holds that we will face increasing extreme weather and climate catastrophes. To develop this more effective way of monitoring and supporting the protection of forests in poor regions and to maintain such a program for a few decades, could greatly contribute to restabilizing the Earth's climate.

In our quest for sustainability, we have the necessary information. What we need is the courage, creativity, and complex thinking to move beyond discussion and planning, and to implement such policies and practices. There are many great examples of successful synergistic approaches from around the globe to draw from, as seen in Elinor Ostrom's work on the commons and successful self-governance, and the potential for cutting Gordian knots and developing synergistic solutions seen in the work of thinkers like Paul Baer and Tim Flannery. Multiple synergistic solutions may shift our thinking away from Gordian knots, towards more effective global self-governance and sustainability.

The case of transitioning to renewable energies in the European Union: case studies in untying the Gordian knot of climate policy

Scientific and ethical consensuses hold that climate change calls for the transition to a much lower-carbon economy, and that we can and should increase many sources of renewable energy. Perhaps we will discover viable new energy sources, as in the dream of harnessing fission. In the meantime, climate science consensus calls for dramatically lowering carbon emissions.

Looking at this situation with the modern lens leads to despair. According to classical, uni-disciplinary ways of thinking, radically shrinking our economy will lead to economic, social and technological loss, even if we can see the ecological gains. In the context of the current disciplinary Diaspora, reductionist thinking blinds us to concepts of integral solutions.

Viewed with complex thinking however, emissions reductions become a more evident proposition, on the one hand apparently necessary, and on the other hand, a more fully, if not completely, win–win scenario, as Paul Baer, Tim Flannery, and others have argued. It is only through transforming our economies, industries, politics and infrastructures to address emissions reductions, that we can also save our economies, social fabric, healthcare, industries, businesses, etc. Every sector is in some respects interdependent on the others. Crucially, this necessarily involves shrinking sectors that deplete resilience and developing those that increase resilience – degrowth in some areas, growth and regrowth in others. We may need some areas of economic degrowth also spurring some areas of economic growth, as well as ecological regrowth and societal flourishing, in a way that allows for more sustainable societies. Reducing fossil fuel use and increasing renewables is one major way to address and transform multiple problems into opportunities. Within the context of complex thinking and our complex planet, this seeming economic loss may be our societal salvation.

Indeed, rather than see climate change as a kind of "external," "single issue," interfering with our other dreams; we might see it as a way better to acknowledge and understand the realistic fabric of our existence – networks, hierarchies, feedbacks, thresholds and all. Climate change provides a context within which to realize a necessary shift towards more realistic societal organization for our realistic world of limits, vulnerability, and change. The transition to lower-carbon and higher renewable energy economies are part and parcel of the changes required in every sector – food systems, environmental stewardship systems, social support systems, institutional systems, political systems, and, therefore, contrary to some common beliefs, the necessary transformation of economic systems.

Coevolution and ecological economics

I explore this through one example, threaded throughout the field of ecological economics in the last two decades, which draws on synergistic solutions between knowledge, value, economic, technological, and ecological systems. In 1994, Richard Norgaard, economist and interdisciplinary environmental scholar of the University of California at Berkeley, put forward one important aspect of the greater complexity framework: the coevolutionary framework. Simply put, the coevolutionary process, Norgaard argued, must necessarily account for the interdependence and coevolutionary forces of five different cross-sector, transdisciplinary threads: values, knowledge, organization, environments, and technologies.[36] In 2005, Norgaard expanded on the framework to show how further threads could be woven into policy solutions.[37]

The coevolutionary process is one of many models that highlight issues of networks and hierarchies, feedbacks and interdependence, and as such, the need to conjoin disciplinary and transdisciplinary work across hierarchical scales. Norgaard's framework has been influential in the fields of ecological economics, and sustainability studies, as it shows how and why certain transdisciplinary links need to be conjoined for policy. The strength of the coevolutionary framework is its focus on complexity principles, as the heart of the model integrates the realities of networks, hierarchies and feedbacks. In this way, coevolution captures some essential features of both vicious and virtuous cycles.

In recent years, others have taken up and expanded on the coevolutionary concept, extending its utility to thinking, in various ways, about more sustainable economies. Timothy Foxon of the University of Leeds in the United Kingdom, for instance, led a team at Oxford University in considering how to bring complex thinking to bear on coevolutionary perspectives for the transition to a low-carbon economy. Foxon builds up complexity principles within and across disciplines, encompassing factors across scales and sectors. In this case, Foxon shows the implications of complex thinking within economics, and then applies this complexity economics to the greater highly transdisciplinary quest to transition to a low-carbon economy.

Economies are complex dynamic systems. Table 11.1 summarizes Foxon's description of the use of complexity principles to explain economic principles.[38] Foxon then contextualizes this within greater social systems, in discussing how to take up these complexity economics principles in conjunction with social, institutional, business, and technological systems. In Table 11.2 he integrates

Table 11.1 Complexity principles and economic principles

Complexity principle	Economic principles
Dynamics	Economies are open, dynamic systems, far from equilibrium
Agents	They are made up of heterogeneous agents, lacking perfect foresight, but able to learn and to adapt over time
Networks	Agents interact through various networks
Emergence	Macro patterns emerge from micro behaviours and interactions
Evolution	Evolutionary processes create novelty and growing order and complexity over time

Table 11.2 Complexity economics for integrated transdisciplinary approaches

Complexity approach in economics	Complexity approach for integrated economic, social, technological, business, and individuals
Coevolutionary approach	Coevolution of technologies, institutions business strategies, and user practices
Coevolutionary multi-level framework	Interactions between micro, meso, and macro levels
Draws on insights from three transdisciplinary research areas within ecological economics	1. Socio-technical transitions (Kemp, Rotmans, Geels) 2. Technologoical innovation systems (Jacobsson, Bergek, Hekkert) 3. Co-evolution of technologies and institutions (Freeman, Nelson)

hierarchy theories, looking at three hierarchical levels, the microscopic, mesoscopic, and macroscopic levels.[39]

Foxon and his colleagues have looked at several case studies. For instance, they compared the multifaceted strategies used in three European nations to help high-carbon industries shift to a greater focus on renewable energies. In the three case studies, net decrease of the fossil fuel sector and net increase of the renewables sector were both negligible. However, these were pioneering examples, producing nonetheless valuable insights and some successes. Foxon explained the results:

> In Germany, incumbent energy firms initially lobbied heavily against the introduction of support mechanisms for renewable energy, as they saw these as threatening their core business. However, these support mechanisms enabled new local energy firms to develop wind energy and other renewables, which the large energy firms were compelled to attach to their networks. Eventually, the large energy utilities recognised the potential of wind energy, but, by that point, the wind energy market was dominated by local energy firms.
>
> In the UK, renewable support mechanisms were introduced, but these were overshadowed by the politically dominant themes of privatisation of energy firms and liberalisation of energy markets, which meant that neither incumbent energy firms nor new entrant firms were willing or able to invest significantly in wind energy.
>
> In Spain, on the other hand, the incumbent energy firms saw renewable energy as an opportunity and so lobbied in favour of support mechanisms and invested heavily in wind energy in their local regions, creating a virtuous cycle.[40]

The study seemed to illustrate two points, according to Foxon. First, the wider institutional and regulatory frameworks and conditions can make a difference as to whether or not various actors succeed in putting into place virtuous cycles involving the promotion of renewable energy technologies.

Second, in general, actors with power under the current system will act to delay or prevent changes to institutions or regulations that are likely to diminish their power. In the examples Foxon looked at, energy companies tended to prioritize their own self-interests over the interests of the common good. Yet, if they could find ways to foster virtuous cycles and maintain their own power, they might well participate.

The second point has greater relevance to the challenge of implementing wide-ranging actions to promote sustainability. Corporations have the power to support or impede synergistic solutions. Typically, at least until now, when they do not see a win in it for themselves, they may impede these approaches, often to disastrous effect. When the global and long-term stakes are very high, this amounts to what many commonly think of as the tragedy of the commons – when short-term self-interests override the common good, including long-term self-interests.

Of course, in a capitalist system businesses follow the bottom line of profits and market competition. As noted above, since the economic crisis of 2007 to 2008, ExxonMobil's profits rose, and again grew by 57 percent from 2009 to

2010. Moreover, in 2010, the company invested even more than it's total annual profits for that year in new oil drilling and expansion into "nontraditional," energy markets – which seems to infer the even more environmentally devastating and higher carbon dioxide emissions inducing practices of mining tar sands, hydrological fracturing or "fracking," and the like.

Virtuous cycles, it seems, only succeed when they are successfully contextualized within the greater political, economic, technological, and social realities and challenges. Some businesses and corporations, including energy corporations, have put forth some genuine efforts to strategize for the transition to a low-carbon economy. Importantly, there have been some small-scale successes, as Foxon outlines.

Foxon acknowledges the major political challenges to transitioning to a low-carbon economy, but he holds that the complexity principles in the coevolutionary framework will help to effect change.

> If, as some ecological economists argue (Jackson, 2009; Victor, 2008), maintaining and widening prosperity means abandoning traditional models of economic growth, then a coevolutionary approach could help to understand how to stimulate more ecologically-beneficial forms of innovation that contribute to growing prosperity.[41]

In this, his work converges beautifully with parallel efforts such as: Baer *et al.*'s "Greenhouse Development Rights framework," Flannery's solutions to our "coal conundrum," and Morin's vision for integrated sustainable solutions in his 2011 book, *The Way*. While integral work appears more challenging, in fact, once we figure out how to get past certain political juggernauts, these synergistic solutions appear to be promising approaches for almost everybody in the short-term, and everyone else in the slightly longer-term; these solutions appear to be more effective and more sustainable. Isolated, short-term, individualistic approaches have failed. Integral approaches may lead to a convergence of more effective practices, a more sustainable way of life.

Interdependence and solidarity

> So, will the century twenty-first
> Be with the growth of fat accursed,
> Or will we have the luck to see
> The world move to maturity.
> When on this planet we call native,
> Our growth gets mostly qualitative.
> The price that we will have to pay
> For going the maturer way,
> Is to abandon the pretense
> Of violent national defense.
> (Kenneth Boulding, 1992, from
> "A Ballade of Maturity"[42])

The above transitions – creating societal scale self-organization, utilizing integral approaches, aiming for appropriately mid-ranged societal complexification, and transforming vicious cycles to virtuous ones – cannot be achieved without deep and thorough social solidarity. Luckily, it is becoming increasingly apparent that this is so. Once again there is no need to reinvent wheels, and in fact there is a long and vibrant literature on the intricacies of strengthening communities – there is a rich history of literature indicating that solidarity is the very fabric of a sustainable society.

The recent rapid decrease, since the 1970s and quite precipitously in the last few years, of equity, justice, and economic status in the United States has underscored for the millions left behind that life is not sustainable for some until it is sustainable for all. The shift to "sustainable" societies, will not be possible without the degrowth of certain unsustainable industries, such as oil, coal, and gas monopolies. The shift is also impossible, without the growth of an entire spectrum of more workable, sustainable lifestyles and visions.

Perhaps one of the deepest lessons of complexity theories is the need for solidarity in a world of interdependence. The power dynamics of the 1 and 99 percent are very real and elites currently enjoy extraordinary wealth while ever-growing margins of people suffer from joblessness or homelessness on one end of the spectrum of disenfranchisement, and hunger, torture, or imprisonment on the other. However, one lesson of nonlinearity and systemic change is that such dynamics can be short-lived. Particularities of time and space determine who suffers where and when in the greater social networks of humanity.

Yet, if we expand the scope just slightly to all of humanity, over a time period of several decades, in some crucial ways the distinction of the 1 percent and the 99 percent diminishes or dissolves. In a not too distant future, in perhaps increasingly substantial ways – 99 percent truly becomes 100 percent. This is in no way to minimize the current extreme disparities in wealth, quality of life, luxury, and suffering. The disparity of wealth now is greater than at any time since the Gilded Age, and it is growing rapidly. Many Americans are now without health insurance, jobs, or homes, and an entire spectrum of society has never had these things. Around the planet a billion people live in misery. And many thousands have perished in the first paroxysms of climate change.

Yet, in the longer-term these distinctions will fade, as the fate of the climate will ultimately be the fate of all. We will either choose a sustainable world, or we will find ourselves in a world in which no one would choose to live.

12 Conclusion

In the early twenty-first century, we are presented with panoply of fears, risks, and perils. Pick your peril – from daily dramas, to Harold Camping's warnings of the Rapture, to the next pandemic, to the very real suffering of poverty, wars, and environmental collapse. Whatever your flavor of fear, it is increasingly clear that the world is nothing if not highly dynamic.

No one can argue that we live in a comforting, stable, simple world. Yet we increasingly have better science and scholarship available to get a clearer picture of the extraordinary nature of our world's complexity. Moreover, as various major environmental studies have shown, such as the IPCC and the MEA, the general environmental trends in the Anthropocene are clearly not good.

I set out on this voyage to explore whether the nascent field of complexity has anything to offer to our current environmental crises, such as climate change, mass extinctions, oceanic malaise, and the rapid depletion of resources like fresh water, aquifers, and topsoil. Drawing from complexity theories throughout many disciplines, I extracted a complex dynamic systems framework that seems to have some bearing on social systems, environmental systems, and the way they conjoin in socioecological issues.

While I do not have definitive conclusions to offer, I have some tentative ones worth exploring further. First, not everything in our world is seamlessly interconnected, and we suffer from a great lack of interconnection in our ideas, politics, values, and public discourse as argued by Slavoj Zizek. Yet clearly much about our world is deeply interdependent, and, specifically, humans are entirely dependent upon nature.

Second, complexity illuminates the need to compliment the myopia of disciplines with a more fully transdisciplinary vision of our world. Focusing on dynamics and interconnections as they do, complexity theories also provide some of the substance and blueprint for that more transdisicplinary vision. This transdisciplinary vision strengthens our capacity to improve our societies and our environments, partly by clarifying how these are deeply intertwined. No longer can we compartmentalize social, economic, political, and environmental issues. The problems are largely interdependent, they must be conceived in their interactions, and it appears that we must also conceive of the solutions in their ensemble.

The significance of social issues to environmental issues highlights the intrinsic importance of all areas of human lives to the resolution of our major environmental crises, such as social power dynamics, socioeconomic class, culture, politics, economics, and ethics. The significance of environmental issues to social issues is often "invisible" just until it collapses. For decades we have witnessed the slow decline of topsoil and aquifers. Yet, networks, nested hierarchies, and vulnerability alert us to the risks, and nonlinearity reminds us that we must act before thresholds.

Third, emergence in complex systems shows us the extreme importance of learning, adaptation, and strategy to living and conscious systems. Inherent to emergent properties is the process of learning. The human mind is extraordinarily complex, the most complex object that we know of, and if it possesses many contradictory qualities, one of these is a capacity for learning, monitoring, modifying, strategy, and change. Moreover, human nature involves the capacity for rapture, awe, enchantment, compassion, creativity, and vivid imagination. We can put all of these qualities to the service of a better worldview and another world.

Fourth, the principle of self-organization offers us a profound window into life's mysteries, showing us just how much deeper some of life's mysteries remain. We may choose to benefit from the humility, as well as fascination that this knowledge offers us. Complex dynamic systems theories help us to see the world, not as a big set of objects, but as a community of complex living, conscious, and ethical subjects. We may learn to see ecosystems not as abstract backdrops, but rather as extraordinarily complex constellations of life forms capable of emotions, consciousness, and intelligence. Self-organizational processes show the contingency and strength, the vulnerability and resilience, the intricacy and dynamics of life. They teach us the need to live better within our ecological, planetary contexts, to develop biophilia, transform our institutions and lifestyles, and rejuvenate our sense of wonder and beauty.

Fifth, the principle of complexification is profoundly humbling and reorienting. As phenomena self-organize, emerge, and proliferate into novel and evolving forms, we are not just alienated actors, but homo sapiens, intelligent stewards of a beautiful, mystical world.

Sixth, more generally, the more we learn about complexity, the more it highlights the dangers of simple thinking and the promise of complex thinking. Complexity highlights the problems of fundamentalism, ideologies, and everyday over simplifying. The principles of unknowability, uncertainty, and complexification open up the promise of learning once again the qualities of reverence, wonder, and responsibility. A complex world is one of vulnerability, risk, and the specter of collapse. But there are two sides to the coin. A world of vulnerability and risk is also a world with the potential for and even tendency toward resilience, opportunity, and sustainability.

Complexity may be undefinable, but we might say the same of humans, the mind, love, happiness, beauty, meaning, and just about everything that is most important in our lives. Complexity theories have been called a "grab bag of any and all theories." Perhaps complexity theories provide a lens with which to study our world, one toolbox that might contribute to exploring any and all ways we might come to peace with our planet. Diverse groups are utilizing specific complexity principles and concepts, for myriad, often counteracting, purposes. As we get a fuller view of complexity theories writ large, they are revealing the imperative of social and ecological interdependence. In the face of growing environmental and social crises, perhaps this complexity lens may help us to realize the imperative of solidarity.

Notes

1 Introduction

1 G. Chui, "'Unified Theory' is Getting Closer, Hawking Predicts," *San Jose Mercury News, Morning Final Edition*, 23 September 2000, p. 29A.
2 A.-L. Barabási, *Linked: How Everything is Connected to Everything Else and What it Means for Business, Science and Everyday Life*, New York: Plume, 2003.
3 E. Morin (2011) "Re: Routledge, Ch 1." Email: 2 December 2011.
4 I. Wallerstein, *The Uncertainties of Knowledge*, Philadelphia: Temple University Press, 2004, p. 38.
5 E. Morin, *Science Avec Conscience*, Paris: Seuil, 1982.
6 S. Schneider, 20 September 2007, personal communication.
7 S. Schneider, 20 September 2007, personal communication. See also, for instance, A. Dahan Dalmedico, "Models and Simulations in Climate Change: Historical, Epistemologiccal, Anthropological, and Political Aspects," in Angela N. H. Creager *et al.* (eds) *Science without laws: model systems, cases, exemplary narratives*, Durham, NC: Duke University Press, 2007.
8 F. S. Chapin, III, G. P. Kofinas, and C. Folke (eds) *Principles of Ecosystem Stewardship: Resilience-Based Natural Resource Management in a Changing World*, New York: Springer, 2009.
9 C. S. Holling, "Resilience of ecosystems: Local surprise and global change," in: *Sustainable Development and the Biosphere.* Clark, W. C. and Munn, R. E. (eds). Cambridge University Press, Cambridge, 1986, 292–317, cited in F. S. Chapin, III *et al.*, "Resilience and Vulnerability of Northern Regions to Social and Environmental Change," *Ambio*, August 2004, vol. 33, no. 6, 344–349.
10 Ibid.
11 K. Boulding, "General Systems Theory: The Skeleton of Science," *Management Science*, 1956, vol. 2, no. 3, 197–208.

2 Elucidating complexity theories

1 Oliver Wendell Holmes, Jr. is one of the most widely cited US Supreme Court Justices who served from 1902–1932. In the 1927 case Buck vs. Bell, during the eugenics movement, Holmes argued for the forced sterilization of Carrie Buck and other women deemed to be of lesser intelligence, reminding us of the many challenges as we seek "simplicity on the other side of complexity."
2 T. F. H. Allen, personal communication.
3 K. Richardson, "Systems Theories and Complexity: Part 1," E:CO, 2004, 75–79.
4 D. Hammond, *The Science of Synthesis: Exploring the Social Implications of General Systems Theory*, Colorado: University Press of Colorado, 2003.

5 J. Macy, *Mutual Causality in Buddhism and General Systems Theory: The Dharma of Natural System*, Albany: State University of New York Press, 1991.

6 E. Morin, *La Complexité humaine*, Paris: Seuil, 1994.

7 R. Abraham, "The Genesis of Complexity," 2002, p. 8, www.ralph-abraham.org/articles/titles.shtml (accessed October 22, 2011)

8 N. Wiener, *Cybernetics or Control and Communication in the Animal and the Machine*, Cambridge, Massachusetts: MIT Press, 1948 and 1961.

9 See, for instance, J.-P. Dupuy, *On the Origins of Cognitive Science: The Mechanization of the Mind*, translated by M. B. De Bevoise, Cambridge, Massachusetts: MIT Press, 2009, and N. Kathryn Hayles, *How We Became Postmodern: Virtual Bodies in Cybernetics, Literature and Informatics*, Chicago: University of Chicago Press, 1999.

10 E. Morin, *On Complexity*, Cresskill, New Jersey: Hampton Press, 2008, pp. 16–17.

11 J.-P. Dupuy, *Ordres et désordres, enquête sur un nouveau paradigme*, Paris: Seuil, 1982.

12 E. Morin advocates the former and Timothy F. H. Allen the latter, for instance.

13 See, for instance, the work of science and technology studies scholars such as S. Jasanoff and B. Latour.

14 See, for instance, D. Ruelle, *Chance and Chaos*, Princeton, NJ: Princeton University Press, 1991, and D. Aubin and A. Dahan-Dalmedico, "Writing the History of Dynamical Systems and Chaos: Longue Duree and Revolution, Disciplines and Cultures," *Historia Mathematica*, 29, 2002, 1–67.

15 See, for instance, I. Wallerstein, *The Uncertainties of Knowledge*, Philadelphia: Temple University Press, 2004, and P. Galison and D. Stump, eds, *The Disunity of Science: Boundaries, Contexts and Power*, Stanford, California: Stanford University Press, 1996.

16 *Oxford English Dictionary*, "Theory," 1989 edition (accessed online November 10, 2008).

17 K. Boulding, "General systems theory: The skeleton of science," Management Science, 2, The Institute for Management Sciences, now the Institute for Operations Research and the Management Sciences, 901 Elkridge Landing Road, Suite 400, Linthicum, Maryland 21090, USA, 1956, 197–208, in E:CO Annual Volume 6 2004 pp. 418–431.

18 J.-C. Lugan, *La Systémique Sociale*, Paris: Presses Universitaires de France, 1993, and S. J. Kline, *Conceptual Foundations for Multidisicplinary Thinking*, Stanford, California: Stanford University Press, 1994.

19 K. Boulding, op. cit., p. 425.

20 E. Morin, "Restricted Complexity, Generalized Complexity," Presented at the Colloquium "Intelligence de la Complexite: Epistemologie et pragmatique," Cerisy-La-Salle, France, 26 June 2005, translated from French by Carlos Gershenson, 24 p., p. 1.

21 E. Morin, op. cit., p. 10.

22 Ibid.

23 Ibid.

24 C. Merchant, *The Death of Nature: Women, Ecology and the Scientific Revolution*, New York: Harper Collins Publishers, 1980.

25 R. Norgaard, *Development Betrayed: The end of progress and a coevolutionary revisioning of the future*, New York: Routledge, 1994.

26 See, for instance, S. Zizek, *The Parallax View*, Cambridge, Massachusetts: MIT Press, 2006.

27 See A. Weisman, *The World Without Us*, New York: St. Martin's Press, 2007.

28 See, for instance, T. F. H. Allen and T. W. Hoekstra, *Toward a Unified Ecology*, New York: Columbia University Press, and the work of the Resilience Alliance, online, www.resalliance.org/.

29 J. H. Holland, *Emergence: From Chaos to Order*, Oxford University Press, 1998, p. 3.

30 See, for instance, A. J. Zellmer, T. F. H. Allen, and K. Kesseboehmer, "The nature of

ecological complexity: A protocol for building the narrative," *Ecological Complexity*, vol. 3, 2006, 171–182.

31 See, for instance, K. Richardson, P. Cilliers, and M. Lissack, "Complexity Science: A 'Gray' Science for the 'Stuff in Between,'" *Emergence*, vol. 3 no. 2, 2001, 6–18: L. H. Gunderson and C. S. Holling, (eds) *Panarchy: Understanding Transformations in Human and Natural Systems*, Washington: Island Press, 2002; T. F. H. Allen and T. W. Hoekstra, *Toward a Unified Ecology*, New York: University of Columbia Press, 1992; and P. Dumouchel and J.-P. Dupuy, eds, *L'Auto-Organisation de la Physique au Politique*, Paris: Seuil, 1983, and E. Morin, *La Méthode*, vols 1–6, published between 1977–2006.

32 J. Monod, *Le Hasard et la Nécessité*, Paris: Seuil, p. 183; D. Andler, A. Fagot-Largeault, and B. Saint-Sernin, 2002. *Philosophie des sciences, tome 2*. Paris: Folio; D. Bertrand Saint-Sernin (Author) › Visit Amazon's Bertrand Saint-Sernin PageChalmers, "Strong and Weak Emergence," in P. Clayton and P. Davies, *The Re-emergence of Emergence*, Oxford: Oxford University Press, 2006; and E. Morin *La Complexité Humaine*, Paris: Flammarion, 1994.

33 T. F. H. Allen, personal communication.

34 Ibid.

3 Complexity in the natural sciences

1 M. Mitchell, *Complexity: A Guided Tour*, Oxford: Oxford University Press, 2009, p. 299.

2 A. Hubler, lecture at the Santa Fe Institute Complex Systems Summer School, July 2005.

3 M. Mitchell, op. cit., p. 95.

4 See, for instance, M. Mitchell, op. cit.

5 J. Horgan, "From Complexity to Perplexity," *Scientific American*, 1995, 272, 6: 74–79.

6 M. Mitchell, op. cit., pp. 94–111.

7 Ibid., p. 101.

8 Ibid., p. 102.

9 Ibid., pp. 293–294.

10 Melanie Mitchell, personal communication.

11 Ibid.

12 Ibid.

13 Timothy F. H. Allen, personal communication.

14 M. Mitchell, op. cit., p. 13.

15 J. Holland, *Complexity: The emerging science at the edge of order and chaos*. Harmondsworth: Penguin, 1994.

16 M. Waldrop, *Complexity: The emerging science at the edge of order and chaos.* Simon & Schuster: New York, 1992.

17 See E. Morin, 1986, p. 104.

18 J. H. Brown, G. B. West, and B. J. Enquist, "Yes, West, Brown and Enquist's model of allometric scaling is both mathematically correct and biologically relevant," *Functional Ecology* 19, 2005, 735–738.

19 J. Gleick, *Chaos*, New York: Penguin Books, 1987.

20 H. Poincaré, "Science and Method," Chicago: St. Augustine's Press, 1903.

21 E. Lorenz, "Deterministic Nonperiodic Flow," *Journal of the Atmospheric Sciences*, March, 20(2), 1963, pp. 130–141.

22 C. Song, S. Havlin, and H. Makse, "Self-similarity of Complex Networks," *Nature* 433, 2005, 392–395.

23 A.-L. Barabási, *Linked: How Everything Is Connected to Everything Else and What It Means*, New York: Plume, 2002, p. 51.

24 M. Granovetter, "The Strength of Weak Ties," *American Journal of Sociology*, May 1973, vol. 78, no. 6, 1360–1380.

25 Google Scholar, accessed 1 June 2011.

26 N. Martinez, 2007, personal communication.

27 J. Dunne, 2012, personal communication.

28 R. Williams and N. Martinez, "Simple rules yield complex food webs," Letters to Nature, Nature 404, 180–183, 9 March 2000.

29 U. Brose, R. Williams, and N. Martinez, "Allometric scaling enhances stability in complex food webs," Ecology Letters, vol. 9, no. 11, November 2006.

30 M. Pascual and J. A. Dunne, "From small to large ecological networks in a dynamic world," pp. 3–24, in *Ecological Networks: Linking Structure to Dynamics in Food Webs*, M. Pascual and J. A. Dunne, (eds) Oxford University Press.

31 R. Williams and N. Martinez, op. cit.; J. A. Dunne *et al.*, "Compilation and Network Analyses of Cambrian Food Webs," *PLOS Biology*, vol. 6, no. 4, 29 April 2008.

32 U. Brose *et al.*, op. cit.

33 J. A. Dunne, R. Williams, and N. Martinez, "Network structure and biodiversity loss in food webs: robustness increases with connectance," *Ecology Letters*, vol 5, no. 4, 2002.

34 See, for instance, E. Berlow *et al.*, "Simple prediction of interaction strengths in complex food webs," *Proceedings of the National Academy of Sciences*, 6 January 2009, vol. 106, no. 1, 187–191; and M. Pascual, J. A. Dunne, and S. A. Levin, "Ecological Networks: Linking Structure to Dynamics in Food Webs," in M. Pasquale and J. Dunne, op. cit.

35 R. Horn, conference poster, *History of the Ideas of Cybernetics and Systems Science, v.1.0.* hornbob@earthlink.net, 2006.

36 Ibid.

37 A. Rosenbleuth, A. Wiener, and J. Bigelow, "Behavior, Purpose and Teleology," *Philosophy of Science* 10, 1943, pp. 18–24.

38 H. Simon, "The architecture of complexity," reprinted in *Emergence: Complexity and organization* vol. 7, 2005, 1962, 3–4.

39 Ibid., p. 138.

40 T. F. H. Allen and T. W. Hoekstra, *Toward a Unified Ecology*, New York: University of Columbia Press, 1992.

41 Ibid., p. 2.

42 J. H. Holland, *Emergence: From Chaos to Order*, Oxford University Press, 1998, p. 3.

43 Ibid.

44 Ibid., p. 4.

45 Ibid., p. 4.

46 Ibid., p. 225.

47 Ibid., p. 225.

48 Ibid., pp. 225–226.

49 Ibid., p. 225.

50 Ibid., p. 48.

51 Ibid., p. 49.

52 Ibid., pp. 50–53.

53 Ibid., p. 92.

54 Ibid., p. 92.

55 Ibid., p. 93.

56 H. Morowitz, *The Emergence of Everything.* Oxford: Oxford University Press, 2002, pp. 25–38.

57 J. Goldstein, "Emergence as Construct: History and Issues," *Emergence: Complexity + Organization*, 1, 1, 1999, 49–72.

58 P. Bak, C. Tang, and K. Wiesenfeld, "Self-Organized Criticality," *Physical Review A* 38, 1, 1988.

59 S. Kaufmann, *At Home in the Universe: The Search for the Laws of Self-organization and Complexity*, New York: Oxford University Press, 1995, p. 15.
60 Ibid., p. 47.
61 Ibid., p. 62.
62 J. Monod, *Chance and Necessity: An essay on the natural philosophy of modern biology.* New York: Knopf, 1971, 1970.
63 Generally speaking, complexity scientists say that they have not as yet established "a complexity science." "Many do not believe that there is yet a 'science of complexity,' at least not in the usual sense of the word science – complex systems often seems to be a fragmented subject rather than a unified whole." M. Mitchell, 2009, p. 299.
64 E. Morin, *La Méthode: Tome I: La Nature de la Nature*, Paris: Editions du Seuil, 1977, pp. 62–63.
65 Ibid., pp. 94–95.
66 H. Atlan, *Le Cristal et la Fumée: Essai Sur L'organisation Du Vivant*, Paris: Seuil, 1986.
67 P. S. Laplace, *Oeuvres, VII, Théorie analytique des probabilités*, 1812–1820, Online. www.todayinsci.com/L/Laplace_Pierre/LaplacePierre-Quotations.htm   (accessed January 5, 2012).
68 E. Morin, op. cit., pp. 88–89.
69 Ibid., p. 92.
70 See, for instance, on the former, T. Flannery, *The Future Eaters*, 1994, and on the latter, J. Adams, *Vegetation-Climate Interaction: How Plants Make the Global Environment*, second edn, New York: Springer, pp. 170–171.
71 D. Gordon in M. Mitchell. *Complexity: A Guided Tour*, Oxford University Press, p. 294.
72 M. McCormick, "Immanuel Kant: Metaphysics," in *Internet Encyclopedia of Philosophy.* Online. www.iep.utm.edu/kantmeta (accessed June 10, 2011).
73 H. Atlan, op. cit., p. 21.
74 C. Wolfe, "Endowed Molecules and Emergent Organization: The Maupertuis-Diderot Debate," *Early Science and Medicine*, vol. 15, 2010, 38–65, p. 38.
75 Ibid.
76 Stanford University Press. Online. www.sup.org/book.cgi?id=377 (accessed January 17, 2012).
77 See, for instance, Atlan's list of French-speaking thinkers on this issue: C. Castoriadis, E. Morin, J. Piaget, J. Schlanger, M. Serres, and I. Stengers in H. Atlan, op. cit.
78 Ibid., pp. 23–24.
79 Ibid., p. 227.
80 Ibid., p. 275.
81 Ibid., p. 275.
82 M. Mitchell, op. cit., pp. 299–300.
83 Ibid., p. 300.
84 Ibid., p. 300.

4 Complexity in social theory

1 R. H. McGuire, *Breaking Down Cultural Complexity: Inequality and Heterogeneity*, New York: Academic Press Inc., 1983, p. 115, in J. Tainter, *The Collapse of Complex Societies*, Cambridge: Cambridge University Press, 1988.
2 See, for instance, the National Wildlife Federation, "The American Prairie: Going, Going, Gone?: a status report on the American Prairie," 2001, and W. Mitsch and J. Gosselink, *Wetlands*, 4th edn, Hoboken, NJ: John Wiley and Sons, Inc., 2007.
3 Eloquently described, for instance, in G. Brechin's *Imperial San Francisco: Urban Power, Earthly Ruin*, Berkeley: University of California Press.
4 M. Davis, *Ecology of Fear: Los Angeles and the Imagination of Disaster*, New York: Vintage, 1998, p. 5.

5 J. McPhee, "Los Angeles Against the Mountains," 1989, in J. McPhee, *The Second John McPhee Reader*, New York: The Noonday Press, Farrar, Straus, and Giroux, 1996, p. 258.

6 Ibid., pp. 259–260.

7 N. Rescher, *Complexity: A philosophical overview*, New Brunswick, NJ: Transaction Publishers, 1998.

8 R. Frost, "Mending Wall," 1914.

9 T. Morton, *The Ecological Thought*, Boston: Harvard University Press, 2010.

10 See, for instance, the Millennium Ecosystem Assessment, among many environmental reports in the last decade.

11 See, for instance, Secretariat of the Convention on Biological Diversity, *Scientific Synthesis of the Impacts of Ocean Acidification on Marine Biodiversity*. Montreal, Technical Series No. 46, 2009, 61 pages; G. E. Nilsson, *et al.*, "Near-future CO_2 levels alter fish behaviour by interfering with neurotransmitter function," *Nature Climate Change*, 2012, published online January 15, 2012; and A. D. Rogers and D. d'A. Laffoley, 2011. *International Earth system expert workshop on ocean stresses and impacts*. Summary report. IPSO Oxford, 18 pages.

12 S. Sim and B. van Loon, *Introducing Critical Theory: A graphic guide*, London: Icon Books, 2009, pp. 167–173.

13 Ibid., p. 171.

14 Ibid., p. 168.

15 P. Cilliers, *Complexity and Postmodernism*, London: Routledge, 1998, pp. 80–81.

16 Ibid., p. 172.

17 Ibid., p. 168.

18 C. Merchant, *The Death of Nature: Women, Ecology and the Scientific Revolution*, San Francisco: Harper, 1980, 2nd edn 1990, p. xviii.

19 R. B. Norgaard, *Development Betrayed: The end of progress and a coevolutionary envisioning of the future*, New York: Routledge, 1994.

20 Ibid., p. 229.

21 S. Zizek, *The Parallax View*, Boston: MIT Press, 2006.

22 D. M. Boje, "What Happened on the Way to Postmodern?," *Qualitative Research in Organizations and Management: An International Journal*, 2006, 1, 1, 22–40, p. 3.

23 B. Latour, *We Have Never Been Modern*, trans. by C. Porter, Cambridge, Massachusetts: Harvard University Press, 1993, 2nd edn 1991.

24 E. Morin, *La Méthode: Tome I: La Nature de la Nature*, Paris: Seuil, 1977.

25 T. F. H. Allen and T. W. Hoekstra, *Toward a Unified Ecology*, New York: University of Columbia Press, 1992.

26 L. H. Gunderson and C. S. Holling (eds) *Panarchy: Understanding Transformations in Human and Natural Systems*, Washington: Island Press, 2002.

27 B. Latour, *Reassembling the Social: An introduction to actor-network-theory*, Oxford: Clarendon, 2005.

28 Ibid.

29 Ibid., p. 9.

30 M. Davis, "The Flames of New York," *New Left Review*, 2001, pp. 37–38.

31 P. Crabtree, "Anticipations: The Remarkable Forecasts of H. G. Wells," *World Futures Society*, Sep-Oct 2007, 40–46.

32 U. Beck, *Risk Society: Towards a New Modernity*, London: Sage, 1992, pp. 12–13.

33 Ibid.

34 F. Bateman, "Labor Inputs and Productivity in American Dairy Agriculture 1950–1910," *Journal of Economic History* 29, 1969, 206–29, in J. Tainter, *The Collapse of Complex Societies*, 1988, Cambridge: Cambridge University Press, p. 95.

35 J. Tainter, op. cit., p. 93.

36 J. Tainter, op. cit., p. 94.

37 Ibid., p. 22.

38 Ibid., p. 23.
39 R. H. McGuire, *Breaking Down Cultural Complexity: Inequality and Heterogenity*, 1983, p. 115, in J. Tainter, op. cit., p. 23.
40 Ibid.
41 T. F. H. Allen, J. Tainter, and T. Hoekstra, *Supply-Side Sustainability*, New York: Columbia University Press, 2003.
42 J. Diamond, *Collapse: How Societies Choose to Fail or Succeed*, New York: Viking Books, 2005, p. 23.
43 Ibid., 421–440.
44 K. Knight (ed.) *The MacIntyre Reader*, Indiana: University of Notre Dame Press, 1998.
45 See, for instance, P. McAnany and N. Yoffee (eds) *Questioning Collapse: Human Resilience, Ecological Vulnerability, and the Aftermath of Empire*, New York: Cambridge University Press, 2010.
46 Ibid., p. 142.
47 Ibid.
48 Ibid.
49 R. Smith, "Engine of Eco Collapse," *Capitalism, Nature, Socialism*, December 2005, p. 28.
50 Ibid.

5 Towards transdisciplinarity

1 "La complexite ne s'analyse pas; elle se concoit." Jean-Louis Le Moigne, 1994. *Le constructivisme: tome 1: des fondements*, ESF editeur, Paris, p. 19.
2 See, for instance, T. Flannery, *The Eternal Frontier: An Ecological History of North America and its Peoples*, New York: Grove Press, 2001, and T. Flannery, *The Future Eaters: An Ecological History of the Australasian Lands and People*, Australia: Reed Books, 1994.
3 E. O. Wilson, *The Diversity of Life*, Cambridge: Harvard University Press, 1992.
4 Ibid.
5 J. K. Sheldon, testimony before the House Committee on Resources, US Congress, 28 April 2004.
6 I. Wallerstein, *The Uncertainties of Knowledge*, Philadelphia: Temple University Press, 2004.
7 IUCN/UNEP/WWF, "Caring for the Earth: A Strategy for Sustainable Living," Switzerland: Gland, 1991. Online. http://gcmd.nasa.gov/records/GCMD_IUCN_CARING.html (accessed October 3, 2011).
8 A. D. Rogers, and D. d'A. Laffoley, "International earth system expert workshop on ocean stresses and impacts: Summary report," Oxford: IPSO, 2011, 18 pages.
9 Ibid.
10 T. S. Eliot, *After Strange Gods: A Primer of Modern Heresy*, London: Faber & Faber Limited, 1934, pp. 19–20.
11 *Oxford English Dictionary, "Transdisciplinary,"* Online. Available with subscription (accessed 15 January 2009).
12 Ibid. (accessed 9 September 2011).
13 See, for instance, P. Leavy, *Essentials of Transdisciplinary Research: Using Problem-centered methodologies*, Walnut Creek, CA: Left Coast Press, pp. 18–23.
14 J. T. Klein, *Interdisciplinarity: History, theory and practice*, Detroit: Wayne State University Press, 1990, p. 64.
15 Leavy, op. cit., pp. 24–25.
16 L. de Freitas, E. Morin, and B. Nicolescu (eds) *Charter of Transdisciplinarity*, translated from the French by K.-C. Voss, adopted at the First World Congress of Trandisciplinarity, Convento da Arrábida, Portugal, 2–6 November 1994, pp. 1–2.

17 J. T. Klein, op. cit.
18 M. Maruyama, p. 66 in J. T. Klein, op. cit.
19 R. J. Lawrence and C. Després, "Futures of Transdisciplinarity," *Futures* May 2004, vol. 36, no. 4, 397–405, p. 400.
20 Ibid., pp. 399–400.
21 E. Morin, *Science Avec Conscience*, Paris: Seuil,1982.
22 Ibid., p. xix.
23 Ibid., p. 3.
24 R. Fumerton, "Foundationalist Theories of Epistemic Justification," *The Stanford Encyclopedia of Philosophy (Summer 2010 Edition)*, Edward N. Zalta (ed.) Online. http://plato.stanford.edu/archives/sum2010/entries/jjustepifoundational/ (accessed November 14, 2010).
25 E. Morin, *La Méthode: Tome I: La Nature de la Nature*, Paris: Seuil, 1977, pp. 51–57.
26 E. Morin, ibid., p. 91.
27 Ibid., pp. 52–53.
28 J. Monod, *Chance and Necessity: An essay on the natural philosophy of modern biology.* New York: Knopf, 1971, 1970, p. 180.
29 A.-L. Barabási, *Linked: How Everything is Connected to Everything Else and What it Means for Business, Science and Everyday Life*, New York: Plume, 2002, p. 51.
30 E. Morin, *La Méthode: Tome I: La Nature de la Nature*, Paris: Seuil, 1977, p. 111.
31 S. J. Kline, *Conceptual Foundations for Multidisciplinary Thinking*, Stanford University Press, 1995, pp. 49–68.
32 Ibid., p. 90.
33 L. H. Gunderson and C. S. Holling (eds) *Panarchy: Understanding Transformations in Human and Natural Systems*, Washington: Island Press, 2002, p. 364; see also the Resilience Alliance. Online. www.resalliance.org/ (accessed online January 10, 2012).
34 Ibid., p. 436.
35 Ibid., p. 401.
36 L. H. Gunderson, op. cit., p. 364.
37 Ibid., p. 422, (Arthur *et al.* 1997; Holland 1995; Hartvigsen *et al.* 1998; Levin 1998; Milne 1998).
38 Ibid., p. 422 (Levin 1998, 1999).
39 S. Carpenter, 2002, in L. H. Gunderson and C. S. Holling (eds) op. cit., pp. 395–417.
40 N. Milne, 1998, in L. H. Gunderson and C. S. Holling (eds) op. cit.
41 L. H. Gunderson and C. S. Holling, (eds), op. cit.
42 Ibid., p. 423.
43 M. Biagioli (ed.) *Intro to Science Studies Reader*, New York: Routledge, 2003, 1999. p. xi.
44 Ibid., p. xiv.
45 A. Goldman, "Social Epistemology," *The Stanford Encyclopedia of Philosophy*, Summer 2010, E. N. Zalta (ed.). Online. http://plato.stanford.edu/archives/sum2010/entries/epistemology-social/ (accessed January 10, 2011).
46 Ibid.
47 IUCN/UNEP/WWF, "Caring for the Earth: A Strategy for Sustainable Living," Gland, Switzerland, 1991. Online. http://gcmd.nasa.gov/records/GCMD_IUCN_CARING.html (accessed October 3, 2011).
48 Ibid., p. 76.
49 "Development," Dictionary.com. Online. http://dictionary.reference.com/browse/development (accessed January 3, 2012).
50 International Institute for sustainable Development, "What is sustainable development?" Online. www.iisd.org/sd/ (accessed January 18, 2012).
51 L. de Freitas, op. cit., pp. 1–2.

6 Complexity in philosophy: complexification and the limits to knowledge

1 E. Morin, *La Méthode: Tome III: La connaissance de la connaissance: Anthropologie de la connaissance*, Editions du Seuil, 1986, p. 222. "Nous nous rendons compte desormais que l'inconscience des limites de la connaissance etait la plus grande limite de la connaissance."
2 P. Feyerabend, *Against Method*, New York: Verso Books, 1975, p. 280.
3 S. Zizek, *The Parallax View*, Cambridge, Massachusetts: MIT Press, 2006, p. 4.
4 N. Rescher, *Complexity: A philosophical overview*, New Brunswick, NJ: Transaction Publishers, 1998, p. 1.
5 P. de Chardin, *The Future of Man*, Paris: Seuil, 1959, translated, New York: Harper Collins, 1964, p. 111.
6 K. Boulding, *Ecodynamics: A new view of societal evolution*, Beverly Hills, CA: Sage Publications, 1978, 1981, p. 32.
7 Ibid.
8 N. Rescher, op. cit., p. 1.
9 Ibid., pp. xiv–xvi.
10 A. N. Whitehead in P. Durbin (ed.) *Philosophy of Science: An Introduction*, New York: McGraw Hill Book Company, 1968, p. 218.
11 E. Harris in P. Durbin (ed.) *Philosophy of Science: An Introduction*, New York: McGraw Hill Book Company, 1968, p. 216.
12 Ibid.
13 J. Dupre, *Human nature and the limits of science*, Oxford: Clarendon Press, 2001, p. 1.
14 M. Bunge, "The Sign of Complexity," in K. Niekerk and H. Buhl (eds) *The Significance of Complexity: Approaching a Complex World Through Science*, Ashgate: Aldershot, 2004, 3–20.
15 N. Rescher, *The Limits to Science*, Pittsburg: Pittsburg University Press, 1999, 1984, p. 52.
16 P. Allen, "What is Complexity Science: Knowledge to the Limits of Knowledge," *Emergence*, 3, 1, 2000, 24–42, p. 25.
17 J. Barrow, *Impossibility: The Limits of Science and the Science of Limits*, Oxford: Oxford University Press, 1999.
18 N. Rescher, 1984, op. cit., pp. 1–4.
19 Ibid.
20 J. Barrow, op. cit., p. 73.
21 K. Richardson, op. cit.
22 E. Morin, *La Méthode: Tome III: La connaissance de la connaissance: Anthropologie de la connaissance*, Editions du Seuil, 1986, pp. 222–230.
23 N. Rescher, 1984, op. cit., pp. 64–65.
24 E. Morin in J.-L. Le Moigne, *Le Constructivisme: Tome I*, "La connaissance n'est pas faite pour essayer de dissoudre le mystere des choses, mais au contraire pour le reveler," 1994, p. 41.
25 M. Mitchell, *Complexity: A Guided Tour*, Oxford University Press, 2009, p. ix.
26 R. Descartes, *A Discourse on the Method*, translated by I. Maclean, Oxford: Oxford Univeristy Press, 1637/2006, p. 17, in M. Mitchell, *Complexity: A Guided Tour*, Oxford University Press, 2009, p. ix.
27 H. Atlan, personal communication, September 7, 2006.
28 H. Atlan, personal communication. September 7, 2006.
29 Dupre, op. cit., p. 1.
30 Y. Bar-Yam (ed.) *Dynamics of Complex Systems: Studies in nonlinearity*, Reading, New York: Perseus Books, 1997, p. 788.
31 K. Richardson, "The Hegemony of the Physical Sciences: An exploration in complexity thinking," *Futures*, vol. 37, 2005, 615–653.
32 Ibid.

33 Ibid.
34 Y. Bar-Yam, op. cit., p. 789.
35 J.-L. Le Moigne, *Le constructivisme, tome 1: des fondements*, ESF editeur, 1994, pp. 113–134.
36 D. Mulvaney and J. Wells, *Biotechnology, the life science industry, and the environment: An annotated bibliography*, University of California, Berkeley: Institute of International Studies, pp. 8–9.
37 R. Lewontin, *Biology as Ideology: The Doctrine of DNA*, New York: Harper Perennial, 1991, p. 32.
38 Ibid., p. 135.
39 Ibid.
40 H. R. Maturana, G. Uribe, and S. Frenk, "A Biological Theory of Relativistic Color Coding in the Primate Retina," Archivos de Biologia y Medicina Experimentales, Suplemento No. 1, Santiago, Chile, 1968, p. xxii, in N. K. Hayles, *How We Became Posthuman: Virtual Bodies in Cybernetics, Literature and Informatics*, Chicago: University of Chicago Press, 1999, p. 135.
41 Ibid., p. 131.
42 Ibid.
43 H. R. Maturana and Francisco J. Varela, *Autopoeisis and Cognition: The Realization of the Living* Dordrecht: D. Reidel, 1980, p. 136, in N. K. Hayles, *How We Became Posthuman: Virtual Bodies in Cybernetics, Literature and Informatics*, 1999, p. 136.
44 N. K. Hayles, op. cit., p. 139.
45 P. Cilliers, *Complexity and Postmodernism*, London: Routledge, 1998.
46 T. F. H. Allen and A. Zellmer, *Two Faces of Complexity*, unpublished book finished in 2007.
47 M. Bradie, "Science and metaphor," *Biology and Philosophy*, vol. 14, 1999, 159–166, p. 160, in K. Richardson, op. cit.
48 K. Richardson, op. cit.
49 R. B. Norgaard and P. Baer, "Collectively Seeing Complex Systems: The nature of the problem," *Bioscience*, vol. 55, no. 11, Nov. 2005, 953–960.
50 R. Strohman, 2004, personal communication.
51 N. Goodman, *Ways of Worldmaking*, Indianapolis: Hackett, 1978.

7 Complexity in ethics

1 T. F. H. Allen, J. Tainter, and T. W. Hoekstra, *Supply Side Sustainability*, New York: Columbia University Press, 2003, p. 417.
2 An exception is E. Morin's book, *La Méthode , Vol. 6, L'Ethique*, Paris: Seuil, 2006.
3 E. Ostrom, *Governing the Commons: The Evolution of Institutions for Collective Action*, London: Cambridge University Press, 1990; and E. Ostrom and J. Walker (eds) *Trust and Reciprocity: Interdisciplinary Lessons for Experimental Research* Vol. VI in the Trust Series, Russell Sage Foundation, 2003.
4 A. Leopold, *A Sand County Almanac: With essays on conservation from Round River*, Oxford: Oxford University Press, 1966, 1949, p. 240.
5 Ibid., p. 240.
6 Ibid., pp. 240–241.
7 Ibid., p. 261.
8 Ibid., p. 278.
9 C. Larrère, "L'Ethiques de l'Environnement," in S. Laugier, *Multitudes: Un deuxième âge de l'écologie politique? Multitudes* 24, 2006, 75–84, p. 82.
10 Ibid., pp. 83–84.
11 A. Leopold, op. cit., p. 239.
12 R. Elliot, "Environmental Ethics," in P. Singer, *A Companion to Ethics*, Malden Massachusetts: Blackwell Publishing, 1993, 1991, 284–293.

13 Ibid.
14 Ibid., p. 284.
15 Ibid., pp. 284–285.
16 Ibid., pp. 284–285.
17 Ibid., p. 292.
18 Ibid., p. 293.
19 A. Light and E. Katz (eds) *Environmental Pragmatism*, in *Environmental Philosophies Series*, A. Brennan (ed.) London: Routledge, 1996, p. 1.
20 S. J. Kline, *Conceptual Foundations for Multidisciplinary Thinking*, Stanford University Press, 1995.
21 A. Light and E. Katz, op. cit., p. 4.
22 Ibid., p. 2.
23 Ibid., p. 5.
24 Ibid., p. 5.
25 Ibid., p. 5.
26 Ibid., p. 335.
27 See, for instance, T. F. H. Allen, T. Hoekstra, and J. Tainter, op. cit.
28 M. Sagoff, in A. Light and E. Katz, op cit., p. 335.
29 H. Jonas, *Le Principe Responsabilité: Une éthique pour la civilisation technique*, traduit de l'allemand par Jean Greisch, Paris: Cerf, 1979, 1991, pp. 253–253.
30 Ibid., p. 35.
31 Ibid., p. 36.
32 Ibid., p. 37.
33 C. Gilligan, "In a Different Voice," Harvard University Press, 1982, 1983, in J. Toronto, "Au-delà d'une Différence de Genre: Vers une théorie du care," pp. 25–49, p. 37, p. 44, in P. Paperman and S. Laugier (eds) *Le Souci des Autres: Ethique et politique du care*, Editions de l'Ecole des Hautes Etudes en Sciences Sociales: Paris, 2006, p. 38.
34 J. Toronto, op. cit., p. 38.
35 Ibid.
36 Ibid., p. 38.
37 Ibid., p. 38.
38 "M. Jouan, "H. Frankfurt et la Métaphysique du Care: Vers une éthique 'au-delà du bien et du mal'," in P. Paperman and S. Laugier, op. cit., pp. 203–226.
39 C. Merchant, "Fish First!: The changing ethics of ecosystem management," *Human Ecology Review*, vol. no. 1, 1988, 25–30, p. 29. See also C. Merchant, *Reinventing Eden: The Fate of Nature in Western Culture*, New York: Routledge.
40 Ibid., p. 25.
41 Ibid.
42 Ibid.
43 C. Larrère, "L'Ethiques de l'Environnement," in S. Laugier, *Multitudes: Un deuxième âge de l'écologie politique? Multitudes*, 24:75–84, 2006, pp. 83–84.
44 Dr. M. L. King Jr., "Beyond Vietnam: A Time to Break Silence," excerpt of the speech at the meeting of Clergy and Laity Concerned, at Riverside Church in New York City, 4 April 1967.

8 Earth in the Anthropocene

1 Millennium Ecosystem Assessment, *Ecosystems and Human Well-being: Synthesis*, Washington, DC: Island Press, 2005, p. 1.
2 The Great Transition Initiative. Online. http://gtinitiative.org (accessed January 4, 2012).
3 United States Energy Information Administration. Online. www.indexmundi.com/energy.aspx (accessed September 25, 2011).

4 J. Zalasiewicz *et al.*, "Are we now living in the Anthropocene?," *GSA Today*, vol. 18, no. 2, 2008, p. 5.

5 P. Vitousek *et al.*, "Human Domination of Earth's Ecosystems," Science, *25 July 1997*, Vol. 277 no. 5325, 494–499.

6 A. D. Rogers and D. d'A. Laffoley, "International earth system expert workshop on ocean stresses and impacts: Summary report," Oxford: IPSO, 2011, 18 pages.

7 International Panel on Climate Change (IPCC), Fourth Assessment Report (FAR), *Climate Change 2007: The Physical Science Basis. Contribution of Working Group I to the Fourth Assessment Report of the Intergovernmental Panel on Climate Change*, S. Solomon, D. Qin, M. Manning, Z. Chen, M. Marquis, K. B. Averyt, M. Tignor, and H. L. Miller (eds) New York, NY, USA, 2007.

8 E. Monnin *et al.*, "Atmospheric CO_2 Concentrations over the Last Glacial Termination," Science, 5 January 2001, vol. 291, no. 5501, pp. 112–114.

9 Millennium Ecosystem Assessment, "Living Beyond Our Means: Natural Assets and Human Well-Being, Board Statement," March 2005, p. 1.

10 G. J. Hay, "Bridging scales and epistemologies: An introduction," *International Journal of Applied Earth Observation and Geoinformation* 7, 2005, 249–252.

11 S. Jasanoff in W. Reid *et al.* (eds) "Bridging Scales and Knowledge Systems Concepts and Applications in Ecosystem Assessment: Final Report," p. 298. Online. www.maweb.org/en/Bridging.aspx (accessed 10 January 2012).

12 W. Reid *et al.* (eds), op. cit., p. 299.

13 I. Hacking in W. Reid *et al.* (eds), op. cit., p. 299.

14 C. Miller and P. Erickson, in W. Reid *et al.* (eds), op. cit., pp. 299–300.

15 W. Reid *et al.* (eds), op. cit., p. 300.

16 Ibid., p. 298.

17 Ibid., p. 302.

18 Ibid., p. 312.

19 *Oxford English Dictionary: A Dictionary of Environment and Conservation in Earth and Environmental Sciences*, "Connectivity," Online with subscription, 2007.

20 Ibid.

21 Ibid., "Threshold."

22 *Oxford Reference online: A Dictionary of Biology in Biological Sciences*, "Threshold," Online with subscription, 2007.

23 P. Groffman *et al.*, "Ecological Thresholds: The Key to Successful Environmental Management or an Important Concept with No Practical Application?," *Ecosystems*, vol. 9, 2006, 1–13.

24 Ibid.

25 T. Lenton *et al.*, "Tipping elements in the Earth's Climate System," in *Proceedings of the National Academy of Sciences of the United States of America*, 105, 6, February 12, 2008, 1786–1793.

26 P. Groffman *et al.*, op. cit., p. 13.

27 *Oxford Reference online*, "Surprise," *Encyclopedia of Global Change in Science*, 2007 edition. Online with subscription.

28 B. Walker, C. S. Holling, S. R. Carpenter, and A. Kinzig, "Resilience, adaptability and transformability in socio-ecological systems," *Ecology and Society*, 9, 2, 5, 2004. Online. www.ecologyandsociety.org/vol. 9/iss2/art5/ (accessed July 5, 2008).

29 IUCN/UNEP/WWF, "Caring for the Earth: A Strategy for Sustainable Living," Switzerland: Gland, 1991. Online. http://gcmd.nasa.gov/records/GCMD_IUCN_CARING.html (accessed October 3, 2011).

30 Ibid.

9 Complexity and climate change

1 National Academy of Sciences, *Report of an* Ad hoc *Study Group of Carbon Dioxide and Climate: A scientific assessment to the National Academy of Science*, Washington, DC, 1979.

2 National Oceanic and Atmospheric Administration, National Climate Data Center, "Fifteen Warmest Years on Record." Online. www.noaanews.noaa.gov/stories2011/20110112_globalstats_sup.html (accessed October 5, 2011).

3 "Hurricane!" PBS documentary NOVA, 1988.

4 J. Masters, "2010–2011: Earth's most extreme weather since 1816?" Online posting. www.wunderground.com/blog/JeffMasters/comment.html?entrynum=1831 (accessed June 30, 2011).

5 Ibid.

6 Ibid.

7 Union of Concerned Scientists, "Year of Extremes Underscores Need for Better Preparedness, Emissions Reductions," November 9, 2011. Online. www.ucsusa.org/news/press_release/year-of-extremes-underscores-preparedness-emissions.html (accessed February 10, 2012).

8 International Panel on Climate Change (IPCC), "Summary for Policymakers," in: *Climate Change 2007: Impacts, Adaptation and Vulnerability. Contribution of Working Group II to the Fourth Assessment Report of the Intergovernmental Panel on Climate Change*, M. L. Parry, O. F. Canziani, J. P. Palutikof, P. J. van der Linden, and C. E. Hanson (eds) Cambridge, UK: Cambridge University Press, 7–22, 2007, p. 22.

9 National Academy of Sciences, "Radiative Forcing of Climate Change: Expanding the Concept and Addressing Uncertainties," *Committee on Radiative Forcing Effects on Climate, Climate Research Committee, National Research Council*, Executive Summary, pp. 1–2, 2005. Online. www.nap.edu.

10 Ibid.

11 International Panel on Climate Change (IPCC), *Climate Change 2001: The Scientific Basis. Contribution of Working Group I to the Third Assessment Report of the Intergovernmental Panel on Climate Change*, J. T. Houghton, Y. Ding, D. F. Griggs, M., Noguer, P. J. van der Linden, X. Dai, K. Maskell, and C. A. Johnson (eds) Cambridge, UK: Cambridge University Press, 2001.

12 Ibid.

13 National Academy of Sciences, *Executive Summary: Understanding Climate Feedbacks*, 2003, p. 1.

14 Ibid., pp. 8–13.

15 IPCC 2007, op. cit.

16 R. W. Lindsay and J. Zhang, in J. Turner, J. E. Overland, and J. E. Walsh, "An Arctic and Antarctic Perspective on Recent Climate Change," *International Journal of Climatology* 27, 2005, 277–293.

17 J. C. Stroeve *et al.*, "Tracking the Arctic's shrinking ice cover: Another extreme September minimum in 2004," *Geophysical Research Letters* 32, 25 Februrary 2005.

18 R. Kwok, H. J. Zwally, and D. Yi, "ICES at observations of Arctic sea ice: A first look," *Geophysical Research Letters* 31, August 18, 2004.

19 B. C. Forbes, N. Fresco, A. Schvidenko, K. Danell and F. S. Chapin, III. "Geographic Variations in Anthropogenic Drivers that Influence the Vulnerability and Resilience of Social-Ecological Systems" *Ambio*, vol. 33, no. 6, August 2004, pp. 377–381.

20 Ibid.

21 M. Maslin, Y. Malhi, O. Phillips, and S. Cowling, "New Views on an Old Forest: Assessing the Longevity, Resilience and Future of the Amazon Rainforest," *Transactions of the Institute of British Geography*, 30, 2005, 477–499.

22 G. A. Shields, "Marinoan Meltdown," *Nature* 1, June 2008, 351–353; and M. J.

Kennedy, D. Mrofka, and C. von der Borch, "Snowball Earth termination by destabilization of equatorial permafrost methane clathrate," *Nature* 453, May 29, 2008, 642–645.

23 C. Thompson, J. Beringer, F. S. Chapin III, and A. D. McGuire, "Structural Complexity and Land-Surface Energy Exchange Along a Gradient from Arctic Tundra to Boreal Forest," *Journal of Vegetation Science* 15, 2004, 397–406.

24 J. Shukla, C. Nobre, and P. Sellers, "Amazon deforestation and climate change," *Science* 247, 1990, 1322–1325.

25 Ibid.

26 C. Jeffrey and K. M. Walter, "Siberian Permafrost Decomposition and Climate Change," United Nations Development Programme and the London School of Economics and Political Science, Development and Transition, 2008.

27 S. Connor, "Shock as Retreat of Arctic Sea Ice Releases Deadly Greenhouse Gas: Russian research team astonished after finding 'fountains' of methane bubbling to surface," *Independent*, UK, December 14, 2011.

28 M. Winton, "Amplified Arctic Climate Change," *Geophysical Research Letters* 33, 2006, p. 4.

29 Ibid.

30 I. Fung, lecture at the Energy Resources Group colloquium, UC Berkeley, October 2008.

31 National Academy of Sciences, op. cit., p. 10.

32 J. Hansen and L. Nazarenko, "Soot climate forcing via snow and ice albedos," *Proceedings of the National Academy of Sciences*, vol. 101, no. 2, January 13, 2004, 427.

33 L. R. Belyea and A. J. Baird, "Beyond the Limits to Peat Bog Growth: Cross-Scale Feedback in Peatland Development," *Ecological Monographs*, vol. 73, no. 3, 2006, pp. 299–322.

34 Ibid., p. 299.

35 H. Atlan, personal communication, September 7, 2007.

36 S. Schneider, "Abrupt Non-Linear Climate Change, Irreversibility, and Surprise," document for the Working Party on Global and Structural Policies Organization for Economic Cooperation and Development, Workshop on the Benefits of Climate Policy: Improving Information for Policy Makers, held December 12–13, 2002, published 2003. Online. http://stephenschneider.stanford.edu/index.html (accessed online November 8, 2008).

37 R. Kerr, "Is Battered Arctic Sea Ice Down for the Count," *Science*, 318–315, October 2007, 33–34.

38 Ibid.

39 R. W. Lindsay and J. Zhang, "The Thinning of Arctic Sea Ice, 1988–2003: Have We Passed a Tipping Point?" *Journal of Climate* 18, November 15, 2005, 4879–4894.

40 Ibid., p. 4879.

41 S. Schneider and C. Azar, *Are Uncertainties in Climate and Energy Systems a Justification for Stronger Near-Term Mitigation Policies?* Pew Center on Global Climate Change, October 2001, p. 14.

42 Ibid., p. 24.

43 L. Capra, "Abrupt Climate Change as Triggering Mechanisms of Massive Volcanic Collapses," *Journal of Volcanology and Geothermal Research*, 155, 2006, 329–333, p. 329.

44 S. Schneider, "Abrupt Non-Linear Climate Change, Irreversibility and Surprise," Paper prepared for the OECD Project on the Benefits of Climate Policy, 12–13 December 2002, Paris, 2003, pp. 5–6. Online. http://stephenschneider.stanford.edu/index.html (accessed November 8, 2008).

45 M. Torn and J. Harte, "Missing Feedbacks, asymmetric uncertainties, and the underestimation of future warming," *Geophysical Research Letters* 33, 2006.

46 National Academy of Sciences, op. cit., p. 13.

47 International Panel on Climate Change (IPCC), Fourth Assessment Report (FAR), *Climate Change 2007: The Physical Science Basis. Contribution of Working Group I to the Fourth Assessment Report of the Intergovernmental Panel on Climate Change*, S. Solomon, D. Qin, M. Manning, Z. Chen, M. Marquis, K. B. Averyt, M. Tignor, and H. L. Miller (eds) New York, NY, USA, 2007; International Panel on Climate Change (IPCC), Fourth Assessment Report (FAR), *Climate Change 2007: Impacts, Adaptation and Vulnerability, Contribution of Working Group II to the Fourth Assessment Report of the Intergovernmental Panel on Climate Change*, M. L. Parry, O. F. Canziani, J. P. Palutikof, P. J. van der Linden, and C. E. Hanson (eds) New York, NY, USA, 2007; International Panel on Climate Change (IPCC), Fourth Assessment Report (FAR), *Climate Change 2007: Mitigation. Contribution of Working Group III to the Fourth Assessment, Report of the Intergovernmental Panel on Climate Change*, B. Metz, O. R. Davidson, P. R. Bosch, R. Dave, and L. A. Meyer (eds) New York, 2007.
48 Union of Concerned Scientists, "The IPCC: Who Are They and Why Do Their Climate Reports Matter?" Online. www.ucsusa.org/global_warming/science/the-ipcc. html (accessed May 5, 2008).
49 S. Schneider and C. Azar, *Are Uncertainties in Climate and Energy Systems a Justification for Stronger Near-Term Mitigation Policies?* Pew Center on Global Climate Change, October 2001, p. 7.
50 S. Schneider and K. Kuntz-Duriseti. (2002). "Chapter 2: Uncertainty and Climate Change Policy," in S. H. Schneider, A. Rosencranz, and J. O. Niles, (eds), *Climate Change Policy: A Survey*. Island Press, Washington, DC, p. 54.
51 K. Vincent, "Uncertainty in adaptive capacity and the importance of scale," *Global Environmental Change* V, 17, 2007, pp. 12–13.
52 Ibid.
53 S. Dessai, K. O'Brien, and M. Hulme, "Editorial: On uncertainty and climate change," *Global Environmental Change*, V.17, 2007, 1–3, p. 1.
54 S. Schneider and K. Kuntz-Duriseti, op. cit., p. 54.
55 Ibid.
56 S. Schneider, 2003, op. cit.
57 J. Bohannon, "Profile: Brian O'Neill, Trying to Lasso Climate Uncertainty: An expert on climate and population looks for a way to help society avoid a 'Wile E. Coyote' catastrophe'," *Science* 213, 2006, 243–244, p. 243.
58 Ibid., 244.
59 S. Dessai, 2007, op. cit.
60 S. Dessai, 2007, op. cit., pp. 8–9.
61 J. Bohannon, op. cit., p. 243.
62 Ibid., pp. 243–244.
63 J. Bohannon, op. cit., p. 244.
64 Ibid.
65 H. D. Minh., R. Swart, L. Bernstein, and A. Petersen, "Uncertainty Management in the IPCC: Agreeing to Disagree," *Global Environmental Change* 17, 3, 2007, 8–11.
66 Ibid., p. 8.
67 J. T. Houghton, "Newsletter: Science and the Environment," *New Scientist*, June 1993, p. 4, in S. Shackley and B. Wynne, "Representing Uncertainty in Global Climate Change Science and Policy: Boundary-Ordering Devices and Authority," *Science, Technology and Human Values*, vol 21, n.3, Summer 1996, 275–302, p. 281.
68 Ibid., p. 3.
69 K. Shrader-Frechette, "Throwing out the Bathwater of Positivism, Keeping the Baby of Objectivity: Relativism and Advocacy in Conservation Biology," *Conservation Biology* 10, 3, June 1996, 912–914.
70 S. Shackley and B. Wynne, "Representing Uncertainty in Global Climate Change Science and Policy: Boundary-Ordering Devices and Authority," *Science, Technology & Human Values* 21, 3, 1996, 275–302.

71 Ibid., p. 282.

72 H. D. Minh, op. cit.

73 H. D. Minh, op. cit.

74 R. H. Moss and S. H. Schneider, "Uncertainties in the IPCC TAR: Recommendations to Lead Authors for More Consistent Assessment and Reporting," in R. Pachauri, T. Taniguchi, and K. Tanaka (eds) *Guidance Papers on the Cross Cutting Issues of the Third Assessment Report of the IPCC*, Geneva, Switzerland: World Meteorological Organization, 2000, 33–51.

75 Ibid.

76 IPCC 2007 WGI, pp. 17–18.

77 IPCC 2007 WGII, p. 8.

78 Ibid.

79 Ibid., p. 21.

80 Ibid., p. 173 and p. 177.

81 IPCC 2007 WGIII, pp. 34–36.

82 IPCC 2007 WGII, p. 20.

83 Ibid., p. 8.

84 IPCC 2007 WGIII, p. 20.

85 J. C. Stroeve *et al.*, op. cit.; J. C. Stroeve *et al.*, "Arctic sea ice decline: Faster than forecast," *Geophysical Research Letters* 34, 1 May 2007; and J. C. Stroeve *et al.*, "Arctic Sea Ice Extent Plummets in 2007," *EOS* 89, 2, 2008, 13–20.

86 [1] An antiquated religion, [2] a meadow, [3] Greek sea god capable of changing into many different forms, and [4] another god known to blow a horn or shell.

10 American dreams, ecological nightmares, and new visions

1 K. Boulding, *The Skills of the Economist*, Cleveland: Howard Allen, 1958, in D. Hammond, *The Science of Synthesis*, Boulder: The University Press of Colorado, p. 199.

2 A. Campbell, P. E. Converse, and W. L. Rodgers, *The Quality of American Life: Perceptions, evaluations, and satisfactions*, Russell Sage Foundation, 1976, p. 3.

3 Ibid.

4 Ibid.

5 S. Connor, "Shock as Retreat of Arctic Sea Ice Releases Deadly Greenhouse Gas: Russian research team astonished after finding 'fountains' of methane bubbling to surface," *Independent*, UK, 14 December 2011.

6 N. Mead, "China vs. US energy consumption," *Guardian News*. Online, posted online Tuesday August 3, 2010, based on data from the International Energy Agency, www. guardian.co.uk/business/datablog/2010/aug/03/us-china-energy-consumption-data (accessed January 9, 2012).

7 R. W. Tillerson, "ExxonMobile Corporation News Release," 31 January 2011. Online. www.exxonmobil.com/Corporate/.../news_release_earnings4q10.pdf (accessed December 3, 2011).

8 Ibid.

9 K. Cobb, "The price of oil is rising, and may never fall: The Energy Slaves," *Le Monde Diplomatique*, English version, May 2006. Online. http://mondediplo. com/2006/05/08energyslaves (accessed January 9, 2012). I have yet to find the original data on how this claim was calculated.

10 K. Boulding, *The Meaning of the Twentieth Century: The Great Transition*, New York: Harper and Row, 1964, pp. 149–150.

11 M. L. King, Jr., "Beyond Vietnam," Speech to Clergy and Laity Concerned, Riverside Church, New York City, 4 April 1967.

12 R. H. Beinecke, "Introduction: Leadership for Wicked Problems," *The Innovation Journal: The Public Sector Innovation Journal*, Vol. 14, 1, 2009, 1–17.

13 J. C. Camillus, "Strategy as a Wicked Problem," *Harvard Business Review*, May 2008.
14 Ibid.
15 From McKinsey Climate Change Special Initiative, in talk by Eric Beinhocker, "Escaping the Last Malthusian Trap: Complex systems, climate change and economic growth," Oxford, November 27, 2008, McKinsey and Company, Inc.
16 R. Wolff, *Democracy Now*, radio and television show, December 2, 2011.
17 A. de Botton, speech, "A Kinder, Gentler Philosophy of Success," TED talks. Online. www.ted.com/talks/alain_de_botton_a_kinder_gentler_philosophy_of_success.html (accessed December 23, 2011).
18 E. Morin, *La Voie*, Paris: Fayard, 2011, p. 12.

11 Complexity and sustainability: wicked problems, Gordian knots, and synergistic solutions

1 J. Didion, *Slouching Towards Bethlehem*, New York: Farrar, Straus, and Giroux, 1968.
2 International Panel on Climate Change (IPCC), Fourth Assessment Report (FAR), Climate Change 2007: Mitigation. Contribution of Working Group III to the Fourth Assessment, Report of the Intergovernmental Panel on Climate Change, B. Metz, O. R. Davidson, P. R. Bosch, R. Dave, and L. A. Meyer (eds) New York, 2007, pp. 34–36.
3 R. B. Fuller, in collaboration with E. J. Applewhite, "Synergetics: Explorations in the Geometry of Thinking by R. Buckminster Fuller," first published by Macmillan Publishing Co. Inc. 1975. Online. www.rwgrayprojects.com/synergetics/synergetics.html, def 100.01, (accessed online September 12, 2011).
4 California Institute of Integral Studies website: Mission Statement. Online. www.ciis.edu/About_CIIS/CIIS_at_a_Glance/Mission_Statement.html (accessed on September 12, 2011).
5 Integral Institute website. Online. www.integralinstitute.org/ (accessed September 12, 2011).
6 A. J. Zellmer, T. F. H. Allen, and K. Kesseboehmer, "The nature of ecological complexity: A protocol for building the narrative," *Ecological Complexity*, vol. 3, 2006, 171–182.
7 S. Vanderheiden (ed.) *Political Theory and Global Climate Change*, Boston, MIT Press, 2008.
8 S. Gardiner, "A Perfect Moral Storm: Climate Change, Intergenerational Ethics and the Problem of Moral Corruption," *Environmental Values* 15, 2006, 397–413.
9 P. Taylor, *Unruly Complexity*, Chicago: University of Chicago Press, 2005, p. xiv.
10 Ibid., p. xvii.
11 Ibid., p. xviii.
12 Ibid., p. 7.
13 Ibid., p. 16.
14 Ibid., p. 30.
15 Ibid., p. 164.
16 T. F. H. Allen Allen, J. Tainter, and T. W. Hoekstra, *Supply Side Sustainability*, New York: Columbia University Press, 2003.
17 P. Feyerabend, *Against Method*, New York: Verso Books, 1975.
18 T. F. H. Allen, J. Tainter, and T. W. Hoekstra, op. cit., p. 22.
19 Ibid.
20 Ibid., p. 23.
21 T. F. H. Allen, J. Tainter, and T. W. Hoekstra, op. cit., p. 380.
22 P. Canadell *et al.*, *Global Carbon Budget 2007* (last update September 26, 2008). Online.   www.globalcarbonproject.org/global/pdf/GCP_CarbonBudget_2007.pdf (accessed September 29, 2011).

23 P. Singer, *One World: The Ethics of Globalization*, 2002, Yale University Press.

24 S. Kartha, P. Baer, and D. Cornland, "Cutting the Gordian knot: Adequacy, Realism and Equity," EcoEquity, 2004. Online. www.ecoequity.org/docs/gordianknot.pdf (accessed October 1, 2008).

25 P. Baer, T. Athanasiou, S. Kartha, and E. Kemp-Benedict, *The Greenhouse Development Rights Framework: The right to develop in a climate constrained world, revised 2nd edition*, Heinrich Boll Foundation, Christian Aid, EcoEquity, and the Stockholm Environment Institute, 2008. Online. www.ecoequity.org (accessed December 5, 2011).

26 Ibid.

27 Ibid., pp. 9–10.

28 Ibid., p. 9.

29 T. Flannery, *Now or Never: Why we must act now to end climate change and create a sustainable future*, New York: Atlantic Monthly Press, 2009, p. 10.

30 Ibid., p. 13.

31 Ibid., p. 55.

32 Ibid., pp. 55–56.

33 Ibid., p. 64.

34 Ibid., p. 70.

35 Ibid., p. 76.

36 R. B. Norgaard, *Development Betrayed: The end of progress and a coevolutionary envisioning of the future*, New York: Routledge, 1994.

37 Ibid.

38 T. J. Foxon, "A coevolutionary framework for analysing a transition to a sustainable low carbon economy," *Ecological Economics*, 70, 2011, 2258–2267.

39 Adapted from T. J. Foxon, op. cit.

40 T. J. Foxon, personal communication, January 22, 2012.

41 T. J. Foxon, op. cit., p. 2264.

42 K. Boulding, in D. Hammond, *The Science of Synthesis*, Boulder: The University Press of Colorado, p. 197 and p. 233.

Bibliography

Abraham, R., "The Genesis of Complexity," 2002. Online. www.ralph-abraham.org/articles/titles.shtml (accessed October 22, 2011).

Allen, P., "What is Complexity Science: Knowledge to the Limits of Knowledge," *Emergence*, 3, 1, 2000, 24–42.

Allen, T. F. H. and T. W. Hoekstra, *Toward a Unified Ecology*, New York: University of Columbia Press, 1992.

Allen, T., J. Tainter, and T. W. Hoekstra, *Supply Side Sustainability*, New York: Columbia University Press, 2003.

Andler, D., A. Fagot-Largeault, and B. Saint-Sernin (eds) *Philosophie des Sciences II*, Folio Essais: Paris, 2002

Atlan, H., *Le Cristal et la Fumée: Essai Sur L'organisation Du Vivant*, Paris: Seuil, 1986.

Aubin, D. and A. Dahan-Dalmedico, "Writing the History of Dynamical Systems and Chaos: Longue Duree and Revolution, Disciplines and Cultures," *Historia Mathematica*, 29, 2002, 1–67.

Baer, P., T. Athanasiou, S. Kartha, and E. Kemp-Benedict, *The Greenhouse Development Rights Framework: The right to develop in a climate constrained world, revised 2nd edition*, Heinrich Boll Foundation, Christian Aid, EcoEquity, and the Stockholm Environment Institute, 2008. Online. www.ecoequity.org/docs/TheGDRsFramework.pdf (accessed December 5, 2000).

Bak, P., C. Tang, and K. Wiesenfeld, "Self-Organized Criticality," *Physical Review A* 38, 1, 1988.

Bar-Yam, Y. (ed.) *Dynamics of Complex Systems: Studies in nonlinearity*, Reading, New York: Perseus Books, 1997.

Barabási, A.-L., *Linked: How Everything is Connected to Everything Else and What it Means for Business, Science and Everyday Life*, New York: Plume, 2002.

Barrow, J., *Impossibility: The Limits of Science and the Science of Limits*, Oxford: Oxford University Press, 1999.

Beck, U., *Risk Society: Towards a New Modernity*, London: Sage, 1992.

Beinecke, R. H., "Introduction: Leadership for Wicked Problems," *The Innovation Journal: The Public Sector Innovation Journal*, Vol. 14, 1, 2009, 1–17.

Belyea, L. R. and A. J. Baird, "Beyond the Limits to Peat Bog Growth: Cross-Scale Feedback in Peatland Development," *Ecological Monographs*, 73(3), 2006, pp. 299–322.

Berlow, E. *et al.*, "Simple prediction of interaction strengths in complex food webs," *Proceedings of the National Academy of Sciences*, January 6, 2009, vol. 106, no. 1, 187–191.

Biagioli, M. (ed.) *The Science Studies Reader*, New York: Routledge, 2003, 1999.

Bohannon, J. "Profile: Brian O'Neill, Trying to Lasso Climate Uncertainty: An expert on climate and population looks for a way to help society avoid a 'Wile E. Coyote' catastrophe," *Science* 213, 2006, 243–244.

Boje, D. M., "What Happened on the Way to Postmodern?" *Qualitative Research in Organizations and Management: An International Journal*, 2006, 1, 1, 22–40.

Boulding, K., *Ecodynamics: A new view of societal evolution*, Beverly Hills, CA: Sage Publications, 1978, 1981.

Boulding, K., "General Systems Theory: The Skeleton of Science," *Management Science*, 1956, vol. 2, no. 3, 197–208.

Boulding, K., *The Meaning of the Twentieth Century: The Great Transition*, New York: Harper and Row, 1964.

Botton, A. de, speech, "A Kinder, Gentler Philosophy of Success," TED talks. Online. www.ted.com/talks/alain_de_botton_a_kinder_gentler_philosophy_of_success.html (accessed December 23, 2011).

Brose, U., R. Williams, and N. Martinez, "Allometric scaling enhances stability in complex food webs," *Ecology Letters*, vol. 9, no. 11, November 2006.

Brown, J. H., G. B. West, and B. J. Enquist, "Yes, West, Brown and Enquist's model of allometric scaling is both mathematically correct and biologically relevant," *Functional Ecology* vol. 19, 2005, 735–738.

California Institute of Integral Studies website. Online. www.ciis.edu/about_ciis/ciis_at_a_glance/mission_statement.html (accessed on September 12, 2011).

Campbell, A., P. E. Converse, and W. L. Rodgers, *The quality of American life: perceptions, evaluations, and satisfactions*, Russell Sage Foundation, 1976.

Camillus, J. C., "Strategy as a Wicked Problem," *Harvard Business Review*, May 2008.

Canadell, P., *et al.*, *Global Carbon Budget 2007* (last update September 26, 2008). Online. www.globalcarbonproject.org/global/pdf/GCP_CarbonBudget_2007.pdf (accessed September 29, 2011).

Capra, L. "Abrupt Climate Change as Triggering Mechanisms of Massive Volcanic Collapses," *Journal of Volcanology and Geothermal Research*, 155, 2006, 329–333.

Chalmers, D., "Strong and Weak Emergence," in P. Clayton and P. Davies, *The Re-emergence of Emergence*, Oxford: Oxford University Press, 2006.

Chapin, III, F. S., G. P. Kofinas, and C. Folke (eds) *Principles of Ecosystem Stewardship: Resilience-Based Natural Resource Management in a Changing World*, New York: Springer, 2009.

Chapin, III, F. S. *et al.*, "Resilience and Vulnerability of Northern Regions to Social and Environmental Change," *Ambio*, August 2004, vol. 33, no. 6, 344–349.

Chui, G., " 'Unified Theory' is Getting Closer, Hawking Predicts," *San Jose Mercury News, Morning Final Edition*, September 23, 2000, p. 29A.

Cilliers, P., *Complexity and Postmodernism*, London: Routledge, 1998.

Cobb, K., "The price of oil is rising, and may never fall: The Energy Slaves," *Le Monde Diplomatique*, English version, May 2006, http://mondediplo.com/2006/05/08 energyslaves (accessed online January 9, 2012).

Connor, S., "Shock as Retreat of Arctic Sea Ice Releases Deadly Greenhouse Gas: Russian research team astonished after finding 'fountains' of methane bubbling to surface", *Independent*, UK, December 14, 2011.

Crabtree, P., "Anticipations: The Remarkable Forecasts of H. G. Wells," *World Futures Society*, September–October 2007, 40–46.

Dahan-Dalmedico, A., "Models and Simulations in Climate Change: Historical, Epistemological, Anthropological, and Political Aspects," in A. N. H. Creager *et al.* (eds)

Science without laws: model systems, cases, exemplary narratives, Durham, NC: Duke University Press, 2007.

Davis, M., *Ecology of Fear: Los Angeles and the Imagination of Disaster*, New York: Vintage, 1998.

Davis, M. "The Flames of New York," *New Left Review*, 2001, pp. 34–50.

Dessai, S., K. O'Brien, and M. Hulme, "Editorial: On uncertainty climate change", *Global Environmental Change*, V.17, 2007, 1–3.

"Development," Dictionary.com. Online. http://dictionary.reference.com/browse/development (accessed January 3, 2012).

Diamond, J., *Collapse: How Societies Choose to Fail or Succeed*, New York: Viking Books, 2005.

Didion, J., *Slouching Towards Bethlehem*, New York: Farrar, Straus, and Giroux, 1968.

Dumouchel, P. and J.-P. Dupuy (eds) *L'Auto-Organisation de la Physique au Politique*, Paris: Seuil, 1983.

Dunne, J. A., *et al.*, "Compilation and Network Analyses of Cambrian Food Webs," *PLOS Biology*, vol. 6, no. 4, April 29, 2008.

Dupré, J., *Human Nature and the Limits of Science*, Oxford: Clarendon Press, 2001.

Dupuy, J.-P., *Pour un Catastrophisme Eclairé: Quand l'impossible est certain*, Collection La couleur des idées, Paris: Seuil, 2002.

Dupuy, J.-P., *Ordres et désordres, enquête sur un nouveau paradigme*, Paris: Seuil, 1982.

Elliot, R., "Environmental Ethics," in P. Singer, *A Companion to Ethics*, Malden Massachusetts: Blackwell Publishing, 1993, 1991, 284–293.

Eliot, T. S., *After Strange Gods: A Primer of Modern Heresy*, London: Faber & Faber Limited, 1934.

Feyerabend, P., *Against Method*, New York: Verso Books, 1975.

Flannery, T., *Now or Never: Why we must act now to end climate change and create a sustainable future*, New York: Atlantic Monthly Press, 2009.

Flannery, T., *The Eternal Frontier: An Ecological History of North America and its Peoples*, New York: Grove Press, 2001.

Flannery, T., *The Future Eaters: An Ecological History of the Australasian Lands and People*, Australia: Reed Books, 1994.

Forbes, B. C., N. Fresco, A. Schvidenko, K. Danell, and F. S. Chapin, III, "Geographic Variations in Anthropogenic Drivers that Influence the Vulnerability and Resilience of Social-Ecological Systems," *Ambio* vol. 33, no. 6, August 2004, pp. 377–381.

Freitas, L. de, E. Morin, and B. Nicolescu (eds) *Charter of Transdisciplinarity*, translated from the French by K.-C. Voss, adopted at the First World Congress of Trandiscipli-narity, Convento da Arrábida, Portugal, November 2–6, 1994.

Foxon, T. J., "A coevolutionary framework for analysing a transition to a sustainable low carbon economy," *Ecological Economics*, 70, 2011, 2258–2267.

Frost, R., "Mending Wall," 1914.

Fuller, R. B., in collaboration with E. J. Applewhite, "Synergetics: Explorations in the Geometry of Thinking by R. Buckminster Fuller," first published by Macmillan Publishing Co. Inc. 1975. Online. www.rwgrayprojects.com/synergetics/synergetics.html, def 100.01, (accessed October 11, 2011).

Fumerton, R., "Foundationalist Theories of Epistemic Justification," *The Stanford Encyclopedia of Philosophy (Summer 2010 Edition)*, Edward N. Zalta (ed.) Online. http://plato.stanford.edu/archives/sum2010/entries/jjustepifoundational/ (accessed November 14, 2010).

Fung, I., UC Berkeley lecture at the Energy Resources Group, October 2008.

Gardiner, S., "A Perfect Moral Storm: Climate Change, Intergenerational Ethics and the Problem of Moral Corruption," *Environmental Values* 15, 2006, 397–413.

Gleick, J., *Chaos*, New York: Penguin Books, 1987. The Great Transition Initiative. Online. http://gtinitiative.org (accessed January 4, 2012).

Goldman, A., "Social Epistemology," *The Stanford Encyclopedia of Philosophy (Summer 2010 Edition)*, E. N. Zalta (ed.). Online. http://plato.stanford.edu/archives/sum2010/entries/epistemology-social/ (accessed January 10, 2011).

Goldstein, J., "Emergence as a Construct: History and Issues," *Emergence*, vol. 1, no. 1, 1999, 49–72.

Goodman, N., *Ways of Worldmaking*, Indianapolis: Hackett, 1978.

Granovetter, M., "The Strength of Weak Ties," *American Journal of Sociology*, vol. 78, no. 6, May 1973, 1360–1380.

Groffman, P., *et al.*, "Ecological Thresholds: The Key to Successful Environmental Management or an Important Concept with No Practical Application?" *Ecosystems* 9, 2006, 1–13.

Gunderson, L. H. and C. S. Holling (eds) *Panarchy: Understanding Transformations in Human and Natural Systems*, Washington: Island Press, 2002.

Hammond, D., *The Science of Synthesis: Exploring the Social Implications of General Systems Theory*, Boulder: University Press of Colorado, 2003.

Hansen, J. and L. Nazarenko, "Soot climate forcing via snow and ice albedos," *Proceedings of the National Academy of Sciences*, vol. 101, no. 2, January 13, 2004, 427.

Hayles, N. K., *How We Became Posthuman: Virtual Bodies in Cybernetics, Literature and Informatics*, Chicago: University of Chicago Press, 1999.

Hay, G. J., "Bridging scales and epistemologies: An introduction," *International Journal of Applied Earth Observation and Geoinformation* 7, 2005, 249–252.

Higgins, P., *et al.*, *Dynamics of Climate and Ecosystem Coupling: Abrupt changes and multiple equilibria*. Phil. Trans. R. Soc. Lond. B. 357, 2002, 647–655.

Holland, J. H., *Complexity: the emerging science at the edge of order and chaos*, Harmondsworth, England: Penguin, 1994.

Holland, J. H., *Emergence: From Chaos to Order*, Oxford University Press, 1998.

Horgan, J. "From Complexity to Perplexity," *Scientific American*, vol. 272, no. 6, June 1995, 74–79.

Horn, R. *History of the Ideas of Cybernetics and Systems Science, poster v.1.0*. hornbob@earthlink.net, 2006.

Houghton, J. T., "Newsletter: Science and the Environment," *New Scientist*, June 1993, p. 4, in S. Shackley and B. Wynne, "Representing Uncertainty in Global Climate Change Science and Policy: Boundary-Ordering Devices and Authority," *Science, Technology and Human Values*, vol. 21, no. 3, Summer 1996, 275–302.

"Hurricane!" PBS documentary NOVA, 1988.

Integral Institute website. Online. www.integralinstitute.org (accessed September 12, 2011).

International Panel on Climate Change, "Publications and Data." Online. www.ipcc.ch/ipccreports/index.htm (accessed May 5, 2008).

International Panel on Climate Change (IPCC), *Climate Change 2001: The Scientific Basis. Contribution of Working Group I to the Third Assessment Report of the Intergovernmental Panel on Climate Change*, J. T. Houghton, Y. Ding, D. F. Griggs, M. Noguer, P. J. van der Linden, X. Dai, K. Maskell, and C. A. Johnson (eds) Cambridge, UK: Cambridge University Press, 2001.

International Panel on Climate Change (IPCC), Fourth Assessment Report (FAR),

Climate Change 2007: The Physical Science Basis. Contribution of Working Group I to the Fourth Assessment Report of the Intergovernmental Panel on Climate Change, S. Solomon, D. Qin, M. Manning, Z. Chen, M. Marquis, K. B. Averyt, M. Tignor, and H. L. Miller (eds) New York, NY, USA, 2007.

International Panel on Climate Change (IPCC), Fourth Assessment Report (FAR), *Climate Change 2007: Impacts, Adaptation and Vulnerability, Contribution of Working Group II to the Fourth Assessment Report of the Intergovernmental Panel on Climate Change*, M. L. Parry, O. F. Canziani, J. P. Palutikof, P. J. van der Linden, and C. E. Hanson (eds) New York, NY, USA, 2007.

International Panel on Climate Change (IPCC), Fourth Assessment Report (FAR), *Climate Change 2007: Mitigation. Contribution of Working Group III to the Fourth Assessment, Report of the Intergovernmental Panel on Climate Change*, B. Metz, O. R. Davidson, P. R. Bosch, R. Dave, and L. A. Meyer (eds) New York, NY, USA, 2007.

IUCN/UNEP/WWF, "Caring for the Earth: A Strategy for Sustainable Living," Switzerland: Gland, 1991. Online. http://gcmd.nasa.gov/records/GCMD_IUCN_CARING.html (accessed October 3, 2011).

Jasanoff, S., in C. Miller and P. Erickson (2004). "Chapter 16: The Politics of Bridging Scales and Epistemologies: Science and democracy in global environmental governance," in the Millennium Ecosystem Assessment Final Report of *Bridging Scales and Epistemologies*. Online. www.millenniumassessment.org/en/Bridging.aspx (accessed January 4, 2008).

Jeffrey, C. and K. M. Walter, "Siberian Permafrost Decomposition and Climate Change," United Nations Development Programme and the London School of Economics and Political Science, Development and Transition, 2008.

Jonas, H., *Le Principe Responsabilité: Une éthique pour la civilisation technique*, traduit de l'allemand par Jean Greisch, Paris: Cerf, 1979, 1991.

Kartha, S., P. Baer, and D. Cornland, "Cutting the Gordian knot: Adequacy, Realism and Equity," EcoEquity, 2004. Online. www.ecoequity.org/docs/gordianknot.pdf (accessed October 1, 2008).

Kauffman, S. A., *At Home in the Universe: The Search for the Laws of Self-organization and Complexity*, New York: Oxford University Press, 1995.

Kennedy, M. J., D. Mrofka, and C. von der Borch, "Snowball Earth termination by destabilization of equatorial permafrost methane clathrate," *Nature* 453, May 29, 2008, 642–645.

Kerr, R. "Is Battered Arctic Sea Ice Down for the Count," *Science* 318: 5, October 2007, 33–34.

King, Jr., M. L., "Beyond Vietnam," Speech to Clergy and Laity Concerned, Riverside Church, New York City, April 4, 1967.

Klein, J. T., *Interdisciplinarity: History, theory and practice*, Detroit: Wayne State University Press, 1990.

Kline, S. J., *Conceptual Foundations for Multidisciplinary Thinking*, Stanford University Press, 1995.

Knight, K. (ed.) *The MacIntyre Reader*, Indiana: University of Notre Dame Press, 1998.

Kwok, R., H. J. Zwally, and D. Yi, "ICES at observations of Arctic sea ice: A first look", *Geophysical Research Letters* 31, August 18, 2004.

Laplace, P. S., *Oeuvres, VII, Théorie analytique des probabilités*, 1812–1820, Online. www.todayinsci.com/L/Laplace_Pierre/LaplacePierre-Quotations.htm (accessed January 5, 2012).

Larrère, C., "L'Ethiques de l'Environnement," in S. Laugier, *Multitudes: Un deuxième âge de l'écologie politique? Multitudes* 24, 2006, 75–84.

Latour, B., *We Have Never Been Modern*, trans. by C. Porter, Cambridge, Massachusetts: Harvard University Press, 1993, 2nd edn 1991.

Latour, B. *Reassembling the Social: An introduction to actor-network-theory*, Oxford: Clarendon, 2005.

Lawrence, R. J., and C. Després, "Futures of Transdisciplinarity," *Futures* May 2004, vol. 36, no. 4, 397–405.

Leavy, P., *Essentials of Transdisciplinary Research: Using Problem-centered methodologies*, Walnut Creek, CA: Left Coast Press.

Le Moigne, J.-L., *Le Constructivisme: Tome II Des épistémologies*, Paris: ESF editeur, 1995.

Le Moigne, J.-L. *Le Constructivisme: Tome I Des fondements*, Paris: ESF editeur, 1995.

Lenton, T. *et al.*, "Tipping elements in the Earth's Climate System," in *Proceedings of the National Academy of Sciences of the United States of America*, 105, 6, February 12, 2008, 1786–1793.

Leopold, A., *A Sand County Almanac: With essays on conservation from Round River*, Oxford: Oxford University Press, 1966, 1949.

Light, A., and E. Katz (eds) *Environmental Pragmatism*, in *Environmental Philosophies Series*, A. Brennan (ed.) London: Routledge, 1996.

Lindsay, R. W. and J. Zhang, in J. Turner, J. E. Overland, and J. E. Walsh, "An Arctic and Antarctic Perspective on Recent Climate Change," *International Journal of Climatology* 27, 2005, 277–293.

Lindsay, R. W., and J. Zhang, "The Thinning of Arctic Sea Ice, 1988–2003: Have We Passed a Tipping Point?" *Journal of Climate*, vol. 18, November 15, 2005, 4879–4894.

Lipsitz, G., "Chapter 1: The Possessive Investment in Whiteness," in *The Possessive Investment In Whiteness*, Philadelphia, Temple University Press, 2006.

Lorenz, E., "Deterministic Nonperiodic Flow," *Journal of the Atmospheric Sciences*, March, vol. 20, no. 2, 1963, pp. 130–141.

Maslin, M., Y. Malhi, O. Phillips, and S. Cowling, "New Views on an Old Forest: Assessing the Longevity, Resilience and Future of the Amazon Rainforest," *Transactions of the Institute of British Geography*, 30, 2005, 477–499.

Masters, J., "2010–2011: Earth's most extreme weather since 1816?" Online posting. www.wunderground.com/blog/JeffMasters/comment.html?entrynum=1831 (accessed June 30, 2011).

Maturana, H. R., and Francisco J. Varela, *Autopoeisis and Cognition: The Realization of the Living*, Dordrecht: D. Reidel, 1980.

McAnany, P., and N. Yoffee (eds) *Questioning Collapse: Human Resilience, Ecological Vulnerability, and the Aftermath of Empire*, New York: Cambridge University Press, 2010.

McCormick, M., "Immanuel Kant: Metaphysics", in *Internet Encyclopedia of Philosophy.* Online. www.iep.utm.edu/kantmeta (accessed June 10, 2011).

McKinsey Climate Change Special Initiative, in talk by Eric Beinhocker, "Escaping the Last Malthusian Trap: Complex systems, climate change and economic growth," Oxford, McKinsey and Company, Inc., November 27, 2008.

McPhee, J., "Los Angeles Against the Mountains," 1989, in J. McPhee, *The Second John McPhee Reader*, New York: The Noonday Press, Farrar, Straus, and Giroux, 1996.

Mead, N., "China vs. US energy consumption," *Guardian News.* Online, posted online Tuesday 3 August 2010, based on data from the International Energy Agency, www. guardian.co.uk/business/datablog/2010/aug/03/us-china-energy-consumption-data (accessed January 9, 2012).

Merchant, C., *The Death of Nature: Women, Ecology and the Scientific Revolution*, San Francisco: Harper, 1980, 2nd edn 1990.

Merchant, C., "Fish First!: The changing ethics of ecosystem management," *Human Ecology Review* 4(1), 1988, 25–30.

Millennium Ecosystem Assessment, *Ecosystems and Human Well-being: Synthesis*, Washington, DC: Island Press, 2005.

Millennium Ecosystem Assessment, "Living Beyond Our Means: Natural Assets and Human Well-Being, Board Statement," March 2005.

Minh, H. D., R. Swart, L. Bernstein, and A. Petersen, "Uncertainty Management in the IPCC: Agreeing to Disagree," *Global Environmental Change* 17, 3, 2007, 8–11.

Mitchell, M., *Complexity: A Guided Tour*, Oxford: Oxford University Press, 2009.

Mitsch, W., and J. Gosselink, *Wetlands*, 4th edn, Hoboken, NJ: John Wiley and Sons, Inc., 2007.

Monnin, E., *et al.*, "Atmospheric CO2 Concentrations over the Last Glacial Termination," Science, 5 January 2001, vol. 291, no. 5501, pp. 112–114.

Monod, J., *Chance and Necessity: An essay on the natural philosophy of modern biology*, New York: Knopf, 1971, 1970.

Morin, E., *La Voie*, Paris: Fayard, 2011.

Morin, E., *La Complexité Humaine*, Paris: Flammarion, 1994.

Morin, E., *La Méthode: Tome I: La Nature de la Nature*, Paris: Seuil, 1977.

Morin, E., *La Méthode: Tome III: La connaissance de la connaissance: Anthropologie de la connaissance*, Editions du Seuil, 1986.

Morin, E., *Science avec conscience*, Paris: Seuil, 1982.

Morin, E., "La Complexité Restreinte, complexité générale," in *Intelligence de la Complexité: Epistémologie et Pragmatique*, Paris: L'Aube, 2007.

Morin, E., *On Complexity*, Cresskill, New Jersey: Hampton Press, 2008.

Morin, E., "Re: Routledge, Ch 1." Email: December 2, 2011.

Morowitz, H., *The Emergence of Everything*, Oxford: Oxford University Press, 2002.

Moss, R. H., and S. H. Schneider, "Uncertainties in the IPCC TAR: Recommendations to Lead Authors for More Consistent Assessment and Reporting," in R. Pachauri, T. Taniguchi, and K. Tanaka (eds) *Guidance Papers on the Cross Cutting Issues of the Third Assessment Report of the IPCC*, Geneva, Switzerland: World Meteorological Organization, 2000, 33–51.

Mulvaney, D. and J. Wells, *Biotechnology, The Life Science Industry, and the Environment: An annotated bibliography*, University of California at Berkeley: Institute of International Studies, 2004.

National Academy of Sciences, *Report of an Ad hoc Study Group of Carbon Dioxide and Climate: A scientific assessment to the National Academy of Science*, Washington, DC, 1979.

National Academy of Sciences, *Executive Summary: Understanding Climate Feedbacks*, 2003.

National Academy of Sciences, "Radiative Forcing of Climate Change: Expanding the Concept and Addressing Uncertainties," *Committee on Radiative Forcing Effects on Climate, Climate Research Committee, National Research Council*, Executive Summary, pp. 1–2, 2005. Online. www.nap.edu (accessed March 9, 2008).

National Wildlife Federation, "The American Prairie: Going, Going, Gone?: a status report on the American Prairie," 2001.

Norgaard, R. B., *Development Betrayed: The end of progress and a coevolutionary envisioning of the future*, New York: Routledge, 1994.

Norgaard, R. B. and P. Baer., "Collectively Seeing Complex Systems: The nature of the Problem," *Bioscience* 55, 11, 2005, 953–960.

Ostrom, E., *Governing the Commons: The Evolution of Institutions for Collective Action*, London: Cambridge University Press, 1990.

Ostrom, E. and J. Walker (eds) *Trust and Reciprocity: Interdisciplinary Lessons for Experimental Research*, Vol. VI in the Trust Series, Russell Sage Foundation, 2003.

Oxford English Dictionary online. 1989 edition.

Oxford Reference online. 2008 edition. *A Dictionary of Environment and Conservation in Earth & Environmental Sciences.*

Oxford Reference online. 2007 edition. *Encyclopedia of Global Change in Science.*

Oxford Reference online. 2007 edition. *A Dictionary of Environment and Conservation in Earth & Environmental Sciences.*

Oxford Reference online. 2007 edition. *A Dictionary of Biology in Biological Sciences.*

Oxford English Dictionary: A Dictionary of Environment and Conservation in Earth and Environmental Sciences, "Connectivity," Online with subscription, 2007.

Oxford Reference online, "Surprise," *Encyclopedia of Global Change in Science*. Online with subscription, 2007.

Pascual, M. and J. A. Dunne, "From small to large ecological networks in a dynamic world," pp. 3–24, in *Ecological Networks: Linking Structure to Dynamics in Food Webs*, M. Pascual and J. A. Dunne (eds) Oxford: Oxford University Press, 2005.

Poincaré, H., "Science and Method," Chicago: St. Augustine's Press, 1903.

Reid, W. *et al.* (eds) "Bridging Scales and Knowledge Systems Concepts and Applications in Ecosystem Assessment: Final Report," Online. www.maweb.org/en/Bridging. aspx (accessed January 10, 2012).

Rescher, N., *Complexity: A philosophical overview*, New Brunswick, NJ: Transaction Publishers, 1998.

Rescher, N., *The Limits to Science*, Pittsburg, PA: Pittsburg University Press, 1999, 1984.

Richardson, K., "The Hegemony of the Physical Sciences: An exploration in complexity thinking," *Futures*, vol. 37, 2005, 615–653.

Richardson, K., P. Cilliers, and M. Lissack, "Complexity Science: A 'Grey' Science for the 'Stuff in Between,'" *Emergence*, vol. 3 no. 2, 2001, 6–18.

Rogers, A. D. and D. d'A. Laffoley, "International earth system expert workshop on ocean stresses and impacts: Summary report," Oxford: IPSO, 2011, 18 pages.

Rosenbluth, A., A. Wiener, and J. Bigelow, "Behavior, Purpose and Teleology," *Philosophy of Science*, 10, 1943, pp. 18–24.

Ruelle, D., *Chance and Chaos*, Princeton, NJ: Princeton University Press, 1991.

Scanlon, T. M., *What We Owe to Each Other*. Cambridge, Massachusetts: The Belknap Press of Harvard University Press, 1998.

Schneider, S., "Abrupt Non-Linear Climate Change, Irreversibility and Surprise," Paper prepared for the OECD Project on the Benefits of Climate Policy, December 12–13, 2002, Paris, 2003. Online. http://stephenschneider.stanford.edu/index.html (accessed online November 8, 2008).

Schneider, S. "Abrupt Non-Linear Climate Change, Irreversibility and Surprise," Paper prepared for the OECD Project on the Benefits of Climate Policy, 12–13 December 2002, Paris, 2003.

Schneider, S. and K. Kuntz-Duriseti, "Chapter 2: Uncertainty and Climate Change Policy," in Schneider, S. H., A. Rosencranz, and J. O. Niles (eds) *Climate Change Policy: A Survey*, Washington, DC: Island Press, 2002.

Schneider, S. and C. Azar, *Are Uncertainties in Climate and Energy Systems a Justification for Stronger Near-Term Mitigation Policies?* Pew Center on Global Climate Change, October 2001.

Shackley, S. and B. Wynne, "Representing Uncertainty in Global Climate Change Science and Policy: Boundary-Ordering Devices and Authority," *Science, Technology & Human Values* 21, 3, 1996, 275–302.

Sheldon, J. K., testimony before the House Committee on Resources, US Congress, April 28, 2004.

Shields, G. A., "Marinoan Meltdown," *Nature* 1, June 2008, 351–353.

Shrader-Frechette, K., "Throwing out the Bathwater of Positivism, Keeping the Baby of Objectivity: Relativism and Advocacy in Conservation Biology," *Conservation Biology* 10, 3, June 1996, 912–914.

Shukla, J., C. Nobre, and P. Sellers, "Amazon deforestation and climate change," *Science* 247, 1990, 1322–1325.

Sim, S., and B. van Loon, *Introducing Critical Theory: A graphic guide*, London: Icon Books, 2009.

Simon, H., "The architecture of complexity," reprinted in *Emergence: Complexity and Organization*, vol. 7, no. 3–4, 2005, 1962.

Singer, P., *One World: The Ethics of Globalization*, 2002, Yale University Press.

Smith, R., "Engine of Eco Collapse," *Capitalism, Nature, Socialism*, December 2005.

Snow Magazine, December 23, 2010, "Mammoth Mountain: deepest snow in North America." Online. www.snowmagazine.com/news/1658-mammoth-mountain-deepest-snow-in-n-america (accessed June 27, 2011).

Song, C., S. Havlin, and H. Makse, "Self-similarity of Complex Networks," *Nature* 433, 2005, 392–395.

Stroeve, J. C. *et al.*, "Tracking the Arctic's shrinking ice cover: Another extreme September minimum in 2004," *Geophysical Research Letters* 32, February 25, 2005.

Stroeve, J. C. *et al.*, "Arctic sea ice decline: Faster than forecast," *Geophysical Research Letters* 34, May 1, 2007.

Stroeve, J. C. *et al.*, "Arctic Sea Ice Extent Plummets in 2007," *EOS*, vol. 89, no. 2, 2008, 13–20.

Tainter, J., *The Collapse of Complex Societies*, Cambridge, UK: Cambridge University Press, 1988.

Taylor, P., *Unruly Complexity*, Chicago: University of Chicago Press, 2005.

Thompson, C., J. Beringer, F. S. Chapin III, and A. D. McGuire, "Structural Complexity and Land-Surface Energy Exchange Along a Gradient from Arctic Tundra to Boreal Forest," *Journal of Vegetation Science* 15, 2004, 397–406.

Tillerson, R. W., "ExxonMobile Corporation News Release," 31 January 2011. Online. www.exxonmobil.com/Corporate/.../news_release_earnings4q10.pdf (accessed December 3, 2011).

Torn, M. and J. Harte, "Missing Feedbacks, asymmetric uncertainties, and the underestimation of future warming," *Geophysical Research Letters* 33, 2006.

Union of Concerned Scientists, "The IPCC: Who Are They and Why Do Their Climate Reports Matter?" Online. www.ucsusa.org/global_warming/science/the-ipcc.html (accessed May 5, 2008).

Union of Concerned Scientists, "Year of Extremes Underscores Need for Better Preparedness, Emissions Reductions," November 9, 2011. Online. www.ucsusa.org/news/press_release/year-of-extremes-underscores-preparedness-emissions.html (accessed 10 February 2012).

United States Energy Information Administration. Online. www.indexmundi.com/energy. aspx (accessed September 25, 2011).

Vanderheiden, S., (ed.) *Political Theory and Global Climate Change*, Cambridge, MA: MIT Press, 2008.

Vincent, K., "Uncertainty in adaptive capacity and the importance of scale," *Global Environmental Change*, 17, 2007, 12–24.

Vitousek, P. *et al.*, "Human Domination of Earth's Ecosystems," Science, vol. 277, no. 5325, 25 July 1997, 494–499.

Waldrop, M., *Complexity: The emerging science at the edge of order and chaos*, New York: Simon & Schuster, 1992.

Walker, B., C. S. Holling, S. R. Carpenter, and A. Kinzig, "Resilience, adaptability and transformability in socio-ecological systems," *Ecology and Society*, 9, 2, 5, 2004. Online. www.ecologyandsociety.org/vol. 9/iss2/art5/ (accessed July 5, 2008).

Wallerstein, I., *The Uncertainties of Knowledge*, Philadelphia: Temple University Press, 2004.

Williams, R. and N. Martinez, "Simple rules yield complex food webs," Letters to Nature, *Nature* 404, 180–183, March 9, 2000.

Winton, M., "Amplified Arctic Climate Change," *Geophysical Research Letters* 33, 2006.

Wolfe, C., "Endowed Molecules and Emergent Organization: The Maupertuis-Diderot Debate," *Early Science and Medicine*, vol. 15, 2010, 38–65.

Wolff, R., *Democracy Now* radio and television show, December 2, 2011.

Zalasiewicz, J. *et al.*, "Are we now living in the Anthropocene?" *GSA Today*, vol. 18, no. 2, 2008.

Zellmer, A. J., T. F. H. Allen, and K. Kesseboehmer, "The nature of ecological complexity: A protocol for building the narrative," *Ecological Complexity* 3, 2006, 171–182.

Zizek, S., *The Parallax View*, Cambridge, MA: MIT Press, 2006.

Index

Cite ≈ p.9

p.17 Cent. Science & "Post-Normal Science" - p.10
new? Complexity defined - p.35
Complex systems ecological studies p.16

p.19 - Central proposition of Book
p.18 Book proposes to give an overview of ...
p.22 - lack of Kge of Complexity

p.31 - "Transdisciplinary Complexity" interrelated elements
p.31   "Complex thinking" meaning
p.32 Fundamental vs Relative Complexity.
p.33/34 Restrained & generalized complexity
p.34 3 principles of classical rejection of complexity
p.228 Definition of SUSTAINABILITY
p.229 Planning for " " " "
p.32 Systems not objects, but self-organizing Subjects
p.37 Physical Processes = buildup & release
p.78 Advancing Complexity Studies: k-12, univ., Govt, etc for Sustainability
p.236 - Climate. Mainstream vs complexity frameworks
p.62 Networks → Everywhere !!